BUÑUEL

John Baxter

BUÑUEL

FOURTH ESTATE

LONDON

First published in Great Britain in 1994 by
Fourth Estate Limited
289 Westbourne Grove
London W11 2QA

A catalogue record for this book is available from the British Library.

ISBN 1–85702–179–7

Typeset by York House Typographic Ltd, London W13
Printed in Great Britain by the Bath Press Ltd, Avon

List of Illustrations

Acknowledgements

I am deeply grateful to Juan Luis Buñuel for his assistance with this book. Without his memories of his father and his unstinting access to family records, this portrait would be far less complete. Joyce Kaufman Buñuel also gave an illuminating and incisive picture of her ex-father-in-law. Jean-Claude Carrière's *My Last Breath* is one of the most revealing of all documents on Buñuel's life, so I was doubly appreciative of M. Carrière's recollections of working with Buñuel, and his introductions to other collaborators and friends.

I would thank in particular Catherine Deneuve, Bernard Noisette, Muni, Pierre Lary, Fernando Rey, Silvia Pinal, Jean Sorel, Serge Silberman (and Bruno Silberman, for the introduction), Alain Cuny, Jacques Fraenkel, Rudy Fehr, Jean-Pierre Cassel, Françoise Helmé, my guide to St Bernard, Delphine Seyrig, Stephane Audran, Mauricio Kagel, Arturo Ripstein, Enrique Oetija, Jeanne Moreau, Diego Lopez Rivera and the staff of Estudios Churubusco Azteca S.A. Señor and Señora Jaime Fernandez and Mr and Mrs Dan O'Herlihy were more than generous with both their hospitality and their reminiscences.

Since Luis Buñuel was one of the least interviewed of great film artists, I am more than usually grateful to the friends and fellow scholars who sought out obscure material. Charles Silver generously opened the files of the Museum of Modern Art in New York and Stuart Ng the Warner Brothers Archives in the Doheny Library of USC. Ron Magliozzi's work on Buñuel's time at MoMA was particularly valuable. Marc Vernet gave me access to the original manuscripts of *Un Chien Andalou* and documents about *L'Age d'Or* in the Cinemathèque Française. Bernadette Thorelle was an indefatigable organizer of interviews, and Brian and Mary Troath tireless in discovering original documents and rare books. To Caroline Montel-Glennison, Natalie Young, Chrystel Jaffro, Kelvin Jones, Barbara Johnson, Remi Chikh, Bill Warren, Charles Higham, Pat McGilligan, Annette Morreau, Laurene L'Allinec, Curtis Harrington and Claudine Montel, also the warmest thanks. And to Marie-Dominique Montel, translator and critic, the warmest of all.

1

'God, death, women, wine, dreams.'

– Jean-Claude Carrière, his collaborator and biographer, on Buñuel's obsessions

In 1961, Irish actor Dan O'Herlihy, who had starred in Luis Buñuel's *The Adventures of Robinson Crusoe* a decade before and won an Oscar nomination, sent the script of a novel by the English writer Elleston Trevor to Buñuel's home outside Mexico City, hoping he might direct it with O'Herlihy producing. Since the novel opens with a man murdering his nagging wife as he prepares her supper, then wiping the bloody knife on the bread, O'Herlihy anticipated that the director who had wrung gasps from a generation of filmgoers by drawing a razor across a girl's eyeball in his first film, *Un Chien Andalou (An Andalusian Dog)*, would enjoy it.

Buñuel did find the script interesting, so O'Herlihy took the package to Warner Brothers. 'I've got one of the greatest directors of all time,' he told Bill Orr, Jack Warner's stepson-in-law and head of production.

'Who?'

'Luis Buñuel.'

'Never heard of him,' said Orr.

This was no surprise. Even when Luis Buñuel worked at Warner Brothers in 1944/5 as head of its Spanish Language Department, turning films like the Barbara Stanwyck/George Brent *My Reputation* into *El Que Diran* for the Latin market, he had barely been visible. Nobody knew him as the director of two milestones of Surrealism, *Un Chien Andalou* and *L'Age d'Or (The Golden Age)*; an intimate of André Breton, Salvador Dali, Max Ernst and Man Ray; a man who had enjoyed orgies with Charlie Chaplin and spied for Republican Spain. Buñuel drove home every evening to his bungalow in the San Fernando Valley and his wife and two sons. That he was a wild man in chains was evidenced only by his study, where he kept a small but discriminatingly assembled collection of guns.

Buñuel had been living in Mexico since 1945, cranking out rhumba musicals and domestic comedies, occupying a small walled house in suburban Mexico City and socializing almost entirely with fellow Spanish Republican exiles. The occasional personal film – *El*, *The Criminal Life of Archibaldo de la Cruz*, *Nazarin* – aired the obsessions that drove him: Communism, sexual fetishism, hatred of the Franco regime that had forced him into exile in 1936, and his equal loathing of the Catholic Church – which was none the less a fundamental theme of his work. It took another heretic and renegade to understand and appreciate the contradictions of his character. 'He is a deeply Christian man who hates God as only a Christian can,' Orson Welles told critic and director Peter Bogdanovich, 'and, of course, he's very Spanish. I see him as the most supremely religious director in the history of the movies.'

Warners' decision to turn down Buñuel would be a fateful one. It meant he would be available later in 1961 to accept an offer to return to Spain and make his most controversial film, *Viridiana*.

In May 1960 Buñuel had taken his newest film, *The Young One*, to Cannes. A fable about racism and sexuality set on an island off the Carolina coast, it had been pseudonymously produced by George Pepper and written by Hugo Butler, both of whom, like Buñuel, had fled to Mexico from Hollywood's anti-Communist blacklist.

The competition at Cannes from Fellini's *La Dolce Vita*, Antonioni's *L'Avventura* and Bergman's *The Virgin Spring* was intense, but since the jury included two old acquaintances from Paris, Henry Miller and Georges Simenon, Buñuel was optimistic. Unfortunately Simenon took a liking to *La Dolce Vita* and, as chairman, pushed through its Palme d'Or as Best Film. No prizes were awarded for Best Director and Best Actor, although *The Young One* and *The Virgin Spring* were singled out as 'too good to be judged'.

Buñuel retired to one of Cannes's many hotel bars to consider this puzzling result over a Martini. He was tracked down by some young Spanish film-makers and critics, among them Carlos Saura, director of the official Spanish entry, *Los Golfos*.

In Spain, Buñuel's standing approached that of legend. All Spanish film magazines, wrote the critic José Luis Egea at the time, contained 'two categorical statements. One, an obvious one, namely that Spanish cinema was in a bad state, that it was a barren desert due to lack of freedom. Another, hypothetical, unverifiable, based on faith, suggested that there was a certain Luis Buñuel, exiled in Mexico, who gave the true measure of what Spanish cinema should be.'

Saura and the others asked Buñuel if he would consider coming back. He could be a rallying point, a role model, an inspiration. Luis listened sceptically. 'I know that as a good patriot I have to return to Spain and help,' he told Francisco Aranda later, 'but maybe I am not a good patriot. I am tired and too old to begin something else there.'

But he liked the young men. 'If Spanish youth is like the ones I've met here,' he wrote to his wife Jeanne, 'then Spain is getting better.' But they lacked the stamina of Buñuel's own generation. A lifetime of half a dozen martinis a day, plus a bottle or two of wine, had given him a head for liquor that his admirers lacked. He deplored their weakness as, one by one, they staggered away or passed out. 'It's the strontium', he told Saura. 'The new generation is weak; no good for anything.'

Back in Mexico, to their astonishment, Buñuel informed Jeanne, his son Juan Luis, who was also his assistant, and his Republican friends that he had agreed to make a film in Spain. The Franco government would not oppose his return. In 1955 Spain had finally joined the United Nations and was eager to sanitize its image. Buñuel was 'ripe', says historian John Hopewell, 'for a symbolic act of rehabilitation.' The state censor would have to accept the script, but once he had, the film would receive the generous 50 per cent subsidy given to any production in the 'national interest'.

Buñuel's family, who had followed him to Madrid, Paris, New York and Los Angeles, were resigned to his move, but fellow Republican exiles were vociferous, even hostile. Some accused Luis of collaboration. 'Buñuel, the false genius,' wrote one, 'is going to Spain to serve Franco a film.' Another said: 'We have had until now three citadels, three rocks: Pablo Casals, Picasso and Buñuel. Some of us have believed that none of these three men would return to Madrid during the Franco regime. Well, with this film which he is leaving to direct in Spain, the Buñuel citadel has fallen.' Luis brushed them off. He already had an idea for the plot. Inhibited since childhood by a fear of women, he often fantasized about using drugs or hypnotism to render them helpless. A beautiful Englishwoman in the street reminded him of Victoria Eugenia, Spain's beautiful English-born blonde queen during the 1910s, who had featured in his boyhood sexual fantasies. The idea of making love to her as she lay in a trance led him, he wrote in his autobiographical *My Last Breath*, to the story of 'a young woman [. . .] drugged by an old man; [. . .] completely at the mercy of someone who, otherwise, could never have held her in his arms. It struck me that the woman should be pure, and I made her a novice [nun].'

His resentment of the Church triggered a vision of the nun becoming the mistress of a rowdy household which turned on its head the pious exactitude of the convent. Perhaps the nun would throw the house open to beggars. 'Then,' said Buñuel, warming gleefully to his fantasy with the schoolboy relish for sacrilege and scatology he never, for all his exterior sternness, lost, 'I thought that I'd enjoy seeing the beggars dine in the manor dining-room, on a great table covered with an embroidered cloth and candles. Suddenly I realized that they were in the position of a picture, evoking Leonardo da Vinci's *Last Supper*. Finally I linked the Hallelujah Chorus with the beggars' dance and orgy, which became more startling like this than if I underlined it with rock and roll.' He gave his heroine and the film the name of an obscure medieval saint, always depicted carrying a crown of thorns, a cross and nails: *Viridiana*.

Technically *Viridiana* was a production of the Films 59 group which funded Saura's *Los Golfos*. Most of its executives were old friends of Buñuel: Ricardo Muñoz Suay, a militant Communist student leader before the 1936 Spanish Civil War, now a staid businessman (and later cultural minister of independent Catalonia), director Juan Antonio Bardem, Pedro Portabella, and Domingo Dominguin, brother of Spain's most famous *torero*, Luis Miguel Dominguin. Another company in the group, UNINCI, would distribute.

Shortly after Cannes, Buñuel wrote to Portabella, outlining his plot of *Viridiana* and predicting that the beggars' banquet would have audiences applauding. He barely hinted at its potential for scandal. 'It could pass for a white film,' he said, 'although I must say it is full of darker intentions.' Anyone who knew Buñuel would have been warned, but he had been in exile for twenty-four years. Many had forgotten how a Fascist and anti-Semitic mob, incensed at its sacrilegious scenes, had wrecked the Parisian cinema that showed *L'Age d'Or*, and how Buñuel had called *Un Chien Andalou* 'not a film, but an incitement to murder'. The Surrealists had thought of themselves as cultural terrorists: 'We descend to the streets with guns in our hands,' Breton had declared. Surrealism in Europe might have been consigned to the museums and history books, but in Luis Buñuel it remained alive and dangerous.

In December 1961, Buñuel, a Mexican citizen for ten years, went to Paris and applied for a visa at the Spanish Embassy on rue Pépinière from where, in 1936/7, he had operated as a courier and spy for the Republican government. The visa was issued without comment. His sister Conchita met him at Port Bou on the French frontier, just in case news of his 'rehabilitation' had not reached the border guards, but there was no problem. They travelled to Barcelona and on to Zaragoza, where Luis's mother, brothers and sisters lived. There, he was reminded for the first time, and tragically, of how long he had been away. His mother, the beautiful and vigorous woman of his youth, was, in the words of Buñuel's son Juan Luis, 'a walking ghost', wandering in senile dementia.

Worse was to come. Of Buñuel's old friends, many, like Federico García Lorca, had died in a civil war notorious for brutality on both sides. Of those who had remained in Spain, most had collaborated with Franco, including Luis's other close friend of pre-war Madrid, Salvador Dali, who had become the clown of Franco's regime, with his house declared a national shrine.

Toledo, Buñuel's favourite city, where he had established the mock medieval Order of Toledo for his friends among the pre-war Communists and Surrealists, had been shattered in the battle between the Falange and the Republic. The Order's favourite meeting place, the Posada de la Sangre, the Inn of Blood, had been reduced to rubble. Luis felt as lost as his mother. Of his old life, only the ghosts remained. When the actor Jaime Fernandez asked about his experience of going back to Spain, Luis told him morosely: 'Every corner kills a memory for me.'

In Madrid, he installed himself in a tiny apartment on the seventeenth floor of the Hotel Torre de Madrid. There, in monastic surroundings, he set up house. A man of rigid habits, he rose at dawn every morning from the hard bed or the floor where he slept for his chronic sciatica. After a walk and a morning of writing, he took the first martini of the day precisely at noon, lunched at one, and went to sleep at nine.

Afternoons were spent in cafés like the Vienna on Callé Victor Pradera. His growing deafness and his protruding eyes, the lid of the right one slightly drooping, hooding it in a knowing half-wink, conveyed courteous indifference. Friends of the old days who remembered all-night drinking bouts, practical jokes, passionate intellectual arguments and visits to the city's brothels were puzzled by this subdued Buñuel. 'He rumbled amiably,' wrote one, 'drank martinis and stubbed out cigarettes in an ashtray.' Luis recalled his last conversation with André Breton, the Pope of Surrealism and his mentor during the pre-war days in Paris. 'I can still see the sadness and vulnerability in Breton's eyes when he told me that no one could be scandalized any more.'

It was a skilful performance. Many were misled. And Luis Buñuel dearly loved to mislead.

At the Café Vienna, Francisco 'Paco' Rabal, the young actor who played his Christ-like hero in *Nazarin*, re-introduced Luis Buñuel to someone he had not seen for years, the Mexican businessman Gustavo Alatriste, who would become the producer of *Viridiana*.

There was a near-Surrealist appropriateness in the meeting. 'I've enjoyed working with everyone,' Buñuel said later, 'but most of all with

Alatriste. A curious character. One of the first times we found ourselves together he told me: "They can say what they like about me, that I'm a serious type, that I'm a bastard, that I'm a thief, but one thing they'll never say is that I'm a bad salesman."'

The son of a cockfight manager, Alatriste had got rich in property and publishing. His hobby was movie actresses, of whom he romanced many and married a few, including the blonde Mexican star Silvia Pinal. It was Pinal who indirectly brought about *Viridiana*. She decided he should expand into film production with a film for her, and that Buñuel should direct it. 'I rang up Buñuel and said: "We must make a film together. My husband Gustavo will produce it. Do you have a story you'd like to do with me?" Luis said: "No, but I can think of one. Why should your husband suddenly decide he wants to go into movies?" And I said, "He loves me." Buñuel, a devout believer like all Surrealists in the power of sex, conceded: "This is a good reason."'

Alatriste had never produced a film before, but the calf offered by Franco to his prodigal son was generously fatted, and he could see that the man who put up front money would make a fortune. He contributed most of the 6 million pesetas and, full of optimism, offered Buñuel four times his usual fee. In return, Buñuel was happy to accept Pinal as his star. Whether she could act was beside the point. More important to Buñuel were her legs and feet; pale, smooth, tantalizing. A life-long foot fetishist, he longed to see them in black stockings and close-fitting shoes.

Viridiana swelled with Buñuel's imagination into a raunchy and gaudily decorated fable, ripe with fetish and sacrilege. Once the Franco government had read the script, he was taken by Juan-Miguel Dominguin to see the Under-Secretary of Cinema, José Muñoz-Fontan. Primed to be obliging to the returning penitent, Muñoz-Fontan returned it with a few courteous suggestions. There was no trouble with the central story, but some details were a little . . . strong? Perhaps Don Jaime could die of a heart attack rather than hanging himself with a skipping rope whose wooden handles looked a little too much like penises? And Viridiana praying beside a crown of thorns, the nail and the hammer was provocative. So was her attempted rape by one of the beggars.

'As for the ending,' said Muñoz-Fontan, 'she simply can't sleep with her cousin *and* the maid.'

'What if they sit down to a three-handed card game?' Buñuel suggested. As a means of satirizing his double-dealing pro-Franco friends, this was even better than a sexual threesome. Muñoz-Fontan was delighted, and the script was approved.

Shooting on *Viridiana* started on 4 February 1961. Nobody noticed. Madrid was preoccupied by the filming of *King of Kings* at the vast Samuel Bronston studios outside the city. Buñuel's modest production was dwarfed by Nicholas Ray's 480-million-peseta epic in which Christ was played by the young American actor Jeffrey Hunter.

'If you had 480 millions,' someone asked Buñuel, 'what would you do?'

'I would throw Franco out of Spain,' he said. Then why was he making a film for the dictator he hated? The hooded eyes became even more secretive. Wait and see.

On the cross, Hunter's Christ revealed discreetly shaved armpits. Cynics dubbed the film '*I Was a Teenage Jesus*'. Buñuel had no truck with such bourgeois good taste. Instead of having costumes made for his beggars, he went to Madrid's garbage dumps and bought clothes off the backs of the rag pickers. Even they were embarrassed by their greasiness. The extra playing the leper who tries to rape Viridiana was a genuine beggar and alcoholic who fused the lights on his first day by pissing on the fuse box. When he came to do his scenes with Pinal, she complained of his smell. Drunk, he had crapped in his pants. Buñuel sent him to hospital, with an assistant on guard. Three days later, cleaned up and dried out, he played his part superbly.

In Mexico, where a film that took more than eighteen days to shoot was sure to lose money, Buñuel had learnt to work quickly and economically. By March, *Viridiana* was shot. So confident were the Spanish government that they entered it in Cannes without seeing even a metre. With any other director, this would have been a risk. With Buñuel, it was an invitation to disaster.

Had Luis planned *Viridiana* from the start as a Trojan horse with which to deliver a cargo of destruction into the heart of Fascist Spain? He said not. 'At first I was astonished by the scandal of *Viridiana*. My intention was not to provoke. I was more inclined to believe that people are actually imperturbable.'

Juan Luis Buñuel knows better. 'Of *course* he knew what he was doing. He always did. If he told anyone he didn't, it would be with a twinkle in his eye. We knew there would be trouble, so I took a duplicate negative to Paris. Dominguin also managed bullfighters, including one named Pedret. I loaded up a small van with the negatives and threw the capes and swords and our suitcases on top, and we drove up through Barcelona and across the border to Lunel, where there was a bullfight. I got on the train with the negatives and took them to Paris.'

A rough cut without sound was shown to Cannes director Robert Favre le Bret, who accepted it. The finished print barely made it to the festival. It was not shown until 3 p.m. on 17 May, the last day of the festival. There was no time for a Madrid screening. The jury, with little faith in a film made under Spanish censorship, had already chosen its winners but after the showing it unanimously added *Viridiana* to the list. Buñuel, ill in Paris with Ménière's Syndrome, the inner ear condition that destroyed his hearing in later life, was represented by Pinal at the award presentation. She rang him with the news that it had shared the Palme d'Or for Best Film and won its own special French critics' prize for Black Humour. Muñoz-Fontan, who still had not seen the film, walked proudly on stage to accept the Palme d'Or. At first Luis refused to believe it. 'They couldn't have,' he said incredulously. 'It's ridiculous.' The Franco regime was even more stupid than he had imagined.

It took a day for the scandal to explode, but when it did, the world knew about it. In *L'Osservatore Romano*, the Vatican's mouthpiece, a Spanish Dominican named Fierro excoriated *Viridiana* as 'sacrilegious and blasphemous'. Muñoz-Fontan saw it for the first time and realized that, apart from accepting his suggestion of the card game, Luis had made none of the promised changes.

Franco did not see it at the time; the Vatican's fury was enough. He disciplined all twenty members of the Cannes delegation and replaced Muñoz-Fontan with Jesús Sueros. *Viridiana* and Buñuel were comprehensively condemned. Any negatives and prints of the film in Spain were seized or burned, UNINCI was liquidated and all Buñuel films suppressed.

In his little house in suburban Mexico City, Luis sipped his lunchtime Martini, more than content. His critics retired in confusion. His old friend, the Mexican artist Alberto Isaac, published an apologetic cartoon. In the first panel, the director is coming ashore in Spain while Franco lays out a welcome mat. Across the seas, a protester yells: 'Buñuel is a traitor.' In panel two, Buñuel presents Franco with a box marked '*Viridiana*'. 'Kill Buñuel!' the critic calls. Panel three: the box has exploded in Franco's face. The critic is silenced. Isaac entitled it: '*Veni, Vidi, Vici*'. I came, I saw, I conquered.

2

'Listen to the newborn infant's cry in the hour of birth – see
the death struggles in the final hour – and then declare
whether what begins and ends in this way can be intended
to be enjoyment.'
– Sören Kierkegaard

'Remember Luis had five servants in that house when he was fourteen,'
said his one-time daughter-in-law Joyce. 'He even had someone to carry
his violin for him when he went to music lessons.'

One does not associate Luis Buñuel with servants – or for that matter,
with the violin. His image when he first became internationally
recognizable was of a balding, expressionless man in an open-necked
check shirt and mis-buttoned cardigan, slouched alone in a café at
midday, cigarette smouldering in one hand, a glass in the other, staring
with protruding but hooded eyes at passers-by. Politically, he was of the
far left, his Communism the commitment of a lifetime. And his hostility
to the Catholic Church in which he was raised was near-pathological.
None of these are characteristics usually associated with the Spanish
landed gentry.

Yet Buñuel was typical of the country and the class that produced him.
Aragon, in the north-east, had dominated fifteenth-century Spain.
Ferdinand of Aragon ruled the country with Isabella of Castile and sent
Columbus to America. Their daughter Catherine married Henry VIII of
England. By the nineteenth century, however, the region had declined
into rural desolation, its people drawn away by Madrid and Barcelona.

Despite its lost glory, however, the Aragon in which Luis Buñuel grew
up was still feudal. Social divisions were pronounced. 'The respectful
subordination of the peasants to the big landowners was deeply rooted
in tradition,' Luis wrote in *My Last Breath*, 'and seemed unshakeable.'
Morality, charity and education were, as they had been for centuries, in
the hands of the Church. The *señoritos* and *señoritas* of the landed

gentry were left to live as they saw fit, ruled only by their flexible and partial consciences.

Some *señoritos* were pious, others drunks and rapists. All were expected to fight duels over abstract questions of honour. Many, including Luis's father, considered themselves political liberals, in that they did not mistreat their tenants, and the beggars and gypsies who presented themselves at the gate could usually be sure of a meal. Every Friday a dozen local poor would line up against the church wall opposite the Buñuel house and receive bread and a 10-centavo coin. By Aragonese standards this was enlightened, even if those who received the largesse were expected to kiss the servant's hand.

Organized labour, however, was regarded as Godless insanity. Although Zaragoza, the capital of Aragon, was known as 'the pearl of unionism', during his childhood Luis saw demonstrations there put down ruthlessly by the mounted Guardia Civil. He would be a Communist for most of his adult life, socializing and working almost exclusively with fellow-believers, but his politics would always carry a whiff of disdain for the common worker. He remained, as he had been born, a *señorito*.

Buñuel celebrated the *señorito* character often in his films, particularly in Don Francisco Galvan in *El*, in the hero of *The Criminal Life of Archibaldo de la Cruz*, but best of all in *Tristana*'s Don Lope. A middle-aged gentleman living on a skimpy private income, Lope declines to work, but out of conviction rather than laziness; a *señorito* does not soil his hands. In the same spirit he rebuffs a dealer who offers him a better deal for some family silver because of the respect in which he holds him. He wants no favours from tradesmen.

His sense of right and wrong cuts casually across the laws of State and Church. He disparages the tendency among duellists to stop at first blood. In his day, one fought on to the death. As for the Church, he loathes its sanctimony and pomp. 'The real priests are people like us,' he growls. 'People who defend the innocent; the enemies of hypocrisy, injustice and filthy lucre.'

Don Lope has decided to respect all the Commandments except for those that deal with sex. And though all women are fair game, he exempts virgins and the wives of friends. This said, he quickly seduces his own virginal ward, Tristana, although the infraction leads to his destruction. Rules, even one's own, are made for the obedience of fools and the guidance of the wise.

That Buñuel wins our sympathy for these deluded, sometimes unbalanced men says much for his understanding of the *señorito* character. He ran his own life in much the same way, with a disregard for money, a strict conception of honour, and a lack of concern for any morality but his own. Like Archibaldo and Francisco Galvan, he was driven all his life by two primary forces, sexual desire and a fascination with death. Yet the world saw him as a man loyal to his friends, loving to his family, meticulous in his work. All he asked was that people take him completely at his own valuation.

Few people, least of all Buñuel, have found much of interest in Calanda, the Buñuels' home town, which lies 100 kilometres south-east of Zaragoza. In Luis's day the population was about 5000. The train passed 18 kilometres away, at Alcaniz. The last part of the journey was by horse-drawn carriage through the sort of landscape most of us think of when we visualize Spain : flat, dry, dusty country of wheat fields, olive groves and vineyards under a cloudless blue sky, with the foothills of the Sierra a few kilometres away to offer a little variety.

The history of Calanda is as flat as its geography. Francisco Goya was born nearby, but the fact that Buñuel later shared his fascination with the horrors of the unconscious (and, like him, went deaf in middle age) hardly justifies generalisations about a prevailing local philosophy. Otherwise, Calanda gave its name to a distinctive dance, the *jota*. And the town had a miracle. In 1640 Miguel Juan Pellicer's leg was amputated after a cartwheel crushed it. The pious Miguel rubbed his stump every day with oil from the lamp that burned before the image of the Virgin of Pilar in the local church until she re-attached the leg.

Its only other distinction is an annual rite in Easter week. Most Spanish towns have some variation on the Easter parade, with teams of local men, often dressed as *penitentes*, hauling a top-heavy image of the Virgin through the streets, accompanied by a blaring band. It is only in Calanda that men, women and children go into the streets, not to carry a statue but to beat drums, symbolizing the darkness and thunder that covered the earth when Christ died. From the night of Good Friday to the morning of Easter Sunday, as many as 3000 people pound an unceasing hypnotic rhythm until their hands bleed.

Such rituals fascinated Luis: he would be a life-long connoisseur of ceremonies. He learned the code of the church bells for masses, vespers, the angelus at midday, sometimes rung to signal a fire but usually when someone was dying: the measured *toque de agonia* for the death throes of an adult and a lighter bronze bell for a dying child. Belfries and bells turn up often in his films, usually to mark high points of madness, and the Calanda drums roar often as a symbol of revelation.

Houses in Calanda have red-tiled roofs and walls stuccoed in brown or white. Large double doors with heavy black iron hinges open on to shadowy interiors. Another gate, equally forbidding, leads to a court-yard. Luis was born in such a house on 22 February 1900. He was the first child of Leonardo Buñuel and Maria Portoles. There would be six more: Maria in 1901, Alicia in 1902, Conchita in 1904, Leonardo in 1910, Margarita in 1912 and Alfonso in 1915.

By Calanda standards the house and the life lived in it were lavish. Leonardo had bought his home from the noble Ram de Viu family just before Luis was born, having demolished his family's cottage at La Torre, on the edge of town, prior to reconstruction. It was a gesture typical of a man determined to make his mark. The Buñuels were an old local family but had never been rich. Luis's uncle became a pharmacist. Leonardo had run away from home at fourteen to join the army as a bugle boy. Bored with this, he signed up with four friends to fight in Cuba in the Spanish-American War. The elegant handwriting he displayed in filling out his application got him a clerk's job in Havana; fortunately for him, since most of his company marched inland and later died of yellow fever. After the war Leonardo stayed on in Havana to open a hardware and gun shop with two friends, Casteleiro and Vizoso. They made a fortune importing European goods into the Caribbean.

Not much is known about Leonardo's time in Cuba, although Luis used to joke that, if his father's potency in Spain was any indication, he must have had plenty of bastard cousins running around Havana. Conchita Mendez, Luis's student fiancée, claimed to have met a sea captain who remembered Leonardo. 'He used to crack nuts with his head,' he recalled, offering a rather different picture of Luis's stern, formal father.

In 1899 Cuba won its independence. Leonardo, then forty-three, sold his interest and decided it was time to settle down. He returned to Calanda and with typical *señorito* brashness announced that he would marry the prettiest, healthiest woman in town. His choice was Maria Portoles, daughter of a local landlord. She was seventeen, certainly pretty, and judging from the sturdy children she bore him, obviously in good health. For their honeymoon they went to Paris, where Luis was conceived in the Hôtel Ronceray, in passage Jouffroy. The little hotel would always have a special significance for Buñuel. On his first visit to Paris he stayed there, and part of his last film, *That Obscure Object of Desire*, was shot in passage Jouffroy.

As a young man Leonardo, though short, had been dramatically handsome, with dark hair swept back from his forehead, heavy black moustache and piercing grey-green eyes, but the tropics aged him. By the time Luis knew him, he was roly-poly, almost bald, and his moustache was white. He still affected the panama, cane and powerful cigars of his Cuban days, however, as well as the confidence of someone used to being obeyed.

Soon after Luis was born, Leonardo tired of sleepy Calanda and moved the family to Zaragoza, renting a large apartment at 29 Paseo de la Independencia. The flat, which took up a whole floor and had ten balconies, had previously been the police headquarters. While the Buñuels lived in Zaragoza Leonardo rebuilt his old country home at La Torre in more opulent style. Not afraid to display his money, he loaded the house with statuary and other decoration which Luis parodied in the house of the crazed landowner in *El*. Most of Luis's childhood was spent in Zaragoza, with summers and every Holy Week in Calanda, and frequent holidays on the north-western sea coast at Vega de Pas, near Santander.

'The fact of the matter', said Buñuel, 'is that my father did absolutely nothing.' Every day he got up, bathed, read his paper, smoked cigars and ate the meals prepared for him. If he went out, it was only for a stroll. The most he or his sons would carry in the street was a jar of caviare. For anything else, they sent a servant.

Luis wrote: 'We were undoubtedly the last scions of an ancient way of life characterized by the rare business transaction, a strict obedience to natural cycles, and a completely fossilized mode of thought. The only industry in the region was olive oil; everything else – cloth, metals, medicines – came from the outside world. Local artisans supplied only our most pressing needs; there was a blacksmith, a coppersmith, a few tinsmiths, a saddler, some bricklayers, a weaver and a baker. Agriculture was semi-feudal; tenant farmers worked the land and gave half their harvest to their proprietors.' Calanda had two churches. Seven priests controlled charity, morality and education.

Essentially it was a society of women, of the sort that Federico Garcia Lorca, who, like Buñuel and Salvador Dali, was brought up in the same way, reflected in his play *The House of Bernarda Alba*. A matriarchal mother imposed absolute rule over the servants and children. As Luis's mother, Doña Maria, grew older, her sons and daughters became more rather than less respectful. In his twenties, when he was technically head of the family, Luis still came to her to beg money for his enterprises. Mostly she refused. And when he started a family of his own, it was she who had his son Juan Luis baptized, despite his furious objections.

According to Juan Luis, Buñuel remembered Don Leonardo as 'a kind man, but quite old'. They were always distant. The one recreation they shared was long walks around the estate, with Don Leonardo stopping at every olive tree to inspect the bark and fruit, upending every rock to examine the insects underneath. Since Aragon had a tradition of banditry and insurrection, he carried a gun from the private arsenal expected of a wealthy landowner.

Luis came to love such walks, and to enjoy firearms, though more for their beauty than their capacity to kill. Death, not killing, fascinated him. One of his earliest memories was of finding a dead donkey in one of the olive groves while on a walk with his father. Vultures and dogs tore its rotted carcass. Don Leonardo explained that the peasants preferred to let nature dispose of the dead. Absorbed, Luis sensed 'some obscure metaphysical significance' in the ragged, stinking remains and the skulking scavengers. He had to be dragged away.

After this, Luis became engrossed in animals, and accumulated a menagerie. 'He had a rat as big as a hare,' recalled his sister Conchita, 'which was perfectly repulsive with its vixen tail, but which we treated as one of the family. Whenever we went anywhere we took it in a parrot's cage [. . .] We always kept some animal. Monkeys, parrots, falcons, toads and frogs, some sort of snake, a large African lizard [. . .] I still remember the ram, Gregorio, who practically crushed my femur and pelvis when I was about ten years old [. . .] We were already a little older when we had a hat box full of grey mice. They belonged to Luis, but he allowed us to look at them once a day. He had selected several couples which, well fed and housed, procreated without cease.'

At six, Luis entered the College of the Brothers of the Sacred Heart. He switched a year later to the Jesuit Colegio del Salvador, where he stayed until he was sixteen. His marks were average; poor for mathematics but adequate for French, Latin, politeness and neatness. He served at Mass, sang in the choir and took Communion every day. Although he came to hate religion, he never lost the habits of Jesuit discipline. 'Discipline was very important to him,' said Joyce Buñuel. 'He used to say, "Liberty is discipline." '

From childhood, Buñuel was solitary. As the eldest son of an important local landowner, he could not socialize with the children of Calanda. Time out of school was spent with his brothers and sisters, and with the occasional visiting cousin. As a result, he would always attach great importance to family rituals and ceremonies, and to institutions with a quasi-family atmosphere. The sense of a secret society inherited from his Jesuit education would also attract him to Surrealism and Communism, and lead him to set up his own Order of Toledo. As a minor secret agent during the Spanish Civil War, he revealed a faintly comic taste for intrigue and deception. All his life he enjoyed disguises. In his twenties he would walk around Paris and Madrid in the habit of a priest and, occasionally, of a nun. Twice in his own films, at the end of *El* and the start of *The Phantom of Liberty*, he appeared in a monk's robe. In Mexico City, married with a family, he would still dress up as a *conquistador* for a party.

During one of the infrequent Buñuel family conclaves, when he was thirteen or fourteen, Luis led Conchita, always his favourite among his brothers and sisters, and a group of cousins on an expedition to Foz, a village near Calanda. Deferential to the offspring of the quality, the locals fed them cakes and sweet wine. Half-drunk, the children wandered to an old cemetery, where many of the tombs were in a state of decay. Luis lay down on a slab and invited the others to cut him open. Then, with only a stub of candle, they descended into the cave-like vaults. The candle quickly went out and they were lost. As the others became hungry, Luis offered to let them eat him. Rescued at last, they were carried home sleepily in a cart. Far from being punished, however, they were lionized, particularly Luis, whom Don Leonardo praised for his self-sacrifice in offering himself to be devoured. Nobody could know quite how pleasurable a sensation this proposal produced in Luis. A sense of imminent death accompanied by a reeling erotic stupor came to dominate his life. 'Death', he wrote, 'along with profound religious faith and the awakening of sexuality constituted the dominating force of my adolescence.' The Surrealist idea of *l'amour fou*, passion so delirious that it transcends distance and even death, would fascinate him. Meanwhile, he fantasized about drugging women and then having sex with them. He also recalls as a young man witnessing a primitive autopsy. One of the Buñuel shepherds had been stabbed and Luis insisted on observing the village doctor and town barber at work in the local church. A bottle of brandy was passed around to the sound of sawed bones and cracking ribs. Luis got so drunk that he had to be carried home half-conscious.

At sixteen Luis experienced a seismic upheaval in his character. What had been passionate devotion to the Church turned almost overnight to contempt. Despite good grades, he left the Jesuit college and graduated two years later from the local high school.

Luis was always vague about the exact motives for this change of heart. He told José de la Colina and Tomás Pérez Turrent, two critics who interviewed him in the 1970s, that Darwin's *Origin of Species* made him 'take a sharp turn', but his wife Jeanne is probably closer when she writes, 'He hated the spiritual power of the Church, and its money.' Luis himself said only that his apostasy began with simple scepticism at the fables fed to him by the Church. His upbringing had turned him into a classic nineteenth-century pragmatist, with an informed intellectual interest in the material world, based on careful observation. He had watched insects, plants and animals, and seen a logical order in their lives and deaths. To convince him, a religious system needed to be rational, and to dove-tail with nature.

His first doubts about Catholicism were not philosophical but practical. If there was to be a literal Day of Judgement, for example, when the dead would rise, how could one earth hold the corpse of every person who had died since the beginning of time? The Church's standard response, 'Because God has decreed it', was insufficient.

Luis also distrusted a God so manifestly lacking the will to expunge his enemies. Perhaps, whispered the Tempter, He did not have the power. By deserting the Church, Luis challenged God to strike him down. Every apostate has his or her own method of throwing down the gauntlet. The anarchists ritually muttered, 'I shit on God.' American expatriate publisher Harry Crosby, whom Luis knew in Paris in the 1920s, had the Crucifixion tattooed under his left foot so that he would defile the central incident of Catholicism with every step he took. Luis, more prosaically, drank most of a bottle of cheap brandy and vomited it up during Mass. No bolt of lightning vulcanized him to the pew, and his scorn ripened into a hatred of the Church that would flourish for almost seventy years and generate one of the most consistently vituperative anti-ecclesiastical bodies of work in the history of art.

All his life, Buñuel would be drawn to stories of men who challenged God. Gilles de Rais, the hero of Huysmans's *Là-Bas*, the Marquis de Sade, the heroes of Lewis's *The Monk* and Moral's *Don Juan Tenorio* thrilled him with their reckless insubordination; he would film, or consider filming, most of them. They fed his conviction that he had been right to abandon the Church. That Tenorio and particularly de Rais, who is mainly remembered as Joan of Arc's lieutenant, could indulge every vice but repent and escape damnation, emphasized how the Church stacked the odds for salvation in favour of those rich and well enough informed to buy redemption with a death-bed confession.

Paradoxically Luis's departure robbed the Church of a potential zealot. With his medieval obsessiveness, his tendency to self-abnegation, his scorn of material comfort, he was set fair to become a religious ascetic. Even before his loss of faith, he had embarked on a monastic regime. He gave up meat and fresh bread, and took to wearing thin clothing and sandals even in Aragon's icy winters. He washed obsessively, both hands and feet, and developed his body with exercise, in particular boxing, at which he became Calanda's outstanding, indeed only, expert.

When a strong erotic nature collides with religious belief, one often reinforces, then devours, the other. The intellectual energy that Luis had expended on God quickly gave way to a sex drive he described as 'stronger than hunger'.

Satisfaction with a real partner, however, was still in the future. The favourite sexual pastime of young Spanish blades was *en cerrar a mujer* – to lock up a girl. If they met a pretty girl in the street without her *duenna*, they showered her with extravagant compliments – *piropos* – until she was forced to run indoors. Young Luis would boast, 'I locked up seven girls today' but, like the rest, he would never dare touch them. For the *señorito* there were only two kinds of sex – in the brothel or with a wife – and he could not afford either. Traditionally the young men of Calanda paid a twice-yearly visit to a Zaragoza brothel, but Luis had neither the money nor the courage for this. Instead he pored over erotic magazines. On holiday in Santander he peeked at girls undressing next to him in the flimsy bathing huts until they began to thrust hatpins through the peepholes, a detail he featured in *El*.

Leaving the Church changed Luis's intellectual habits as well. Until then, he had coasted along on the usual teenage reading: Sherlock Holmes and Nick Carter, with the occasional Spanish *feuilleton*. Afterwards, Darwin, Nietzsche, Kropotkin and novelists of the Spanish realist tradition replaced them. Luis never went back to reading for recreation. In his seventies, the books on his shelves were histories of the Church, some Surrealist poetry, and Henri Fabre's pioneering texts on insects. If one wanted sex, action and travel to exotic lands, they were more easily found in the real world.

Like many men who leave the Church in adolescence, Buñuel spent the rest of his life seeking an alternative belief system. At first he thought science might provide a focus. Sensuality followed, then Surrealism, Communism, and finally the cinema. None provided exactly what he needed. Nor could he lose himself, as many Spaniards did, in patriotism. By his own specialized definition, Buñuel was a patriot, but he placed his belief in the national temperament and in certain old friends rather than in Spain itself, that 'closed and isolated society', as he called it, where 'each day was so like the next that they seemed to have been ordered for all eternity'. Physically and spiritually Buñuel lived always in exile, fleeing from a Spain and a Church which, nevertheless, as his films made obvious, lurked always at his shoulder.

In 1912, sensing that war in Europe was imminent and that money might be made from it, Leonardo Buñuel returned to Cuba and tried to re-enter his old business. Had he been successful, Luis's life would have been very different, but his partners refused, and he returned disconsolate to Spain, leaving them to become millionaires. Luis, instead of falling heir to a commercial fortune, would inherit nothing but land and responsibilities, and would need to find a career.

His first idea was music. At thirteen, of his own volition, he had taken up the violin. He also played the ocarina, and could pick out tunes on the piano. Later, in Paris, he learned – improbably – the banjo. At sixteen, he became fascinated by Wagner. Now he badgered his father to let him study composition at the Schola Cantorum in Paris. Don Leonardo sensibly refused. No son of his was going to become a Rodolfo starving in some *La Bohème* garret.

As an alternative, Luis suggested entomology. The family gave this a little more thought. Phylloxera had just ravaged Spain's wine industry, but although a local liberal landowner, Don Luis Gonzales, imported an agronomist who set up a microscope in the Calanda town hall to show everyone the mites that caused the disease, growers stubbornly refused to uproot their vines. When Gonzales tore out his own, the locals sent death threats. A Buñuel who knew insects might make a useful manager of the estate, but Don Leonardo urged his son to think about agricultural engineering. 'The aristocratic thing to do in Spain is to study to be an engineer or a diplomat,' Luis wrote. 'The only young men who had access to these careers were those who, besides having the necessary intelligence and application, had sufficient funds, as the cost was excessive for the modest Spanish way of living.' The title of Doctor of Engineering was mainly honorific, but with it one could go into commerce, even politics. Reluctantly Luis agreed, mostly to put the stultifying life of Zaragoza and Calanda behind him, and in October 1917 he arrived in Madrid to enrol in the University's Engineering School.

3

'Madrid is above all the city of cafés.'
— John dos Passos, *Journey Between Wars*

Luis had been to Madrid only once before, briefly, with his father, and although by international standards it was still a small city of fewer than a million people, its size scared him. While Don Leonardo, natty with his Cuban straw hat and cane, had strolled along the Calle d'Alcala, pointing out the sights, Luis thrust his hands into his pockets and turned his back, pretending not to know him.

Compared to Paris or Berlin, Madrid, like Spain itself, was a backwater. Despite an embarrassment of engineers, 'the Madrid Spaniards,' complained Paris-based American editor and writer Robert McAlmon, 'are not accustomed to machinery or to industrialization. They have sky-scrapers but they are rickety; they have elevators but they seldom work and then inspire one with fear of a crash; they have flush water-closets but even in the first-class hotels they are often clogged and dirty. The Spaniard is not modernized. Even tram cars are operated more as they were in smaller American cities some twenty years back.'

Doña Maria came to Madrid with Luis to help him find a place to stay. Neither liked the boarding houses they saw. The food was the basic daily plate of *cocido a la Madrileña*; chickpeas and cabbage boiled with a little bacon, *chorizo* sausage and stringy chicken. Hygiene was worse. Anything unwanted was simply tossed on the floor and, with the staff shortage, usually stayed there. Doña Maria also suspected, rightly, that boys in such places quickly fell into drinking and whoring.

Fortunately Don Bartolomeo Esteban, a family friend, had given Luis a recommendation to the Residencia de Estudiantes. The 'Resi', as it was known, had been launched by Alberto Jimenez Fraud at the invitation of Francisco Giner de los Rios, a liberal educator who admired the Oxbridge system; gentleman students, informal tutors, residential colleges. He aimed to give out-of-town students an environment where they could form the sort of relationships that, as at Oxbridge, would provide the foundation of life-long careers. According to Lorca's biographer Ian Gibson, 'Fraud selected the students carefully to ensure that there was always a balance between the "two cultures" [. . .] The warden and his collaborators felt themselves to be missionaries in the cause of a new Spain.' The Residencia's modish reputation was sustained by guest lecturers and performers like Le Corbusier, Einstein, the economist John Maynard Keynes, Stravinsky, Poulenc and Ravel.

The Residencia had opened in the autumn of 1910 on Fortuny Street, at the north end of the Paseo de la Castellana, the wide avenue that, even more than it does today, divided Madrid. Once the fields where it stood had been a popular place for duels. By the time Luis arrived, they were occupied by a cluster of halls of residence for 150 students. Standing on a hill above large gardens with ornamental ponds and groves of poplars, the three-storeyed red-brick buildings, known as 'pavilions', with big windows and wide wooden eaves painted green, shared a fanciful architectural style of turrets, towers and long balconies. One was nicknamed 'The Transatlantic Liner'.

Rooms were cheap: 7 pesetas a day, or 4 if you shared, which most did. Meals were included. The floors were tiled, the windows and furniture plain wood. Here and there, a pot or a tapestry provided a splash of colour in an intentionally austere environment. Alcohol was banned – everyone drank tea – and the floors were spotless. Doña Maria instantly approved the plain atmosphere and tough management, and installed Luis in a single room, for which the family paid directly by the semester. He also got an inadequate 20 pesetas a week to spend. 'Without the Residencia,' Luis said, 'my life would have been very different.'

Luis enrolled in the 1918 class of the University's Engineering School, specializing in agricultural engineering. In fact he had no intention of learning how to build culverts and irrigation systems. He expected to transfer quickly to agronomy and on into the world of insects. In Spain's hidebound academia, however, even a career in the natural sciences demanded the extensive study of mathematics. Luis did well in biology, but his maths grades were dismal. Nor did he make much of an effort to improve them. As a friend at the Residencia, José Bello y Lasierra, says: 'For two years, Luis didn't do very much at all.'

Most of his energy went into sports. The Resi's emblem was 'The Blond Athlete', the head of a handsome young Greek, adapted from a fifth-century B.C. Athenian sculpture, and residents lived up to it with football, running, hockey, tennis and sun-bathing. The physique Luis had developed in Calanda matured quickly. At eighteen he was vain about his strong arms and the hairless muscular torso which a doctor friend, Gregorio Maranon, to Buñuel's delight, declared 'perfect'. He even went to the trouble of having himself photographed front and back as a record.

'I was always a morning person,' Luis said. 'Already . . . in Madrid, I was getting up just when the night people were just going to bed.' In the grounds and on a track used by the cavalry of the Guardia Civil, he ran every morning in all weathers, always barefoot and bare-chested. He turned up at breakfast in running clothes, carrying his javelin, and would invite other students to stand on his stomach to demonstrate the strength of his muscles.

Team sports did not interest him but he worked out with a heavy sawdust-filled 'medicine ball', threw the javelin, arm-wrestled in cafés and, above all, boxed. He claimed to have been amateur champion of Spain in 1921, though later he acknowledged that he fought in the ring only twice. The first match went to him by default because his opponent did not show up, and in the second, against a man named Naval, he was disqualified for lack of effort. 'If the truth be known,' he admitted, 'I spent the entire five rounds worrying about how to protect my face.'

Surprisingly for a man who would show almost total disregard for clothes in later life, Luis as a student was sartorially vain. He always wore a jacket and, often, a tie, though his heavily muscled neck meant that he was more comfortable wearing collar-less shirts and the light sweaters his mother sent him. Dali's 1924 portrait of him catches him in what was probably a typical outfit of the period, including one of Doña Maria's jumpers.

Like most students in this city of cafés, Buñuel often idled time away after class over one coffee and an infinite number of glasses of water in the Gijon, the Granja del Henar, the Castilla, the Fornos, the Kutz or the Montana. Occasionally he went to the Platerias, where a political *peña* attracted the Aragonian anarchist Angel Samblancat and left-wing poets like Eugenio d'Ors, the biographer of Goya.

The *peña*, a semi-formal gathering which usually convened from three to five in the afternoon, and after nine at night, often around a particular individual, was central to café life. It merged with the less structured *tertulia*, strictly speaking a casual meeting for a drink, although John Hopewell defines it as 'the café get-together where banter sharpened a taste for paradox, irony, and the anecdote which builds on itself to climb to the absurd'. The fragmentary narratives of *The Discreet Charm of the Bourgeoisie* and *The Phantom of Liberty*, where incidents flow into one another, spiralling to a giddy apotheosis of illogic, bear its signature.

Spain was as backward intellectually as it was mechanically. The composer Edgard Varèse assured Robert McAlmon that 'there would be a renaissance in Spain' whilst cavilling '[it] will not start from what Americans or the French conceive as "modern". It will be another directional development from the later middle ages.' During Luis's time in Madrid, there was little sign of this new age. Musicologist John Brande Trend asked a priest/librarian at the University of Seville if he could see the catalogue: 'See the catalogue?' the priest hissed. 'See the *catalogue*!'

The Spanish avant-garde, such as it was, was embodied in the Generation of '98 — older intellectuals like Miguel de Unamuno, the argumentative and morbid philosopher who had been exiled to the Canaries by the right-wing government for his dissident opinions, and José Ortega y Gasset. The young had little time for them, and most Spanish artists quickly moved to Paris, their intellectual capital. Pablo Picasso had already made a name for himself there, as had Joan Miró and Juan Gris. They had been followed by a handful of others, mostly lesser painters: Hernando Viñes, Joaquin Peinado, Manuel Angeles Ortiz, Pancho Cossio, Francisco Borés, Ismael de la Serna, Rafael Barradas, José Maria Uzelay. Those who remained in Madrid became known as the Generation of '27. The tabloid *Gaceta Literaria*, edited by the energetic Ernesto Giménez Caballero, documented their doings.

In 1918 the Chilean poet Vicente Huidobro had spent five months in Madrid spreading the gospel of Cubism and Dada. The result was the formation of the Ultraistas, an avant-garde group launched in 1918 by Guillermo de la Torre, the poet who wrote its 1920 manifesto, and centred on Ramon Gómez de la Serna, who ran a *peña* on Saturday evenings in the cellar of the Café Pombo near the Puerta del Sol. Twelve years older than Luis and already a published novelist and biographer, Gómez de la Serna properly belonged to the Generation of '98, but his enthusiasms for machine art, film and the French avant-garde placed him with the Ultraists. His *peña* attracted the Argentinian Jorge Luis Borges, playwright and designer Edgar Neville, Rafael Alberti, an artist who discovered a talent for poetry, and, before long, two men who were to have a profound effect on Buñuel's career, the painter Salvador Dali and the poet and playwright Federico Garcia Lorca.

Garcia Lorca arrived at the Resi in the spring of 1919, when Luis had been there for two years. He was twenty-one, with a trusting, almost girlish face and an electric smile. Always dressed in suit and tie, he came from a wealthy Granadian family with an artistic tradition. He had already published poems, which had plenty of admirers in Madrid.

Luis probably met Lorca on his first exploratory visit; most new arrivals ate a meal in the dining room, a chance to look one another over and check out the food. Immediately impressed, Luis wrote: 'Federico was brilliant and charming, with a visible desire for sartorial elegance – his ties were always in impeccable taste. With his dark, shining eyes, he had a magnetism that few could resist.'

Lorca was also homosexual – a fact that, even in relatively cosmopolitan Madrid, was best kept secret. Luis certainly did not realize that Lorca was *maricon*. Despite his own taste for cross-dressing, he detested homosexuality. To win a bet he flirted with one of Madrid's few well-known gays, letting himself be picked up at a bus stop and coaxing 25 pesetas out of the man 'for school books'. He even indulged in gay-bashing, accosting a man in a public lavatory and luring him outside to be beaten by other Residencistas. For years, Buñuel refused to believe that Lorca was gay, and his eventual discovery of his hero's sexual nature had a seismic effect on their friendship.

'From time to time,' said Jean-Claude Carrière, Buñuel's scriptwriting collaborator and 'ghost writer' of *My Last Breath*, 'I've tried to imagine what [Buñuel] was like at eighteen. He was probably hard to please and not so easy to live with; somebody already not so charming. Not only a night-club habitué. You can't become somebody else overnight.' Even so, Luis idled away much of his first year in Madrid. Most evenings he was probably drunk. He had discovered the pleasures of alcohol and also the useful fact that he had a good head for it; the foundation of a lifetime's pleasurable drinking.

He also found how to satisfy his craving for sex, which had become more than irritating. 'No sooner would I sit down in a railway carriage,' he wrote, 'than erotic images filled my mind. All I could do was succumb, only to find them still there, and sometimes even stronger, afterwards.' Exactly what he succumbed to is not clear, but certainly during his more virile days he was a frequent client of prostitutes. As a result of this wild life the end of term almost always found him broke. Every time he went home for holidays, his mother had to be persuaded to pay off the previous term's debts, a transaction kept from Don Leonardo.

The *peñas* admitted no women, and Luis followed his friends in regarding them, except for casual lust, as an adjunct to life rather than an integral part of it. Mistresses and fiancées were kept well away from one's friends, a rule Luis followed meticulously until he was married. For five of his years as a student he was technically engaged to Conchita Mendez, a poet who later married his friend Manuel Altolaguirre, but it is unlikely, from the evidence of later liaisons, that the relationship ever went beyond a certain formal, virginal cordiality. Neither Conchita nor the engagement rates even a mention in his memoirs.

Luis's fascination with the intimate relationship of sex and death persisted and expanded. On a midnight visit to the grave of the poet Mariano José de Larra in the San Martin cemetery with a group led by Eugenio D'Ors, Luis wandered away from the others and stepped down into a tomb. Through the broken top of a coffin, he could see a woman's dirty hair where it had, as he believed, continued to grow after death. He would use the image in *The Phantom of Liberty*, where the exhumed body of a princess is as pink and fresh as in life.

What attracted Luis in this case was less the association with death than the necrophilic attraction of a beautiful but inanimate woman, an image that was fast becoming his sexual ideal. Buñuel always believed he had the power to hypnotize women, to read and influence their minds. Simply by willing it, he could draw a woman to his table or reel off the most private details about her.

In 1921 Luis spent a few days in Toledo with the philologist Antonio Solalinde. Most Spaniards regarded the twelfth-century city 70 kilometres south of Madrid as the repository and museum of Spain's medieval glory. Cut off from the world by the steep banks of the muddy Tejo River which had gouged a gorge through the soft rock around three sides of the city, it retained its air of medieval isolation. Waves of Roman and Moorish domination had created a palimpsest of architectural styles, dominated by the Gothic cathedral and the Moorish fortress of the Alcazar, once commanded by El Cid.

Toledo spawned legends. This was La Mancha, the windmill-dotted homeland of Don Quixote, and the city's narrow, twisting, cobbled streets and medieval inns more than lived up to the imagination of Cervantes. It had also been the home of the mysterious El Greco, whose homoerotic Crucifixions and scenes of martyrdom made explicit the Spanish Church's preoccupation with the flesh and its mortification.

Buñuel and Solalinde spent much of their time in the city's cafés and brothels. In one of the bordellos, Luis tried out his recently discovered skill in hypnosis. When he was finished with a girl, he hypnotized her and sent her to call on Solalinde.

They also went to a performance of *Don Juan Tenorio*, a play by the nineteenth-century dramatist José Zorrilla y Moral. Tenorio, a young tearaway, and his friend Mejia bet on which one of them can perform the most evil deeds in a year. Tenorio wins by raping or murdering most of the cast, but is saved from damnation by a love from beyond the grave. The play, with its catalogue of rapes and murders, and cynical attitude to sin and redemption, impressed Luis forcibly.

From 1920 to 1922, Luis was Lorca's acolyte. Both were part of a Resi group that met in each other's rooms to drink tea, argue and read poetry. 'At times [Lorca] and I would improvise plays and even operas!' Buñuel recalled. For someone who had never had close friends, it was a heady experience, made more so when, in 1921, Lorca casually dedicated a group of eleven poems to him – easy enough for someone so prolific, but for Luis immensely flattering.

Although the turnout varied, the group numbered about a dozen, some of whom – significantly not the most brilliant – were to become life-long friends of Buñuel. José Moreno Villa, Guillermo de la Torre and José Bello, known as 'Pepin', would always be close.

Dali made some notes on a typical evening's conversation in Room 3 at the Resi. Buñuel began by remarking: 'Wonderful evening! Weather which was yearning for rain. You cannot imagine what joy it causes me, despite the literature.'

Lorca responded: 'My friend, I feel for you with all sincerity. Yesterday you were stirred before the lilies on the canal and later under the light of the moon; if we'd stayed there you would have ended up by saying foolish things. If I remember rightly, you recited, though in a low voice, those lines of Verlaine which begin "*La lune . . . boît*".'

Guillermo de la Torre burst into the room with a curse by the Italian Futurist poet F. T. Marinetti: 'Universal hatred for the moon!' He went on, 'What's the point of your having been born under the wings of aeroplanes? And you dare call yourselves avant-garde. I'm leaving, leaving straight away because I fear contact with you will convert me into some antediluvian being and above all because my sensibility does not allow me to stay silent . . . '

Conversation like this must have been heavy going, especially for Luis, for whom banter never held much appeal. He also keenly felt his lack of education. Although he was furiously reading the moderns, he never did catch up, his taste always drawing him back to nineteenth-century realism and accounts of natural phenomena.

Lorca knew how to undercut ponderous undergraduate humour with irony, a lesson Luis learned well, and put into practice later. On particularly dull nights Lorca offered his party trick. Lying back on a couch, he folded his hands and slipped into a death-like trance. The others prepared his body, placed it in an improvised coffin and carried it downstairs and into the streets, at which point Lorca usually lost his composure and began to giggle.

Pepin Bello, though peripheral, was more important than he appeared, both to the group and to Buñuel. Most dismissed him as a cheerful nonentity, almost a buffoon, but in fact he was neither. He had arrived in 1915 at the Resi where he would stay for almost a decade without taking a degree. He spent most of his time strolling the streets doing nothing, which he called *ruismo*, though his sharp eye often saw things his more self-absorbed friends missed. His presence injected into the contrived conversation of the group a touch of the streets, and of madness. 'He was witty, sharp and someone to whom extraordinary things happened,' Rafael Alberti said. 'All the business of donkeys and pianos, most of that came from him [. . .] Bello was full of imagination – and the *putrefactos* [rotting donkeys] came from Pepin. It was then that Dali drew the *putrefactos*, but the person who had talked most about all this was Bello.'

Some in Madrid knew of and were intrigued by the new ideas being propounded in Paris by André Breton, successor and heir of Tristan Tzara, inventor of Dada. Breton came to Madrid in 1923 to open an exhibition by Francis Picabia. The following year he published his First Surrealist Manifesto. During the Great War Breton had worked in a psychiatric hospital and seen the effect of mania. He also read Freud, but in the light of earlier poets and writers classified in their time as 'decadent': Baudelaire, Comte de Lautréamont, the Marquis de Sade. 'I believe,' he wrote, 'in the future transmutation of those two seemingly contradictory states, dream and reality, into a sort of absolute reality, *surrealité*.' He went on: 'Let us not mince words. The marvellous is always beautiful, anything marvellous is beautiful, in fact only the marvellous is beautiful.' Louis Aragon, Breton's lieutenant, announced: 'One madness more has been given to man. Surrealism, son of frenzy and darkness.' On 18 April 1925, Aragon also lectured at the Residencia on Surrealism. It's likely Buñuel was there, since, shortly afterwards, he began to speak knowledgeably about the new movement.

If Lorca was the Resi's star until 1922, he was eclipsed thereafter by Salvador Dali. Dali was eighteen when he arrived, Buñuel twenty-two and Lorca twenty-four. Dali's father, also Salvador, was one of the richest men in Figueras, on the plains of Catalonia, not far from the Mediterranean, and the family owned property on the coast, at Cadaques, a fishing village just south of the French border.

From birth, Dali was disturbed and eccentric. A brother (yet another Salvador) died a year before he was born, and Dali lived in his shadow. His father erected a life-size statue of himself and his dead son in the local churchyard. *He* was the real Salvador; 'all my life,' said the second, 'I felt myself a fake'. Obsessively attached to his mother, Dali grew up with only the sketchiest grasp of the practical. When he arrived at the Resi, he could not read the time, buy anything in a shop, or travel on a train alone. Emotionally infantile, he was terrified of grasshoppers and anally fixated on his own excrement. As a result of his mother's tireless encouragement, however, he was a precociously brilliant artist.

Impatient of his son's oddities, his father tried to drive Salvador into rationality. When his mother died, it seemed a perfect time to push him from the nest. Dali senior also had his own agenda; he intended to remarry almost immediately, and didn't want a disapproving son looking over his shoulder. He enrolled Salvador in the Art School of Madrid University and sent him to live at the Residencia.

The students had their first glimpse of Dali in September 1921 when he came with his father to look over the place. With his shaggy haircut, long sideburns, wide-brimmed hat and doleful expression, he made a startling impression. Both wore mourning, but Dali had embellished his with a hunting jacket and plus-fours buttoned at the knee, with puttees wound loosely round his calves to reveal expanses of hairy flesh. The mock Tyrolean oddity of that first appearance earned him the nickname 'The Czechoslovakian Painter'.

Various Residencistas, including Bello and Buñuel, claim responsibility for discovering Dali's genius. Bello said: 'I was walking past his pavilion one morning and I looked in the window and saw him at work. There were pieces of paper everywhere. I asked him what he was doing. He said: "Drawing". I looked, and they were wonderful. I went back to the others, and said: "That weird Catalan kid can draw".' The revelation didn't take long, since within a week of his arrival he was designing posters for the Residencia.

Despite his paralysing shyness, Dali was soon adopted into the Room 3 group. Between Lorca, Buñuel and Dali a friendship sprang up. Arrogant, visionary, over-sexed, committed to a concept of creativity they barely understood, they were ripe for a revelation that provincial Madrid was ill-equipped to offer. They compromised by looking to one another for the enlightenment they had hoped to find in art. Inevitably they were disappointed, and the disappointment eventually turned to jealousy and, in the case of Dali and Buñuel, hatred.

When the Art Academy suspended Dali and some others in 1922 after they stirred up demonstrations when a favourite teacher failed to win a staff post, Luis persuaded a friend, Dr Barnadas, King Alfonso's personal trainer, to put in a good word. It didn't work, however, and Dali was sent back to Figueras for the rest of the year, where, since it was election time, he was promptly arrested as someone likely to disturb public order and jailed for a month.

Later, Dali brushed off these setbacks as if they had never happened. In fact they changed the direction of his career. His adolescent innocence was burned away. He became more manipulative, aware that the friends who could get you into trouble could also further your career.

Throughout 1924/5, however, the three were as intimate as brothers. They sniggered together over scatology, pooled their allowances to get drunk, sketched, played word-games and wove malicious rhymes around the cultural heroes of the day. For the moment Dali was content to be led, although his voice, unexpectedly deep and confident, and the eccentric clothes he wore, indifferent to the reaction of those around him, suggested the unyielding nature that would eventually wear down Lorca and Luis, both of whom Dali would use, then discard, in his single-minded search for fame.

Lorca was immediately attracted to Dali and set out to seduce him, intellectually and physically. The former was easy. Dali acknowledged Lorca's 'irresistible personal influence'. He blazed, he said, 'like a mad and fiery diamond'. At times Dali could become so furiously jealous of Lorca's imagination and flair that he would 'set off at a run, and nobody would see me for three days'.

For his part, Federico talked about 'my friend and inseparable companion, Salvador Dali'. When the three went on excursions to fairgrounds, it was more often Lorca and Dali, not Buñuel, who had themselves snapped against the painted backdrops of planes and boats usually reserved for lovers.

Lorca and Dali were ingenious and audacious schemers. Running out of money on one occasion, they declared a Resi room a 'desert', furnished it with a cabin and an angel (manufactured by Dali from a camera tripod, with celluloid collars for wings) and, opening the windows, begged food and drink from passers-by. Their 'installation' became one of the sights of Madrid. Gawkers poured through, bringing refreshments and company.

Dali also invited Lorca to Cadaques for the holidays, while Lorca, on the pretext of having him design some of the short plays he was writing, encouraged a deeper friendship which he hoped might develop into something more physical. To those at the Resi who sensed Lorca's sexuality, the trend of their relationship was obvious. Would Dali succumb? Everyone wondered what went on behind that dark face, snake-smooth and impassive, but Salvador gave nothing away, except perhaps in the portraits he painted of other Residencistas. His 1924 picture of Buñuel, which poses him against a bare abstract landscape of leafless trees and white buildings, geometric and featureless, lingers on Luis's sceptical eyes and sensual lips, the cruel, almost sneering tilt of which betrays Dali's nervous admiration.

In April 1925 Lorca began a poem called 'Ode to Salvador Dali', summing up the memories of his summer at Cadaques. Dali, 'with an olive-smooth voice [. . .] and love for all that is explicable', serves as a symbol of the region but obviously Lorca means to celebrate much more than Catalonia. Buñuel, still not entirely certain about Lorca's designs on Dali, became furiously jealous, and all the more so when a part of the poem was published in the *Gaceta*. Unable openly to attack the content, he fixed on its infidelity to Surrealism. 'Federico wants to make surrealist things,' he wrote, 'but they are false, made with the intelligence, which is incapable of finding what the instinct finds.'

Luis was doubly frustrated by the increasing intimacy of his two friends. Not only did Lorca and Dali share a sexual bond; they were both artists, while Luis had yet to discover a talent for anything but admiration. He was slipping behind them, less and less part of their lives. At the end of 1925, Dali returned to the Resi. He was soon exhibiting alongside artists much older than himself in the Society of Iberian Artists in Madrid, where his work was excellently reviewed. But the Madrid art school scene, with its conventional thinking, was beginning to chafe his expanding imagination. Lorca wanted him to design his play *Mariana Pineda*. Josep Dalmau had offered him a show in his Barcelona Gallery for December 1926. Dali was emerging.

The final shedding of the chrysalis took place when he confronted the examination panel at the Art Academy in the summer of 1926. They asked him to nominate a subject so that he could be examined in art theory. He snapped, 'No. Given that none of the professors at the Escuela de Bellas Artes has the competence to judge me, I withdraw.' The school needed no further encouragement, and Dali was expelled. For the next three years he would paint, and scheme how to get to Paris.

Dali's departure from the Resi and Lorca's increasing involvement in his own projects, sometimes with Dali, left Luis feeling disconsolate and lost. Alone amongst the trio, he had not discovered a talent. Nor did he possess Pepin Bello's languid detachment. Halfway through his course, he and some other Resi students had gone with their history professor Americo Castro on a day trip to the ancient university city of Salamanca. When Luis harped on French culture and his enthusiasms of the time, Jean Cocteau and Guillaume Apollinaire, Castro wondered why he was sticking with agronomy when, with even a second-rate liberal arts degree, he could walk into a job as Spanish instructor in a French university. Sensing a way out of his impasse, Luis had switched to philosophy, history and literature, though he never dared tell his father.

In 1923, Buñuel had also launched a fraternal group he called the Order of Toledo, a clique which combined the rituals of the Church with the clannishness of the aristocracy and the intellectual conceit of the Room 3 group at the Resi.

The idea came to him in a dream. He imagined he was in Toledo, drunk, with friends. They met another party, and the combined group caroused around the old city. Staggering into a cathedral, they were surrounded by singing birds. A voice ordered Luis to return to the Church – not to regain his faith but to rob the Carmelites. A concierge let him into the convent, and Luis confessed drunkenly to a monk that he wanted to join the order. He was shown back to the street.

On March 19, 1923, the feast of St Joseph, he invited some friends from the Resi to meet him in Toledo. There, at the Posada de Sangre, which Cervantes had used as a setting for his *La Ilustre Fergona (The Illustrious Chambermaid)*, he announced the formation of the Order, organized in not entirely sarcastic imitation of the fraternities that infested Spanish high society. He was the Grand Master; Lorca and his younger brother Paquito were among the founders. Alberti and Bello were knights – *caballeros* – as was Dali, who drew a group portrait on the inn's whitewashed wall, but was later, after his falling-out with Buñuel, marked 'Demoted' in the Order's records. Others were Squires, or Friends of the Squires, or Friends of the Friends of the Squires.

The only membership requirement was a devotion to Toledo equal to Luis's, the sole duty that of turning up for occasional drunken nocturnal revels when the group drank, ate and joked its way around the town in search of its many oddities. Members were forbidden to wash during these events, which began with a ritual visit to the Hospital of San Juan Bautista and a few moments' meditation at the Tomb of Cardinal Tavera, with its statue by Alonso Berruguete. The wax-like image of a gaunt old man, sculpted when the flesh had already settled to the bones in death, appealed to Luis's sombre sense of occasion. Later, in *Tristana*, he would show Catherine Deneuve absorbed in contemplation of the same face.

After this, the hunt was on for eccentricity. There was no shortage. Late one night, Buñuel and Eduardo Ugarte followed the sound of children chanting multiplication tables. They found the source, an open window, but when Luis hoisted himself on Ugarte's shoulders, he found only darkness and silence. On another trip, a blind man took him to his house which, since the whole of his family was also blind, had no lights on at all.* The walls were covered in Victorian funerary pictures of graveyards, woven from human hair.

Over the years most of Buñuel's friends and collaborators would be inducted into the Order. Its irregular meetings became famous, although nobody was ever quite sure of its founder's motives in setting it up. Friends who mocked it received a frosty stare, as did those who got too drunk or riotous. On one level, the Order was simply a more elaborate version of the deadpan jokes that amused Luis all his life. On another, however, it preserved the integrity and essence of the Resi group, but on Luis's own terms, and with himself at its head.

In May 1923, at the age of sixty-eight, Don Leonardo Buñuel died suddenly of pneumonia in Zaragoza. Luis had hurried to his bedside, making out that he was in town to take readings of the stars for a course. He helped dress his father's corpse, slitting his boots to squeeze them on to his swollen feet, and sat up all night with the body, drinking brandy and smoking.

Hearing what sounded like a chair falling over, he turned back into the room to see Don Leonardo standing with arms outstretched. The hallucination lasted only ten seconds, but it scared Luis sufficiently for him to sleep with a pistol under his pillow when he occupied his father's bed on the day after the funeral. The dream returned throughout his life. Half a century later, Juan Luis, sharing an apartment with him in the Torre de Madrid, was woken by his father's cry. Buñuel had dreamed of his father and his mother standing over him, holding hands, their eyes shining, looking down at him, an image he would use in *The Discreet Charm of the Bourgeoisie*.

For days after the funeral Buñuel remained in Zaragoza. He sat at his father's desk, smoked his cigars, even wore his boots. He sensed that his life was falling into a pattern of loss. Surviving, relatively unscathed, the failure of his faith and the death of his father proved that his inner resources could absorb much – even the loss of country.

He finished his philosophy degree at the end of 1924 but did not bother to take his doctorate. Teaching Spanish in a provincial French university no longer held much appeal, besides which his French was still rudimentary. However, the League of Nations was launching a Society for Intellectual Co-operation, based in Paris. Recommended by the director of the Residencia, Buñuel applied to be the (unpaid) secretary of its Spanish representative, Eugenio d'Ors. Nobody turns down free help,

---

* Luis does not seem to have connected the two events: in the house of the blind, presumably, lessons would take place in darkness.

so even though the organization did not yet exist, Buñuel was told to go to Paris, read the papers to improve his French and English, and await orders. With Doña Maria's blessing – diplomacy was an entirely suitable job for her son – and her promise of a monthly cheque, he left for France.

4

'No more painters, no more writers, no more musicians, no more sculptors, no more religions, no more republicans, no more royalists, no more imperialists, no more anarchists, no more socialists, no more bolsheviks, no more politicians, no more proletarians, no more democrats, no more armies, no more police, no more nations, no more of these idiocies, no more, no more, NOTHING, NOTHING, NOTHING.

'Thus we hope that the novelty which will be the same thing as what we no longer want will come into being less rotten, less immediately GROTESQUE.'

– Louis Aragon, 1920 (translated by Richard Howard)

Buñuel came to Paris in January 1925 with only the sketchiest idea of what he would do there. The International Society of Intellectual Co-operation had told him to wait for their call. It never came.

One place in the French capital spoke to him of his family and Zaragoza. Like an insect called back across hundreds of miles to its hive, Buñuel checked into the little Hôtel Ronceray in passage Jouffroy, one of the shopping arcades of northern Paris that burrow through the blocks between the Bourse and Montmartre, where his parents had spent their honeymoon in 1899. He may have slept in the bed where they conceived him; it would not have been out of character.

He found his way with equal speed to Montparnasse. The suburb south of the Seine on a slope rising behind the Jardins du Luxembourg had become home to the artists of Paris after tourists and developers made Montmartre, the Quartier Latin and the rest of the Left Bank too expensive. Its frontier was boulevard Montparnasse, long and wide, one of the triumphs of Baron Haussmann's remodelling of the city. Its trademark was the café. The boulevard was lined with them, from the Closerie des Lilas at the top of the Luxembourg to the intersection with rue Vavin where the Dôme, the Select, the Rotonde and, a few years after Luis arrived, the most elegant of them all, La Coupole, spilled rattan tables and chairs on to the pavements.

Paris had always been Buñuel's spiritual home but in those first weeks of 1925 he also came to feel he belonged there socially and intellectually. In the 1960s, when he returned to work in France and could easily have stayed at the Crillon or the George V, he rented a small apartment in the Hôtel L'Aiglon at 232 boulevard Raspail. There, with the cafés only a few minutes away and Montparnasse cemetery below his window, he felt at home. Every expatriate group had its favourite hang-out. The Spanish adopted the Rotonde, where Buñuel, dropping in three days after his arrival, was surprised to find Miguel de Unamuno holding court; friends had chartered a boat to rescue him from his Canarian exile. Regulars at his *peña* included the Basque writer Miliena and the Catalan Juan Castanyer, although most were painters attracted to Paris by Picasso's success, among them Francisco Borés, Hernando Viñes, Ismael de la Serna, Joaquin 'Paquin' Peinado and another Catalan, Francisco Cossio. Like most racial minorities, the Spaniards in Paris were triumphantly, even arrogantly nationalistic. Only Viñes, whose French wife Loulou had literary connections, and Castanyer, who preferred to be known as 'Jean Castanier' and was to become Jean Renoir's collaborator and friend, were, figuratively at any rate, welcome on the other side of boulevard Montparnasse. Buñuel agreed with the notoriously changeable and argumentative Unamuno about almost nothing, but the Rotonde was close enough to the cafés of Madrid for him to feel at home, and he joined his circle.

'The society of Montparnasse was not dedicated to remunerative efforts', said American journalist Waverly Root. 'It was centred on the café terrace, and the personal relationships that were built up there were the products of long hours of café sitting'. There were few better meeting places for young foreigners with a taste for drinking and chat developed in the cafés of Madrid or New York, and no particular urge to work. Hemingway wrote to Sherwood Anderson: 'we sit outside the Dôme Café [. . .] warmed up against one of those charcoal brazziers and it's so damned cold outside and the brazzier makes it warm and we drink rum punch, hot, and the rhum enters into us like the Holy Spirit'.

Café owners did not relish their establishments becoming foreigners' clubs, but since French clients mostly came after five, they tolerated the expatriates. Out of 42.2 million people in France in 1927, 2.5 million were foreigners. But however welcoming the attitude of the waiters and café proprietors, Paris's prevailing attitude towards émigrés, especially those with money, was one of resentment. In April 1924 the franc was devalued. In December 1925 it stood at fifteen to the dollar, but by July 1927 the rate had sunk to forty-nine. Douglas Goldring saw drunken American tourists in Montmartre throwing handfuls of coins and bills at the feet of the 'natives'.

'We won the war, didn't we?' they shouted. 'Here's your cheap franc!'

The Montmartrois spat and swore, but they picked up the money. Most of them needed it to eat. While Buñuel drank Moët et Chandon champagne in the Rotonde at 11 francs a bottle, across Paris George Orwell was washing dishes in a hotel on rue Royale, living on bread and wine and sleeping in a bug-infested doss-house, the only food and lodging unskilled workers could afford. Buñuel did notice that French buses were covered with posters warning people not to waste bread, but at most it was an interesting detail. Even when he discovered Communism, social conscience was never his strong suit.

What was Buñuel like at twenty-six? The most famous of Man Ray's 1929 photographs shows an aggressive young man with a bruiser's glare and a labourer's collarless striped shirt. By capturing him bending forward, Ray suggests the heavy shoulders, thick lips and dark, protruding eyes of a young bull. The pensive effeminacy of Dali's portrait had disappeared. Seeing Luis in 1931, Count de Foxa would describe him as 'that man of brutish aspect and curly hair'. Whatever he would turn into, the Buñuel of 1926 was, under his new suit and behind the ingratiating smile and punctilious good manners, a dangerous man. His letters to Pepin Bello reveal a personality in which pride is compromised by ego, confidence by arrogance, conviction by prejudice, reserve by shyness, and a friendly nature by near-pathological jealousy.

When the *peña* broke up at 2 a.m. Buñuel would often stroll back with Unamuno to his home in the fashionable area around the Etoile, at the top of the Champs-Elysées. It was on these two-hour walks through a Paris reclaimed by its workers that Buñuel first experienced French xenophobia. Burly, speaking almost no French, often drunk, already a little hard of hearing and dressed, as his diplomatic ambitions demanded, *à la mode*, in spats, three-piece suit and a bowler, he epitomized the clichéd *métèque* or half-breed. A friend remembers him moving cautiously around the city at night, sticking to the brightly lit centre of the pavement. Still, fights were unavoidable, and Buñuel relished the excuse for violence.

He found himself unaccountably attracted as well to Unamuno's dour philosophy. The author of *The Tragic Sense of Life* believed that 'suffering is the substance of life and the root of personality'. Buñuel found himself nodding in silent affirmation. 'All religion', he went on, 'has sprung historically from the cult of the dead.' Buñuel could only agree.

At the Rotonde a medical student named Angulo introduced him to the cheap student hotels around the Sorbonne. By February 1926, he had a room at 1 *bis*, place de la Sorbonne. Shortly afterwards, he moved across boulevard St Michel to the St Pierre, a cheap student hotel in the narrow rue des Ecoles de Médecine. There was a Greek restaurant opposite, and a Chinese *cabaret* next door, where Buñuel became a regular. He befriended one of the Chinese hostesses who, though she never slept with him, shared his enthusiasm for wine and educated him about life in their adopted country. It is ironic that Buñuel, always the outsider, would receive his introduction to French culture from someone who was herself an alien.

As a sort of diplomat-in-waiting, Buñuel was sufficiently reputable to be introduced around the established Spanish community. He visited an elderly Juan Gris at his home in the suburbs, where he would die in 1927. Picasso worked in rue de la Boëtie but Luis met him at the rue Vercingétorix studio of Manolo Angeles Ortiz. He did not share the common admiration for Picasso, partly out of scorn at the painter's intellectualizing of his work but mostly because he suspected, rightly, that Picasso regarded everyone, even his admirers, as expendable in pursuit of reputation and commercial success. Although they remained distantly friendly, and he would help Picasso to hang *Guernica* in 1937, Buñuel could not bring himself to like either the picture or its painter. He rightly sensed that Picasso had no real interest in the struggle against Franco, merely using it for his own ends.

Apart from these visits, Buñuel's days passed in a haze of alcohol and conversation. He studied French but spent just as much time learning dances like the Java. He drank not only for the buzz, but because a doctor friend had prescribed champagne for his frequent head colds. Immersed in the Spanish sub-culture, Buñuel was not fully aware of two events late in 1926 that would materially affect his career. On 14 September the Surrealists, who had launched their magazine *La Révolution Surréaliste* the previous December, held their first art show at Galerie Loeb. Picasso was in it, along with Hans Arp, Max Ernst and the writers Philippe Soupault, Robert Desnos, René Crevel and Paul Eluard and his wife Gala, many of whom would become Buñuel's most intimate friends and enemies; in some cases both. And on 7 October, at the Music Hall des Champs-Elysées, the black American *Revue Nègre* opened, headlined by the pyrogenic dancer whom Buñuel would later call 'that bitch Josephine Baker'.

*

Considering the importance the Surrealists would have for Buñuel and he for them, it took a long time for them to find each other. He knew their writing from the literary magazines and through Gómez de la Serna, who was their Spanish correspondent. At the Residencia he and Dali had read Benjamin Péret and 'almost piss[ed] themselves laughing'. Buñuel is off-hand about his early contact. 'Until 1927,' he told Spanish writer Max Aub, 'I thought they were nothing but a lot of fags.' This was a pose. Like *le tout Paris*, he knew the legends and read about the Surrealists' stormier activities. But in 1926 Surrealism was mostly a literary movement. Its members were almost entirely poets and journalists. Buñuel, with his poor French and lack of literary background, was hardly suited to the complex word-games and structured evocation of dream states that occupied their *séances*. In other respects, however, Buñuel was made for the Surrealists. Their violence and anti-clericalism, as well as their *penchant* for subversion, betrayal and delusion, were exactly to his taste. Although André Breton would decree in 1927 that all members should join the French Communist Party as the only political group whose ideals corresponded even slightly with those of the movement, its real roots were in anarchism. Less *for* anything than *against* everything, the Surrealists embraced radical cultural change for its own sake. The *New Yorker*'s correspondent Janet Flanner wrote disapprovingly of their belief that 'art must not be beautiful but should on the contrary shock and dismay the eye of the beholder'. She slated their 'violent anti-Catholicism, usually demonstrated by [. . .] insulting priests and spitting on nuns on the Saint-Germain streets' and their 'sadistic physical practices [among which] street brawling was considered an essential'.

Cultural terrorists, the Surrealists aimed to prick inflated reputations. They wrote insulting letters to public figures and, sometimes singly but mostly as a group, turned up at concerts and plays to disrupt the performance. In July 1923 Breton burst on stage at the Théâtre Michel during a Tristan Tzara play, slapped fellow-member René Crevel and broke Pierre de Massot's arm with a walking stick. Louis Aragon, Benjamin Péret and Paul Eluard joined in the mêlée.

One could rely on some sort of *bagarre* at most fringe artistic events, and the *gratin* never missed anything organized or endorsed by Jean Cocteau, whose ostentatious aestheticism and homosexuality, which Breton loathed, were bound to get the Surrealists out. 'There was always a question as to which end of the auditorium attracted most attention,' wrote Robert McAlmon. 'Surrealists and enemies of Cocteau would be shouting down the actors and the play from all parts of the house, and the drinkers at the bar retaliated by shouting at the Surrealists to pipe down.'

Shrewd entrepreneurs invited, even manipulated, these *scandales*. In 1923 the American arts enthusiast Margaret Anderson, who published the *Little Review* and supported the Ballets Suédois, asked avant-garde American composer George Antheil to perform his *Sonata Sauvage*, *Airplane Sonata* and *Mechanisms* on 4 October at the Théâtre des Champs-Elysées in support of the Ballets. The stage was dazzlingly bright as Antheil walked to the piano. He saw movie cameras set up around the theatre but was too preoccupied by the possibility of attack to speculate on what they might be doing there. Just in case, he wore a gun in a shoulder holster.

James Joyce, Picasso, all the composers of Les Six, the Polignacs, the Prince of Monaco, many Surrealists and Man Ray were in the audience. Many applauded loudly, especially Erik Satie and Darius Milhaud, but during *Mechanisms* people in the gallery began heaving seats into the stalls. Antheil kept playing, consoling himself that he could always shoot his way out.

It was not until a year later, when he saw Marcel L'Herbier's film *L'Inhumaine*, about a sensational soprano, that Antheil realized he had been used. The soprano, who entertains artists and tycoons in a futuristic country villa and is murdered by a jealous rajah, only to be revived by another lover who has fortuitously invented a machine to bring back the dead, was played by Georgette LeBlanc, mistress of Maurice Maeterlinck and a great friend of Margaret Anderson's. Rather than hire a theatre and a crowd for a scene in which an audience riots over her late appearance, Anderson set up Antheil's concert and filmed it.

Jean-Claude Carrière believes that, in some intangible sense, Buñuel and the other Surrealists were drawn to Paris by a common disgust with the times that only Surrealism could answer. 'There is absolutely no reason,' he says, 'why Benjamin Péret came from Toulouse to join the group, why Max Ernst comes from Germany, why and how Man Ray comes from the States and Buñuel from Spain, and they get together [. . .] There are probably billions of little *hazards* and coincidences. But something was calling them together. It was something they shared already before belonging to the same group.'

Joining them, however, or even meeting them, was difficult. They were a brotherhood, and a close one, for which Breton, a burly, solemn man habitually dressed in bottle-green tweed and seldom without his pipe, set a rigorous agenda, dictating the schedule of *séances* and exhibitions, guiding discussions, literally laying down the law with the dogmatism of his gendarme father. Dissidents risked expulsion. Georges Ribemont-Dessaignes, himself expelled from the group, said that 'about [Breton], there lurked the odour of the secret society'. He compared him to some cultural terrorist carrying a bomb that he proposed to plant in the middle of bourgeois European life. 'We descend to the street,' Breton wrote, confirming this vision, 'with pistols in our hands.'

Ostentatiously anti-bourgeois, the Surrealists seldom went to the Rotonde or the Dôme. Instead they met twice daily, at lunch and after dinner, in the Café Cyrano on place Blanche, a smoky Montmartre bar haunted by whores and pimps. Later they adjourned round the corner to Breton's cluttered apartment at 42 rue Fontaine. A few, however, particularly Eluard and Aragon, did visit Montparnasse. Buñuel might have wangled an introduction, but his interests continued to be focused on the Spanish in Paris and his friends in Madrid. He was still a rootless young *Madrileño* with a career, if such it could be called, as a diplomat and bureaucrat.

By the end of 1926, however, it was clear that hopes of a secretary job were illusory. Buñuel went to Spain on 11 November and returned on 22 December with confirmation that his diplomatic career was over before it had begun. 'The League of Nations didn't have the money. France (which was going to pay) didn't have any more money.' His stay in Paris had been wasted. Or perhaps not entirely. 'During that period of two years when I was supposed to initiate myself into international politics,' Buñuel wrote later, 'I devoted myself to the cinema.'

5

'German man is the supreme example of demoniac man. Demonaic indeed seems the abyss which cannot be filled, the yearning which cannot be assuaged, the thirst which cannot be slaked.'
– Leopold Ziegler, *Das Heilige Reich der Deutschen*.

It is typical of Buñuel to compress into one sentence a process that took at least two years and was to change his life. Surrounded by artists, he had become more and more drawn to an artistic life, but he had no skill in painting and his experiments in literature were fragmentary. In Spain Lorca's reputation was growing, while Dali was regarded as the new *wunderkind*. Of the Residencia trio, only he remained unknown. Nor did it help his state of mind to hear from Bello that Lorca was actively trying to seduce Dali.

It was against this background and driven more by jealousy, frustration and a need to make a living that Buñuel fell, almost by accident, into the cinema. As a boy he had seen movies in Zaragoza. Many were Italian melodramas, but he also remembered the trick films of Méliès and the comedies of the French comedian Max Linder, whose deft acrobatics, frock-coat and silk hat Chaplin was to imitate before he discovered his tramp persona. At one point a colleague tried to persuade Luis's father to invest in a chain of cinemas but Don Leonardo, who had never seen a film in his life, declined, depriving his son of yet another opportunity to inherit a fortune.

Initially, movies for Luis were a way honourably to kill time in Paris; it wasn't really loafing to go to the press screening of a film. He began with morning previews of American films at the Salle Wagram, near the Champs-Elysées, where most of the big cinemas were. He borrowed a press card – probably from Cossio, who reviewed them for *La Gaceta Literaria*.

At night he usually went to one of the tiny Left Bank *cinémas d'art et d'essai* near the Sorbonne. Armand Tallier and his partner had opened

Studio des Ursulines in January 1926 on a side-street off rue Gay Lussac. They aimed, they wrote, 'to recruit our public from among the elite of writers, artists and intellectuals of the Latin Quarter'. It became the preferred first-run house for films like von Stroheim's *Greed* and Dreyer's *La Passion de Jeanne D'Arc*. Buñuel also patronized the Vieux-Colombier. Launched in 1924 when Jean Tedesco turned the old Vieux-Colombier theatre into a cinema, it specialized in revivals of foreign films, especially German, which had been badly received on their first run. Audiences whistled Murnau's *The Last Man* at the Aubert-Palace but it was a hit for Tedesco.

The visual bravura of these Expressionist films with their dramatic lighting and stylized acting fascinated Buñuel. 'You can't imagine what the cinema of that time was like,' he told Elena Poniatowska. 'Two thousand metres of film contained five hundred metres of subtitles. The first film without subtitles I ever saw was Lupu Pick's *Le Rail (The Railway)*.* It put me into a real stupor. It confirmed me in my idea of consecrating myself to the cinema.'

The film that most impressed Buñuel in his early days in Paris was Fritz Lang's 1921 *Der müde Tod (The Weary Death)*, also known as *Destiny* and *The Three Lights*. A sombre fable in three episodes, it had flopped on its first Paris release but came into its own when the Vieux-Colombier reissued it in 1926. A young woman whose man has been taken by Death begs him to reconsider. Death offers to exchange the man's life for that of another in three exotic locations: Italy under the Borgias, an Arabian Nights harem and a court in ancient China.

'I didn't like the film,' Buñuel said, 'but it convinced me that the cinema could arouse the artistic emotions.' He was moved 'not [by] the three interpolated stories, but the figure of Death, his arrival in a Flemish village, the dialogue with the girl'. In its matter-of-fact acceptance of life and death in a setting of quotidian reality it prefigures many of Buñuel's own films, especially *Nazarin*. His admiration for Lang lasted for decades, and when he finally met him in Los Angeles in 1972, he asked him, somewhat to his own surprise, for a signed photograph.

In the mid-1920s Paris harboured three or four groups of avant-garde film-makers, all eyeing one another with mutual suspicion. The 'official' one, poetic, literary, painterly, influenced by the Germans, aspired to a visual sumptuousness and symbolist language to rival the painters, writers and composers whom its directors respected: Debussy, Morreau, Mallarmé, Baudelaire, Poe. The leading lights when Buñuel arrived in

---

* The French title of *Scherben (Shattered)* about a railwayman's daughter seduced by an inspector.

Paris were Marcel L'Herbier, Germaine Dulac, Louis Delluc, Abel Gance and Jean Epstein. The latest hit of this self-conscious group had been L'Herbier's *L'Inhumaine* in 1924. Robert Mallet-Stevens designed a villa for the film and Fernand Léger the scientist's laboratory. Darius Milhaud wrote its music.

The avant-garde lived as they worked, disdaining the everyday. L'Herbier perched on a couch while he directed and wore small circular prescription dark glasses to protect his weak sight. Germaine Dulac lived in elegant seclusion. Arriving to interview her for an American magazine, Henry Miller was ushered into a book-lined, cathedral-like study furnished with antique sea charts and tanks of exotic fish. Dulac received him dressed in men's clothes and seated at a desk raised on a daïs. Recognizing that he was in the company of 'one of the celebrated Lesbiennes of Paris and all Europe', Miller abandoned the idea of an article and started to push his actress wife June Mansfield, stressing her bisexual appeal.

While Epstein, Gance, L'Herbier and especially Dulac had many friends and sponsors among the American expatriates and dilettantes, the Surrealists, not surprisingly, despised their work and especially their life-style. They were in two minds about the cinema anyway. Breton called it 'the first great open bridge which binds the day to the night' but gave unqualified acceptance only to films which had been created without artifice, and whose poetic moments were therefore naive and accidental.

Robert Desnos, the only one of the group to write regularly on the cinema (for the magazine *Le Merle*), praised Mack Sennett and the cheapest American action films and serials. Breton admired the World War I thriller serials *Judex*, *Fantomas* and *Les Vampires*. 'It's in *Les Vampires* that one should search for the great reality of this century,' he wrote. 'Beyond fashion. Beyond taste.' It was a sauce to his enthusiasm that the creator of these accidental masterpieces, Louis Feuillade, knew nothing of the avant-garde and was a typical suburban family man, proud of his box office success.

It was one thing to relish the vigor of Pearl White serials and Mack Sennett two-reelers or the naive poetry of Feuillade, but quite another to employ film to convey a Surrealist idea. To spend a year raising money and painstakingly creating a film would be to sell out to the very establishment they were sworn to subvert. A few film-makers compromised by exploiting cinema tricks to achieve an effect consistent with the ideals of Dada, Tristan Tzara's post-World War I movement out of which Surrealism had developed. Slowing the camera down or running it backwards, as René Clair did in *Entr'Acte* and *Paris Qui Dort (Paris*

Sleeps), and Cocteau in all his films, interfered amusingly with reality as Tzara had with his cut-up texts and Braque with his collages, but until 1928 the Surrealist interest in cinema ended there.

The only form of cinema that seriously tempted the Surrealists was pornography, which combined scandal and eroticism, always ruling preoccupations, with the casual production methods of slapstick. René Crevel outlined a Surrealist porn film called *The Geography Lesson* in which the map of Europe, and in particular phallic Italy, runs amok in a class of schoolgirls, and in 1929 Eluard wrote hotly from Marseille to his wife Gala about the porn screenings he had seen, promising her an excursion to the same cinema.

Late in 1925, Buñuel, who knew Jean Epstein's writing on film from the magazine *L'Esprit Nouveau*, went to see him with an introduction from Guillermo de Torre, who had published some of the director's pieces in the journals *Ultra* and *Tablero*. Polish-born, Epstein started in cinema as a critic and editor, and directed almost a dozen films before he was thirty. When Luis met him he was working for Alexandre Kamenka, the Russian émigré producer who had funded four of them. Kamenka's Albatros Films, a small studio at Montreuil-sous-Bois in a working-class suburb of Paris, had become an informal hang-out for film and theatre people who fled from Russia after the Revolution.

Like his colleagues, Epstein tried to cut a figure. He affected the high-laced riding boots and megaphone of Cecil B. DeMille. Unfortunately, short and slight, with a beaky nose, piercing eyes and unruly curly hair, he looked more like Woody Allen. Thinking Buñuel wanted an interview, Epstein explained that he was leaving Kamenka to set up his own company with his screenwriter sister Marie. Waiting to finance his next project, he and two friends, Camille Bardoux and Alex Alain, had launched a film school, the Académie de Cinema. When Epstein figured out that Buñuel was really looking for a job, he urged him to sign up. Buñuel did, as student No. 19, and persuaded the sons of José Maria Uzelay and another painter named Regoyos to join him.

Buñuel quickly saw that the school, like many such institutions, was a scam. Almost all the students were White Russians who knew no French and even less about films. They had enrolled because their student credentials earned them *carnet rouge* residence permits.

A poor director of actors, Epstein favoured the Expressionist style. 'For the first few weeks we did exercises and improvisations,' recalled Buñuel, 'on the order of "You are condemned to death. It's the night before your execution".' Epstein would then detail one student to act despairing, careless or desperate.

Epstein finished his last Kamenka film, *Les Aventures de Robert Macaire (The Adventures of Robert Macaire)*. Bored with emoting with the White Russians, and hearing Epstein had found money for the new film, an adaptation of George Sand's novel *Mauprat*, Buñuel took the bus to Montreuil-sous-Bois. He offered to sweep floors and run errands in return for a job. Taking note of his husky build, Epstein signed him up.

The story of a brute transformed by love, *Mauprat* was a compromise between the stage-bound period melodramas Epstein directed for Kamenka and the more significant films he intended to make when he could find the money. They shot at the Epinay studios, as well as around Paris, and on locations at châteaux in Romorantin and Châteauroux. Buñuel operated a waterfall, played bit parts as a priest, a gendarme and nobleman in an elaborately frogged coat, and did the occasional stunt, including a three-metre fall after being shot in a battle.

He quickly became friendly with the crew, particularly cameraman Albert Duverger, who had shot part of Gance's audacious *La Roue (The Wheel)*, and who would shoot both *Un Chien Andalou* and *L'Age D'Or*. He also got to know some of the performers, including Maurice Schultz and Sandra Milovanov, but whereas most newcomers to film-making find the process glamorous and fascinating, Buñuel could not help seeing its ridiculous side. Whether because he never got the plot straight – was it Louis XV or XVI they were fighting for? – or because he put off the actors in dramatic moments by making them giggle, he was less than the perfect assistant.

Nor did his admiration for avant-garde film increase as he watched Epstein striding around in his uniform of high boots, baggy riding breeches and a tweed coat over a gaudy sweater and plaid scarf.

A fanatical pictorialist, Epstein was obsessed with the well-framed close-up and the position of his characters within the frame. 'Noticing a drop of dew on a leaf by the roadside,' he wrote, 'we would stop and film the drop of dew on the leaf and then insert it somewhere or other.' Despite Buñuel's friendship with Duverger, his interest in the aesthetics of film-making was, as it remained all his life, sketchy. 'I remember,' he wrote later, 'Gabriel Figueroa [his Mexican cameraman] setting up an aesthetically perfect frame with Popocatepetl in the background, crowned with its habitual white cloud, but instead of proceeding I turned the camera around to focus on a thoroughly banal scene that seemed far more appropriate to me.'

Mauprat was released early in 1926. Epstein produced and directed two more films, *Six et Demionze (Six and Half Eleven)* and *La Glace à*

Trois Faces (The Mirror with Three Faces), both released in 1927, but Buñuel was not offered a job on either. Instead he scuffled for work on the fringes of the avant-garde. At the start of 1926, Hernando Viñes asked if he was interested in joining some other unemployed émigrés in presenting a puppet production of Manuel de Falla's *El Retablo de Maese Pedro* in Amsterdam. Commissioned by the Princesse de Polignac in 1919, the piece, based on an episode from *Don Quixote*, had been performed only once, in her palace, but Willem Mengelberg was interested in giving its public world premiere with the Concertgebouw Orchestra.

The *Retablo* was a small puppet theatre like a Punch and Judy show. All the characters were marionettes whose voices were provided by singers behind the scenes, a workable idea for a private showing but not feasible in a large theatre. Buñuel suggested using four live mimes who would act as the audience of Maese Pedro and interrupt the show. He roped in his friends, including Cossio, Peinado, and his cousin Rafael Saura as Don Quixote. A newspaperman, a medical student and members of the Viñes family made up the number.

Hector Dufrance, Thomas Salignac and Vera Janocopulos of the Opéra Comique sang the roles, but the rest of the production was scratch, with masks and decor scrounged, improvised, and only where absolutely necessary commissioned. Presented on 26 and 27 April, *El Retablo de Maese Pedro* was a success, with Buñuel credited as 'Scenic Director'. Despite the fact that he rehearsed for a fortnight at Viñes's home in Paris, he appears not to have been paid, but, like most of the non-professional cast, to have worked for the free trip to Amsterdam. 'I must say we didn't do so badly,' he said later, 'and both my friends and I gave all our efforts to succeed in such a disproportionate enterprise. None of the public suspected that the plastic part of the spectacle was an experiment, for once not catastrophic, of Spanish improvisation.' In fact, this is not entirely true. Showing his usual disregard for technique, Buñuel forgot that the show needed extra lights to be visible on a large stage. The first performance took place in near-darkness and he had to work overtime with a lighting designer to prepare the second.

In May Dali arrived in Paris with his stepmother and sister for a brief holiday. His father, almost reconciled to the idea that Salvador might be a genius, had financed the trip, while prudently refusing his son money for more than a few weeks. Nobody in Madrid had forgotten the fate of another local painter, Ramon Pitxot, who had died in Paris the year before, broke and destroyed by his decadent life.

Behind Dali's pose as the flighty aesthete was his usual concentration on what was good for Salvador. 'I knew that the road to success led through Paris,' he wrote later. 'But in 1925 Paris was far from Figueras, far away, mysterious and big. I landed there one morning [in 1926] with my sister and my aunt to judge its distance and size, as a boxer does during a round of studying his opponent.' The boxing metaphor is interesting, since Buñuel was at the station to meet him. Luis found Salvador vibrating with the thrill of being in Paris at last. He remained, however, uneducated and sometimes infantile in practical matters. Buñuel was amused to see that, when the Dalis crossed the street, his stepmother would take the hands of the other two and trill, 'Come on, children!'

Dali had letters of introduction to Breton and the poet Max Jacob, though he did not present either. Buñuel was ready to reintroduce him to mutual friends in the Spanish colony, such as Viñes and Borés, but Dali insisted that his first call, like a visiting prince paying ritual obeisance to the local ruler, should be on Picasso. Ortiz accompanied him.

'I have come to see you before visiting the Louvre,' Dali told him fawningly.

'Quite right,' responded Picasso.

Dali had brought a small painting to show him. After examining it, Picasso led him round his studio, displaying, without comment, his accumulated work. After the tour he gave Dali a searching look which seemed to say, 'You get the idea?' Dali responded with a glance that confirmed, 'Yes, I've got it!' After that, his move to Paris was just a matter of time.

6

'I realized the pleasure of cruelty. [. . .] There was a girl lodging close by I wanted to do things to. I loitered outside the door, hoping to see her. I didn't want to do anything about it [. . .] but I was happy.'
– Graham Greene, *Journey Without Maps*

Dali's departure from Paris left Luis feeling more adrift than ever. Whatever it was that his friend had got from Picasso continued to elude him. 1927 was an arid year, the most dispiriting of Buñuel's early life. All the same, it was filled with incident. Peinado got both of them jobs as extras on the film of *Carmen* with Raquel Meller being made at Albatros. 'He arrived like a gust of wind at La Rotonde,' said Buñuel, 'and we were all swept up.' Peinado and Viñes played guitarists, but Buñuel's looks won him a grandiose stage Spaniard costume and a scene with the star. 'Carmen was sitting motionless at a table, her head in her hands. [Director Jacques] Feyder told me to do something, anything, some kind of gallant gesture. I did, but unfortunately the one I chose was an Aragonian *pizco*, a real hard pinch, which got me a resounding slap.'

Often with Juan Vicens de la Slave, a friend from Zaragoza who managed Leon Sanchez Cuesta's Spanish bookstore at 10 rue Gay Lussac, next to the Spanish School of the Sorbonne, Buñuel haunted the Bal Bullier, the *bal musette* or dance hall opposite the Closerie des Lilas. Its band specialized in the shimmy and fox-trot (known locally as *le fox*), and the dim alcoves and corners made it a popular pick-up spot, especially with Latins.

Buñuel liked American jazz, of which he had built a record collection in Madrid. He even took up the banjo and started playing the violin again. But his enthusiasm for the Bullier was not musical. Naive, repressed, uncomfortable around women, he was both shocked and titillated by the public kissing and fondling common between lovers in France. The Bullier offered an outlet for his imaginings. While more aggressive friends flirted in the shadows, he showed off on the floor, not because he was a good dancer but because it was the only way he could get physically close to women.

'I taught Luis the tango in the kitchen of my place in Paris,' his eventual wife said in her memoirs. 'Although Luis played the violin he couldn't keep a beat, so we compromised with the fox-trot. To tell the truth Luis didn't like to dance. He liked to get me in his arms.' Since *bal musette* etiquette forbade conversation with a partner as an invasion of privacy, places like the Bullier offered the same anonymous satisfactions as a brothel.

Buñuel's sexuality increasingly found expression in fetishism. Frightened to accept total sexual contact, the fetishist concentrates his desires on one part of the body, or on an object which becomes invested with erotic power, to the extent that orgasm may be impossible without it. Buñuel's fetishism was connected with feet, calves and high-heeled shoes, a classic sexual displacement in which the foot slipping into the shoe is a metaphor for the sexual act.

In 1954, André Bazin asked Buñuel why, of all the images in Robert Bresson's *Les Anges du Péché (The Angels of Sin)*, he should best remember one of a nun's feet being kissed, since it was not characteristic of the film. Seeing that Bazin hoped for some sort of sexual credo, Buñuel said: 'I know what you mean [. . .] Throughout Bresson's whole film I had a feeling of something about to happen, which attracted me a lot, and in the final scene, sure enough, it came disturbingly into the open. For this reason I only remembered the kissing of the dead nun's feet. But having said this, I don't *myself* feel like kissing the feet of dead nuns, of green cows, or any other sort of feet.'

Buñuel's fetishism, like his fantasies of drugged and hypnotized women, was a means of displacing his taste for sexual violence. The Cuban critic and novelist G. Cabrera Infante rightly calls him 'a sublimated sadist'. Like Sade's heroines, his female characters, often blonde, innocent, occasionally virginal, are dominated, seduced or raped by older protectors. Others, sexually mature, are thrust into predominantly male societies and forced to satisfy its demands.

Jean-Claude Carrière acknowledges Buñuel's taste for sexual cruelty but doubts it ever went beyond his imagination. 'You never know, of course: in the intimacy . . . But he never told me, and nobody ever told me anything that could give this impression that he was either a sadist or a repressed sadist. Maybe we all are. If you think of it, he was much closer to the masochists than to the sadists. *Belle de Jour* is the exact portrait of a masochistic woman, and very precise. Many psychiatrists like [Jacques] Lacan just present and screen the film instead of talking about the case of feminine masochism.

'He *was* a sadist in one way: he loved Sade as a writer very much. Probably Sade was the number one reading in his life. When he read *Les 120 Journées de Sodome (The 120 Days of Sodom)*, when he came to Paris he discovered a new territory that he couldn't suspect before that, that didn't exist. Sade was a real revelation for him, and he kept a secret love for Sade as a writer I think during his whole life.'

Buñuel himself later insisted on the gap between being stimulated by Sade and acting out those fantasies. 'In practice I am neither a sadist nor a masochist. I am only these things in theory, and I don't accept these elements as anything more than elements of struggle and violence.' Later he added, 'Sade only committed his crimes in his imagination, as a way to free himself of criminal desires. The imagination can permit all liberties. It is quite another thing for you to commit the act. The imagination is free, but man is not.' All the same, his morbid fascination with rotted corpses and the primitive autopsies of Calanda suggests more than casual interest.

When he arrived in Paris, Luis knew nothing of Sade. He said he was 'about twenty-five' when he first read him, but twenty-eight seems more likely, since he discovered him via Roland Tual, one of the friends he made on the fringes of Surrealism. Tual, dark, slight and intense (as were most of the Breton group), was close to Eluard. Though more a collector and enthusiast than an artist, he often turned out with the group for *scandales*.

Lunching at his home with Buñuel, Desnos mentioned Sade's *Les 120 Journées de Sodome, ou L'Ecole de Libertinage*. Luis confessed that, despite his supposed liberal education, he had read nothing of Sade, least of all this *magnum opus* that the Marquis never lived to complete. Tual then produced his copy of the 1904 first edition, issued for the Club des Bibliophiles with 'scientific annotations' by Dr Eugen Duhren. So sulphurous was the Marquis's reputation that, even in liberal France, only five copies were printed. Tual's had belonged to Proust and had been read by André Gide, among others, but he lent it to Luis.*

The novel describes how four sensualists, the Duc de Blangis, his brother the Bishop of X***, the President de Curval and M. Durcet, lock themselves in the Duc's castle at Selligny with four women who have 'spent their lives in the most excessive debauchery and who were now in fine frame to report exactly on all these pursuits'. The idea is for these

---

* Eluard and Breton introduced Luis to a bookseller in rue Bonaparte from whom he ordered *Justine*, but it never turned up.

women to recount every erotic or cruel act they have experienced or can imagine, but the party becomes an orgy when the men begin to enact the perversions, including torture and murder.

The Enlightenment had proposed a Divine Order inhabited by Natural Man and the Noble Savage, in whom animal passions were balanced and controlled by a rational and compassionate soul conferred by God. Sade rejected all these propositions. Is there any evil of which man is not capable? He thinks not; once imagined, any act becomes forever a potentiality. 'What we are doing here is only the image of what we would like to do,' says one of his debauchees. 'To attack the sun, to deprive the universe of it, or to use it to set the world ablaze – these would be crimes indeed.'

If God exists, how could He not intervene to punish cruelties like these? Sade's explanation is simple: God does not exist. 'The idea of God is the sole wrong for which I cannot forgive mankind,' he wrote. To Sade, our greatest dignity and true role in life is to resist any curb on personal freedom, whether by law, religion or our fellow man. The murderer has the absolute right to kill, the victim the same right to defend himself, the parent of the victim to exact revenge. 'What he demands,' wrote Simone de Beauvoir, 'is that, in the struggle between irreconcilable existences, each one engage himself concretely in the name of his own existence.'

To many modern philosophers, particularly the Existentialists, Sade was the first philosopher to articulate a rational vision of man. His atheism and materialism echoed Buñuel's mechanistic and entomological view of life. 'In Sade,' he said, 'I discovered a world of extraordinary subversion, one that included everything: from insects to social customs, sex, theology [. . .] In short, I was utterly dazzled.'

In 1927 Paris was going through a clean-up campaign spearheaded by Jean Chiappe, its Prefect of Police, a man with, according to the English writer Richard le Gallienne, who lived in Paris during the 1920s, 'a drill sergeant bent', intent on making Paris 'moral'. He disapproved of everything from excessive noise (not the traffic but the cries of street market vendors) to the growing number of immigrants. Foreign art particularly excited his contempt. In 1930 he would ban Sergei Eisenstein's *The General Line* and refuse the director an extension of his *carnet rouge*.

A dapper little man who enjoyed holidaying at the same expensive Monte Carlo resorts as Charlie Chaplin and Josephine Baker, Chiappe, it was widely understood, could be persuaded to look the other way with a few well-placed bribes. As a result opium and heroin were widely available in Paris, and bordellos, call-girls, abortionists and porn film producers openly advertised in 'naughty' weeklies like *La Vie Parisienne*.

There is little doubt Buñuel visited the brothels of Paris, as he had those in Madrid.* There was also a brief involvement with a girl named Rita who soon after shot her lover, then committed suicide. Meanwhile, however, he had met the woman he was to marry. He was visiting Viñes one night in his studio when Peinado, who shared it, arrived back from anatomy class with two fellow students, Hélène Tasnon and Jeanne Rucar. Jeanne, a gymnastics teacher, had won a bronze medal in the 1924 Olympics. She was athletic, with good legs and a calm, abstracted face. Attracted, Luis took Peinado aside and said urgently: 'I've got those pills that get women excited if they're dissolved in wine. Let's give them to these girls.' Peinado was indignant. 'These are respectable girls from good families! Jeanne's father is a friend of mine.'

This astonished Luis. In Madrid, any girl who even sat down with the men at a *peña* automatically forfeited her reputation. To come unchaperoned to an artist's studio was to announce yourself as a whore.

It is indicative of his formal and constrained sexual nature that, once Jeanne Rucar had been established as a 'good girl', Luis embarked on a courtship that would have gratified the stiffest Aragonese family. He called on her parents, who were almost as strict as any Spaniards, and requested permission to take her out. Her sister Georgette was appointed chaperone and the three began regular Sunday afternoon promenades, although Georgette, less placid than Jeanne and short-tempered, soon took to leaving them alone and arranging to meet only when they went home. Nevertheless, sex was confined to kisses, and the two did not go to bed until they married.

Away from this relationship, Buñuel's sexual eccentricities flourished, dominated by elements of cross-dressing and fetishism. Not content with playing a monk in *Mauprat*, he enjoyed dressing as a nun. There were plenty of opportunities for this in a city that delighted in costume balls, and Buñuel often put on a starched coif and long robe, completing the effect with full make-up and a saintly expression.

Accompanied by Viñes or Vicens de la Slave in a monk's habit, he would stroll around Paris. On a bus they would covertly pinch or feel up a woman and, when she turned to protest, either look pious or wink at her knowingly. Buñuel justified his behaviour as anti-clerical but he also

---

* He was in good company. Though Breton would never go near such places, other Surrealists like Aragon often arranged to meet André Malraux, Drieu la Rochelle and Emmanuel Berl in the bars of brothels, particularly one in rue de Provence where Berl was a regular. They liked the atmosphere.

found it sexually exciting. He and Vicens de la Slave even arrived in their outfits at the Rucar home when the two double-dated Jeanne and Georgette at a ball.

Luis also tried, without Jeanne, to attend the most notorious of Paris's costume balls, Le Bal des Quat'zarts, thrown by the city's art students and models. Traditionally everyone dressed outrageously, some in little more than a coat of body paint, and after midnight the event descended into orgy. He paid a large amount for tickets, and he and Vicens de la Slave joined students from the Académie Julien for dinner beforehand. During the meal one of them opened his trousers, arranged his genitals on a plate and walked round the room displaying them, a gesture which shook even Luis. He was eager for the high jinks of the ball but when they arrived at Salle Wagram their tickets turned out to be forgeries and they were turned away.

Early in 1927 Buñuel ordered some headed stationery identifying him as 'Luis Buñuel, *Metteur en scène Cinématographique*'. His address was simply (and evasively) given as 'Paris' although by then he was back on place de la Sorbonne, at 3 *bis*. Film work was sparse to non-existent, so he tried writing. His model remained Gómez de la Serna, although he increasingly drew on that most Surrealist of all raw materials, his dreams.

Palace of Ice, a fragment from 1927, is essentially a nightmare transcribed. The wind blows through a ruined Zaragoza, looted by Napoleon. A hanged corpse sways in the wind. It is Buñuel. A woman files her nails, then rips out the corpse's eyes and throws them into the street, where one of Napoleon's troops bayonets them. A passage in a long letter to Pepin Bello who had written to congratulate Buñuel on the saint's day of Zaragoza's patron saint, San Valero, shared the same dream imagery. Walking with his father through the wind-swept city, they meet half-naked priests whose moustaches became entangled with those of Don Leonardo.

He also jotted down the occasional film idea, although these were mostly scenes that might later be fitted into a larger structure. One of them, which he called, in bad schoolboy Latin, *La Sancta Misa Vaticanae*, was actually thought up by his brother Leonardo. It satirized Catholic ritual as a sport, with altars set up around St Peter's Square and priests competing to say the fastest Mass while altar boys toss sacred objects back and forth, sometimes collapsing from exhaustion. One Moses Rendueles from Huesca wins by performing a Mass in one-and-three-quarter minutes and is given a monstrance as a prize. The episode displays the same casual irreverence and covert awe as Federico

Fellini's ecclesiastical fashion show in *Roma*, which Buñuel admired sufficiently as to cable his congratulations.

Dali had settled back into his niche in Barcelona, supported by his father and accepted by almost everyone at his own valuation as Spain's greatest young talent, destined soon to sweep Picasso from his pedestal. Lorca, his career limping, was in Granada but he and Dali kept up a voluminous and, on Lorca's side at least, romantic correspondence. In February Dali had started his obligatory nine months' national service, although by pulling some strings, as Buñuel had done a few years before, he was able to work only half-days and sleep at home.

Lorca continued to court Dali with jobs designing sets for his plays and commissions to draw covers for the magazine he edited. Dali obliged, but with reluctance. Paris had given him new tastes and fresh ambitions. Until the end of his military service he was stuck in Spain, but once that was over he could think of returning to France, this time in triumph, and with Buñuel as his bridge to acceptance in the most prestigious of artistic coteries, the Surrealists. Around this time he painted one of his most important canvases, *Honey is Sweeter than Blood*. On a beach sown with spikes lies the head of Lorca which throws the shadow of Dali's profile. Nearby are a headless female dummy, the rotting body of a donkey buzzing with flies, and parts of a dismembered corpse which resemble Buñuel; to Dali, nobody was indispensable.

In the hope of earning some money, Buñuel began sending film reviews to *La Gaceta Literaria*. The first film he reviewed, not surprisingly, was Lang's *Metropolis*, which had opened in Paris on 10 January 1926. He admired its futuristic fantasy but not the mawkish melodrama, which he credits, rightly, to Lang's writer wife, Thea von Harbou. Giménez Caballero published his ambivalent notice on 1 May with a Peinado drawing. Buñuel followed it with the description of a programme of early Lumière films and more recent experimental work presented at the Ursulines. He particularly praised Alberto Cavalcanti's *Rien Que les Heures (As Time Goes By)*, with its dream-like images of the city and nature. All his life, Buñuel found any kind of creative writing hard, and often described himself as 'agraphic'. His reviews, flat as college essays, mostly imitate the style of well-regarded critics like Jacques Brunius, a cadet Surrealist. But getting them published at all was a triumph of sorts, and he recognized a way he might win some artistic credibility.

Once their courtship had progressed as far as dating, Jeanne and Luis went to the movies – frequently to the same one over and over, Jeanne complained. One they saw more than once was von Stroheim's *Greed*, an obvious influence on Buñuel's own work. Despite this, his review dwells mainly on how many metres of stock were exposed and how much ended up on the cutting-room floor. In its preoccupation with technique it appears suffused with nostalgia for his own film-making days, now, it probably seemed, behind him for good.

On 7 April Gance's *Napoleon* opened at the Opéra de Paris. With its triptych sequences and its thundering score it was touted by the avant-garde as the apotheosis of film art. Buñuel praised it, although in common with the Surrealists he found Gance's work pretentious, like the man himself. Gance had shown himself expert at running with the hare while hunting with the hounds. He even screen-tested Jean Chiappe to play the older Napoleon.

By the summer Buñuel was losing hope of a career in the arts. Castanyer had opened a restaurant, Le Catalan, in the narrow rue des Grands Augustins, opposite the studio where Picasso would paint *Guernica*, so Vicens de la Slave suggested he and Luis start their own *cabaret* on boulevard Raspail. Hoping that Doña Maria would finance it, Buñuel decided to go back to Spain for a few weeks. To make a little money and to keep his reputation bright, he offered to bring some avant-garde films. Armand Tallier, the manager of the Studio des Ursulines, helped him to choose, and Pepin Bello arranged a projection at the Residencia.

The programme, presented under the auspices of the Sociedad de Cursos y Conferencias, was a hit. Seeing *tout Madrid* out front, Giménez Caballero decided to start the Ciné Club de Madrid, which would launch many film-makers in Spain, including Buñuel himself.

For his provincial audience Buñuel had chosen the flashiest material, full of trickery, especially slow motion. As well as the Clair/Picabia/Satie *Entr'acte*, which was the hit of the evening, he had brought some early studies by Marey of a bullet emerging from the barrel of a gun, *Rien Que les Heures* and the dream sequence from Renoir's *La Fille de L'Eau (The Water Nymph)* of 1925. The Renoir impressed the *Madrileños* as much as it had the Surrealists. A delirious Catherine Hessling wanders in slow motion through a forest in a filmy gown, leaping backwards into trees, fleeing down a colonnade and across a bare ruined landscape until rescued by her lover on a white horse and whisked into the stormy sky – all images Cocteau would plagiarize for *La Belle et la Bête (Beauty and the Beast)*.

The delight of his audience reminded Buñuel how far Madrid lagged behind the rest of Europe in artistic experiment. In 1930, when *Variétés*, the Belgian Surrealist magazine, published a map of the world with 'significant' countries reproduced disproportionately large, Paris was the capital, Russia, Labrador and Easter Island enormous, but Spain was simply left out. The elegance of the crowd brought out all Luis's most seditious instincts, and he suggested to Bello that they announce a menstruation contest and award prizes. 'But like so many other Surrealist acts,' he sighed, 'this one never happened.'

After the screening, Ortega y Gasset and Juan Ramon Jimenez complimented Buñuel. Jimenez was particularly enthusiastic. Spain's leading Modernist poet, who would win the Nobel Prize for Literature in 1956, he was famous for his 1917 *Platero y Yo (Platero and Me)*, a novel about a boy and his donkey which would become a classic of children's literature in Spain. Ortega y Gasset told Buñuel he would have liked to try movies had he been a little younger, an oddly middle-aged comment for a man of only forty. Ramon Gómez de la Serna was also keen. For the first time Buñuel realized the power of his reputation, however little deserved, as someone who had 'made it' in Paris.

He must have been both hurt and angry that neither Dali nor Lorca attended. But both were busy with the Barcelona premiere of Lorca's *Mariana Pineda*, for which Dali had done the sets. Afterwards, the Dali family invited Lorca to join them on a seaside holiday at Cadaques. He and Salvador stayed there until July. Neither would have been happy at Buñuel's sudden reappearance in Madrid nor the fuss it occasioned. Ian Gibson thinks that Lorca must have read the report on Buñuel's lecture in the 1 June 1927 issue of *La Gaceta Literaria*. Pepin Bello, or perhaps Dali, or even Buñuel himself, may have told him he was at work on a book of 'narrations', to be called *Polisaños* (literally *Multi-isms*). 'The title suggests that Buñuel wished to express the spirit of the many "isms" then current in Europe,' says Gibson, 'and with which he felt himself increasingly identified.'

Doña Maria refused Luis money for the *cabaret*: a *señorito* had no business running a bar. Dejected, he thought again about the movies. As long as Gómez de la Serna was enthusiastic, he suggested they write a film together. *El Mundo por Diez Centimos (The World for Ten Cents)* was inspired by *Rien Que les Heures*. It would begin with a newspaper being produced. A man buys a copy and, as he reads each story, the film would dramatize it, with the headline as its introduction. At the end, the man throws the paper away. 'I worked with him for two days,' Luis said. 'I only gave some shape to the storyline, which was by Ramon.'

He was shrewd to choose Gómez de la Serna. As the only Spaniard in the Académie Française, his name gave an instant entrée to the best Parisian circles. He also introduced Buñuel to an Aragonese group, the Junta del Centenario de Goya en Zaragoza, who were interested in backing a film for the centenary of the painter's death. On 24 June 1927 the Junta paid Buñuel 750 pesetas for a one-page summary. Ramon del Valle-Inclan was also contemplating such a film, so Buñuel went to see him at the Fine Arts League in Madrid. The playwright was happy to withdraw. Buñuel hung around Madrid for a few days, hoping an outline for *The World for Ten Cents* would materialize, but it was still unfinished when he returned to Paris.

7

'A terrace of autumn. A white villa placed like something
on the watch at the terminal of the walk in the bitter
odour.'
– Léon-Paul Fargue (translated by Wallace Stevens)

Buñuel returned to Paris more confident than he had left. As Ian Gibson
writes, he was 'beginning to see himself [. . .] as one of the principal
Spanish representatives of the Parisian avant-garde, a John the Baptist to
the uninitiated barbarians south of the Pyrenees, for whom [he] was not
jeslow to express his petulant scorn'. There was a general impression in
Madrid – which Luis did nothing to scotch – that his circle of Parisian
friends included some, if not all, the Surrealists. As a sign of his optimism
he moved into a new part of the city. The 13th *arrondissement* was
middle-class and quiet. Unlike the cramped hotels of the area around the
Sorbonne, the Hôtel des Terrasses at the intersection of rue de la Glacière
and boulevard Auguste Blanqui was a new building in modified Art
Deco, the roof dominated by the two-storey tinted windows of a rooftop
cabaret and the balustrades of the terraces that gave it its name.

A man with an eye to his image might well choose such a flashy hotel,
one whose rates he could afford since it was on a busy corner, opposite
the elevated line of the Métro. He may also have been attracted by the
proximity of the Cités des Artistes, blocks of small apartments and
studios, many with their own leafy courtyards, which the city of Paris
funded for the use of artists. Viñes and other members of the Spanish
colony may have had their studios here. Many other artists worked in
the area, including the photographer Brassai, whose studio was in rue de
la Glacière. The change of address marked Buñuel's graduation from
newcomer to seasoned Parisian, since few tourists wandered into this
suburb of small corner cafés and markets. In September he was already
addressing letters from 'La Glacière'. At the Terrasses he started work on
his new projects. As well as *Goya*, he had *Polisaños*, and a cod version of
Hamlet, which he called a play but probably meant to be filmed.

Described as a 'tragic comedy', it is an exercise in flip absurdism, styled after Max Linder and Douglas Fairbanks, both of whom sent up period subjects by mixing them with contemporary technology. The inspiration was probably a playlet called *Buster Keaton's Stroll* which Lorca had written in 1925 in response to a collage of Keaton press clippings sent to him by Dali. Buñuel's Hamlet smokes cigarettes and sends telegrams. The heroine sings a song in gibberish and the ghost doubles as butler. Buñuel's invention flagged quickly. He got to Act IV but the entire piece could hardly have played more than half an hour and its relentless facetiousness would by then have worn out any audience. Inscribing it 'Paris, le 6 Juillet 1927, Hôtel des Terrasses', he put the manuscript away. It was not discovered until 1986.

Now that his relationship with Jeanne was established, Luis adopted a more proprietory attitude towards her. After watching one of her gymnastics classes at Mme Poppart's academy, he solemnly told her that such displays in brief costumes were indecent, and ordered her to resign. She obeyed. At the Rucar house one day her father told her, 'Jeanne, play something of Strauss for Luis.' When she obliged, Buñuel grumbled, 'The way you play the piano it would be better if you gave it up altogether.' Shortly afterwards, he met her teacher, a personable young man, and told her to stop taking lessons. Jeanne again acquiesced, and never played again. 'I never opposed anything Luis asked of me,' she said. But sixty years later, when she wrote a memoir of their marriage, a book Arturo Ripstein called, 'a long-considered revenge, carefully knitted over sixty years', she called it *Woman Without a Piano*.

Out of a job, Jeanne asked how she was supposed to support herself. A few days later Buñuel told her that Vicens de la Slave needed an assistant in the Spanish Bookshop at 300 francs a month. Although this was less than she earned teaching, Jeanne took the job. Some time later she noticed that her salary did not appear in the shop's cash book. Vicens de la Slave, under pressure, confessed that Buñuel was paying it out of his own pocket. Jeanne was furious, but did not dare confront him. Later, when the shop ran into difficulties, Georgette bought out Vicens, and Jeanne continued to work there until she married Luis.

In July, Buñuel, like most Parisians, left the city for a holiday. He spent it in Brittany. While he was there, news reached him from Madrid of the reverberation of his visit and the less than enthusiastic reaction of Lorca and Dali. On 28 July he wrote to Bello: 'I have received a revolting letter from Federico and his acolyte Dali.' 'Revolting' was probably an overstatement but he enjoyed the fact that '*asquerosa*' – revolting or disgusting – was also the name of a village where the Lorca family owned land. He improvised a little poem.

> Dali is writing me revolting letters.
> He's revolting.
> With Federico that makes two revolting types.
> One because he's from Asquerosa and the other because he's revolting.

The letter Dali and Lorca wrote to Buñuel has not survived but if it was anything like the others that the Surrealists (including Dali and Buñuel) fired off at cultural heroes they thought inflated, it was designed to take Luis down a peg or two. The fact that Dali and Lorca would have collaborated on it underlined the growing bond between them. It made Buñuel jealous, and also fearful that the two would sabotage his reputation in the only place where it remained high.

Back in Paris in September he wrote to Bello: 'Federico sticks in my craw incredibly. I thought that the boyfriend [Dali] was putrescent but now I see that the other is even worse. It's his awful aestheticism that has distanced him from us. His extreme narcissism was already enough to make a pure friendship with him impossible. It's his look-out. The trouble is that his work may suffer as a result.

'Dali is deeply influenced by him. He believes himself to be a genius, thanks to the love Federico professes for him. He's written to me saying, "Federico is better than ever. He's the great man, his drawings have genius. I'm producing amazing work, etc." And then, of course [Dali's] successes in Barcelona are so easily achieved. How I'd love to see him arrive here and renew himself far from the dire influence of Garcia! Because Dali is a real male and very talented.'

With its mixture of false solicitude for Dali's artistic well-being and sneering at Lorca's talent, the letter reads like the classic *cri-de-cœur* of a discarded lover. In any event, Buñuel had no reason to worry that Lorca was alienating Dali's affections. Unbeknown to Luis, Lorca had, during his stay in Cadaques, finally tried to sodomize Salvador, with catastrophic results for their friendship.

Lorca wrote to Dali in July, apologizing for his appalling behaviour. Later Dali said that Lorca was 'madly in love with me. He tried to screw me twice [. . .] I was extremely annoyed, because I wasn't homosexual, and I wasn't interested in giving in.' Somewhat undercutting his pose of aggrieved innocence, he added: 'Besides, it hurts.'

In case either Dali or Lorca had done anything to tarnish his image in Madrid, Buñuel worked furiously to burnish it. On 22 July he wrote to Bello: 'I am working ten hours a day. I am neglecting my book – *Polisaños* – for want of time. I have thought up two stupendous scenarios, but I haven't had time to write them. In the spring I shall make a film in Greece. For this winter in Spain: project with Ramon [Gómez de la Serna]. Project with Sanchez Mejias [Ignacio].'

The film in Greece would have been funded in part by a Basque shipbuilder who had ambitions as a producer, but nothing came of it. 'Ignacio' was the matador Ignacio Sanchez Mejias whom Buñuel had known in his Madrid café days. 'Ignacio was a friend of all the poets of my generation,' he said. 'He liked to mix with intellectuals, he bought drinks and dinner from time to time. An intelligent guy, interesting.' Retiring at the height of his career, Mejias devoted himself to the arts as writer, actor and financier. At the end of 1927 he organized a famous trip to Seville by seven Madrid writers, including Lorca, for a gala recital and discussion.

In 1925 he acted in the film *La Malquerida (The Badly Loved)* and in December 1927 he had just finished writing a play, *Sinrazón (Without Reason)*, inspired by Freud and set in an asylum for the insane. Buñuel said later: 'In my beginnings I always had contact with [the] milieux [of insanity and mental hospitals]. Freud interested himself in *Chien Andalou* and Jung considered its author like an invalid suffering from *dementia praecox*.' He may have proposed filming *Sinrazón*, but if so, it never went beyond discussion.

Late in the summer Buñuel did start work on a film, though it was not a project of his own. Through Albert Duverger, who was photographing it, he had been offered a job as assistant on *La Sirène des Tropiques (The Siren of the Tropics)*, a vehicle for Josephine Baker to cash in on her overnight fame. The money came from Maurice Nalpas, Gance's producer. Henri Etievant directed, but not to Buñuel's satisfaction or anyone else's, to judge from a letter to Bello on 5 September in which he remarked that the film was moving along 'if the *metteur en scène* does not change, which I would like.'

In a script cooked up by the fashionable novelist Maurice Dekobra with some additions from Baker's manager/lover Pepito Abatino, Baker plays a West Indian girl named Papitou who is pursued by a horny trader until she is rescued by a French adventurer, to whom she demonstrates the local tribal dance, a sort of Charleston. After stowing away on a ship to France in pursuit of her lover, she is soon performing her dance in Paris's music halls.

The film was shot in the forest of Fontainebleau and a comically artificial West Indian village built in the Francœur studios. On first seeing this creation, Baker remarked, 'We could use some manure around here.' Her leading man was Russian-born Pierre Batcheff, a highly strung *jeune premier* with a brooding screen presence. He had been in L'Herbier's *Feu Matthias Pascal (The Late Matthias Pascal)* and played the firebrand general Lazare Hoche in *Napoleon*. After seeing him opposite Chaplin's long-time mistress and star Edna Purviance in *Education de Prince*, Rex Ingram, the Hollywood director who worked with both Ramon Navarro and Rudolph Valentino and had now relocated in Nice, told him he had both the talent and looks to succeed in Hollywood as a Latin lover. Everything pointed to a promising career. Batcheff, however, was a drug addict who would die of an overdose in 1932.

On 23 August, the day Buñuel finished shooting interiors on *Sirène*, two anarchists, Nicola Sacco and Bartolomeo Vanzetti, were executed in Boston for their alleged involvement in a spurious bomb plot. In Paris, the Communists organized huge demonstrations which turned into riots. Buñuel went to the Champs-Elysées with an electrician from *Sirène* and watched as a group of rioters pissed out the eternal flame on the grave of the Unknown Soldier under the Arc de Triomphe. It took ten days to clean up the ruined boulevards, during which time Chiappe's men, goaded by patriotic protests over the Unknown Soldier incident, rounded up the usual suspects.

On 5 September the *Sirène* unit left for Dieppe to film Baker stowing away. Her ego inflated by an abrupt rise from chorus girl to star, the star had behaved impossibly. Since the clubs where she performed did not close until 6 a.m., she often flounced on to the set hours late, announcing her arrival by smashing perfume *flacons* against the walls of her dressing room. Ultra-violet radiation from the big lamps gave her 'Klieg eyes', making her temper still worse. Halfway through the film, she demanded a fur coat as the price of completing it. After one tantrum, triggered by the fact that her dog was sick (Baker seldom went anywhere without one or two members of her menagerie, which included a piglet), Buñuel remarked to Batcheff, with whom he had become friendly: 'Well, I guess that's the movies.' Batcheff snapped 'That's *your* movie, not mine.'

Buñuel claimed later that he left *La Sirène des Tropiques* before the end of exteriors but it is evident that he stayed until shooting finished in October. Meanwhile, he had become even closer to Batcheff and his pretty young wife Denise, who worked as a publicist on *Feu Matthias Pascal* and had ambitions to produce. She remembers Batcheff coming home from the shooting of *Sirène* to tell her excitedly about a young Spanish assistant who 'had in his head a film that would revolutionize the world'. She was even more impressed when she met Buñuel. 'His open and generous face with its olive complexion was lit up by two big but very soft green eyes. His large square jaw was the only visible sign of his potential for violence. He emanated a tranquillity, a calm and assurance, letting one guess at an immense humour. He expressed himself in colourful language, and burst out with a loud and prolonged laugh when he could not find the French word he was searching for; then his face would split in two. That loud laugh contrasted with a voice that was soft and a little husky. He gave the impression of someone getting ready to play an enormous joke.'

The Batcheffs had good connections in the film business. Jacques Prévert, Jean Renoir, René Clair, Jacques Brunius and the management of the magazine *La Revue du Cinéma* were all friends. Buñuel became a regular visitor to their home. For the first time, he sensed his career was heading in the right direction.

8

'Irony, as I have said, is nakedness; it is the gymnast who hides behind the pain of Saint Sebastian.'
– Salvador Dali, *Saint Sebastian* (translated by Ian Gibson)

Although Denise Batcheff implies that Buñuel was thinking about *Un Chien Andalou* at the time of *Sirène*, she was anticipating by a year. It would take Dali to isolate and identify the vision circulating like a virus in his imagination. At the time, *Goya* looked more promising. The Centennial Committee liked his outline and asked for an expanded treatment. In September 1927 Buñuel wrote to Leon Sanchez Cuesta requesting some documents about eighteenth-century Spanish court life. Marie Epstein helped him draft the eighty-five-page outline. There was nothing experimental about it. So conventional was the treatment, in fact, that Buñuel later offered it to Paramount in Hollywood as a biopic, to be called *Goya and the Duchess of Alba*.

On 8 November Buñuel wrote to Bello: 'I start with Epstein again soon, hoping that Ramon will send me his work.' He was being optimistic. Epstein had promised him a place as 'assistant assistant' on *The Fall of the House of Usher*, a version of the Poe classic which Marie had padded with episodes from *The Oval Portrait* and other stories, but so far nobody had offered the money to make it.

As for *The World for Ten Cents*, Gómez de la Serna continued to temporize. 'The —— promised me I would have it here by the 15th of last month,' Luis wrote irritably to Bello, 'but so far there is no news of it.' In a typical young man's recital of wishes, plans and remote possibilities, he went on: 'I pin all my hopes on making my debut [. . .] but without the scenario I can do nothing. As soon as I have it I will have to work on it for a month, with another two to sort out the company and to make a start on it. Because of this, if all goes well I won't start my first film at least until March. I will bring German, French and Spanish actors, a friend or two – you, if you like.'

At the end of 1927 Epstein was still financing *Usher*, so Buñuel returned briefly to Madrid. There was work there, though not the kind he wanted. On 8 November Giménez Caballero appointed him editor of the cinema pages of *La Gaceta Literaria*. He had also been put in charge of the movie page of the Paris journal *Cahiers d'Art*. 'I have to devise the [*Gaceta*] page, find contributors, decide on rejections, give news and interviews, etc. . . . ,' he told Bello when he got back to Paris. 'Nearly every day brings letters from Giménez Caballero, who is very nice and gives me practically complete freedom.' As for *Cahiers d'Art*, 'there too, I am in charge of the movie page, and responsible for accepting and rejecting articles. This opens every door in Paris to me. I begin with the next issue. Maybe you already know that it is the best modern art magazine in Paris. I am very grateful to the director, M. [Christian] Zervos, for the honour.'

Letters like this were meant to be read aloud at the *peña* and handed around; something he could rely on Bello to do. Giménez Caballero helped by introducing Buñuel in the paper as 'chief of the cinema page which we shall periodically present to our readers', explaining that he had 'accomplished what none of our *cinéastes* has managed; to lodge himself in High Studies of Cinema'. He was vague about Buñuel's qualifications, mentioning only the Gómez de la Serna project and his 'first work as a technician, seen this spring [. . .] in the context of films of the avant-garde'. Evasively, he ended by saying that Buñuel was in Paris 'preparing . . . Preparing what? This is the interrogation mark.'

He was right to be sceptical. Someone with time to see three films a day, as Luis was doing, obviously was not overwhelmed with offers to direct. Nor was either of his new jobs as important as he made out. The *Gaceta*, as Giménez Caballero said, ran cinema pages only intermittently. Buñuel's first and, as it turned out, only job, aside from contributing the occasional review, was to compile a page to coincide with the First National Cinematographic Conference being held that October in Madrid.

As for *Cahiers d'Art*, far from being 'the best modern art magazine in Paris', it was seen by the literati as a slightly disreputable focus of émigré arts journalism. Zervos, a Greek who, with his deputy Efstratios Eleftheriades, had insinuated himself into the Paris art world, was every ambitious newcomer's role model. While he edited and intrigued, Eleftheriades, as 'E. Teriade', won a reputation for argumentative and contrary opinions. To be in charge of *Cahiers d'Art*'s movie page was no special honour, but Buñuel's role was not even that important. His new friend Jacques Brunius wrote most of its cinema pieces, and probably got Luis the job.

Some *Madrileños* were suspicious of Buñuel's overnight fame, but not Dali, particularly when *Cahiers d'Art* reprinted one of his essays in December. To Dali, 'Buñuel', said his biographer, Meredith Etherington-Smith, 'now represented a valuable new channel, through which [he] could be published in Spanish and French, rather than in Catalan, and in magazines which would undoubtedly be read in Paris by the avant-garde, particularly the Surrealists. Such publicity might open an escape route.' Cold-bloodedly, Dali decided to discard Lorca and deliberately cultivate Luis.

To demonstrate his new low opinion of Lorca, Dali had insisted that, while Luis was in Madrid, the three meet to hear Federico read his play *The Love of Don Perlimpin for Belisa in His Garden*. A fable about an impotent husband who magically rediscovers his manhood, it had been finished two years before but not yet performed.

They met in one of the wooden booths in the cellar bar of the Hotel Nacional, and Lorca, 'a superb reader', Buñuel conceded, launched into the text. By the end of the first act, however, Luis was restless, finding it 'hopelessly contrived'. Thumping the table he said, 'That's enough, Federico. It's a piece of shit.'

Lorca paled, closed the manuscript and looked at Dali. 'Buñuel's right,' Dali said as if delivering a death sentence. '*Es una mierda.*'

Distraught, Lorca left the Nacional. In embarrassment Dali and Luis followed, talking loudly so that he wouldn't think they were trailing him. Lorca, apparently oblivious, entered a church, knelt and spread his arms wide, like a penitent. Dali and Buñuel watched for a moment, abashed, then went to a bar.

The next day Buñuel asked Dali what had happened when he went back to the room they shared. 'Everything is sorted out,' Dali said. 'He tried to make love to me but couldn't.'

Buñuel returned to Paris with nothing settled about any film project but with a new sense of solidarity with Dali. Buñuel's plotting, Dali's ambition and Lorca's inept attempts at seduction had split the trio irreparably, leaving Dali established as Buñuel's champion and potential collaborator. They had even talked about making a film together.

In April, Buñuel would write to Bello that he and Lorca had 'rediscovered their intimacy'. But, as if to underline the fact that he now felt himself to be the more powerful of Dali's two friends, he went on to attack Lorca's *Romancero Gitano (Gypsy Ballads)* for its 'approximate modernism'. Although one wonders whether anything Lorca wrote would have pleased him in the circumstances, Buñuel genuinely felt him to be overrated. Lorca was influenced at the time by children's stories and lullabies, the naiveté of which tasted flat on a palate accustomed to

Surrealism and Sade. With mounting viciousness Buñuel announced that *Romancero Gitano* was poetry of the sort produced by 'those homosexual poets of Seville' and not to be compared with 'those exquisite and great poets of today'. It exhibited, he said, the false drama of flamenco. Ending on an image startling for its sexual overtones, he said Lorca's work typified the art that had 'filled Spanish beds with menstrual blood'.

On 10 January 1928 Leon Trotsky and thirty of his followers were expelled from the Communist Party. It was a blow for André Breton, who revered the Bolshevik leader. His Communism was increasingly unpopular among the Surrealists, not only on ideological grounds but because many of them believed that political commitment of any kind fouled the group's ideal. 'Didn't Surrealism die the day Breton and his followers believed it necessary to rally to Communism?' demanded Antonin Artaud, who, with Philippe Soupault, had been ejected the year before for just such resistance to Breton.

In 1927 Eluard, Péret, Aragon and Pierre Unik loyally accepted Party cards at Breton's urging. Breton stopped short of demanding that the other members, then about twenty-five, join as well, though he did expect them to become fellow-travellers. To demonstrate what turncoats could expect, he led a party to the Studio des Ursulines on 9 February 1928 for the première of Germaine Dulac's *The Seashell and the Clergyman*, a symbolist visual poem from an Artaud text.

Artaud had complained of Dulac betraying his work and, although he was no longer officially of the group, Breton and Desnos in particular sympathized. As the titles came on the screen, Breton stood and courteously announced to the packed house: 'I have to say that Mme Germaine Dulac is an arsehole.' There was uproar. Artaud himself, showing signs of the insanity that was to plague his later life, ran amok, smashing mirrors and yelling, '*Goulue! Goulue!*'* Next day Tallier received a letter from Breton thanking him for not having called the police, the first example he had encountered of a manager acting with such forbearance. To the headed notepaper from the Surrealist headquarters at 15 rue de Grenelle, Breton had added a spot of blood for effect.

Breton was right to be grateful, since Chiappe was just waiting for the pretext of a public disturbance to descend on the Surrealists. He was doubly angry, then, when another member, journalist Roger Vailland, wrote articles praising the Prefect, whom he called 'the purifier of our

* '*Greedy! Greedy!*' Since this makes little sense, Artaud may have been saying, '*Gouine!*' (dyke).

capital' and compared to 'a grandfather who showers his grandchildren with presents'. Vailland was called to account at place Blanche. When Georges Ribemont-Dessaignes protested that, like everyone else, Vailland had to earn a living (a view not accepted by most Surrealists, who thought work counter-revolutionary), he was shouted down. Vailland was expelled. Ribemont-Dessaignes later resigned in protest.

Buñuel watched all this from a distance. Whatever he told Dali or his other Madrid friends, he was almost as far from the centre of things, and especially from the Surrealists, as when he first arrived. It is ironic that a man soon to become indelibly identified with the movement and to survive as one of its most faithful followers should, after almost three years in Paris, have encountered mainly its fringes, met none of its principals and attended no meetings. Revelation, however, traditionally precedes conversion, and Surrealism was above all a state of mind demanding no formal rationale, just an impatience with the world and an acceptance that only violence can change it.

Suspecting that Buñuel had exaggerated his intimacy with the Surrealists, Dali urged him to demonstrate his sympathies and attract their attention, as he himself was doing at every opportunity. 'I was prepared to join the Surrealist movement,' Dali wrote. 'I had studied their watchwords and their themes thoroughly, dissecting them down to the smallest bones.' In March he co-authored a pamphlet attacking Catalan art as provincial and old-fashioned. The *Manifest Groc (Yellow Manifesto)* celebrated the machine over man and listed the artists it felt to be part of the new age. They included Eluard, Aragon, Desnos and Breton.* Dali also gave a lecture to artists at Sitges in which he attacked local folklore and suggested that Barcelona's old quarter, the Ramblas, be demolished. Perhaps to demonstrate to Luis how his own healthy influence had triumphed over Lorca's perceived decadence, he also urged his audience to take up sport, to bathe daily and change their underwear.

On one of Buñuel's visits to Cadaques, Dali also persuaded him to indulge in the Surrealist exercise of gratuitously attacking some cultural icon. Buñuel only mentions one such letter, though Dali says that 'insulting letters, co-signed with Buñuel, were sent to the humanist doctors and to all the most distinguished personalities in Spain'.

Composer Manuel de Falla and Juan Ramon Jimenez were obvious targets. Dali and Buñuel selected Jimenez, partly because *Platero and Me* was so well loved, but also because, as a supporter of them both, and of

---

* Lorca had contributed to the Manifesto but when it was published he deleted his name.

Lorca, he was the less suspecting. According to Dali, Jimenez had told them excitedly, 'I've found the group of the future. Dali is a genius, Buñuel is insane, violent, passionate, and he's producing the most extraordinary things. Federico Garcia Lorca is a wonderful poet.'

With misgivings, Buñuel signed the letter. It read:

> Our Distinguished Friend,
>   We believe it is our duty to inform you in a totally disinterested way that your work is deeply repugnant to us because of its immoral, hysterical, arbitrary quality.
>   In particular SHIT! for your facile and ill-intentioned *Platero and Me*, the least donkeyish and the most odious donkey that we have ever encountered.
>   SHIT. Sincerely

Jimenez was flabbergasted, which more than satisfied Dali. 'Most of the time these demonstrations were quite unjust,' he conceded smugly, 'but I intended in this way to assert my "will to power" and to prove that I was still impervious to regret.' Buñuel shared this motive, but he also took a perverse pleasure in the act. He wrote that 'our letter' (which they had made a point of circulating widely) 'was so rude that, when we arrived in Madrid, all the friends of Ramon refused to talk to us. We learned later that Ramon, who was a solitary, had been sick for three days because of our letter.'

To the northern European temperament, the letter and the glee Dali and Buñuel took in writing it seem callous. On one level, Buñuel undoubtedly enjoyed being able to mete out the punishment he had received himself from Dali and Lorca when they wrote to him. There was also a ruthlessness in his character especially towards the weak, which the letter exercised. Filming in the mountains of Las Hurdes a few years later, he would pitilessly observe a donkey like Platero being stung to death by bees. Yet cruelty, sarcasm and gratuitous insult are so integral to the Spanish sense of humour that it is easy to exaggerate Buñuel's pleasure and the injury to Jimenez. As Buñuel never tired of insisting, Anglo-Saxons seldom understood him or his films.

With all Madrid convinced of his influence in Parisian artistic circles, Buñuel was pressed more than ever to maintain the illusion. On 14 February 1928 he wrote to Bello: 'I shall be signing a contract which will oblige me to make a film this summer, and the other party in his turn will commit himself to contributing 50,000 pesetas.' He went on: 'I cannot tell you the name of the party.' This may have been the Goya project, although he confided to Bello in a letter of 21 March that 'the business I was so mysterious about was a work of Claudio de la Torre and the son of Sota de Bilbao'. In the same letter, however, he complained: 'My affairs are going very badly. I did not believe it was going to be so difficult to start. The film in Greece will not now be made, in spite of the fact that it was certain. Ramon has still not sent me his scenario! [. . .] In brief, here I sit in my room with not an idea of what to do.'

Film reviews brought in a little money. He could not find much to praise in Fred Niblo's *Camille* or Victor Fleming's *The Way of All Flesh* with the melodramatic Emil Jannings, but Falconetti as the yearning, submissive Joan of Carl Dreyer's *La Passion de Jeanne d'Arc*, which opened on 20 April, excited him, and he wrote revealingly: 'We all feel the urge to prescribe her a whipping so that we can give her a sweet afterwards. To take away her dessert from her, to punish her childlike integrity, her transparent obstinacy.' Giménez Caballero in October had launched the Ciné Club of Madrid, and Luis persuaded them to book Flaherty's *Moana*, the Man Ray/Desnos *L'Etoile de Mer (The Sea Star)*, Epstein's *Feu Mathias Pascal*, and to reshow *Entr'acte*, which had been such a hit at the Residencia during his talk.

Luis's courtship of Jeanne continued. The Rucars thought him a catch, his impeccable manners evidence of his sensibility. He had the well-raised young man's skill at diverting the middle-aged. He had learned hypnosis, a useful parlour trick, and plenty of family friends were 'put under', among them Mme Tasnon, mother of Jeanne's friend Hélène. Luis persuaded her she was a little dog, and she ran about on all-fours.

Jeanne, who had the normal erotic instincts of a healthy young French woman, endured the formal visits to her house and Sunday promenades chaperoned by Georgette, but not without a glance at girlfriends who found their lovers more satisfying physically than she did the stiff, correct Luis. At the Spanish Bookshop she met the most handsome young Spaniards in Paris, with one of whom, Pepe Moreno Villa, she flirted more than the rest, but when she even hinted they might go further, Moreno Villa backed off. 'I couldn't do that, not with a man like Luis behind you,' he told her. 'If I asked you out he would kill me.' Jeanne took this as a joke – erroneously.

In February Epstein came good on his promise of a job on *The Fall of the House of Usher*, and until March Luis worked as his assistant. Marie's script immersed Poe's already tenebrous tale in an atmosphere of storm-swept heaths and gloomy lakes. The interior of the mansion, re-created at Billancourt, was cavernous, its wide corridors lined with billowing curtains, the ballroom-sized living room swept by hurricane draughts. Usher, pausing only to snatch up and strum a guitar, is painting a portrait of his wife, each stroke of which takes away a fraction of her vitality until she is immured in the canvas.

Buñuel felt humiliated by his role. When the production manager, Maurice Morlot, sent him to buy haemoglobin, a xenophobic pharmacist refused to serve him, more evidence of entrenched racism. Madeleine Usher was played by Abel Gance's wife Marguerite and, although Artaud had begged to play Roderick Usher, Epstein, in the wake of Germaine Dulac's humiliation at the screening of *The Seashell and the Clergyman*, had turned him down. Both acts seemed to Luis to be further evidence of the official avant-garde's clannishness.

To Buñuel's embarrassment, Claudio de la Torre visited the set and wrote a tongue-in-cheek piece for *La Gaceta Literaria* which underlined Luis's menial position. 'We [. . .] discovered a lake, a lot of owls, two or three skeletons. Their owners, slow and pale, gesticulated solemnly before the camera. Epstein's shouts served to indicate our friend to us. "Buñuel. Lights!" Luis Buñuel – who would recognize Madrilene inertia in him now? – rapidly consults his papers. "Buñuel! Number!" Again he consults his fan of papers as if it were the wheel of fortune. "Thirty-two".'

Jeanne often came to see Luis at Billancourt. Once, Epstein drove her back to Paris, and she told him that Luis had proposed. 'I'm very much in love,' she said, 'but I'm scared by his intelligence.'

Epstein said, 'Jeanne, you're equivocating. He's very intelligent but maybe you are more intelligent. He's not the man for you. Don't marry him.'

Buñuel's temper held until the day everyone was given assignments for a Dordogne location trip. Epstein told him to stay behind. 'Abel Gance is going to audition two girls,' he told him, 'and you might be able to give him a hand.' Buñuel snapped that he was assisting him, not Gance, whose work he found pretentious. Epstein, furious, said, 'How can an insignificant asshole like you talk that way about a great director?' As far as he was concerned, their relationship was at an end. He relented enough to drive Buñuel back to Paris but on the way he warned him: 'You be careful. I see Surrealistic tendencies in you. If you want my advice, you'll stay away from them.'

The break with Epstein was disastrous but inevitable. Buñuel knew there was a limit to the amount of time he could spend as anyone's assistant without losing credibility. Also, *Usher's* pictorialism and Gothic sensibility had highlighted the artistic bankruptcy of the avant-garde. If he needed confirmation of this, the Surrealists were happy to oblige. Desnos condemned film-makers whose 'exaggerated respect for art [and] a cult of expression [has] led to [. . .] an avant-garde cinema remarkable for the rapidity with which its productions go out of fashion, its absence of human emotion and the danger into which it leads the whole cinema [. . .] We cast into outer darkness *L'Inhumaine, Panam n'Est Pas Paris (Panama Is Not Paris)*, and *La Chute de la Maison Usher*, in which Epstein's lack of imagination, or rather his paralysed imagination, were exposed.'

Almost at once, Buñuel also lost his job with *Cahiers d'Art*. There too he had been acting more like a Surrealist than a 'responsible' member of the artistic community. Zervos had given him some latitude by publishing a report on the visit to Paris of suave Hollywood actor Adolphe Menjou. Mostly a satirical meditation on the actor's moustache, it was probably inspired by Dali's essay 'Saint Sebastian' in the Catalan *L'Amic de les Arts* of July 1927 which mused on Menjou, Keaton, Tom Mix, and Josephine Baker, whose 'rhythm [. . .] in slow motion,' Dali decided, 'coincides with the purest and slowest growth of a flower produced by the cinematographic process'. Keaton is praised as 'Pure Poetry. Paul Valéry' and Hollywood for magnifying 'the pulchritude and eurhythmics of the standardized implement, aseptic, antiartistic variety shows, concrete, humble, lively, joyous, comforting clarities, to oppose to a sublime, deliquescent, bitter, putrescent art'.

Buñuel ended his piece with an attack on film critics that read like a journalistic paraphrase of Dali filtered through Surrealism. 'Hence the terror of so many judicious people, the dismal "taste for art" which whines against the superficiality of the American cinema, without taking into account that it was the first to realize that cinematic truths do not form a common denominator with those of literature or theatre. Why persist in demanding metaphysics from the cinema, and not recognize that in a well-made film the fact of opening the door or seeing a hand – great monster – taking possession of an object, is capable of enshrining an authentic and unexpected beauty?'

The new piece, *News from Hollywood: Latest*, parodied movie gossip. Mary Pickford had changed her toothpaste; the new portrait of John Gilbert was better than his photographs; the news that Emil Jannings's father's name was not Emil but Andrew had been flashed round the world, etc. What angered Zervos was the final paragraph, which declared that the Ministry of Public Information had banned all cinema magazines as 'pornographic, brutalizing public taste, [and] encouraging the stupid triviality of the fans'. When he tried to cut it, Buñuel resigned. Fortunately Brunius remained on the staff and supported all Luis's films, even assisting on *L'Age d'Or*.

*

Ever since he came to Paris, Buñuel had been writing poetry, but without conviction. A little amateur poetasting seemed demanded by his social position. '[It] seemed to me to be more like the luxury of a *señorito*. Then, as even now, I was opposed to luxury and to the *señoritos*, although, because of my birth, I was one of them.'

Throughout 1927, he'd been working on some dream-based poems. Lorca's success jolted him into thinking of publishing. In March he wrote to him truculently: 'You will be receiving soon from me something that is almost a book of poems. Poetically I am anti-Juan Ramon [Jimenez]. He seems to me the chief of poetic putrefaction. His rottenness is the worst of all [. . .] I have re-read *Platero and Me* and made up my mind: absolutely disgusted.' The book's working title was *Un Chien Andalou*.

On 12 June he wrote to Cuesta again, asking for more photographs of Goya paintings, along with some pictures showing the architecture of the time. In five days, he said, he would be 'presenting [the Goya scenario] to an important film production house'. On 1 August he told Bello: 'In October I will be going to Spain for a cinema congress. It is very probable that I will sign a contract with the "Julio Cesar" [production company] the president of which likes me very much. The "Julio Cesar" has accepted my treatment of *Goya* for which they will pay me 4500 pesetas.'

In September Buñuel's cinema page appeared in the *Gaceta*. Subtitled 'The Seventh Art – Cinema, 1928', it included his long essay on film editing which recycled rhetoric of the time about the poetic value of contrasting images,* the satire *News from Hollywood: Latest*, a review of *La Passion de Jeanne d'Arc* and a brief survey, *New Poets in the Cinema*, as well as an article by Epstein.

His optimism about Goya was dashed. Neither the Julio Cesar company nor anyone else was in a hurry to fund so ambitious a film. The coming of sound was also making everyone uneasy. Warner Brothers had hurriedly added some dialogue sequences and a lavish music score to the John Barrymore *Don Juan*, but no Madrid cinema owner was prepared to invest in sound equipment until he saw it had taken off. The market for costume films was glutted by an oversupply from Germany. One American cinema owner ordered his distributor: 'Don't send me any more of those films where the hero writes his name with a feather.'

Buñuel was reunited with Lorca and made a sort of peace with him, although the poet was feeling increasingly isolated from his generation.

---

* Buñuel knew almost nothing about cutting-room technique. When he got a job re-editing Nazi documentaries in New York he had to ask for help.

When Giménez Caballero asked at the end of the year in a *Gaceta* interview who his 'habitual friends' were in Madrid, Lorca named, somewhat poignantly, 'Dali, Buñuel, Sanchez Ventura, Vicens de la Slave, Pepin Bello, Prados and many others'. But almost none of them lived in Madrid any longer. Most were making their way elsewhere, and two of them, perhaps his closest friends, had gone out of their way to insult and humiliate him. Over the years this sense of isolation ripened into resentment. Later in New York Lorca would say, 'Buñuel and Dali have made a pile of shit called *Un Chien Andalou* and I am the dog.' He was convinced that the film's impotent main character was based on him. In the light of the scene where he is forced to assume the position of a penitent, this may well have been the case.

9

'The Sleep Of Reason Brings Forth Monsters'.
– Title of an etching by Francisco Goya

The failure of the *Goya* and Gómez de la Serna project left Buñuel profoundly depressed. Glumly, he accepted Dali's invitation to join him at the family home for a holiday. Cadaques in 1929 consisted of only a few houses clustered around shingle beaches of black slate. The one road, white with dust, wound through coastal mountains that plunged precipitously into the sea – a favourite setting for Dali's paintings. Not far away was Port Bou, the main exit route for Spaniards in a hurry to leave the country.

For centuries, the vineyards clinging to narrow terraces built on the mountainside by generations of peasants had produced a thin local wine, but now visitors crawled past field after field of dead vines ravaged by phylloxera. The locals scraped a living from fishing and from the tourists, mostly from Paris, who, although Cadaques had only one hotel, the Miramar, had adopted the village as their hideaway. During the summer Dali lived and worked almost permanently in a small fisherman's cottage a kilometre away at Port Lligat.

Buñuel found Dali as ambitious and enthusiastic as he himself was lacklustre and despondent. Surrealism had inflamed Dali's imagination, and he was eager to move on to Paris where he could be at its heart. He badgered Luis to arrange this. But Luis was at his lowest ebb since he left the Residencia. All his projects had come to nothing. He had alienated Epstein, his best contact in the French film business, and severed his relationship with *Cahiers d'Art*. After the *Gaceta*'s Seventh Art issue, he had no serious prospects of a career in film journalism. Logically the next step would be a return to Madrid and a decline into provincial mediocrity as overseer of his family property.

This was the background for Buñuel's suggestion to Dali that they collaborate on a Surrealist film. Dali agreed with enthusiasm. It would be the rocket with which he would astonish Breton and win entry to the group. For Buñuel, however, it was the last throw of the dice, and he approached the project with a desperate fury that Sade might have relished.

He went to Zaragoza to see Doña Maria. His sisters had been promised dowries of 10,000 *duros* (50,000 pesetas) when they married, and Luis, helped by a family attorney, persuaded his mother to give him half that amount, whether on the basis of his plans to marry Jeanne or for a film is not clear. His mother never thought film was a suitable career for a *señorito*. Twenty-five thousand pesetas may have seemed a small price to cure Luis's movie bug and lure him back home where he belonged. She was less than pleased with the success of the film she financed, and always refused to see it.

With a small fortune in his pocket, Buñuel was racked with doubts about spending it. He went back to Paris and, if he is to be believed, blew half the money in *cabarets* and restaurants. If so, he did it quickly, because in January he wrote to Bello that he was getting ready to return to Spain, this time to write a screenplay with Dali. 'Even if the world crumbles about us,' he said, 'this film will begin shooting at the beginning of April with the money which I still have left; and when we start I shall go on adjusting it so that we can keep within the budget and I do not need to ask anyone for economic assistance.'

Back in Cadaques, Buñuel proposed Gómez de la Serna's newspaper project. Dali dismissed it as 'extremely mediocre [and] avant-garde in an incredibly naive sort of way [. . .] I told [Luis] that this film story of his did not have the slightest interest, but that I on the other hand had just written a very short scenario which had the touch of genius.'

This tale of an existing scenario is invented, because both men later detailed their week's work in January as they engaged in the classic Surrealist exercise of free association, turning dreams into reality. Dali instigated the process and was the most expert in it. 'I had understood,' he said, 'that the point [of Surrealism] was to transcribe thought spontaneously, without any rational, aesthetic or moral checks.' It seems unlikely that he would have persisted, however, without Buñuel's dogged persistence and understanding of what could reasonably be put on film.

On the first day, they told one another their most recent dreams. Luis volunteered 'a long, tapering cloud slic[ing] the moon in half, like a razor blade slicing through an eye'. Salvador offered the hand crawling with ants he had dreamed of the previous night. They continued like this for a week. 'Our only rule was very simple,' Buñuel said. 'No idea or image that might lend itself to a rational explanation of any kind would be accepted. We had to open all doors to the irrational and keep only those images that surprised us, without trying to explain why.* The amazing thing was that we never had the slightest disagreement: we spent a week in total identification. "A man fires a double bass," one of us would say. "No", replied the other, and the one who'd proposed the idea accepted the veto and felt it justified. On the other hand, when the image proposed by one was accepted by the other, it immediately seemed luminously right and absolutely necessary to the scenario.'

The film Buñuel shot in the spring of 1929 differs little from their original treatment. After the title 'Once Upon a Time', a man sharpens a razor, steps on to a balcony, looks up at the moon, then draws the blade across a girl's eye. There is another intertitle, 'Eight Years Later', which, like the rest of the titles in the film, is meaningless. A man dressed in frilly clothing and wearing a small box round his neck cycles down a Parisian street. In an apartment a girl is reading a book that includes Vermeer's *The Lacemaker*. As she drops it, the man falls off his bicycle. She runs downstairs and kisses him. Back in the apartment she takes a necktie from the box and places it on her bed with the man's frills, arranging them as if he were wearing them.

The man appears in the room. He is staring at his hand, in the palm of which is a hole crawling with ants. There are quick dissolves from the hole to a woman's armpit, then a sea urchin. Meanwhile, outside in the street, a crowd has gathered round a severed hand lying there. An androgynous girl pokes it with a stick. A policeman picks it up, puts it into a box and gives it to her. Cars roar by on either side, one of which knocks her down.

In the room the man becomes sexually aroused and caresses the girl's breasts and buttocks with drooling abandon. As if in response, her clothes dissolve. She runs to a corner and menaces him with a tennis racquet. The man moves towards her but at the last moment picks up two ropes, to each of which is attached a slab of cork, a melon, two Marist brothers and a grand piano with a dead donkey sandwiched in it. As he struggles to reach her, she slips through the door. He stops it from closing with his hand. On the other side the girl sees it crawling with ants.

The girl finds herself in a room identical to the first, with the man lying on the bed. A stranger rings outside (the 'bell' is a cocktail shaker agitated by two hands poked through holes in the wall) and the girl lets him in. The stranger snatches the man's frills and throws them out of the

---

* This seems slightly naive. Anyone who had read Freud would recognize many of the images and their significance.

window, then orders him to stand against the wall with arms held out as a punishment. From a desk he snatches up two notebooks, one of them bearing the signature of Goya, and makes him hold them in his outstretched hands. As the stranger turns, we see he has the same face as the man. Another title is randomly inserted: 'Sixteen Years Before'. The books turn to revolvers in the man's hands and he shoots the stranger. As he falls, the scene shifts to a park where a naked woman sits with her back to the camera. The man materializes behind her and his hands scrape down her back as he dies. People gather and carry the body away.

Back in the empty room, the girl see a Death's Head moth on the wall. The man appears, once again wearing his frills. He wipes his hand across his face and his mouth disappears. The girl pointedly makes up her mouth with lipstick. Where the man's mouth should be, he now has a patch of hair. She looks in alarm at her armpit, from which the hair has disappeared.

On a beach, the girl and a third man walk along the shingle. Lying in the mud are the frills and the broken box. They examine them without interest, then walk off along the beach. A title, the only one in the film with even a vague logic, announces 'In the Spring'. From the bodies of the man and woman, buried to their chests in a desert, the spikes of new growth have started to emerge.

Although many of the film's images came from the same pool of movie stills, advertising layouts, art prints and visual bric-à-brac which René Magritte, Max Ernst, Man Ray and a dozen other Surrealists had been plundering for years, the more lurid imagery is Dali's. The juxtaposition of rotting donkeys and grand pianos, the severed hand, the woman's naked back, the visual puns with pubic hair, armpits and sea urchins bear his mark. The pianos had a particular significance. In 1934 he would paint *Atmospheric Skull Sodomizing a Grand Piano*, a comment on his attempted seduction by Lorca, whose spirit hovers uninvited over *Un Chien Andalou*. In particular the final tableau recalls Lorca's poem: 'Parched earth/Tranquil earth/Of immense nights/Earth of the dead without eyes/And of arrows'.

Buñuel contributed far less to the film's poetry. The man's attempts to achieve sexual satisfaction while struggling against the self-imposed burden of religious dogma and infantile obsessions reflect his problems, but perhaps those of Dali as well. Other details are more personal. The twin revolvers mirror his (but also the Surrealists') fascination with guns. For background music he chose the tangos to which he danced with Jeanne, padding them out with the 'Liebestod' from Wagner's

Tristan and Isolde. He also supplied most to the framing structure and the Parisian bourgeois setting.

The title is his too. They started with *El Marista de La Ballesta (The Marist Brother of the Ballesta)*. This became *Dangereux de se Pencher en Dedans (Dangerous to Lean Inside)*, a joke on the railway injunction not to lean out of the window. That title is typed on the shooting script, but during filming Buñuel struck it out with the same thick blue pencil he used to cross off shots as they were finished. Scrawled in its place is *Un Chien Andalou*, the provisional title for his unpublished book of poems. It was Buñuel's declaration of independence.

The ease of collaboration impressed him. For the rest of his career he would always work with another writer, replicating the *Chien Andalou* system. Collaborators were encouraged, even ordered, to say 'No' if they disagreed. Work could only continue on the basis of complete equality of ideas. Each session began with Buñuel telling a story, as he had started with Dali by recalling a dream. With Jean-Claude Carrière, who co-wrote all his later films, he enlarged the system. 'Every evening, after we'd rested,' said Carrière, 'we would meet for a drink, and each of us would tell a story. Something we'd just invented. "The imagination is a muscle," Buñuel said. "It has to be exercised".'

In February Buñuel was back in Paris with the completed screenplay, but this gave him little satisfaction. More than ever he realized that making *Un Chien Andalou* was an act of professional desperation. 'I was absolutely sure it was going to be a failure,' he said. The censors would almost certainly ban it, and if they did not, Chiappe would. As for the cultural fringe, it would do Buñuel no good there either, since the film was defiantly anti-avant garde, 'a gob of spit in the face of art', as Henry Miller was to describe *Tropic of Cancer* – in Buñuel's case the art of Dulac, L'Herbier, Epstein.

Under the rules of 1929 Buñuel was right. Censors, the political right, the film industry and the police should have joined forces, as they would in the case of *L'Age d'Or*, to suppress the film and ruin the director. But the rules were about to change as the old avant-garde ran out of steam and a new brash style of personal film swept in with the arrival of sound. 'Hollywood was becoming a deluxe garage,' said Jean Cocteau, 'and its films were more and more like sumptuous makes of automobiles. With *Un Chien Andalou* we were back to the bicycle.'

10

'Morning of wolves and their bite is a tunnel
That you will leave all clad in blood
To blush for the night . . . '
– Paul Eluard (translated by Jesse Browner)

In February Buñuel apologized to Bello for not sending even a card from Cadaques, but they had been writing 'a stupendous scenario, quite without precedent in the history of the cinema. It is something very big. You will love it. I'll begin filming in March.' He and Dali were now, he said, 'more united than ever'.

Buñuel asked Pierre Batcheff to star, telling him 'the subject demands the complete participation of the actor – and also, much later, the complete participation of the public when the film is finished'. It also needed someone who would work for little money. Batcheff agreed to break another contract, and his apartment became Buñuel's head-quarters while he wrote a shooting script. A projector was moved into the living room to screen rushes.

Luis and Pierre often argued all night. Denise was once woken at dawn by them, demanding she settle a disagreement. As she looked from her husband to Luis, the bells in a convent on rue St Oudinot began to toll. 'The face of Buñuel cleared,' she wrote. 'Having been raised by Jesuits, Luis remembered the crystal sonority of convent bells. He went to the window and smiled as he watched the sisters crossing their kitchen garden on the way to morning prayers. I got up, made coffee and rolls. Another day had begun.

'Buñuel asked if he could shave and take a bath. Afterwards he put back on a shirt which might have just come from the laundry. His beige alpaca trousers had not suffered in the night's discussions: the crease was impeccable. Always smiling, with his usual beautiful manners and Oriental gestures, he backed to the door and disappeared.'

As Denise remembers it, Luis ran out of money and the three combed Montparnasse cafés and Montmartre jazz clubs for a backer. It would appear that Ricardo Soriano, a wealthy Spaniard who lived in Biarritz, finally advanced the cash, although, if this is so, Buñuel never mentioned it. Duverger had agreed to shoot the film but after renting space at Billancourt Buñuel could only afford a six-man crew.

Dali, his military service over, insisted on being present for at least part of the shooting. He later claimed he was on the set throughout and was consulted by Buñuel on every scene, but Buñuel insists he came only for the last two days, a version supported by a letter to Bello of 25 March. 'I am immediately starting the film. It will be finished at the beginning of May. Dali will come to Paris in a few days for a long stay. Dali and I are going to do a revue.' Though doubtful that, even at twenty-four, Salvador could survive away from home, his father paid his train fare and gave him spending money. Having seen his incompetence on his previous visit to Paris, Luis met him at the Gare d'Orsay with Jeanne and Georgette, who became his nursemaids. They took him to appointments, arranged his meals, told him what day it was.

When he could slip away from his minders, Dali devoted himself to a quest, mostly unsuccessful, for sex. Although female bodies, and especially naked backs, attracted him and appeared repeatedly in his work, he was so repressed and shy that all his life he achieved satisfaction mostly by masturbating. He had long realized he would always be sexually inadequate. 'Naked, and comparing myself to my friends,' he wrote, 'I found my sex small, sad and soft.' His version of his arrival in Paris is that he had a taxi take him from the station straight to a brothel. The driver delivered him to the famous 12 rue Chabanais, around the corner from the Bibliothèque Nationale. The house that accommodated Edward VII and regular parties of Surrealists (who hid their visits from Breton) had no trouble categorizing Dali's tastes, and he was allowed to watch through the voyeur's peepholes. He left, he said, 'with enough to last me for the rest of my life in the way of accessories to furnish, in less than a minute, no matter what erotic rêverie, even the most exacting'. He also accosted girls in the street. All turned him down, and he spent hours in the Jardins du Luxembourg, a celebrated pick-up spot, weeping with frustration.

Other people were more friendly, Mirò, after having Dali to dinner, advised him to buy a dinner jacket and, a few days later, took him, now in a boiled shirt and *smoking*, to dine at the home of the Duchesse de Dato, an experience that left the young painter tongue-tied. The Russian painter Pavel Tchelitchev and the dealer Pierre Loeb were also there. Dali and Tchelitchev went home together by Métro, but when the Russian got off at the stop before Dali's, Salvador became hysterical at being left alone. Thereafter he took taxis everywhere, ordering them to wait while he went shopping.

Dining him at the Bal Tabarin a few nights later, Goemans pointed out a pale man with thinning hair, doleful eyes and a sad, downturned mouth. He was Paul Eluard, not only an important poet, author of *Capitale de la Douleur (Capital of Pain)*, and a core Surrealist but also, like Breton, a collector and dealer in pictures. He was with Alix Apfel, 'La Pomme', a vivacious Berlin girl with whom he was enjoying, as he confided to his wife Gala, then in a Swiss sanatorium, an affair that was 'going very simply . . . calmly, no exhaustion, onanism for two, etc.'. Such exchanges between Eluard and Gala were typical. It was an open secret that he enjoyed fantasizing about her having sex with other men, and often joined her in bed with her lovers, who had included Max Ernst and Giorgio de Chirico.

Goemans introduced Dali to Eluard, who was soon plotting to bring the young Spaniard and Gala together in what he hoped would be an exciting *partouze*, as the Parisians call sex *à trois*.* When Dali raved about the unique 'mineral' qualities of the Cadaques landscape and especially Cabo Crues, the rocky headland at the end of his beach at Port Lligat, Eluard saw a way, and by the end of the night both he and Goemans had agreed to spend the summer there. In July, when Eluard wrote Gala to discuss holiday plans, he told her: 'Goemans is going to Cadaques, in Spain, with some Spaniards who made a wonderful film.' Impressed by Eluard's evident interest, but perhaps not grasping its subtext, Goemans offered Dali a one-man show for November.

Un Chien Andalou took fifteen days to shoot. After editing, it ran seventeen minutes. The script, neatly typed in Spanish, with the exact focal length of the lenses in many cases indicated in advance, shows how little Buñuel deviated from his concept. With no money for laboratory work, he did all the dissolves and fades by winding back the film or irising down on the image.

Although most of the cast were friends, it was a point of honour with Buñuel to pay each at least a token fee. Jeanne took charge of the budget, making nervous trips by bus and Métro to Billancourt with the payroll in her purse. She also sewed costumes, including Batcheff's frills. Pierre flirted with her until Luis hustled her into another room and locked her in – 'so they can't disturb you,' he explained.

---

* For an amusing inside account of the Surrealist *partouze* in theory and practice, see George Melly's memoir *Rum, Bum and Concertina*, where he describes his own intricate relationship with Edouard and Sybil Mesens.

Then and later, Buñuel mostly shot in sequence. By the time main shooting started he had already filmed the prologue. He used a dead calf's eye for the notorious shot, with the skin around it shaved and made up, but this didn't minimize the impact. He himself was nauseated the first few times he saw it. Pepin Bello would later describe its effect on audiences as 'like the cut of a whip'.

From the start, Buñuel had trouble directing actors, a problem he never overcame. For the next half-century performers would complain of how little guidance he gave them. 'He liked actors,' said Catherine Deneuve, 'but I wouldn't say he loved them. That's why he worked with the same people. He didn't like to get involved.' On *The Adventures of Robinson Crusoe* he would tell Dan O'Herlihy, 'Nothing for *effect*' and, directing the most erotic scene in *Tristana*, order Deneuve, 'Just stand there, and above all don't . . . *perform*.' The best he could do to motivate Batcheff was to order him, 'Stare out the window and look as if you're listening to Wagner. No, no – not like that. Sadder. Much sadder.' When Batcheff stared into the street at the girl playing with the hand, he was told to imagine a military parade was passing or that two drunks were fighting. Because of the neutral motivation the performances of *Chien* achieve the quality of dream to which more prestigious films of the avant-garde aspired in vain.

The park exteriors were left to last, just after the famous scene of the pianos and donkeys. Dali was present for both. In the park he can be seen in the distance, walking away from the camera with Jeanne. For the donkey sequence, he dressed in a Marist outfit to play one of the brothers. The other is the anarchist publisher Jaume Miratvilles, who was passing through Paris *en route* to South America. In the second pair, Dali was replaced by the production manager, Marval. Anyone available and willing was pressed into acting. Fano Messan, a café acquaintance who followed the *garçonne* fad of 1929 by affecting male clothes and cropped hair, played the girl in the street, poking the severed hand.

The donkeys had been slaughtered earlier and stuffed with straw. The script called only for a medium shot of a donkey with one bleeding nostril, but Dali insisted on augmenting the carcasses with rotting fish and filling the eye cavities with oozing wax. Later Buñuel was scornful about Dali's insistence on the accurate re-creation of their dreams but he himself could be obsessive about such details. The ants that crawl on Batcheff's hand were a fat, red-headed variety he'd seen in the Sierra del Guadarrama while on walking tours with Pepin Bello. Buñuel had a friend named Maynar capture some and send them to the documentary director Carlos Velo, a trained biologist, who shipped them to him on a piece of rotten wood in a can.

*

As soon as shooting was finished, Buñuel left for Madrid, where he had promised to present a programme of new American comedies for Giménez Caballero's Film Society. He seems not even to have supervised the shooting of *Chien*'s credits which, as usual in experimental films, were misspelt and incomplete. Even Buñuel's first name is rendered as 'Louis'. The designer, Pierre Schildnecht, is shown as 'Schilzneck', Batcheff as 'Batchef', Simone Mareuil as 'Simonne'. They, with Duverger and Dali, are the only people credited.

On 4 May Buñuel introduced his comedy programme at the Goya Cinema. It included films with Ben Turpin, Harold Lloyd, Buster Keaton, Harry Langdon and Chaplin. 'This session will be something definitive,' he wrote in a note that loyally restates the Surrealist line. 'These lunacies [. . .] are not lunacies at all but what I would call new poetry. Surrealism in the cinema is to be found only in these films. Much more genuine Surrealism than in the films of Man Ray.' In the interval Alberti read his poems.

Dali stayed in Paris. Buñuel visited Mme Rucar before he left and told her, 'While I'm away, only allow Jeanne to go out with Rafael Sanchez Ventura and Salvador. They are the only friends I trust.'

Jeanne came to like the unworldly Dali, if not his bizarre ideas. One evening he asked if she believed in life after death. She thought she probably did.

'*Thinking* is no good,' he said. 'The important thing is to know. We are going to make an experiment, if you agree. I am going to kill you right away and if there is an after-life you are going to appear to me to confirm it.'

Jeanne said, 'You're crazy! It's better if I kill you and you appear to me.'

Dali did not care for this at all, so they decided that the one who died first would tell the other one. Afterwards, Jeanne pondered Luis's faith that nothing could happen to her with Salvador.

As soon as Buñuel returned to Paris, he and Dali showed *Chien* to distributors. Tallier wanted it for the Ursulines if the censors would clear it, but a new Montmartre art cinema, Studio 28, had been launched in 1928 just around the corner from place Blanche, and its owner, Jean Mauclaire, a young left-wing enthusiast for the avant-garde, was also keen. Buñuel submitted the film to the Ministère de l'Instruction Publique for a certificate, though its chances seemed slim in the climate created by Chiappe.

Irritated and frustrated, Dali moped around Paris until May. He took to haunting the Montparnasse cafés with a painting under his arm, hoping to raise money for a longer stay. Desnos ran into him at La Coupole, took him back to his apartment and eventually bought a picture. George Antheil was also interested until he heard Dali's prices: it had not taken Salvador long to learn the market. In May he left, disillusioned with Paris and especially with Luis, whose Surrealist connections had been exposed as mere café acquaintances. Thereafter the two would move further apart until they became enemies, sniping at one another from opposite sides of the world for the next fifty years.

How and when did Buñuel finally make contact with the Surrealists? Luis himself so complicated this question that we will never know for sure. He told the Swiss critic Freddy Buache that Zervos introduced him at La Coupole to Louis Aragon and Man Ray, Carrière that Teriade presented him to Ray, but at Le Dôme, and José de la Colina and Tomás Pérez Turrent that Fernand Léger introduced him at La Coupole to Ray, who then took him to the bar to meet Aragon. Elsewhere, he describes the meeting with Aragon and Ray as one held to plan the preview of *Un Chien Andalou*, which suggests it took place after they had already met. Whichever is true, no meeting took place before July 1929, otherwise Eluard would never have referred vaguely to Buñuel and Dali in his letter of that date as 'some Spaniards who made a wonderful film'. To complicate things still further, Ray, through whom Buñuel met his eventual sponsors Vicomtesse Marie-Laure de Noailles and her husband Charles, makes no mention of introducing him to anyone, although from Luis's frequent references it is clear that the photographer/film-maker was one of his first contacts.

Born Emmanuel Radnitzky in Philadelphia, Ray had been instrumental in launching Dada in the United States. In 1921 he moved to Paris and set up as a portraitist, fashion photographer and photo artist. His pioneer photographic abstractions and short films led him to the Surrealists. In 1928, Desnos had just written the text for Ray's film *L'Etoile de Mer*, the dream-like images of which attracted the attention of the de Noailles. Buñuel may even have targeted him as the one person who could win him the crucial sponsorship he needed to make more films. As a foreigner and a film-maker, Ray was his best conduit to both the Surrealists and potential patrons like the de Noailles. We cannot be sure whether he manipulated and cultivated the connection, but it seems too useful to be coincidence.

In a city that glittered with the rich and artistically sophisticated, the Noailles were by far the most celebrated couple. Both had inherited fortunes but, with her marriage in 1923, Marie-Laure Bischoffsheim, still only twenty-eight when Buñuel met her, also acquired one of France's most distinguished titles. Her artistic credentials were impeccable. A painter and poet herself, she was the grand-daughter of Laure, wife of the Marquis de Sade. The family heirlooms included the manuscript of *Les 120 Journées de Sodome*, preserved in a phallic leather case. Her mother was Proust's inspiration for the Duchesse de Guermantes, and her own childhood playmates included Cocteau, with whom she fell in love at eighteen and who, along with many of his gay circle, remained a lifelong friend.

Dark, not especially pretty, but vivacious and sensual, Marie-Laure was a born hostess, and passionately interested in art and Paris's bohemia. Asked if she had political convictions, she said, 'I have *Parisienne* convictions.' Charles dutifully followed her taste, commissioning her portrait from Foujita, Picasso and, in the 1940s, Balthus, and underwriting a variety of artistic projects for her. Tall, formal, diffident, with a wan smile and a small moustache, Charles de Noailles was decidedly the weaker partner. 'A delightful man,' says François Buot in his biography of Crevel, 'very cultivated, but very cold.' A committee member of France's most select club, the Jockey, his taste ran to formal gardens and eighteenth century furniture and painting, some of which, with his pained agreement, Marie-Laure sold to buy works by Cocteau and the Surrealists.

As well as their château at Fontainebleau, the Noailles had a mansion at 11 place des Etats-Unis in Paris's elegant 16th *arrondissement*, and numerous houses and apartments around Paris. In 1923 they also built a summer villa, St Bernard, on the hills above the Mediterranean at Hyères. A geometric complex of reinforced concrete, it boasted a Cubist walled garden with a Jacques Lipschitz statue and, for Charles, an indoor swimming pool and marble exercise patio. The architect, at Marie-Laure's urging, was Robert Mallet-Stevens, who designed *L'Inhumaine*.

In 1928, the Noailles, in Ray's words, were 'bitten by film', even turning a mirrored eighteenth-century *salon* at place des Etats-Unis into a private cinema. Between 1928 and 1931 Charles commissioned an annual film as a birthday present to Marie-Laure. In 1928 the job went to Marcel L'Herbier, who agreed to shoot a documentary about St Bernard. He took over one of their apartments as an office for his Cinégraphic Company but, deciding that home movies were beneath him, sent his assistant Jacques Manuel to actually film *Biceps et Bijoux (Biceps and Jewels)*. Manuel shot the Noailles and their guests clowning on the sundeck in identical striped jerseys, shorts and sailor hats, supervised by their professional coach. Afterwards they cavorted in the pool and in the evening amused themselves acting out a jewel robbery story written for them for Paul Valéry.

Life at St Bernard, however, was not entirely the idyll it seemed in *Biceps et Bijoux*. Mallet-Stevens, an indifferent domestic architect, had built something closer to an art gallery than a home. The guest rooms, all oriented towards the sea and with private bathrooms, were cell-like. Eluard, when he visited Hyères, preferred a hotel. And while the Noailles were happy to be seen playing at being jewel thieves, Manuel did not film the affairs that flourished among the guests and their host and hostess, nor the nightly parties at which Cocteau and René Crevel smoked opium.

In 1929 the birthday film was commissioned from Man Ray. The Noailles expected another *Biceps et Bijoux*, but instead Ray parodied them. *Le Mystère du Château de Dé (The Mystery of the Chateau of Dice)* was something between a travelogue, a Surrealist exploration of chance and a spoof mystery story, with the Noailles as performers. The couple arrive mysteriously at the house in a mist, find giant dice on the lawn, and are switched into an alternative reality (shot in negative) where they pose awkwardly on the rooftop next to some of its statuary. Later Marie-Laure juggles oranges underwater in the pool. The sponsors acted amused, but their smiles were forced.

While he waited for a censor certificate for *Un Chien Andalou*, Buñuel screened it to anyone who might help get it shown publicly. Since he and Dali were almost unknown, nobody quite knew if the film was genuine Surrealism or simply a sensational rip-off. Denise Batcheff says that Buñuel showed it to Louis Aragon the day after he met him. Aragon, Breton's most trusted confederate, decreed it was indeed Surrealist. Ray then offered to screen it at the invitation-only premiere of *Le Mystère du Château de Dé* on 6 June at the Studio des Ursulines.

If everyone who claimed to have attended that first public screening of *Un Chien Andalou* had been there, the largest modern multiplex would scarcely have held them. Buñuel remembers, probably inaccurately, Picasso, Le Corbusier, Georges Auric, Christian Bérard and Cocteau, but does not mention the Noailles who, as Ray's sponsors and subject, would surely have been present.

He claimed also to have spotted 'the Surrealist group in toto', including Breton, a report echoed by the critic Ado Kyrou. But Georges Sadoul, the only *cinéaste* among the Surrealists, emphatically denied in his *Mon Ami Buñuel, d'Un Chien Andalou à Los Olvidados*, that Breton or more than a handful of the brotherhood attended. 'We did *not* go in a group to acclaim the film, but individually, and the encounter with

Buñuel took place *after* the premiere, which [Breton] didn't attend [. . .] Nobody among us knew the name of Luis Buñuel or Salvador Dali. We had given nobody the right to claim the name of Surrealism. Six months earlier, for having called her dance show *Ballets Surréalistes*, Valeska Gert [. . .] had had to abandon the Comédie des Champs-Elysées under our insults and whistles.' Everyone expected Breton to call down a strike on Studio 28 and *Un Chien Andalou* once he chose to acknowledge the existence of these upstarts.

The screening began at nine-thirty. Polite applause greeted *Le Mystère du Château de Dé*, which everyone recognized as more home movie than art film. During the *entr'acte*, Buñuel went behind the screen where he had set up a gramophone. To accompany the film he had chosen some of the Argentinian tangos he had practised with Jeanne, and the 'Liebestod' from *Tristan and Isolde*. Buñuel says he stayed behind the screen during the showing. Possibly remembering how Antheil had gone on stage armed, he had filled his pockets with stones, intending to pelt anyone who created a scandal. Aragon, however, rejected this account. 'He dreamed it,' he told Max Aub. 'He didn't have stones in his pocket and he wasn't behind the screen. He was only worried about what we would think. But he was wrong, because we were all overflowing with enthusiasm.'

Everyone agreed that there was wild applause after the screening. 'I was stupefied, confused,' Buñuel said. 'I actually believed it was a joke.' Denise Batcheff summed up the most common reaction among his friends. 'My principal preoccupation was to understand how such a soft man as Luis – the only thing he liked was laughing – could have made a movie so cruel and so aggressive.' The best answer came from Aragon, who said, 'There is a deep contradiction between the cruelty of the picture and the horizon of what he imagines.' Aragon was to continue as Buñuel's warmest supporter among the Surrealists. His ex-mistress, English editor/publisher Nancy Cunard, would be responsible for launching *L'Age d'Or* outside France.

Cocteau would later deny having seen *Chien* until months later, the better to excuse stealing some of its images for his own *Sang d'un Poète (Blood of a Poet)*. He would even go further, writing, 'When I conceived [*Sang d'un Poète*], Surrealism did not exist.' But at the time he was as impressed as the rest. 'One summer night,' recalled Antheil, 'Jean Cocteau had phoned my Montparnasse hotel and excitedly told me to come right over to the Right Bank, as he had discovered something of incredible interest and beauty. Knowing Jean to have the best nose in Paris I quickly entered the local subway and met him in front of his hotel inside twenty-five minutes. He immediately took me to a nearby moving picture theatre where, after the regular show, they were to run for him a private showing of a brand-new Surrealist film, *Un Chien Andalou*.'

An astonished Buñuel saw himself transformed overnight into Paris's hottest new talent. Immediately after the Ursulines screening, Pierre Braunberger, a short, bustling young producer and distributor who had just taken over the Panthéon cinema and, with the brothers Marc and Yves Allegret, leased Billancourt studios, bought the theatrical rights to *Un Chien Andalou* for his company Studio-Film, which specialized in experimental cinema. If Buñuel felt uncomfortable at being handled by the man who also distributed Germaine Dulac, he kept it to himself. He also agreed to the Batcheffs' friend Jean-Georges Auriol publishing the script in *La Revue du Cinéma* No. 5, a casual decision that was to have dramatic repercussions.

Charles de Noailles was hooked too. 'Two days later,' Buñuel said, bemused, '[Noailles] sent the assistant director of the Musée de l'Homme [Georges-Henri Rivière] to my hotel to invite me to eat at his house.' Zervos, who had insinuated himself into the deal as Buñuel's agent, fixed the details and assured Noailles on 1 July that the film now had its censorship certificate.

Guests that night included Mme de Chevigne, Jean Hugo and Etienne de Beaumont and their wives, and also composer Francis Poulenc and Cocteau. Buñuel tried not to gape at the liveried servants and the two full-length Goya portraits at the head of the main staircase, nor to jump nervously (as Dali did later) when the wine steward murmured the vintage in his ear as he poured it. Like many aristocrats of the time, Charles and Marie-Laure also affected a slight English accent, which fell awkwardly on the ear of someone whose French was still approximate.

Un Chien Andalou was screened after dinner. On 5 July Charles wrote to Zervos: 'We have shown [the film] to one or two friends last night, and it will be shown again tonight to many people able to do much to advertise it. Buñuel has seen the enthusiasm of the spectators the day before yesterday. I believe that he has been pleased.' Indeed he was. Sitting around the table after dinner, Noailles said: 'We would like to make a film with you . . . two reels, just like *Un Chien Andalou*' – but with a sound track. A few days later they met in Zervos's office to finalize the details of *L'Age d'Or*.

11

'Why did her death remind me of the sublime scorpion
which, surrounded by flames, stabs itself to death?'
– Jean Cocteau on the death of Anna de Noailles

Charles and Marie-Laure de Noailles championed *Un Chien Andalou* as
energetically as Buñuel could have hoped. On 7 July, hiring a print for
another screening, Charles wrote to Braunberger: 'I have already shown
it to some not bad critics and useful people, and I would like to show it
one last time to be sure of all the publicity necessary before it opens at
Studio 28.' With the letter was a generous rental cheque for 1000 francs.
The same day, he explained to Buñuel: 'There will be among others Karl
Dreyer, Jea[n] Lods, Léon-Paul Fargue, René Crevel, Michel Leiris,
[Léon] Moussinac, Jean Tedesco, and various other friends.' But Buñuel
would not be there for this screening. Almost immediately after the first,
he had gathered up the scraps of writing he had done over the years and
some random notes for film scenes, and left for Spain to coax Dali into
collaboration.

Dali had hurried back to Spain for his rendezvous with Goemans and
Eluard. The gallery owner was already at Cadaques with his wife
Camille and Georgette Magritte. The Eluards and their daughter Cécile
arrived in July and checked into the Miramar hotel. To Dali, their arrival
was no more than an advantageous professional opportunity. He was
too naive to grasp Eluard's sophisticated sexual agenda. This changed
on the Eluards' first evening in Cadaques, when Dali met them at the
hotel for drinks, then walked the kilometre back along the beach to his
house with them. Gala, born Helena Deluvina Diakonoff, was a Tartar
Russian, intense, small-breasted and boyish. Her energy seemed concentrated in her eyes, so penetrating, swore Dali, that they could see through
walls. Her impact on Dali was all the greater for Eluard's evident
complaisance. 'Eluard kept telling me about this handsome Dali,' Gala
said, 'I felt he was almost pushing me into his arms before I even saw him.'

The following day, Salvador, dressed in a slashed silk shirt and a pair of swimming trucks turned inside out, shaved his armpits until they bled and tucked a geranium behind his ear. His anality, exacerbated by his rejection in Paris, had become obsessive after his return, and he had spent the first weeks painting a pair of shit-stained underpants. Now he applied fish glue and goat dung as aftershave and went courting. The relationship might have ended there, in revulsion and laughter, had he not glimpsed Gala's naked back on the beach and been jolted into rationality by her beauty. He fled, bathed and presented himself more conventionally.

By the time Buñuel arrived in September, Dali was in love. 'A fantastic woman is in town!' he told him. Fascinated by her back and buttocks, often on display as she sunbathed semi-nude, he had discarded his images of excremental underwear and rotting donkeys, and was now furiously painting Gala from the rear, surrounded by symbols of tumescence and penetration. But Luis, as censorious and formal as Gala was sensual and spontaneous, disliked her almost on sight, and she him. An enthusiast for sturdy, well-formed legs, he confided to her as they strolled on the beach that the sight of a woman with a wide space between her thighs repelled him. Gala greeted this revelation frostily. When they all went swimming, an embarrassed Luis saw that Gala had just such legs.

Superficially Dali and Buñuel seemed as close as ever. They were photographed together in swimming trunks, both tanned, perched on the same rock, Dali staring out to sea, Buñuel's chest pressed against his friend's naked back. But Dali's thoughts were too full of Gala for work, especially when Eluard pointedly returned to Paris, leaving his wife and daughter in Cadaques.

Buñuel and Dali did spend three days desultorily kicking scenes around, but the electricity of the year before had gone. Dali proposed 'a lot of archbishops with their embroidered tiaras bathing amid the rocky cataclysms of Cabo Creus', but Buñuel, who saw nothing gorgeous in Catholic regalia, rejected the idea as insufficiently savage, preferring the prelates as skeletons draped with their robes. He showed Dali his notebook of ideas collected in the months since *Chien*. A literary salon carries on unmoved as a cart-load of drunken farm workers rolls through it; a boy is shot by his father when he causes him to spill tobacco from the cigarette he is rolling. He also had an idea about comparing contemporary decadence to the fall of Rome. But Dali dismissed them all.

As the Gala/Dali affair became public knowledge (even the local paper commented on 'the painter-lovers of Cadaques – and they are legion')

Luis's anger and frustration grew. On a boating picnic a few days later with Salvador, Cécile, Gala and a local friend and reputed witch Lidia Nogueres, he remarked that the landscape reminded him of the unfashionable Valencian painter Sorolla. Dali immediately snapped, 'What? Are you blind?' and began to argue with him. Gala said exasperatedly, 'Oh, you two! Like dogs in rut.'

Throughout the afternoon Gala continued to snipe at Luis, until the violence that had been seething since he arrived exploded. Throwing her down on the sand, Luis began to strangle her. Cécile and Lidia, terrified, hid behind some rocks, while Salvador, equally ineffectual, knelt beside Luis and begged him to stop. Luis did – but only when he had seen the tip of Gala's tongue poke out between her teeth, which he took as a sign of submission. Two days later, Gala left. By then, she had decided to abandon Eluard. She remained with Dali until her death.

On 24 October 1929, less than a month after *Un Chien Andalou* opened, the US stock market crashed. American newspapers were reassuring at Christmas, but still the Paris expatriates melted away, aware that the days of the cheap franc had gone. A catastrophe for hotels, galleries and bars, the Crash was the consummation the Surrealists had devoutly wished for a decade. In the manifesto issued to support Buñuel after *L'Age d'Or*, Breton could not help pointing out that '[the film] complements the present stock-exchange crisis perfectly'.

By November Buñuel was back in Paris, and negotiating with Noailles. He was evasive about the new screenplay, although Charles assumed it was in good shape. Buñuel always said they proposed a budget of 1 million francs for the new film, but initially Charles offered a monthly rate; 12,000 francs a month during shooting and 6000 francs a month during editing, aiming at a final cost 'in the neighbourhood of 350,000 francs'. It was only as the length expanded from two reels to seven that the budget rose closer to the million.

In a letter of 19 November, Noailles laid out the terms, including the division of income 75/25 in the sponsors' favour. All the correspondence hints at urgency. If the film was to be ready for Marie-Laure's birthday, it would need to be finished no later than the early summer. Charles and Marie-Laure were leaving Paris on 2 December and arriving in Hyères around the 5th for a four-month stay. Perhaps Luis and Salvador could join them at St Bernard?

Initially Buñuel was elated. He pounded up the stairs to the Batcheffs' apartment shouting (as Denise remembers it), 'I've got a million – and without interest!' In fact he had only been paid 9000 francs in advance. This, and his doubts about Salvador, prompted second thoughts. Luis began to audition possible pretexts to pull out.

One was provided by Igor Stravinsky, a friend of the Noailles. According to Buñuel (although there is no reference to this in their correspondence), Charles asked that the film's music be composed by Stravinsky, since they had promised him a commission. Supposedly Buñuel refused, either because 'I can't work with geniuses' or because 'he spent all his life on his knees', a reference to Stravinsky's *Symphony of Psalms*, his current work. In any event Charles backed down, so Buñuel was once again forced to negotiate with Dali.

On 14 December he was in Zaragoza and writing to Charles, not entirely truthfully, that he had finished a scenario 'much superior to that of *Chien Andalou*'. Then he went to see Dali. On 15 December the Cadaques paper noted: 'Just arrived from Paris, the painter Salvador Dali has left his house at Llane accompanied by his friend Luis Buñuel, who will stay for a few days in Cadaques.'

With Gala gone, Luis hoped to find Salvador calmer, but he arrived in the midst of a new uproar. Dali *père* was already infuriated by his son's slurs about his stepmother and her real or imagined infidelities. One of his Paris lithographs carried the text 'Sometime I spit for pleasure on the portrait of my mother', and no number of protests from his son that the image was one of Christ and the mother in question the Virgin would mollify him. The affair with Gala Eluard inflamed him even more. Buñuel was just in time to see Dali ordered out of the house by a purple-faced Don Salvador and threatened with disinheritance. Shaken, Dali moved into the Port Lligat cottage. Buñuel joined him.

They were uncomfortable days. Filled with guilt over the break with his father, Dali shaved off most of his hair, leaving only a narrow 'Mohawk' crest and, burying the cuttings on the beach, climbed the hill to take what he imagined would be a last look at Port Lligat. Buñuel, drinking heavily by then, responded by letting his beard grow for the first and almost the last time in his life. With his tan and husky build, it made him look villainous. As if to capture the physical changes that reflected their internal turmoil, they photographed one another in identical poses leaning against the cottage wall.

Working on a script proved almost impossible. Depression and Goemans's demands for pictures to hang in the Paris show drove all thought of films from Dali's mind. Feeling defeated and rejected, Buñuel returned to Paris, putting off invitations to visit St Bernard and participate in the Noailles' gymnastics. With a careful blend of enthusiasm and apology, he wrote: 'I haven't played any sport since I won in 1920 the amateur boxing championship for Spain, and such a pastime will be very agreeable to me', while explaining he could not come just then.

Dali arrived in Paris for his opening on 20 November to find himself welcomed everywhere. Gala was a brilliant agent and publicist: she had even persuaded Breton to write an introduction to the catalogue. Notwithstanding the Crash, negative notices from, among others, Teriade in *Cahiers d'Art*, and the fact that it contained only two new paintings, the show was a success, with most pictures selling for between 6000 and 12,000 francs. The Noailles had become Dali collectors, which kept prices high.

Mauclaire had made the best offer for *Un Chien Andalou*. It opened at Studio 28 on 1 October, supporting Donald Crisp's crime melodrama *The Cop*, with William Boyd (retitled *14.101*), and ran for eight months with a variety of programmes, including Mack Sennett and Harold Lloyd comedies. Cyril Connolly was one of the many foreign intellectuals who made the pilgrimage to see it, in February 1929. 'Studio Vingt-Huit – high up a winding street of Montmartre in the full blasphemy of a freezing Sunday; taxis arriving, friends greeting each other, an excitable afternoon audience. In the hall stands a surrealist bookstall, behind is a bar where a gramophone plays "Ombres Blanches" and disturbing *sardañas* while beyond is a small modern theatre. The lights are lowered and the film begins [. . .] '

He carried back to Britain the legend of a film that rewrote the rule book. 'This contemptuous private world of jealousy and lust, of passion and aridity, whose beautiful occupants patter about like stoats in search of blood, produced an indescribable effect, a tremendous feeling of excitement and liberation. The Id has spoken and, – through the obsolete medium of the silent film, – the spectators had been treated to their first glimpse of the fires of despair and frenzy which were smouldering beneath the complacent post-war world [. . .] With the impression of having witnessed some infinitely ancient horror, Saturn swallowing his sons, we made our way out into the cold of February 1929, that unique and dazzling cold.'*

* Connolly describes the film being 'received with shouts of boos and when a pale young man tried to make a speech, hats and sticks were flung at the screen. In one corner a woman was chanting "*Salopes, salopes, salopes!*" ["Bitches, bitches, bitches!"] and soon the audience began to join in.' There is no other record of any such reaction to *Chien*. In recalling incidents from fifteen years earlier, Connolly may have become confused with the furore over *L'Age d'Or*.

With the devious Braunberger in charge of the books, there was never much chance the film-makers would see a profit, and although Dali continued for years to demand his share of what he imagined was a huge income, the film eventually returned Buñuel only about 8000 francs, making it a financial loss.

The real profit was to Buñuel's reputation. *Un Chien Andalou* had become one of the cultural 'sights' of Paris. When Henry Miller arrived the following March, he visited Studio 28 on his first Sunday.

A copy of the film had not then arrived in the United States, but Lorca, in New York on an extended holiday, heard about it and probably read the enthusiastic review by Eugenio Montes in the *Gaceta*. His first response was anger at what he took to be a personal slur, but this changed to enthusiasm for the movies once he had seen a few other films, including one of the earliest sound comedies, Harold Lloyd's *Welcome Danger*. He began work on a Surrealist screenplay called *Voyage to the Moon*, frankly inspired by *Un Chien Andalou*, though far more outspoken in sexual imagery. The words 'Help! Help! Help!' are superimposed on shots of a vagina, and a body is shown bleeding from the genitals. The screenplay was never finished.

Meanwhile, in Paris, Breton had picked up the reins of his Surrealist leadership again after a summer spent with Eluard during which the two men, each deserted by a long-time lover, succumbed to self-pity and emotional exhaustion. In October he went alone to a public screening at Studio 28 of *Un Chien Andalou*. 'After that operation of reconnaissance,' said Sadoul, 'we believed that he would call for a punitive expedition against the Spanish usurpers. But the film was to be approved by the acknowledged chief of Surrealism.' A few days later, Breton summoned the film-makers to anoint them as official Surrealists.

This took place in November at Café Radio on the corner of rue Coustou and boulevard de Clichy which had replaced the Cyrano as their meeting place. 'Dali had the huge eyes of a gazelle,' recalled Sadoul, 'and the same grace and timidity. Buñuel was athletic, large, with big eyes that protruded a little.'

Breton's invitation to Buñuel and Dali was partly strategic. Battles over politics had depleted the group. Soupault, Artaud, Desnos and Ribemont-Dessaignes had all been purged or had resigned. Aragon was wavering. Breton also saw that Surrealism was changing direction. What had begun as a literary movement was becoming increasingly visual. It now included as many painters as writers. Film-makers had never been admitted before, not even René Clair, but, watching *Un Chien Andalou*, Breton could see where the movement might make a new and even greater impact. By co-opting Buñuel and Dali he brought new forces to bear against the establishment.

The twelfth and last edition of the group's magazine, *La Révolution Surréaliste*, was to be published in December, before being reborn with its political convictions on its sleeve as *Surréalisme au Service de la Révolution*. Passionate for machine products, the Surrealists had welcomed the installation on 28 June of Anatol Marco Josepho's automatic 5-franc Photomaton machines at four locations around Paris. For a portrait of the group, Photomaton snaps of the sixteen members in good standing, including Breton, Eluard, Péret, Aragon, Arp, Ernst, Tanguy, Magritte, Miró and a subdued Dali and Buñuel, all in dark suits and ties, with eyes closed, were arranged as a border to Magritte's painting of a nude with its ironic caption '*Je ne la vois pas cachée dans la fôret*' ('I cannot see her hidden in the forest').

Breton could not know that the admission of Dali and Buñuel would prove disastrous. It confirmed Dali as an official Surrealist, a fact the painter, insisting 'I *am* Surrealism' to anyone who would listen, exploited with a self-aggrandizing life-style and career which by the late forties had largely discredited the movement, leading Breton to coin the anagramatic nickname 'Avida Dollars'. Meanwhile, the Buñuel/Dali films, as the most accessible Surrealist works, won a popularity which the group's writers came to resent. In 1935 Eluard would write despondently that he and Breton had been offered a trip to a Surrealist conference at Santa Cruz de Tenerife in the Canaries, but only if they brought a copy of *Un Chien Andalou* or, better, *L'Age d'Or*. (They went to the Canaries, taking *L'Age d'Or*, but the film was banned and the copy seized by the islands' then-governor, Francisco Franco.)

Buñuel persuaded Dali to spend some of his time in Paris on the script for what they still called 'the film about Rome'. On the last day of the year he left for Hyères and what he feared would be an embarrassing meeting with the Noailles. He was not made more cheerful by knowing the other guests were Auric, Rivière, Cocteau with his current lover, the young writer Jean Desbordes, and the designer Christian Bérard, all of whom, he noted disapprovingly, used opium – even Cocteau, who had just emerged from a detox clinic at St Cloud. Some mornings the tiny rooms stank so pungently of fumes and sweat that one could not enter them.

While the others played and smoked, Buñuel worked on the script, taking time off to participate in calisthenics and to pose in the villa's uniform of striped maillot and shorts with Marie-Laure. (Auric, glass in hand, and wearing a double-breasted suit, looked on sardonically.) A story began to evolve that had more to do with Buñuel's own experience than Dali's firework imagination. Its subject was the one that would preoccupy him all his life: what he later called 'the obstacles which religion, as well as society, oppose to the attainment of love'. The film lacks the almost Martian drama of Dali's vision. Most of its scenes consist of shooting parties, white-tie concerts in private homes, literary salons and public meetings where bureaucrats drone meaningless speeches. Within this structure of formal tedium, sexual desire struggles to assert itself. Henry Miller would call the film 'an exposition of the collision between the sexual instinct innate in man, and his intellect, as the glorification of death and of the lost rhythm of life'. It also hints at Buñuel's own attempts to find sexual release in the teeth of his Jesuit upbringing.

Buñuel and Dali wrangled for decades over their relative contributions to *L'Age d'Or*. Dali always took credit for both films. 'For my arrival in Paris,' he wrote in his autobiography, 'I made two films in collaboration with Luis Buñuel that will remain historic, *Le Chien Andalou* [sic] and *L'Age d'Or*. Since that date, Buñuel has worked alone and produced other movies, thereby rendering me the inestimable service of revealing to the public who was responsible for the genius and who for the elementary aspects.'

Buñuel claimed he left Cadaques with only thirty images, and that Dali later sent him 'a postcard with a few more ideas'. Since nothing survives from the Cadaques meetings, we can never know for sure. The nearest we have is a hand-written document in Dali's notional Espano-French, headed '[illegible] *eschematique de l'escenario*'. Since Dali seldom dated anything, even letters, there is disagreement about when this was written, but minor differences from the film suggest it was Dali's *aide-mémoire* of their discussions. Buñuel circulated a corrected version as a synopsis of *L'Age d'Or*, so he obviously regarded it as a fair summary of what he and Dali had set out to do.

Dali wrote: 'One sees the life of the scorpion. In the landscape where it lives there is a bandit. The bandit, having climbed on a rock, sees a group of archbishops who are singing and sitting in a mineral landscape. The bandit runs to advise that the people from Mallorca have arrived (because in this case the bishops are called Mallorcans).* He knocks at the door of the log cabin where his friends, like himself, are in a strange state of weakness and depression. They take their weapons and leave, all except one of them, who says he is going to die. One by one all fall on the

---

* 'Mallorcans – inhabitants of the island of Mallorca (Spain)' [Dali's footnote]. Pop-eyed, dark-skinned and in-bred, Mallorcans were regarded by most Spaniards at the time as primitives.

ground, tired to death after their walk. The boss of the bandits sits down without hope on the ground. From the place where he is sitting arrives the noise of the sea and he can already see the Mallorcans who by this time are all skeletons sprawled between the stones.

'An enormous marine caravan arrives on this coast, which is desolate and abrupt. The caravan is composed of priests, military men, nuns, ministers, civilians, etc. All of them start to walk through the rocks until they arrive where the boats of the Mallorcans are moored. Imitating the authorities who are walking ahead of the procession, everybody takes off his hat. This is the foundation of Imperial Rome. We are in the process of laying the foundation stone. Piercing cries catch everyone's attention. In the mud, on the ground, a man and a woman are violently devouring one another. They are separated. The man is beaten by the police.

'This man and this woman will be the protagonists of the movie. Thanks to a [illegible] which proves high his personality, and the important humanistic and patriotic mission which he has been given, and left in freedom, from this moment all the activity of the protagonist is taken on a straight line by love. In a scene of love interrupted [illegible] by the violence of a failure he is interrupted by a telephone call from the high person who charges him with the responsibility of the humanitarian mission we have been talking about. This man tells him he is dishonest. Because of him, thousands of old people, innocent children, etc. etc. are dying. The protagonist, who gets only insults, returns to the side of his love; at that moment a very inexplicable fate succeeds in parting them forever.

'After that we see the protagonist throwing out of the window a burning pine tree, an enormous agricultural instrument, an archbishop, a giraffe, and feathers. All this coincides with the time and that precise moment where the survivors of the Château de Selliny walk out into the snow. The Count de Blagis [sic] is obviously Jesus Christ. All this last moment is accompanied by a *paso doble*.'*

Dali's 'postcard' does survive. It is a double-sided sheet covered with suggestions, both drawn and written, for the love scene. Gala's influence is evident; all the images are highly erotic. 'She is almost naked,' he writes of the girl. 'He can see much breast and much ass [. . .] The neckline I see like this [he sketches a low-cut gown]. The shoulder is absolutely naked.' He proposes a haircut like that of Louise Brooks. He also sketches a visual pun, reminiscent of the pubic hair/armpit image of

* 'One sees also other details – a father almost for nothing kills his son, [illegible] a blind man, a dog without feet, slapping a woman, etc. etc.' [Dali's note].

Chien; the lips of a woman lying on her side dissolve into her vagina. (Could Lorca have told him of his *Voyage to the Moon* scenario? The image is almost identical.) He also suggests, graphically, how, during the love scene, the man might peel back the woman's nails and the flesh of her fingers with his teeth. Buñuel did his best to film this, inserting the close-up of a mutilated hand, but it does not approach Dali's Goya-esque vision.

Dali also proposed the scene in which both a statue and a man walking past it have flat stones balanced on their heads, a recurring image in his work. The man's fantasy of the girl sitting on the lavatory with an abstracted, longing expression, and ending with a toilet flushing and shots of lava oozing and exploding, is also archetypically Dali-esque. Buñuel contributed the more classically Surrealist scenes which, in the style of place Blanche, parody middle-class Parisian sensibility. In the most famous of them, a large Normandy cow reclines complacently on the bed in a formal bedroom.

Each day Buñuel read his work to the Noailles in Hyères, and to his relief they were approving and enthusiastic. He was amused that, at the last late-night reading, with its evocation of Sade's protagonists lurching away from their orgy, one of them transformed into Christ, Charles excused himself, explaining that he wanted to be up early for Mass. Various titles were considered, including *Abajo la Constitución (Down with the Constitution)* and *La Bestia Andaluza (The Andalusian Beast)*. The latter title appears on the screenplay, written in Spanish, from which Buñuel shot the film. It was Marie-Laure who, pointing out that she and people like Luis were part of a new Golden Age, suggested *L'Age d'Or*.

For the last issue of *La Révolution Surréaliste* Buñuel responded to a questionnaire on love concocted by Breton, who was preoccupied with the subject following the collapse of his relationship with Suzanne Muzard the previous summer. In the light of Luis's courtship, and fights with Salvador over Gala, his answers are interesting.

Q: What sort of hope do you put in love?
Buñuel: If I'm in love, all hope. If I'm not in love, none.
Q: How do you envisage the passage of the idea of love to the fact of love? Would you sacrifice, willingly or not, your freedom to love? Have you already done so? Have you sacrificed for love a cause which until then you believed you would fight for if requested? Would you accept not to become that which you could have been if it was the price to pay to love fully? How would you judge a man who would betray his convictions to please the women he loved?
Buñuel: (1) For me there is only the fact of love.

(2) I would willingly sacrifice my freedom to love. I have already done so.

(3) For love I would sacrifice a cause but this is to be judged on the spot.

(4) Yes.

(5) I would approve of a man betraying his convictions but despite this I would tell him *not* to betray his convictions. I would even demand it.

Q: Would you deprive yourself for a while of the presence of the loved one, knowing that 'absence makes the heart grow fonder' but at the same time knowing such a strategy is undignified?

Buñuel: I would not part with the one I love at any price.

Q: Do you believe in the victory of admirable love over sordid life or that of sordid life over admirable love?

Buñuel: I don't know.

Buñuel was right to respond with such high-flown sentiments, despite the fact that, even as he put them on paper, he was doing the reverse in real life. The Surrealists valued spontaneity in relationships, especially sexual ones (the sole acceptable excuse for being late to a *séance* was that one had been making love), but too flighty a response would have made Buñuel seem trivial, a far worse sin. Under their cynicism, the Surrealists were still solid men of letters. As Dali (who was not sent the questionnaire) said later: 'Gala was the first to warn me that among the Surrealists I would suffer the same vetoes as elsewhere, and that they were all ultimately bourgeois.' Buñuel had already been put off by the etiquette of place Blanche, which, among other things, demanded that everyone shake hands when they arrived. At first, since the café was often crowded, he greeted only those he could get to and just waved to Breton, barricaded in his corner by the inner circle. But Breton snapped: 'Does Buñuel have something against me?', so Luis went through the formalities. Worse was to come. The Belgian Surrealist magazine *Variétés* asked to reprint the scenario of *Chien*. Buñuel explained that he had promised it to the Batcheffs' friend Auriol for *La Revue du Cinéma* and thought no more about it until Breton invited him to a special meeting at rue Fontaine. When he arrived, he found himself on trial for having supported a capitalist journal over a Surrealist one. 'The question is,' said Breton, 'are you with the police or with us?'

This inquisition had less to do with Buñuel than with Breton's insistence that *La Révolution Surréaliste* should be the movement's journal of record, with first refusal of everything. He had already undermined the Communist magazine *Clarté* for which some of the Surrealists wrote, and there was a long-standing feud with Bataille's

Documents, to which writers like Desnos contributed. Whether or not *Variétés* had been the first to request the script was beside the point. Buñuel should have offered it to *La Révolution Surréaliste* as a matter of form.

Torn between loyalty to the Batcheffs and to Breton, Buñuel spent a sleepless night, after which he sided with the Surrealists. He and Eluard went to Gaston Gallimard, one of France's most powerful men, whose company published *La Revue du Cinéma*. Gallimard refused to withdraw the article, which was already set in type. Stubbornly Buñuel returned with a hammer under his coat, ready to smash the press, but by then copies were on the streets. He compromised by writing to all the French papers, protesting at this infringement of his rights, and by allowing *La Révolution Surréaliste* to print the script too. It appeared in the final issue.

In August 1929 Sergei Eisenstein, his cameraman Eduard Tissé and his friend and assistant Grigori Alexandrov had each been given 25 dollars and allowed out of Russia to study Western film-making. At a Congress of Independent Cinematographers in Switzerland in September they saw *Un Chien Andalou*, introduced by Giménez Caballero. Eisenstein disliked it. It exposed, he said, 'the extent of the disintegration of bourgeois consciousness'. In December they arrived in Paris, where Eisenstein hosted screenings of his new film about the collectivization of Soviet agriculture, *The General Line*. Since the censors refused it a certificate, these private showings were popular. Both the film, filled with erotic and religious symbolism, and its director, a cultivated homosexual who spoke excellent French, surprised and delighted Parisians, even winning over some of the local Czarists.

Eisenstein met Aragon, and on 15 February went with Eluard to the first night of Cocteau's *La Voix Humaine (The Human Voice)* in which Berthe Bovy played the anguished woman pleading on the phone with her ex-lover. Eluard led the now-obligatory Surrealist *scandale*, yelling 'Obscene! Enough! It's Desbordes on the other end of the line.' He was ejected, after having been burnt on the neck with a cigarette. The incident confirmed Eisenstein in his dislike of Surrealism, which he began to mention slightingly in his introductions to *The General Line*.

Alexandrov, the most worldly of the Russian trio, put out feelers for paying work. Some Hollywood studios showed interest, but meanwhile Parisian jeweller Léonard Rosenthal was prepared to commission a short sound film as a showcase for his wife, singer Mira Gily. Alexandrov concocted a script about a girl singing against the background of a storm that symbolized her tumultuous life. Eisenstein agreed to collaborate on it while he haggled with Hollywood, claiming he did so only to learn about sound recording.

Within a year, Buñuel's career was to converge spectacularly with Eisenstein's, but for the moment it was Dali's self-serving ambition that preoccupied him. Salvador's arrival in Paris and acceptance by the Surrealists drove the final wedge between the two old friends. Their separation was dramatized by their contrasting attitudes to Surrealism. Dali saw it as a costume basket from which he could whip up increasingly exuberant outfits. Buñuel, on the other hand, experienced with Surrealism the same revelation Dali had felt with Picasso. It replaced the Church he had rejected. Here was a faith to which he could attach his need to believe, which would gratify his sensual urges, satisfy his artistic ambitions. He became, and remained, a convert, philosophical, ascetic, faithful unto death. At last he had 'got' it. Of the movement he would say later, 'My vision of the world, I have learned there.'

12

'The de Beaumonts were angry with the Lopezes because of me and my film *L'Age d'Or*. Everybody knew that they had fallen out and neither greeted nor saw each other because of me. But I, Dali, imperturbably, went to visit the de Beaumonts and after that I went to see the Lopezes, without knowing anything about these quarrels or, when I knew, not paying them the slightest attention.'
– Salvador Dali, *Diary of a Genius*

Since *Chien*, Buñuel's correspondence with Pepin Bello had fallen off. In May he wrote to bring him up to date. The letter, with its casual 'I don't know if you've heard that de Noailles has given me a million francs to make a talking picture, with complete spiritual freedom', has a new confidence. He invited Bello to the Paris opening, then planned for June, after which, he said, he hoped to take a week off in Toledo for a celebratory revel with the Order. 'You cannot imagine how I've changed,' he wrote, 'and the progress I think I've made, especially in the field of morale and intransigence.' There is nothing so heartening as getting one's own way.

He had hired space at Billancourt again to shoot *L'Age d'Or*. Duverger was once more his cameraman and Schildnecht his designer. Jacques Brunius assisted him and also played a small role in the film, as did Max Ernst, Pierre Prévert and many Spanish friends, including Cossio, Manuel Ortiz, who had designed the *Retablo*, and Jaume Miratvilles, back briefly from his publishing business in South America. Marval, his production manager, played the archbishop who is flung out of the window, and Joseph Artigas, a bantam Catalan ceramicist with a huge moustache, appeared as a dignitary whom many confused with King Victor Emmanuel of Italy, sparking diplomatic protests when the film was screened. Lionel Salem, a specialist in playing Christ for religious films but who secretly admired Sade, gave the proper look of satiety to the Duc de Blangis.

To play his nameless main character, Buñuel hired Gaston Modot, a tall military-looking leading man with a moustache and a commanding baritone who would go on to major roles in Renoir's *La Règle du Jeu* and Carné's *Les Enfants du Paradis*. Buñuel had met him on the set of Feyder's *Carmen* and they had become friends. An amateur painter, writer and guitarist with an enthusiasm for Spain, Modot was a regular in the Montparnasse cafés and knew many of the avant-garde. He welcomed the chance to act in what Buñuel told him was 'a militant film aimed at raping clear consciences'.

The girl was more difficult. Buñuel said off-handedly that an agent sent him two women to try out for the role, but since both Elsa Kuprin and Natalia Lyecht were Russian, and Kuprin, as the daughter of émigré writer Aleksandr Kuprin, was part of the circle around Albatros Films, it is likely that he knew them from his Epstein days. The role finally went to the temperamental amateur Natalia, who adopted the stage name Lya Lys.

Arriving at Billancourt, Buñuel was surprised to find himself sharing the studio with Eisenstein, who was shooting the film with Mira Gily, now called *Romance Sentimentale*. Technically Alexandrov was directing but Eisenstein, though he later denied it, did some shooting. The gardens, swans and grand piano Buñuel saw being filmed by the great Soviet 'realist' soured his view of Eisenstein for life.

In February the Surrealists raided a new cabaret in rue Edgar Quinet, the Bar Maldoror, which took its name from the poems of Isidore Ducasse, Comte de Lautréamont, revered by Breton as a forerunner of Surrealism. Eluard, Sadoul, Tanguy, Aragon and his mistress Elsa Triolet turned up to lend moral support but waited on the pavement while Breton led a party inside to wreck the place. Buñuel says he too was excused from the destruction because, if arrested, he could have been deported, but he showed solidarity by ejecting from the *L'Age d'Or* set a Rumanian journalist who, though a supporter of *Chien*, had written disapprovingly of the Maldoror incident.

After shooting the interiors, Buñuel took the unit, including Ernst, who played the pirate captain, to Figueras and Cabo Creus. Jeanne went with him. In the making of *Chien*, Buñuel had been able to control his effects almost scientifically, manipulating his settings and people, but the more complex *Age* exposed him for the first time to the inconveniences of real film-making. His assistant Claude Heyemann was stopped at the Spanish border and forced to explain boxes of human skeletons and religious vestments to sceptical customs officials. The script called for the dog kicked away by Modot when he is dragged off the girl to be 'torn apart'. An unsuspecting white half-

Samoyed was on hand and Modot was resigned to co-operating, but Jeanne, horrified by their cruelty, stepped in and rescued the animal. Buñuel could not talk her out of it, so the scene was dropped and the animal, christened Dalou, became the first of many Buñuel family dogs.

Buñuel set what was to be the style of a lifetime by shooting *L'Age d'Or* with extraordinary speed. On 23 March he sent Noailles the rest of his schedule: the Tobis studios in Paris from 31 March to 1 April for sound shooting, and to Spain on 3 April. On 2 April he wrote: 'the film is almost finished and in general I'm content'. After shooting, Luis and Jeanne spent a few days at Cadaques with Dali, who had stayed away from the production. At first he admired what Luis had done. 'It looks like an American movie,' he said without irony. However, as it became obvious that Buñuel had found a way to get along without him, the atmosphere chilled. *L'Age d'Or* was, he would decide, 'a caricature and betrayal of the idea', a line he would stick to for fifty years.

In Paris, Buñuel edited the film to its music score, a mélange of Mendelssohn, Mozart, Beethoven, Debussy and Wagner; inevitably, *Tristan and Isolde*. The well-known film composer Georges van Parys contributed *Gallito*, the *paso doble* that accompanies Sade's characters at the end, but asked for anonymity. Buñuel credited him simply as 'X'. For the first time in Buñuel's films the drums of Calanda are heard, roaring out as the Sadeian party emerges from the castle. He also re-recorded most of the dialogue. Eluard did the voice-over where the man, sitting in the garden with the girl, murmurs, as if they were in bed: 'Move your head, the pillow is cooler over here. Are you sleepy?'

Even with the expense of dialogue and music, *L'Age d'Or* only cost 747,409 francs. By instinct a cheap film-maker, not given to extravagant lighting or multiple takes, Buñuel hated waste, on his films or those of anyone else. As a postscript to his letter of 16 June to Charles de Noailles summarizing the money spent to date, he wrote: 'I have seen the film of Einsestein [sic] financed by Roshental [sic]. It's an ignominy. If the author was still in Paris I'd slap him. I'd like to talk to you about this scandalous work. There is no performer but Madame Roshental, only one set, some shots of clouds and a piano. Monsieur Einsestein has drawn half a million to make one of the most miserable things I have seen.'

The Noailles hardly cared. The Crash had not even chipped their enormous fortune. Some months later, Luis presented his accounts to Charles during a visit to Hyères. Next morning he noticed a pile of ashes in the fireplace where his host had burnt them.

*

As Buñuel's letter implies, Eisenstein had left Paris by June. His presence in France had triggered a spate of editorials against foreign influence, and demonstrations from right-wing groups like the Ligue Anti-Juive, the Jeunesse Catholique, the Ligue des Patriotes and the Camelotes du Roi. One of the blue tickets to a private Sorbonne screening of *The General Line* fell into the hands of Jean Chiappe who, remembering the Sacco/Vanzetti riots, ringed the theatre with police. He was disappointed and surprised when the audience emerged laughing. A secret report claimed that Eisenstein was winning friends for the Soviet Union '*par son charme personnel*'. Paradoxically, to a Paris accustomed by the Surrealists to an honest brawl at the theatre, the failure of his audiences to riot made Eisenstein seem even more subversive. 'Be frightened not of Bolsheviks with a dagger in their teeth,' one right-wing paper warned, 'but of those with laughter on their lips.'

In April the Russians had applied for extensions of their *carnets rouges*. Paramount wanted Eisenstein for Hollywood but he needed to stay in Paris during negotiations. They were refused, but after a fuss in the left-wing papers, a petition signed by sixty French artists and intercessions behind the scenes by Roland Tual, who took Eisenstein to see Anatole de Monzio, France's former ambassador to Moscow, they were allowed to stay until 26 April. On 6 May the trio left for Hollywood. Before doing so Eisenstein told a journalist: 'I made a mistake in coming to Paris without donating the necessary sum to the Hospital for Old and Infirm Gendarmes, of which Madame Chiappe is the patron [. . .] (This is one of the best known of the devious ways of bribing Monsieur Chiappe!)' If the Prefect needed more fuel for his hatred of foreign film-makers, this gibe offered it. A fuse had been lit to the charge that would blow up *L'Age d'Or*, and Buñuel and the Noailles with it.

Once again it was Mauclaire who bought Buñuel's film, although he could not show it until the end of the year, when his sound equipment was installed. The technique of sound film was anything but perfect at the time, with some companies issuing sound-tracks on gramophone records and others on the film itself. Many cinema-owners were wary about investing in a fad, so Noailles asked Buñuel to prepare two versions, one of them silent. Given *L'Age d'Or*'s modest amounts of dialogue and eighteen inter-titles, this was no problem. Nancy Cunard, who saw both versions, preferred the silent one.

While they waited for Mauclaire, the Noailles previewed the film widely. Buñuel himself held a private screening, for which Charles and Marie-Laure, out of town, lent him their house in place des Etats-Unis. All the Surrealists were invited but it was mostly the wilder members, including André Thirion and Tzara, who came. Thirion, the most irascible and politically violent of the group, recalled in his memoirs: 'At first I didn't want to go. But curiosity was too strong. Climbing the great staircase between uniformed lackeys, my anger exploded. I went to the buffet to make a scandal, breaking glasses, throwing bottles against the mirrors and the waiters, overturning everything that could be overturned, insults in my mouth.' Buñuel's version of the occasion, which seems more credible, is that everyone got roaring drunk, almost emptied the well-stocked bar, poured any remaining liquor into the sink and smashed a few bottles and glasses in the process. Well-mannered as ever, the Noailles did not mention the ruin, just asked how the screening had gone.

Buñuel now regularly attended lunch and evening Surrealist *séances* at place Blanche. As a mark of favour, Breton cast his horoscope, an elaborate process that took hours and produced a 108-page document which foretold that Luis would die on a distant ocean or from medicine taken by accident.

The group urged him to bring Jeanne to meetings, but Luis preferred to keep her well away from his promiscuous new acquaintances with their flagrantly kept mistresses and sensational liaisons. 'With his Spanish friends he didn't think there was any risk,' she said. 'They had the same attitudes, the same respect for women which said that a friend's girlfriend is someone you don't touch.' It was only when Breton accused him of bourgeois jealousy and possessiveness that Buñuel accepted an invitation. Inevitably, it ended badly.

Jeanne remembers a dinner at the Aragons', Buñuel a meal at Breton's apartment, with Magritte and his wife among the guests. Both agree there was an argument. Jeanne says the subject was politics, 'I gave my opinion,' she recalled, 'which was not exactly that of Luis. He said: "Shut up Jeanne. You don't know anything. What you say is stupid." Aragon tried to defend me. "I don't agree with you, Luis. Jeanne's ideas are original." Luis backed off.'

More credibly, Buñuel recalls that Breton, pathological about the crucifix, which he always called tersely '*cet objet-là*' ('that thing there'), took exception to the religious medal Jeanne wore. This version is borne out by Jeanne's description of the aftermath. 'When we left the Aragon house and walked into the night [Luis] was in an awful mood. As we were passing the front of the Senate* he ripped the medal from around my neck. I understood then that he wanted a wife who would never question him, and he never again took me to meet his French friends.'

* The Senate was on the other side of Paris from Breton's house, but close to Aragon's.

That circle of friends enlarged by the week. It soon included the painter André Derain and the writer Georges Bataille, who had been intrigued by the slicing of the eye in *Un Chien Andalou* and asked Jacques Prévert to introduce him. Soon after, Bataille wrote his famous decadent/erotic novel *The Life of the Eye*. Breton disapproved of almost all these people, but Buñuel, no longer so defensive nor as anxious to placate the Surrealists, was flattered by their attention. Man Ray also photographed both Luis and Jeanne. His shots of her were unremarkable, but those of Luis, in particular his portrait staring bull-like at the camera, were to become famous. Struck by the imbalance in Buñuel's face, Ray made up two composite shots, repeating each profile to show that the right side of his head was almost monstrously larger than the left, an effect that would be accentuated in old age when Buñuel's right eyelid developed a distinctive droop.

Preparing the first issue of *Le Surréalisme au Service de la Révolution*, Breton invited Buñuel to contribute. He set up (but probably did not physically shoot) a photograph, carefully staged and lit, of a bishop in full robes, including mitre and crozier, with his arm round a pretty, troubled girl. He's asking her: '*As-tu froid?*' ('Are you cold?') and, in apparent solicitude, cupping a breast. It was given a full page.

In early July a disconsolate Eluard wrote to Gala: 'Did you see Buñuel's talking film? Everyone's seen it but me, and Buñuel's left for three months.' Luis was in Spain, on a chaste holiday with Jeanne. They swam at San Sebastian and went on to Zaragoza, where the Noailles wrote to him with news of further *L'Age d'Or* previews.

On 9 July they had shown the film to a group of writers, including Edouard Bourdet, Julien Green, the American novelist Carl van Vechten, Pierre de Lacretelle and sculptor Jacques Lipschitz. 'It is going to be a triumph,' Charles told Luis, without mentioning that neither Green nor Lacretelle shared his enthusiasm. 'Without doubt,' Green wrote in his diary, '[Lacretelle] didn't find it reasonable that a cow should sleep on a bed.' He also noted that two other writers who had seen it, Francis de Croisset and François Mauriac, were dubious as well.

The Noailles hired Braunberger's 318-seat Panthéon cinema for a final gala late-morning screening on 22 October. The guest list was a tribute to their prestige and the advance word of *L'Age d'Or*. Picasso, Tanguy, Lipschitz, Tzara, Auric, Gide, Brancusi, Duchamp, Simenon, Nabokov, Gertrude Stein and André Malraux all came, as did the Tuals, the Batcheffs, the Vicens de la Slaves, Breton and Eluard. Dali and Gala were there too, sitting together but, diplomatically, in the row in front of Eluard.

That afternoon, Noailles cabled Buñuel, who was once again in Zaragoza, that the screening had been a huge success. Vicens de la Slave, however, gave him a different account. Charles and Marie-Laure greeted everyone at the door. Although the guests were effusive when they arrived, many left in silence, and one of the Noailles' most formal friends, Prince Jean-Louis de Faucigny-Lucinge, warned Charles that some might not appreciate the film's anti-clericalism. For the first time, the Noailles had an inkling of danger.

Had Buñuel been at the Panthéon and seen the mixed reaction for himself, his future might have been very different. But in the days following the first private previews he had received some offers he found hard to refuse.

One was from Breton. The Second International Conference of Revolutionary Writers was being held at Kharkov in the Ukraine at the end of October. Aragon and his mistress Elsa Triolet, who was Russian, a famous firebrand and former mistress of the poet Mayakovsky, were going, and Breton suggested Buñuel join them. Flattered, Luis agreed, expecting to be back in time for the release of *L'Age d'Or*. Since the impoverished Soviet government did not offer expenses, he persuaded Noailles to contribute 10,000 francs, a year's income for someone like Aragon, to their trip.

At the last minute, however, Buñuel had an even more unexpected proposal. Metro-Goldwyn-Mayer wanted both him and Lya Lys for Hollywood.

Of all the Hollywood studios MGM was the least damaged by the Crash. It showed a profit even for 1931 and 1932, in part because of its strong European distribution. It owned, with Paramount, the Ufa studios outside Berlin, and cinemas in every European capital. But the coming of sound posed more problems for MGM than the Depression. Once, it had been enough to translate the intertitles to create a foreign version. Now a film needed sound tracks in half a dozen European languages. The simplest solution was to dub new dialogue over the old, but MGM, vain of its technical standards, elected initially to re-shoot at least the important French and German versions in Hollywood, using the same sets and costumes but a new cast and, sometimes, a new director. When Garbo, always more popular in Europe than in the United States, appeared with great success in a German version of her first sound film, *Anna Christie*, directed by Jacques Feyder, the wisdom of the decision seemed confirmed.

As one of France's first sound films, *L'Age d'Or* was viewed with interest by American scouts, among them the ebullient L.L. 'Laudy'

Laurence, head of MGM's office in Paris and a friend of Marie-Laure de Noailles. According to Buñuel, he summoned him to his office and told him that, though he did not understand the film, he could not get it out of his mind, and he proposed to send Luis to Hollywood for six months to learn American technique as a prelude to his making films for MGM. The salary would be 250 dollars a week.

Much of this account is suspect, not least the money involved: even Charles Boyer, hired at the same time by MGM as a leading man, only got 400 dollars. Other evidence suggests that MGM was not the least enthusiastic about hiring an avant-garde director who spoke no English. Marie-Laure may have urged Laurence into the offer, since Buñuel says that, in a rider (though not one mentioned in any correspondence between himself and Noailles), Laurence demanded a list of forty influential referees for *L'Age d'Or*. The call for such a testimonial might have been Laurence's way of weaseling out of the deal. If so, it didn't work. Charles de Noailles just smiled and provided some of France's most distinguished signatures.

It is more likely that Buñuel owed the MGM offer to Lya Lys. Marlene Dietrich had created a market for European *femmes fatales*: Tala Birell from Austria, Gwili Andre from Denmark and Anna Sten from Russia all won Hollywood contracts about this time. Many arrived with an impresario and/or lover: Mauritz Stiller with Garbo, Gustav Machaty with Hedy Lamarr, Eugene Frenke with Sten, Dietrich not only with her husband Rudolf Sieber but also with her director/lover Josef von Sternberg, returning to pick up a Hollywood career he had abandoned two years before. An assumption that Luis and Lys were lovers would explain Buñuel's inclusion in the deal for her services.

Laurence (or perhaps Buñuel himself) sugared the pill for the studio by hinting that he would make a fine supervisor of Castilian versions. The Spanish-language market was huge but complex. In 1930 Latin America alone had 6000 cinemas and 160 million spectators. Mexican actor Ramon Novarro directed some Hispanic versions and Carlos Villarias replaced Bela Lugosi in a Spanish-language *Dracula*, but while Latin and South America enjoyed them, European Spaniards resented the assumption that Mexican Spanish was the equal of Castilian. Since the boat that took Buñuel to America also carried ten Spanish actors imported to work on Spanish remakes, as well as Pierre Weill and Claude Autant-Lara, promising assistant directors hired by MGM to make French versions, it is likely that Luis was sold to the front office in Hollywood as a possible dubbing talent.

MGM's offer threw him into confusion. He was eager to see the United States but hesitated to offend Breton by dropping out of the Kharkov trip. Breton, however, urged him to accept. He could be replaced at Kharkov by Sadoul, who was anxious to get out of France. With Jean Caupenne, he had written an insulting letter to a highly honoured student named Keller at the St Cyr military academy, and the French authorities, more dangerous adversaries than other victims of this Surrealist prank, had given them both jail sentences. Aragon agreed with Breton, but Buñuel did explore alternatives. Another friend of the Noailles, the radical deputy Gaston Bergery, offered to negotiate a delay. Buñuel went to see him, taking Aragon, but MGM were adamant.

Aragon and Triolet left for Moscow late in September, picking up Sadoul at the German border. Buñuel made a quick trip to Spain to see his mother, at the cost of missing the Noailles' Panthéon preview of *L'Age d'Or*. Jeanne went with him to Le Havre. She had half hoped he might propose before he left, or maybe even take her with him, but he never offered. 'I was very sad to think that I wouldn't see him for six months,' she said. 'At twenty-two, six months seemed very long.' On 28 October, after a tearful farewell, Luis sailed on the *Leviathan* for New York and a series of experiences that was to transform his life.

13

'I was notorious in Paris, therefore famous. Picasso would
not have become famous in Paris unless he had first become
notorious; the same was absolutely true of Stravinsky. Paris
loves you for giving it a good fight, and an artistic scandal
does not raise aristocratic lorgnettes.'
– George Antheil, *Bad Boy of Music*

In New York, the group had been booked into the Algonquin, the West
44th Street watering-place of Manhattan's intellectuals. With an
Argentinian friend to interpret, Buñuel explored the city, bewitched by
everything: the different way of moving and walking, the films, the
skyscrapers, the clothes, even the policemen's uniforms. The Plaza Hotel
became his hang-out: he spent hours in the companionable oak-panelled
gloom of its bar. Years later, he would tell friends: 'If I am in New York,
that's where you'll find me any afternoon.'

Unfortunately, since Prohibition was still in force, the Plaza could not
supply him with liquor. For that, Luis patronized the city's many speak-
easies. 'I never drank so much in my life,' he says of his first stay in the
United States. Safely out of Jeanne's sight, he also indulged himself with
'taxi girls' who could be hired as casually as a cab from bars and hotels.
He rationalized this as he always did: 'We Spaniards knew of only two
ways to make love – in a brothel or in marriage.'

Five days later, the party boarded the all-first-class Twentieth Century
Limited to Chicago, where they transferred to the equally elite Super
Chief. Many Europeans found American distances appalling, but to Luis
the United States seemed 'the most beautiful place in the world'. At the
end of their three-day trip they arrived at Los Angeles' cavernous Art
Deco Union Station to find three Spaniards, Edgar Neville, the playwright Lopez Rubio and Eduardo Ugarte, waiting to meet them.

Buñuel knew all three from Madrid. Ugarte was also a close friend of
Lorca's. Although his father was a minister in the right-wing government of Primo de Rivera, he had inherited nationalist and left-wing

sympathies from his Basque mother. Stocky, with yellow teeth and a
hairy body but a bald head, he peered suspiciously at the world through
pebble-glass spectacles, asking so many questions that he earned the
nickname 'Ugarte-*que*?' ('Ugarte-what?'). By contrast, Neville was an
aristocrat. As a designer he had revamped the sets of George Hill's
prison drama *The Big House* at MGM for its Spanish remake, *El
Presidio*, before launching into a new career in writing.

After the obligatory tour of Los Angeles, Neville drove Buñuel into
Beverly Hills, telling him, 'You're going to have dinner with the man
you'll be working for.' Luis did not immediately recognize their grey-
haired host as Charlie Chaplin and his girlfriend as Georgia Hale, star of
The Gold Rush. Chaplin, who classed Neville the best raconteur he had
ever heard, had hired him as comedy adviser, and Neville sneaked so
many Spaniards on to the staff that Scott Fitzgerald called Chaplin's
home 'The Spanish House'. Now he had hopes of doing the same for
Buñuel.

Next day Buñuel reported at MGM's Culver City lot. Although Louis B.
Mayer was putatively in charge, creative decisions were taken by
production head Irving Thalberg and his deputy Albert Lewin, from
whom they trickled down to a bureaucracy of producers, directors and
writers. Buñuel never met Thalberg and seldom saw Lewin. The
Supervisor of Spanish Productions was Frank Davis, who, since Buñuel
spoke almost no English, communicated through a Spanish-speaking
Irishman, Tom Kilpatrick. Buñuel and Kilpatrick, a minor screenwriter
(the fantasy *Dr Cyclops* was the peak of his career), became friends.

Davis was as baffled as everyone else by the terms of Buñuel's
agreement. Where did he want to begin? Editing? Camerawork?
Screenwriting? Buñuel said, 'Direction' and, since Clarence Brown was
shooting *Inspiration* with Garbo, Davis sent him to Stage 24 to watch. It
was not a happy set. Garbo, playing a promiscuous artist's model who
nobly renounces high-born young Robert Montgomery, found the story
trite, and Brown, though he was one of Metro's most thoughtful
directors and had handled some of her biggest successes, old-fashioned.
She threatened, not for the first time, to go home to Sweden.

When Buñuel arrived, Garbo was in makeup. Spotting this interloper
from the corner of her eye, she had him thrown out. Offended, Luis
thereafter treated the lot as if he were a tourist, loitering around,
spotting stars, and only showing up regularly on Saturdays at noon –
Hollywood worked a six-day week – for his cheque. Recognizing in
Ugarte a natural partner in mischief, like Vicens de la Slave, he moved
into the ground-floor guest bedroom of his Oakhurst Drive house in

Beverly Hills. An obliging bootlegger supplied him with good gin, explaining how to tell real from fake by shaking the bottle: the real stuff produced bubbles. He bought a Leica camera, a rifle and a Ford, in which he took long drives into the desert. Having travelled this far, he was tempted to keep going. Impressed by Robert Flaherty's images of Polynesia in *White Shadows in the South Seas*, he studied steamship schedules and planned a long, slow Pacific cruise.

For a European used to street life and café society, Los Angeles was a dull place. Joseph Kessel, whose *Belle de Jour* Buñuel would film years later, served his time there in the 1930s and left a summary in his book *Hollywood, Ville Mirage*, that stood for most European visitors. 'Everything had been done by nature and by man to give Hollywood the diversity of grace and charm. But in the enchanted streets, one never hears the cry of a child, nor a dog's bark, nor sees a silhouette at the windows. In these houses, where the interior comfort equals the sumptuous simplicity of the facades, one has no sense of life. Despite being inhabited by ten people, it's as if they were empty and interchange-able. In the great arteries, there are no passers-by. The automobiles roll, roll without stopping, one behind the other, like links in a chain without end, between the empty sidewalks.'

Almost against his will, Buñuel began taking an interest in studio film-making. On the purely technical level, he already inclined towards Hollywood methods. And Breton had also praised a cinema that was innocent, instinctive, an expression of the unconscious. The genre films of the early 1930s approached that ideal. One could take a conventional vehicle, manipulate it to express one's ideas, then launch it at the public, confident they would neither know nor care who directed or wrote it; most people thought the stars made up their lines anyway. Such films exemplified the perfect harmony of self-expression and anonymity. Buñuel would often say that it would not disturb him in the least if every one of his films was burned. Making movies the Hollywood way was the next best thing.

His prejudice against photographic richness for its own sake and directorial flourishes in general was confirmed when he met Josef von Sternberg, who invited him over to Paramount, decoratively the most opulent studio, to see him work. In *My Last Breath*, Buñuel remembered watching him shoot a film with a Chinese setting. 'The place was swarming with crowds of extras who floated down the canals, filled the bridges, and jostled each other in the narrow streets. What was more upsetting, however, was to see his set designer positioning the cameras while Sternberg seemed content just to shout "Action" (so much for *auteurs*).'

True as this description may have been of many Hollywood directors, it could not have applied to von Sternberg. His only thirties' film set in China, *Shanghai Express*, did not begin filming until September 1931, by which time Buñuel was back in Paris. Between October and November 1930 he made only *Dishonored*, set in Vienna. Nor did Sternberg work as Buñuel described. Far from leaving everything to minions, he obsessively placed every pennant and feather personally. The first time Dietrich's daughter Maria saw him in Hollywood, he was on top of *Shanghai Express*'s steam engine, painting in shadows. But many Chinese movies were shot in Hollywood late in 1930, and Buñuel's faulty memory seems to have put Sternberg on the set of one of them.

Buñuel did see *Dishonored* at a preview screening – with, he says, its producer, though the film lists no producer, and von Sternberg almost certainly produced himself – and did not care for it. Its ending, where Dietrich as a Mata Hari clone is shot by a firing squad, struck him as predictable, to the executive's scorn.

'What are you talking about?' he said. 'I'm telling you that's never been done before in the entire history of the cinema.'

To prove his point, Buñuel woke Ugarte and started describing how Dietrich, a Viennese whore, falls into conversation with Gustav von Seyffertitz while a suicide is carried from her apartment building. She says she is not afraid of either life or death, and von Seyffertitz, unbeknown to her the head of Austria's secret service . . .

'Don't bother with any more,' Ugarte said, heading back to bed. 'They shoot her at the end.'

Simply being in Hollywood did not guarantee a social *entrée* to the stars. Buñuel sat next to cross-eyed ex-Sennett comic Ben Turpin at the Metro shoeshine stand and spotted Chaplin's old foil Mack Swain on the lot, but nobody invited him to the picnics and beach parties where stars mingled only with stars. Except for other émigrés like Jacques Feyder, and Autant-Lara, who flourished at MGM, redirecting six features with stars like Buster Keaton and Douglas Fairbanks Jr, Buñuel knew nobody. Almost the only people who spoke Spanish at MGM were the Chicano swing gangs who worked through the night clearing sets and hauling equipment. In Europe he had been at the heart of things, an intimate of Breton, 'the most haunted mind in Europe'. Now he had translated back to his first days in Paris, understanding almost nothing he heard and even less of how to behave.

In this alien world it was a pleasure to meet even an enemy from Europe, and Buñuel went out of his way to contact Eisenstein. The Russians had moved into the home of British writer Ivor Montagu and his wife Hell while they auditioned projects. To neutralize mutterings about 'Godless Bolsheviks', Montagu encouraged them to socialize. With a publicist and a cameraman in tow they visited cultural icons like Garbo, Walt Disney and wonder dog Rin-Tin-Tin, and played tennis ('badly', remarked their host) on Charlie Chaplin's court.

Failing to catch him at home, Buñuel cabled (in French): 'Dear Eisenstein, I came to see you but you had left. I will be very happy to see you again. Will you call me one morning before 10 at CR6668?' They finally met, like many other émigrés, at Chaplin's. It was an uncomfortable encounter. A 'young-man-about-Hollywood', whom Montagu called 'Count B', took Buñuel and Ugarte there one afternoon, then abandoned them. Nobody spoke Spanish and the Russians conveniently forgot their French when Buñuel was around. 'It never occurred to the rest of us to try him out in it', Montagu said vaguely. While the Russians worked on their backhands, the Spaniards played matador with Chaplin's sons, Ugarte acting the bull and Buñuel demonstrating *veronicas* with a handkerchief.

Montagu's PR efforts on Eisenstein's behalf failed and in October Paramount broke his contract. In November he returned from a trip round America to find his visa had also been withdrawn. On 5 December the party crossed the Mexican border *en route* to Mexico City to make *Que Viva Mexico!* with funding from left-wing novelist Upton Sinclair. Unbeknown to Buñuel, this event would have far-reaching consequences for his life and career.

Still hoping to get Buñuel a job with Chaplin, Neville took him to see some rushes of *City Lights*. The scene where Charlie swallows a whistle seemed too long, and Luis whispered as much to Neville, who passed on the opinion, hoping it would persuade Chaplin they needed Buñuel on the team. Chaplin did shorten the sequence, but direct criticism was a tactical error with the vain comic. Buñuel did not get the job and Chaplin bore a grudge for the rest of his life.

Chaplin's position in the Hollywood hierarchy was ambiguous. No name was bigger, but his nymphet wives, his left-wing politics, and most of all his maverick working methods made him an outsider. Always embarrassed by his lack of education, he courted visiting intellectuals, using them as cannon fodder in his skirmishes with the Hollywood establishment. In 1925 he had persuaded Douglas Fairbanks to buy von Sternberg's gloomy apprentice film, *The Salvation Hunters*, and release it through United Artists. Now, in much the same spirit, he took up *Un Chien Andalou*. Buñuel probably gave him the print himself, since he mentions several screenings at Chaplin's house. Most people were horrified by it. Toraichi Kono, Chaplin's Japanese major-domo, fainted the first time he projected the film. In later years Chaplin would frighten his daughter Geraldine by describing scenes.

There is not much doubt that Chaplin exploited Buñuel and had little real interest in the film or its director's career. In 1931, on a visit to France, Chaplin and his mistress for the trip, May Reeves, spent some time with Aziz and Nimet Eloui Bey, wealthy Egyptian friends of Man Ray. Chaplin praised *Chien* to them, and later Reeves asked him about it.

'It's just a stupid film,' Chaplin said.

'Then why say publicly that you find it interesting?'

Chaplin shrugged. 'Oh, one has to keep people amused and look up-to-date.'

Buñuel was not celibate in Hollywood. Who could be? As playwright Enrique Jardiel Poncela joked of the movie capital, 'You can only do two things: lie on the sand and look at the stars, or lie on the stars and look at the sand.' Although Luis denied sleeping with Lya Lys, it is probable they were lovers. 'What a woman!' he said to Max Aub years later, recalling her Californian sexual adventures, including flirting with lesbianism. He admits that a friend of Lys's caught his eye, and that he and Ugarte set up a seduction. Both girls were invited round to Oakhurst Drive. 'We'd laid in all the necessities, right down to the flowers and champagne,' Buñuel said, 'but the two women simply talked for an hour and then politely said goodbye.'

He may have hoped that the assignation with Lys and her friend would turn into an orgy, a form of sex he admitted finding 'tremendously exciting'. Whether he ever participated in orgies or simply fantasized about them is not clear. In 1972, Max Aub recounted a claim by Maxime Alexandre that, in Paris, Luis had often checked into a brothel and enjoyed six or seven whores at a time. Although he never denied frequenting brothels, Buñuel rejected this story. It began, he said, in conversations among the Surrealists about Eluard's taste for *partouzes* and their sexual fantasies in general. However, he could seem more knowledgeable. 'Orgies depend above all on how much you've drunk,' he told Aub later, 'on your resistance and on how much money you have to spend. "Normal" orgies I knew in Hollywood in the thirties, with Lya Lys. My friend Ugarte was there too.'

One such 'normal orgy' was arranged by Chaplin. Buñuel had confessed his interest and Chaplin, no stranger to group sex, offered to lay on a party. Ugarte and Neville were also invited but, rather than hiring girls from one of Hollywood's many smart brothels, Charlie imported three pretty amateurs from Pasadena, a bastion of the bourgeoisie. It was an error. Where professionals would have knuckled down to the job, these girls argued over who would have Chaplin and, when they could not decide, left angrily.

The French censorship board passed *L'Age d'Or* on 1 October with the deletion of a single intertitle, and Mauclaire scheduled it to open at Studio 28 on the 12th. Able at last to capitalize on his investment in Buñuel and Dali, Breton ordered an all-out Surrealist effort. For the opulent twenty-four page gold-covered programme booklet he and Eluard wrote essays, which they signed with the names of thirteen of the group, many of whom had not read them; Dali certainly knew nothing of the pieces, while Péret, another signatory, was in Brazil. The programme advertised Surrealist books and magazines, many of which were on sale in the foyer, next to a small exhibition which included four Dali canvases (lent by the Noailles), four by Ernst, and three each by Arp, Miró, Ray and Tanguy. Also on show was the sole existing example of Bruitist composer Luigi Russolo's Noise Organ lent by Edgard Varèse. Breton mailed a copy of the booklet to Buñuel, who cabled his congratulations from Culver City.

Reviews of *L'Age d'Or* were sparse, but throughout November, supported by two shorts, it played to respectful, if baffled, audiences. Early in December, however, word spread around Paris that some demonstration against the pollution of French culture by Jews and atheist foreign film-makers was planned to coincide with Eisenstein's expulsion from the United States. Revelations in the press about Soviet suppression of religion fanned the flames.

By ill-luck, *L'Age d'Or* became the focus of these attacks. It was the most visible and least understandable film running in Paris at the time, its director and writer were, if not Jewish, then at least Spanish, and though it was not remotely Communist, the Trotskyism of Breton and Mauclaire made it guilty by association. On the night of Wednesday, 3 December a coalition of right-wing rowdies converged on Studio 28. In a report distributed to the British press, Nancy Cunard described what followed.

'The *commissaires* of the League of Patriots and certain representatives of the Anti-Semitic League interrupted the performance by throwing ink at the screen and shouting "We shall see if there are any

Christians left in France!" and "Death to the Jews!" at the moment when one of the characters in the film is shown throwing a monstrance into the river. The demonstrators then lit smoke-bombs [actually fumigation cartridges] and threw stink-bombs into the audience, on whom they hurled themselves with blackjacks, in order to force them to leave the cinema. Later, passing through the Exhibition Hall, they destroyed every breakable object, smashing furniture and windows, slashing the pictures by Dali, Max Ernst, Man Ray, Miró and Tanguy, tearing up the books and magazines on view there (incidentally stealing a few intact) and finally cutting the telephone wires. Nevertheless, the audience remained to see the end of the film and, on their way out, organized and signed a protest against the demonstration. The material damage done was assessed at 80,000 francs.'

For the next few days Parisian papers roared accusations and recriminations. Gaston Bergéry appealed to the Congress on behalf of *L'Age d'Or*, but in vain. The League of Patriots, while repudiating its over-zealous followers, attacked 'the immorality of this Bolshevist spectacle'. In *Figaro*, the paper most vocal against the film, Richard Pierre Bodin said he would 'defy any finished technician to find the faintest artistic value' in *L'Age d'Or*. 'Our Country, the Family and Religion are here trailed in the mud,' he said. 'All those who have safeguarded the grandeur that is France, all those, even if they are atheists, who respect Religion, all those who honour family life and hold childhood sacred, all those who have faith in a race which has enlightened the world, all those sons of France whom you have chosen to defend you against the moral poison of unworthy spectacles appeal to you now to uphold the rights of the censor.' The fact that the censor had passed the film was brushed aside.

On 5 December the Provost of the Municipal Council, de Launay, ordered Mauclaire, who had continued to show the film, to cut the two scenes featuring the archbishops. He obeyed, but the furore continued, as on 8 December the Prefecture demanded he remove 'the passage about Christ'. Mauclaire pointed out that there was no such scene, so the Prefect was content with the deletion from the programme of the remark in Dali's summary that 'the Comte de Blangis is obviously Christ'.

By this time the papers were in full xenophobic cry. *Figaro* urged de Launay to crush Surrealism. On 10 December, in an open letter, he denounced its works as 'refuse' and protested against 'other films of German origin or importation which are shown or going to be shown in the Champs-Elysées quarter, A STONE'S THROW from the Unknown Soldier'. At the height of the furore he wrote to Chiappe: 'We are in greater and greater numbers committed to react against the systematic poisoning of our society and of French youth.' Next morning the press learned that the 'Bolshevist' *L'Age d'Or* was banned, though Mauclaire was not told until that evening. The following day the censorship board met again, and reversed its earlier decision. On 12 December police raided Studio 28 and Buñuel's home, and seized two of the three existing copies of *L'Age d'Or*, although Noailles was able to rescue the negatives and hide them with Jeanne at the Spanish Bookshop.

The furore delighted Breton. His hopes that Buñuel and Dali would heighten the group's visibility were more than realized. This was the scandal to end all scandals. Hurriedly he circulated a questionnaire asking for opinions on the acts of the police. At the same time he and Eluard prepared a leaflet describing the events of 3 December, including photographs of the slashed Dalis and ink-splashed screen, captioned 'A Christian Alphabet'.

In Hollywood Buñuel tried to keep up with the news from Paris. In a letter of 14 December, Noailles reassured him that 'all copies of the film are staying in the hands of your friends of rue Gay-Lussac', but Buñuel was apprehensive. With the scandal at its height, he and some other Spanish expatriates were invited to Christmas dinner with the Spanish actor Tono, Chaplin and Georgia Hale. Everyone had been asked to bring a modest gift to be hung on a large tree. After dinner, Rafael Rivelles Guillen recited a long poem by Eduardo Marquina in memory of the dead of World War I. For Buñuel, drunk and seething over the destruction of his work by patriotic bigots, this was too much. 'When I blow my nose,' he murmured to Ugarte and two other Spanish friends, 'that's the signal to get up. Just follow me and we'll take that ridiculous tree to pieces.'

As the table watched in astonishment, the three attacked the tree. When its green branches resisted, they tore down the gifts and stamped on them. In the hush that followed, Tono's wife said, 'That was unforgivable.' Buñuel responded that it was subversive, a Surrealist act, but in fact it was an outburst of rage at his impotence, stranded here while his work was persecuted on the other side of the world. For New Year's Eve Chaplin invited some of the same guests to his home. When Buñuel arrived, he pointed out his own tree and suggested he work off his frustration right away rather than interrupt dinner.

Anxious to spread the scandal over *L'Age d'Or*, Breton pressed Nancy Cunard to arrange a London showing. She needed no encouragement. Not only did she admire the film, having seen it in various stages of production, but such a screening was another opportunity to infuriate her mother. Lady Maud 'Emerald' Cunard was already embarrassed by her daughter's flamboyant bisexual life-style, Parisian publishing ventures and especially her extremely visible black lovers, notably her Hours Press partner Henry Crowder.

The screening, by invitation only, took place on 2 January 1931. Emerald warned Nancy that she risked prosecution, but that just encouraged her. She hired the Gaumont Theatre, a private preview cinema in Wardour Street, heart of the British film world, and arrived in London with the last surviving print, carefully guarded by Crowder. As the audience filed in, they were handed a four-page summary of the Parisian scandal.

A few days later, Cunard wrote to Breton: 'In all bourgeois security the sole presentation has taken place [. . .] Perhaps a hundred people saw it. None were bored. The film has been sent back today. Five people understood it a little – [five very] fecund people [. . .] but for the rest the audience was "the cream" of all London. There will be some articles *I think*. With the old priests [of the critical establishment] it's a little like getting them to eat iron.'

In fact the few critics at the screening ignored the film. To Crowder, distributing the leaflet, it seemed that cinephiles were outnumbered by Nancy's lovers of both sexes, including the black boxer Bob Scanlon. Afterwards she took some of the guests to a nightclub, but soon left with Scanlon, maximizing the gossip. She and Crowder returned to Paris in January. Shortly after, Emerald wrote through her bank to say she was cutting her daughter's allowance, which to Nancy probably made the evening a success.

One person who did not revel in the *succès du scandale* was Charles de Noailles. The most public of all those associated with *L'Age d'Or*, he was socially the most vulnerable. He tried to maintain his mask of calm in the blizzard of criticism but occasionally it slipped. On 14 December he drafted a long letter to Buñuel filled with well-bred self-pity. 'The *L'Age d'Or* affair has become little by little more venomous. I'm sorry that Studio 28 seems to have transformed into a political demonstration [. . .] Your personality (and your name as well, as you will see from the programme and the clippings) is more and more marginalized in favour of those of the [Surrealist] group and our name since they provoke more scandal. [. . .] We are obliged to avoid all scandal in future. *We must be forgotten.* I see from the papers that Mauclaire is being pursued [by the police] but I don't think it's very important. Will you please ask him *not to mention my name any more*!'

This letter may never have been sent, but his distress is palpable. To make matters worse, the latest film he and Marie-Laure had financed, *Sang d'un Poète*, was generating its own scandal. Cocteau had asked the Noailles and some friends to appear as spectators in a theatre watching and applauding a show from their boxes. When the film was assembled, they found they were clapping the hero's suicide. The censors denied it a certificate, and Cocteau angrily wrote to Noailles' aunt: 'This film is held up for the time being, perhaps forever, because of a vicious cabal directed against your nephew Charles and his wife.'

The same cabal demanded Charles's expulsion from the Jockey Club. If he stayed, the committee told him, there would be no alternative but to disband, since most members would not socialize with him. He resigned. He was also rumoured to have been threatened with excommunication from the Church, which his mother headed off by some manoeuvring behind the scenes at the Vatican, payment of bribes and a promise on her son's behalf to destroy *L'Age d'Or*. Luis refers to this in his letter to Charles of 26 December, but Church files do not mention *L'Age d'Or* except to record a ruling that it was 'essentially pernicious from the social, religious and moral points of view'.

But the rumour that Noailles tried to destroy *L'Age d'Or* has persisted. On 27 January Eluard wrote to Gala that 'very serious things are happening here. To start with, Noailles is calling for the negative and three copies of the film, to have them destroyed. No question of it, of course. Too serious. We'll look after it, rest easy.' This letter is one of the rare references in print to the rumour, which Noailles vehemently denied. All other evidence points to his vigorous defence of the film. In the draft letter of 14 December to Buñuel, he offered to send copies for showing in the United States. As soon as Luis returned, he handed over the negatives and surviving prints. If anyone thought about destroying the film it was Luis, who saw an *auto-da-fé* as the perfect climax not only to the scandal but to his career.

The Noailles were traumatized by the public outrage over *L'Age d'Or* and *Sang d'un Poète*. The avant-garde they had so generously fed seemed to have bitten their hand. There would be no more birthday films, and Charles also wrote to Dali that he would not be buying any more of his paintings for the moment. The letter, not the only one from a patron frightened off by the scandal, made Dali 'foresee the worst difficulties' with his career. His collaboration with Buñuel, engineered with such effort, now looked like a liability. He wrote furiously to Luis, accusing him of taking credit for both films and minimizing his contribution, a complaint that over the years would widen the distance between them into a chasm. In February Luis also received an abusive joint letter from his old friends among the Spanish artists of Montparnasse, including Cossio, Huidobro and Castanayer, threatening him with knifing if he showed himself in Paris again.

It did seem almost pointless to return to France. 'After *L'Age d'Or*, I sometimes thought that my career as a director was finished,' Buñuel said. He *was* certainly finished in Hollywood, where he had never really started. At the end of the year Mayer summoned everyone on the staff to one of the stages. Buñuel watched, first with awe, then amusement, as the diminutive patriarch lectured with blackboard and chalk on 'co-operation' – which, to him, meant everyone doing exactly as they were told.

For some, that meant giving up their jobs. Late in 1930 MGM had reorganized its Foreign Department. Parallel foreign versions were discontinued. *Anna Christie* in German and French had paid off, but remakes of *The Big House* and *The Trial of Mary Dugan* lost money. The studio decided to make its European versions, including those for Spain, at the Joinville studios outside Paris, which Paramount had turned into a dubbing factory. To shed Europeans stockpiled in panic a year earlier, it simply offered them work so trivial that they were driven to break their contracts. Charles Boyer was cast as Jean Harlow's chauffeur in *Red-Headed Woman*, little better than a cameo. He left for France. 'My bitterness with Hollywood was so intense that my ears rang with it.' Another casualty was Lya Lys. She had played in a few French versions for MGM, including *Buster se marie (Buster Gets Married)*, Autant-Lara's remake of *Spite Marriage* with Buster Keaton, but the studio did not renew her contract. After small roles in *Lives of a Bengal Lancer*, *The Return of Doctor X* and *Confessions of a Nazi Spy*, she retired in 1943 and lived the rest of her life in America.

Buñuel jumped before he could be pushed. Charles Brabin had just finished his version of Thornton Wilder's *The Bridge of San Luis Rey*, for which MGM had borrowed French actress Lily Damita. Adding a few minutes of dialogue to justify its release as a talkie, the studio had the star do her lines in Spanish as well. Tom Kilpatrick asked Buñuel to look at the rushes and check her accent.

Buñuel had met Damita through her friend Dolores del Rio but, like most of the stars he saw up close, she did not impress him. 'I'm especially disappointed by [the women],' he wrote to Noailles on 2 December. 'Joan Crawford is really plain. Greta Garbo, very little seen, dresses very humbly. Norma Shearer less than nothing. Lily Damita, quite the opposite, is very pretty but she puts out her tongue when one looks at her.' Damita was famous as the mistress of half the world's millionaires, including Prince Louis Ferdinand, son of the Crown Prince of Germany, and Luis seized on her kiss-and-tell reputation. 'I'm not here as a Spaniard. I'm here as a Frenchman,' he told Kilpatrick. 'And what's more, go tell Thalberg that I don't waste my time listening to whores.'

The next day he resigned. Kilpatrick probably never mentioned the Damita incident to his superiors, since on 27 February Frank Davis wrote to Buñuel, accepting his resignation in the most cordial terms. 'It is only the fact that it has become the policy of this company to suspend the production of pictures in the Spanish language that forces me with deep regret to say, "Hasta la vista". Yours has been one of the most pleasant associations this department has experienced and the fact that you anticipated our situation by voluntarily relieving us of our contractual obligation to you has shown us aside from your many talents, that you are the kind of person that we want with us when we go into production again. Please let us know how you fare on the many voyages you are planning [. . .] '

Buñuel was indeed planning voyages. Far from hurrying back to France to face the music over *L'Age d'Or*, he contemplated a leisurely return on the SS *President Adams*, leaving San Francisco on 30 April for Hawaii, Japan, China, the Philippines, Singapore, Ceylon, Alexandria and Naples, arriving in Marseille early in June.

The news from Spain that General Primo de Rivera's right-wing government had been overturned changed all that. On 14 April 1930 Alfonso XIII would abdicate and a socialist republic be declared. The new government opposed militarism and Spain's servility to the Church. There were riots in Madrid. Government leaders were jailed, churches and priests attacked, and convents burned as the Army, including a minor officer named Francisco Franco, looked on helplessly. Ugarte left immediately for Spain. Buñuel cancelled his berth, took the train for New York and, after a ten-day debauch in its speak-easies as he waited for a boat, sailed on 24 March for France on the *Lafayette* with some other French performers purged by Hollywood.

On board, his truculence persisted. At a birthday party for the captain, the ship's orchestra played both the American and French national anthems. Buñuel refused to stand for the first and ostentatiously put his feet up on the table for the second. He also enjoyed an affair with a wealthy young American, although it ended in tears long before the boat docked. Jeanne was at Le Havre to meet him when he berthed on 1 April, but Luis's thoughts were mostly of Spain.

14

'My sweet darling,
  I stay in this apartment arranging my cards. Lounging
around. The weather is lovely, but I don't have any desire
to go out. A splendid silence.'
– Paul Eluard, letter to Gala, 30 January 1930

Buñuel arrived back to find a city in mourning for lost prosperity. 'Paris was completely finished,' Robert McAlmon recalled, 'with all the old crowd gone and the [Latin] Quarter impossible.' Many galleries, including Goemans', had closed. Heavily mortgaged, Studio 28 limped along for a while, pointedly showing other films which had run foul of the censors. These included a slightly malicious double bill of *La Chute de la Maison Usher* and *Un Chien Andalou*, which paid off unexpectedly. Among the young men who discovered or re-discovered the films on this re-release were George Franju and Henri Langlois, co-founders of the Cinemathèque Française, which would conserve both Buñuel's films and reputation.

The ban of *L'Age d'Or* had done nothing to harm Buñuel's artistic standing. Jean Vigo and Henry Miller both wrote enthusiastic articles about it, and Dutch documentary-maker Joris Ivens sought him out to tell him how impressed he was. The longer the film remained suppressed, the greater became its fame, and Buñuel's. Ironically, however, Mauclaire did not survive. Overwhelmed by debt, he sold Studio 28 and went to China for the League of Nations.

The Noailles were drifting along the Côte d'Azur, ricocheting languidly from friend to friend as they waited out the scandal. At Sanary they dropped in on Aldous Huxley, who asked to see *L'Age d'Or*. Charles had a copy sent from Paris. When they left, Huxley noted that it was 'a relief, *au fond*: for, tho' nice, they have the rich persons' inability to conceive that other people have anything to do than eat lunches and teas in their houses'.

Despite the *L'Age d'Or* scandal, the Crash had robbed the Surrealists of momentum and direction. Eluard and Ernst were preoccupied with women, Crevel with opium and tuberculosis, Sadoul with illness and legal problems, the artists with declining markets, and Breton with art dealing and publishing. He already had plans for *Minotaure*, an opulent magazine to be funded by Swiss publisher Albert Skira which would bring Surrealism to the collecting classes. His apartment was engulfed by Inuit masks, pre-Columbian sculpture, erotica, artifacts created by the inmates of insane asylums and hundreds of paintings. It became even more disordered when Eluard, broke, moved in. The terrorist cell whose members had once boasted of descending to the street with pistols had become an association of distracted intellectuals bedeviled by mid-life crises and the problems of earning a living.

Only Aragon harboured the old revolutionary bacillus. In Kharkov, he, Sadoul and Triolet had been exposed to a virulent socialist ideology that had little in common with the café Communism of place Blanche. The couple stopped off in Brussels for a few days on the way back, leaving Sadoul to bring Breton the bad news.

'I can still see the more than anxious expression Sadoul wore on his return,' recalled Breton, 'and the painful embarrassment that my questions caused him [. . .] Yes, everything had gone smoothly; yes, our goals had been met, but . . . There was, in fact, a very large "but". An hour or two before their departure, they had been asked to sign a document that implied the abandonment, not to say repudiation, of every position we had held until then; rejection of the Second Manifesto [of Surrealism] "to the extent [. . .] that it contradicts dialectical materialism"; denunciation of Freudianism as an "idealist ideology", of Trotskyism as a "social-democratic and counter-revolutionary ideology". To top it off, they had to agree to submit their literary activity "to the discipline and control of the Communist Party" [. . .] This was the first time that I saw open at my feet the abyss that since then has taken on vertiginous proportions.'

Breton and Thirion persuaded Aragon and Sadoul to repudiate their Kharkov statements, but Aragon had lost faith in Surrealism. Fired by this new ideology, he had written *Front Rouge*, a poem urging the shooting of French politicians, including Prime Minister Léon Blum. Now he turned on the Surrealists on their home ground. When Dali offered his latest 'object', a dinner jacket hung with whisky glasses full of milk, Aragon, to the scorn of the group, rose to condemn such waste in a world where children went hungry. He moved quickly towards radical Stalinism and an inevitable break with place Blanche. Breton's abyss became a schism that split the entire movement.

Buñuel too agreed that Surrealism must embrace revolutionary violence, but while Aragon saw this as bowing to the inevitable, adding one's strength to the inexorable force of history, to Buñuel it was an orgiastic surrender to the Dionysian. Surrealism, he believed, would achieve apotheosis in total anarchy. In Spain, crowds were dancing in the streets, celebrating the fall of the Bourbons and the birth of the republic they called '*La Niña Bonita*' ('The Pretty Girl'). Churches were reportedly in flames with their art works inside. The élite of old Spain poured across the border, convinced of inevitable murder. The new regime's turbulence and anti-clericalism seemed made for the Surrealists, and Buñuel urged the whole brotherhood to travel immediately to Madrid and set fire to the Prado.

Breton was horrified, even more so when Buñuel offered to burn the negative of *L'Age d'Or* on the place du Tertre in front of the Sacré Coeur. 'Come now!' he protested. 'Our creations? You can't think of such a thing. What would be left?' For all his talk of terrorism and class war, Breton shared the bourgeois distaste for physical violence. A number of Surrealists would enlist against Franco but he stayed in Paris, explaining he could not jeopardize the future of his young daughter.

Furious at this evident cowardice, Buñuel was inspired to respond to the insulting letter he had received from the Spanish clique in Montparnasse. With Hernando Viñes he went to the Dôme to confront them. As he walked in, one of the group threw a box of matches that hit him on the ear. Snapping, 'Fine. It's war,' Buñuel left, returning the next night carrying a 7.65mm pistol he had brought back from America, and the letter, to convince the police, if it came up, that he had been responding to a threat. He admitted he probably would not have actually shot anyone, though he was ready to let off a few rounds, particularly at Huidobro. However, he did not have the chance. One of Cossio's girlfriends told him they had all gone to the movies.

Impatiently, Buñuel decided to go to Spain. Strikes had paralysed the railways, so, raising a loan, he took a taxi to the border. At Irun he hired another for the drive to Madrid. He had arrived in Paris on Wednesday. The following Friday – Good Friday – he drummed day and night in the streets of Calanda, a delirious reunion with his roots. For Easter Sunday he went to Zaragoza: 'I've never seen such enthusiasm, so many people in the streets.' With Sanchez Ventura and Gaos, a professor at the university, he watched from a café. He felt engulfed, reborn, cleansed. In the penance of Calanda and the revolution, the apostasy of Hollywood was expiated. He was back in Spain, where he belonged. 'My father would have been happy,' he wrote in a revealing note.

Bourgeois panic over the revolution did not last. 'Wealthy business-men stayed at home with shutters closed and doors barred till they found out how a liberated Spain was going to behave,' wrote John Dos Passos in *Journey Between Wars*. 'But the Republic of Honest Men was very well-behaved indeed. Property and persons were respected. Everybody was for law and order in the shape of the new Republican Civil Guard led by the now republican General Sanjurjo. The only outrages were the chipping off the royal arms wherever they could be reached in public buildings and the upsetting of the magnificent bronze statue of Philip III in the Plaza Major. A couple of grandees were hissed and a few nuns were hustled but everything passed off with the greatest good humour.'

Alcala Zamora, the new head of the government, was a white-haired and silver-tongued intellectual who recruited his administration from the same social group as the one it replaced. Manuel Azana, his president of ministers, had even been president of that stuffiest of Madrid clubs, the Ateneo, which the Hall of Congress soon came to resemble. 'The coffee was better,' wrote Dos Passos, 'the seats were more freshly upholstered, the attendants were more elderly and courtly [. . .] It was the best café in Madrid and Madrid is above all a city of cafés.'

Buñuel only stayed fifteen days on his first trip, and spent most of them with his family. He was in Madrid for the declaration of the Republic and the celebrations that followed, but, once it became clear that the revolution was not as sweeping as the newspapers claimed, rather than waste the trip he started looking for someone to distribute *L'Age d'Or*. Victoria Ocampo, the beautiful and aristocratic Argentinian who had funded some avant-garde publishing projects, was interested. She also invited Buñuel to take the film to Buenos Aires, where she was holding a series of conferences on experimental art.

Flattered, he returned to Paris on 27 April and brought Noailles up to date. They also discussed German distributors. None of this suggests that Noailles ever intended to destroy *L'Age d'Or*. Now that the storm seemed to have blown over in France, Buñuel had the negatives of both sound and silent versions moved from the Noailles' hiding place to the laboratory, GM Film, making it easier to produce extra prints. A copy found its way to New York through Iris Barry, librarian of the Museum of Modern Art, later to be a force in Buñuel's life. The Film Society showed it at the museum on 19 March 1933.

Buñuel had no immediate plans to return to Spain. On 30 April he told Noailles that he hoped to find work in the Spanish Language

Department of Paramount. The French government had passed new laws forcing American studios to invest part of their distribution profits in local production. Robert T. Kane, who had supervised Paramount's dubbing programme in Hollywood, was sent to take charge of Joinville and turn out cheap films, mostly remakes of those produced at Ufa in Berlin.

'For two years it was bedlam,' said Michael Powell in an interview. 'European directors from all over were flooding to Paris because they needed people who knew every European language.' Paramount's Foreign Versions Department was run by Rudolf Sieber, Marlene Dietrich's husband. He had gone with her to Hollywood but, having seen that his presence there might impair both her American career and her affair with von Sternberg, and being used to such conflicts of interest with the sexually voracious Marlene, philosophically returned to Europe. Rather than let him become a focus for gossip in Berlin, Paramount found him a job in Paris. Dietrich financed an apartment for him and his mistress.

Buñuel worked at Joinville for most of 1932 and 1933, re-writing Hollywood dialogue under Claudio de la Torre. Other Spanish émigrés on the team included another friend of Victoria Ocampo, Benjamin Fondane, a cadet member of the Surrealists, and Gustavo Duran.

Blond, blue-eyed and handsome, the Catalan Duran impressed even Buñuel with his bizarre biography, and they became friends. When he was ten, his womanizing father and neurasthenic mother left home, dressed for the opera. His father returned alone, having committed his wife to a mental asylum. A week later his mistress moved in. Duran fled to Paris, joined the Communist Party, studied composition under Paul Dukas and Nadia Boulanger, tutored Yehudi Menuhin's children, and befriended Hemingway and André Malraux, who wrote him into *Man's Hope* as 'Manuel' and asked him to score the film version.

Hoping to float his own film, Buñuel turned to Pierre Braunberger who, with the Allegrets, was keeping Billancourt busy. The trio made seven features there in 1931 alone, under literally hand-to-mouth conditions. Braunberger, whose nervous habit of chewing the corners of business papers became worse as business declined, was kept afloat only by emergency injections of capital from his rich German relatives, the Monteux-Reichenbachs. Stars like Raimu, paid by the day, refused to work until the cheque was in their hand. If it had not arrived, Raimu would simply take a nap until it did. Once, Braunberger, viewing rushes while waiting for the money, was handed some papers in the dark. When the lights went up, he found he had eaten Raimu's cheque.

Although the operation was tottering, Buñuel suggested a film of *Wuthering Heights*. It was a shrewd choice. Apart from being a popular romantic melodrama, Emily Brontë's novel, like George du Maurier's *Peter Ibbetson*, was a favourite of the Surrealists for its celebration of *l'amour fou*. Braunberger was interested enough to ask for a treatment.

Since, after the Dali experience, he would not write alone, Buñuel enlisted Pierre Unik, at twenty-two the youngest of the Surrealists, and one of the least typical. His father was a tailor and a rabbi, but Unik was a confirmed atheist and a Communist who edited the Party journal for children. He also lived out of Paris, in Reims, and was not so directly influenced by Breton.

In 1928, as part of a series of discussions about sex with the group, Unik admitted he always asked a woman what sort of sex she preferred. 'I think that is absolutely colossal, really phenomenal,' Breton blustered. 'Talk about complications.'

When Unik asked why he was so surprised, Breton replied, 'Because her preferences have nothing to do with it.' Although Luis's sexual attitudes were closer to Breton's than to Unik's, the two became friends. They spent long evenings playing mildly erotic Surrealist games with Unik's mistress Agnes Capri, the photographer Denise Bellon and a beautiful librarian named Yolande Olivero whose limp, in Luis's eyes, only added to her attractiveness.

Buñuel and Unik were helped on *Wuthering Heights* by Sadoul, who remembers spending a few weeks in July 1932 with his wife Nora, Luis and Unik at an inn at Cernay-la-Ville, in the valley of the Chevreuse, working on the adaptation. Buñuel visualized Katharine Hepburn as Cathy. Sadoul did not think the script was ever finished, but in August Buñuel told Charles de Noailles that Braunberger 'liked [the script] a lot'.

With its first winter approaching and the honeymoon period over, the Spanish Republic was in trouble. Life might continue tranquilly in the cities but the peasants were demanding promised land reforms. The coalition that crushed the Bourbons began to fragment into anarchists, socialists, Communists, Catalan separatists and even less well-defined splinter groups, leavened now with carpetbaggers and opportunists. Some poorer communities with nothing to lose had become anarcho-syndicalist enclaves. They were threatening to declare themselves free communes and shoot the Guardia Civil which, with the Army demoralized and still essentially in sympathy with the Bourbons, was the only force for order. Appalling cruelties were committed on both sides. What had looked at first like a standard socialist revolution was emerging as something more typically Spanish.

On 22 November *L'Age d'Or* was shown for the first time in Spain. The nervous Guardia had formally banned it, but a much mellowed Lorca, Guillermo de la Torre and Ricardo Urgoiti, a fledgling film producer and distributor whose father owned Spain's major daily, *El Sol*, set up a private screening at the Cine Palacio de la Prensa. Buñuel was there and, provident as ever, collected 5 pesetas at the door from everyone to cover transport and customs duty. Before the screening, he offered a typically truculent introduction. 'What I want is you *not* to like the film, to protest. I should be sorry if it pleased you.' Count Agustin de Foxa wrote up the screening in his diaries. 'Left-wing intellectuals and ladies were there. The most recent film of Buñuel vibrated on the silver screen. That man of brutish aspect and curly hair had photographed the subconscious [. . .] In the interval the conversation was about Freud, about Picasso, about the friends in Paris [. . .] Afterwards they showed *Un Chien Andalou*. The public shuddered, making their seats creak, when an enormous eye appeared on the screen and was cut coldly by a razor, the drops of liquid from the iris leaping on to the metal. Hysterical shouts were heard.' The reaction was all Buñuel could have hoped: revulsion and approval at the same time.

He enjoyed his second visit to Republican Spain more that the first. Just the year before, Gómez de la Serna had written an inflammatory exchange into his play *El Hijo Surrealista (The Surrealist Son)*:

'If you even knew what being a surrealist means!'
'It is the spirit of permanent revolution.'

Buñuel revelled in this atmosphere of revolt and anarchy. He wrote in *My Last Breath* of his generation of Spanish intellectuals that 'our political consciousness had been more or less asleep for so long that they were only just beginning to stir. Most of us did not come fully awake until [. . .] just before the proclamation of the Republic.' This is usually taken as evidence of a Pauline conversion to Communism, but the story of his involvement with Communism and, in particular, the Party, is more complex and revealing.

Buñuel knew and worked with Communists all his adult life. Apart from those within Surrealism, Yves Allegret was an active Trotskyist and prime mover behind the guerrilla October Group theatre, whose members included Castanayer. The Rumanian photographer Eliazar Teodoresco, who, as Eli Lotar, shot *Las Hurdes*, was also a Communist, as was Frank Davis, his MGM supervisor with whom he worked again in the late 1930s. Most of his team at the Museum of Modern Art in New York between 1941 and 1943 were Communists, and in Mexico Buñuel made films with George Dancigers, Hugo Butler, George Pepper, Gabriel Figueroa, Zachary Scott and scores of others who never disguised their affiliations.

Buñuel, however, would always deny joining the Party. He agreed he was a sympathizer and that he attended Party meetings, especially at the Communist paper *L'Humanité*, often with Aragon, who, he said, would get him past the guards on the door, saying, 'This is Comrade Buñuel. He's with us.' In public, however, he spoke of the Party with reserve. 'The Communists are the least wicked,' he'd say of Paris's political factions. 'It's Communism where there's the least evil.' Asked why he did not join, he said flippantly that he couldn't stand long-winded discussions.

Many people, however, including Aragon, insisted that Buñuel was a secret Party member. In his biography of Buñuel, Francisco Aranda said 'In 1926/7 [. . .] the main Surrealist group declared their adherence to Communism and loyally paid up their subscriptions [. . .] Buñuel's subscription [. . .] lapsed after he came to America in 1937.' If one adjusts Aranda's erroneous dates of these events, this would make Buñuel a Party member from 1929 to 1938. Pressed by Max Aub to comment on a claim in a Spanish magazine that Buñuel joined the Spanish Party in 1932 and stayed in until 1935, Aragon said, 'I can't know if he belonged to a foreign Party. All I know is that he belonged to the French Party.'

Most Communists automatically assumed Buñuel to be one of their own, an impression Luis did nothing to dispel. Ricardo Muñoz Suay remembers him always using the standard members' code for the Party, 'How goes it with the widow?' or 'Well, how's it going with the friends of the widow?' Aragon may have got Buñuel into some Communist meetings, but it is unlikely that he would have been admitted to others he describes without a Party card. His comment to Penelope Gilliatt that he left the Museum of Modern Art because of 'Dali's information that I was a member of the French Communist Party' does not imply Dali lied, and a decision to relocate in Mexico in 1945 stemmed from an expectation of being 'named'.

Why did Buñuel deny his Communism? Partly it was the anarchist's natural revulsion for any social organization. 'As usual,' he wrote in *My Last Breath* of his involvement, or lack of it, in the Spanish Civil War, 'I was torn between my intellectual (and emotional) attraction to anarchy and my fundamental need for order and peace.' As a purist of Surrealism, he also believed, like Artaud, that politics had no place in the movement.

Buñuel's Communism was less political than mystical. Like Aragon, he turned to Marx when Surrealism ceased to satisfy all his intellectual and emotional needs. 'Communist orthodoxy [. . .] supplies a felt lack of religion,' says Elsa Triolet's biographer Lachlan Mackinnon of Aragon's conversion. 'Surrealism [. . .] was at its weakest when it came to explaining the purpose of human life. Those who survived it were either heroic individualists like André Breton or psychotics like Salvador Dali. Life had given Aragon no reason to believe in anything in particular before and he might be thought to have been in a gambler's position. The Soviet order could at least offer him a world-view that honoured [. . .] his gift.'

Buñuel did not, like Aragon, move directly from Surrealism to Communism. He lacked, among other things, the advantage of a resident ideologue which Aragon enjoyed with Triolet. For the next four years he would swing indecisively between Breton's version of pure artistic violence and the more structured revolutionary thought of Marx.

Whatever his formal politics, however, Buñuel was shaken by the idealism of the new Republic. His first reaction to the enthusiasm and commitment of men like Lorca and Ugarte was a revulsion for conventional capitalist cinema. 'I was disoriented,' he wrote back in France, 'but I didn't want to make any more films; the whole *milieu* repelled me; the public, the critics, the producers, etc.'

He could afford the luxury of these convictions because there was no film work in Paris anyway. From a new apartment at 39 rue Pascal he wrote to Charles de Noailles on 27 January 1932 that 'film production is doing very badly in Paris. Braunberger is looking for new capital; there's no money to finish *Fantomas* and after that film he will close the studios for some months. At Pathé-Natan the same thing is happening. Spanish production has halted for some time at Paramount.' With Braunberger's failure, *Wuthering Heights* was shelved. It would not resurface for twenty years.

The same letter went on: 'I'm going to try to be hired as a director for Russia, something that won't be very difficult, according to some people in the know.' The 'some people' were Aragon and Communist cadre Paul Vaillant-Couturier, and the film a version of André Gide's novel *Les Caves du Vatican*, which *L'Humanité* had just serialized.

The Communists were doing their best to recruit France's intellectual élite. Picasso, for his own reasons, professed to be convinced, but Gide, a classic homosexual aesthete, had little interest in politics. Triolet, Aragon and Vaillant-Couturier managed to tempt him into at least a flirtation. Ambushing him at a Soviet Embassy reception, Aragon, whom Gide had helped early in his career (not entirely selflessly: Aragon was both handsome and bisexual), offered as bait the possibility of a Russian film of his book, with Buñuel directing.

A labyrinthine story of intrigue in Rome, with an enormous cast and a period setting, *Les Caves du Vatican* was no project for Buñuel, although its anti-clericalism and the eccentric main character, Lafcadio Wluiki, a blond Nietzschean *Übermensch* who stabs his thigh with a penknife every time he betrays his emotions, might have drawn his interest. Buñuel said he collaborated on a script with Gide for three days, but without either of them believing it would work. Buñuel knew it was technically beyond him, while Gide feared that Aragon was full of 'terrible repressions' which would have doomed any joint project. Unik and Sadoul tried to help, but it petered out. When Gide went to Moscow a few years later, he returned disillusioned, and promptly recanted on any belief of socialism he had harboured.

On 16 January the police seized copies of Aragon's book *Persécuté Persécuteur* which contained *Front Rouge*, and he was charged with inciting mutiny and murder. Despite their differences with him, the Surrealists defended the poem, only to have Aragon on 10 March denounce them in *L'Humanité* and affirm his commitment to the Party. Breton attacked his apostasy with a furious pamphlet, *Misère de la Poésie*.

Relations between the Surrealists and the Communists continued to deteriorate. At Kharkov, it had been decided to launch an International Union of Revolutionary Artists. Breton had been considering such a project for months under exactly this name but, confident that, once in, he could subvert it and take control, he swallowed his pride and agreed to bring the Surrealists into its French chapter, the Association des Écrivains et des Artistes Révolutionnaires (AEAR).

Before they could join, however, a piece by Dali in *Le Surréalisme au Service de la Révolution* 4 in December 1931 stirred the Communists to fury. Entitled *Rêverie*, it described his fantasies as he masturbated in front of a little girl. Aragon, Sadoul and Unik were called before a Party official (probably Vaillant-Couturier who headed the AEAR) and ordered to repudiate the Surrealists. When they refused, he raged, 'You stink of bourgeois rottenness!' Breton was forced to defend Dali, and the scandal held up Surrealist entry to the AEAR until the end of 1932.

Buñuel received an anguished *pneumatique* at 8 a.m. one March morning and hurried round to Aragon's apartment in rue Campagne-Première. Aragon was desperate, caught between the Communists, Breton, and Triolet who, furious at his vacillation, had walked out. Luis consoled him and the disasters blew over, at least for the moment. The two men remained friends long afterwards. 'He had a soul of iron under that precious and elegant exterior,' Buñuel said. Although ready to discard any memento to which he felt too attached, he always kept proudly his inscribed copy of *Persécuté Persécuteur* in which Aragon thanked him as a friend who would come to one's aid 'when you thought your final hour had come'.

Aragon was right to be grateful. By siding with him, Buñuel sacrificed his own standing with the Surrealists. In late February or early March Eluard wrote to Gala: 'I think that a break with Aragon is to be feared. I haven't seen him in a fortnight. Sadoul and Buñuel are supporting him and we might lose them too. Unik and [Maxime] Alexandre are wavering between us. How many of us will be left?' Shortly after, he wrote again: 'The break with A[ragon], Bun[uel], Unik, Sadoul and Alexandre seems to have been effected. Sadoul alone had the courage to write a parting letter to Breton.' By the summer, Aragon realized he had no future in Paris. Triolet found him a job in Moscow on the French edition of the Soviet magazine *International Literature*. To finance the trip, he sold the manuscript of *Persécuté Persécuteur*. Buñuel acted as go-between with Charles de Noailles, who bought it for 3000 francs.

For the first half of 1932 Buñuel lived a curious life. Because he had kept his options open with every group, he could move from the terse rivalries of place Blanche to house-parties at St Bernard and Stalinist cell meetings in the Paris *banlieue*. At a gathering of foreign workers in Montreuil-sous-Bois the guests included Ramon Casanellas, one of the anarchists involved in the March 1921 assassination of Spanish Prime Minister Eduardo Dato. Buñuel could still remember a cab driver showing him bullet-holes in a Madrid wall. When, bored with the meeting as usual, Luis tried to leave, the speaker called out to him, 'If you go now and Casanellas is arrested, we'll know you're the traitor.' Resigned, Buñuel kept his seat.

By contrast, he also spent a week in February at Hyères as part of a group that included Milhaud, Poulenc, Auric, Markevitch, Giacometti, Unik, Henri Sauguet, Bérard, Cocteau and his newest protégé, the young conductor Roger Desormière. Urged by the Noailles to improvise, Buñuel, Giacometti and Unik created (in an hour, according to Buñuel) a giant cardboard giraffe, each spot hinged to reveal a text. Guests were called out before dinner to read the *pensées*, which included 'An orchestra of one hundred musicians playing *Die Walküre* in a basement' and 'Christ is laughing hysterically', an image Buñuel would recall in *Nazarin*. When they came out after dinner, the giraffe had disappeared and the Noailles never referred to its fate, although Unik published the texts in *Surréalisme au Service de la Révolution* 6.

It was probably during this weekend (since none of their letters mention it) that Charles tried to boost Luis's flagging career. He had found a possible sponsor for *Wuthering Heights*, an Egyptian princess, but Buñuel cried off, offering Noailles an excuse he knew he would accept; that, as a committed Surrealist, he was disgusted by the thought of commercialism.

Charles then suggested Luis accompany his brother-in-law, the Prince de Ligne, Governor General of the Belgian Congo, on an expedition across sub-Saharan Africa. A couple of hundred people, mostly anthropologists, geographers and zoologists, would trek from Dakar to Djibouti. Noailles thought Buñuel might make a documentary about the trip, as Marc Allegret had done with *Le Voyage au Congo* a few years before, during an African journey with Gide. It was a shrewd proposal from the unworldly Charles who, as an enthusiast for gardens, saw better than anyone that Luis had not lost his scientist's fascination with the physical world: *L'Age d'Or* opened, after all, with an extract from a documentary on scorpions.

The idea of a foreign trip tempted Buñuel, but he just was not that interested in Africa. Another Surrealist, Michel Leiris, went instead, and was as disappointed as, one suspects, Buñuel would have been. 'One doesn't come so close to people by approaching their customs,' Leiris wrote three years later in *L'Afrique Fantôme*. 'They remain, after all our inquiries, obstinately closed [. . .] I haven't slept with a black woman. That's how European I've remained!'

Buñuel did embrace a muddled plan to relaunch *L'Age d'Or* by cutting it to about 600 metres and changing the name to a phrase from Marx's Communist Manifesto, *In the Icy Waters of Egoist Calculation*. Dali protested, but since Braunberger seemed interested in distributing the edited version, the Noailles agreed. Buñuel delivered it at the end of the summer. However, on 24 September 1932 he wrote to Charles that, three days before, Braunberger had submitted what he called 'my *new* film *The Icy Waters*, etc.' to the censor, but that, after consulting Chiappe, she had refused it a visa. Breton would recall seeing the film with its new 'childishly reassuring' label in workers' cinemas, but there is no reliable evidence that it was ever shown in public, nor does a copy survive.

15

'In ourselves the explosion.'
– René Char

'To be frank,' Buñuel wrote in *My Last Breath* of leaving the Surrealists, 'it wasn't just the political dissension [. . .] that cooled my ardour for the movement, but also their increasing snobbery, their strange attraction to the aristocracy.' For so close a friend of the Noailles to complain of 'attraction to the aristocracy' sounds hypocritical, but perhaps he meant to distinguish between his genuine friendship with Charles and Marie-Laure, the only aristos he knew personally, and the general pursuit by Breton and Eluard of wealthy patronage and high *ton*.

He had also criticized Breton and Eluard for allowing their photographs to be displayed in a bookstore on boulevard Raspail when *L'Immaculée Conception* was published. They brushed off the charge of self-aggrandizement; it was just publicity. Buñuel also disliked the lush production and 'arty' character of Breton's magazine *Minotaure*, but since it was not launched until 1934 this cannot have influenced his decision to leave.

He was right to say he abandoned the Surrealist movement rather than Surrealism itself. His loyalty to individual members would never flag, nor would his belief in Breton's original impulse, to recognize the primacy of dreams and the subconscious.

Never having been totally in the group made it easier for Buñuel to slip out, and to remain on good terms with many of them. Eluard, however, now Breton's closest lieutenant, regarded him as a traitor, and Gala, with Dali's encouragement, egged him on. 'Let Dali rest easy as to Buñuel, Unik, Alexandre, Sadoul, Giacometti,' Eluard reassured her in March 1932. 'There is no question that anyone among us will keep in touch with them. We wouldn't tolerate it.' The anti-Breton group, however, did keep up with Buñuel. Roger Vitrac, whom Breton disliked, and the radical André Thirion remained his friends. Eluard had warned that Thirion cared only for politics, not art, but Buñuel found common ground with him, even helping with geographical details on the maps of Spain he updated in expectation of Franco's overthrow. Buñuel maintained many of these relationships all his life. 'He was the only one of the Surrealist group who was a friend with all the others until the end', said Jean-Claude Carrière. 'In the sixties in Paris he would go and see Aragon as well as Breton.'

In early 1932 Pierre Batcheff, in the middle of a party, abruptly confided to his wife, 'I want you to know the reason for my extravagances and crazy behaviour. I'm a drug addict. I've been on drugs since the age of fifteen, in Switzerland, when I was an extra for the Piteoffs.' On 12 April, he slipped away from Denise and Jacques Prévert during a night out in Montparnasse. When Denise got home she found him in a coma from an overdose. A suicide note explained that he could not go on causing pain to the people he loved. Prévert called Theodore Fraenkel, both a doctor and a Surrealist, but he could only declare Batcheff past help.

This was not the only suicide to impinge of Buñuel's work. Simone Mareuil would set herself afire with petrol in a Parisian park, and Miroslava Stern killed herself shortly after starring in *The Criminal Life of Archibaldo de la Cruz*. Buñuel, characteristically, shrugged off the deaths. In his memoirs he would describe Batcheff as dying on the day *Un Chien Andalou* finished shooting.* Part of this was his studied hostility to all emotion, but a growing alienation from Paris played its part. Increasingly his thoughts were of Spain.

After a period of shock, the right wing was resisting the new Spanish republic. In August a group of generals led by Janjurjo failed in a counter-revolution in Seville after a prostitute leaked their plans.

The political life of Republican Spain defied logical analysis. The revolutionaries were a loose coalition of Trotskyists, Stalinists, Catalan separatists, and anarchists (reported to number 2 million in Spain at the time), with little in common except revulsion for the old regime, and in particular its primary institutions, the monarchy, the military and the Church. It was equally simplistic to label the right-wing Falange or Phalanx and its emerging leader Franco as 'Fascists'. Though he accepted help from Mussolini and Hitler, Franco, as George Orwell wrote in *Homage to Catalonia*, 'was not strictly comparable with [either]'. Franco did not lead a revolution but a 'military mutiny backed up by the aristocracy and the Church [. . .] not so much to impose

* This error first surfaced in Dali's memoirs, along with the one that Batcheff, a heroin user, 'reeked of ether'.

Fascism as to restore feudalism'. Despite repeated efforts to educate him in Fascism, Franco never believed it could work in Spain. His ideal was the Spain of Buñuel's childhood, or at least his biased perception of it, a pious and disciplined country with power concentrated in the cities, and the peasantry at work in the fields, their spiritual and intellectual welfare in the hands of the Church. Hundreds of thousands of Spaniards would die in his attempt to achieve it.

After the first elation, the popular front fragmented into mutually distrustful camps. The two biggest labour unions, the anarcho-syndicalist Confederación Nacional de Trabajador and its socialist partner the Unión General de Trabajadores, both had private militias, as did the Trotskyist Partido Obrero de Unificación Marxista, which, though one of the smallest unions, was endorsed by the British Communist Party. In practice the lines between groups were vague. As Bernard Crick explains in his biography of Orwell, 'Communists would join the UGT and POUM members would join the CNT. As the CNT had led the revolution in Catalonia, its alliance there with the cautious UGT worked badly. The CNT anarchists in Catalonia had their own militia, but some preferred to enlist with the POUM militia, which was a slightly more disciplined body and must have been one of the most politically conscious militias ever. The Communists helpfully simplified the situation by calling everyone in the POUM and their militias "Trotskyists". Some had been, like their leader Andres Nin, and a few still were in spirit; but Nin had broken with Trotsky long before [. . .] The POUM was an independent Marxist force.' Into the same seething alphabet soup went a second Communist union (PSUC), the student union (FUE), its right-wing rival JONS, a secret military underground, UME, and scores more.

Having lived out of Spain for so long, Buñuel belonged to another group looked on with suspicion by almost everyone, the repatriates. Some returned in search of political or moral rebirth. Others saw rich pickings. The cafés were full of the latter, 'the type of Spaniard,' said John dos Passos in *Journey Between Wars*, 'who's hated in Mexico as a *gachupin*, people with gimlet eyes and greedy predatory lines on their faces, jerkwater importers and exporters, small brokers, loan sharks, commissionmerchants, pawnbrokers, men who knew how to make two *duros* grow where one had grown before. They'd never been much before under the monarchy, mostly they'd had to scrape up their livings in America; at home the hierarchy, the bishops, the duchesses, the grandees and the Bourbons high-hatted them off the map, but now the feudal paraphernalia was gone, the *gachupines* were on top of the world.'

*

As in Russia, the revolutionaries in Spain knew that education and the arts would be crucial in welding a hundred isolated and ignorant regions into a modern nation. An astonishing 32.4 per cent of Spaniards were illiterate. The Bourbons had built only 11,128 schools in thirty years. In two and a half years the Republic created 13,570. Almost no Spaniard had read a Spanish book or seen a Spanish play. When Lorca, fast becoming the laureate of the new regime, suggested setting up a travelling student theatre to bring Cervantes, Lope de Vega and Calderón to the culture-starved provinces, Ugarte formed a company of young actors known as La Barraca, 'The Barn', after its headquarters on the Madrid University campus.

Meanwhile, brushfire insurrections were exploding all over Spain. Inspired by the news from Madrid, peasants who had endured centuries of exploitation rallied behind a local firebrand, disarmed or killed the Guardia Civil, deconsecrated the local church and convent, unfrocked its clergy, turned its treasures into negotiable gold and declared themselves independent. In the process old scores were settled, almost always in blood. Blood would become the motif of a revolution that had begun and, it seemed to the more optimistic, ended in 1931 almost without casualties. Watching both sides slaughter their enemies, Manuel Azana lamented that the Spanish were driven by 'hatred, distilled during years in the hearts of the dispossessed; hatred by the proud, little disposed to accept the "insolence" of the poor; hatred of counter-posed ideologies, a kind of *odium theologicum* with which one sought to justify intolerance and fanaticism.'

In the summer of 1932, however, life in the new republic seemed to be settling down after a hard first winter. Franco, who was becoming a focus of revolt in the Army, was sacked from his job as director of the Army Academy. A year later he would be exiled to the Balearic Islands as Governor. In July Buñuel made a longer and more relaxed visit. He saw Ugarte and Lorca in Madrid. They posed for a photograph with Luis, formal and unsmiling in tight blue suits; men of substance in the new Spain. They probably tried to enrol him in their activities. Certainly Luis knew about the Barraca, since he would take advantage of it when he made *Las Hurdes* the following year.

Not all his old friends had sided with the Republic. Cossio, Huidobro and Eugenio Montes supported the Falange. So did Giménez Caballero, who became Franco's speech-writer and, as one of the General's biographers calls him, his 'court jester'. Loyalties could change with bewildering speed. Count Augustin de Foxa and Rafael Alberti were on their way to a screening of *L'Age d'Or* when a friend told them that José Antonio Primo de Rivera, son of the ex-dictator and now leader of the

Fascists, was addressing a rally. Foxa went, and was converted to the Falange. Alberti saw the film, and went on to be one of the most inflammatory of Communists. Stephen Spender described him in *The Thirties and After* as 'a massive leonine figure, dressed in blue dungarees, with flowing hair and Michelangelo features, leaping on a chair and shouting with passionate fury to everyone'.

Dali had spent most of 1931 in Paris, confecting Surrealist trifles and knick-knacks for the shrinking art market. When he did return to Spain, he too sided with the old regime. Buñuel called on him a year later to find him working on a large statue of a woman on all-fours. When Buñuel asked about his politics, Dali slapped her buttocks and said, 'This matters more than all the republics in the world.' He confessed to finding Hitler erotically fascinating, and dreamt of him 'as a woman. His flesh, which I had imagined whiter than white, ravished me.' Franco would leave Dali in peace, eventually declaring his villa a museum and national monument.

With much to think about, Buñuel went home to Zaragoza. In August he wrote to Charles de Noailles: 'I've spent fifteen days in a village in the Spanish Pyrenees, really admirable and anti-touristic. Impossible to find oneself in a solitude more grand and desolate [. . .] Pierre Unik came to see me down there.' The village was Huesca, Aragon's capital in the twelfth century and site of a famous medieval university. Sleepy and backward in 1932, Huesca would become notorious as one end of the Huesca-Zaragoza line in the Aragonian front of the Civil War.

Buñuel seems to have gone there on the invitation of anarchist art teacher Ramon Acin, whom he had met in Zaragoza and who may have been a friend of another Huescaño, Pepin Bello. Among other things, they discussed the problems of the Spanish film industry. Drained of talent by Hollywood and enfeebled by the American studios' policy of suppressing national production by barring local films from its theatres, Spain's cinema lagged a decade behind the rest of Europe. According to Buñuel, Acin, seized by a particularly Spanish mixture of superstition, braggadocio and revolutionary fervour, announced, 'If I win the lottery, I'll give you the money to make a film.' In other versions, Acin, drinking on a terrace with Buñuel, decided to buy a lottery ticket from a passing vendor but found he didn't have the money. Luis paid for it, telling him, 'If you win, give me the money to make a short film.'

After Huesca, Buñuel took Unik to Toledo and ritually inducted him into the Order. On this visit, Luis renewed his friendship with Alberti, now rated as a poet second only to Lorca but better known as a Communist firebrand. This was dangerous company. As usual, Buñuel shrugged off the risk of guilt by association and got on with drinking and joking, but everyone felt a suppressed violence. 'The situation was asphyxiating,' Buñuel agreed. 'There was a feeling that things would explode.' He startled everyone by sneaking off with the inn's sheets and appearing robed in them at the top of some church steps as a ghost.

As usual, they finished with a gargantuan breakfast of omelettes, pork with fried eggs, partridge and Yepes wine at the Venta de Aires outside town. On their way back to their hotel, Buñuel, Unik, Alberti and his wife Maria-Teresa Léon were crossing a square dominated by a giant stone crucifix when two cadets from Franco's Alcazar military academy playfully grabbed Maria-Teresa. Since two nearby Guardia showed no inclination to intervene, Unik and Buñuel knocked down the cadets and kicked them. They expected to be arrested, but the Guardia just stood by, then advised them to leave Toledo as soon as possible. This fight, conducted in the shadow, awesome but exhilarating, of '*cet objet-là*', seemed to Buñuel the very typus of those hallucinatory events the Order was founded to encourage. The following summer, when Sadoul visited him in Madrid, he described it in detail and even drew the crucifix for him.

Wisely not relying on Acin's good luck for a film. Buñuel returned to Joinville at the end of the summer. Sieber had left to flirt with production, then emigrate to California, where Dietrich installed him on a chicken ranch. Buñuel took over his job. On 14 November he wrote to Charles de Noailles that he had been director of Spanish dubbing at Paramount for six months. Since the studio was usually in uproar during the day, he worked from six at night to two in the morning. This was to be one of the last letters to the Noailles for some years. Already he seemed to have relocated mentally and emotionally in Spain.

The winter of 1932/3 tested the Spanish Republic almost beyond endurance. As land reform lagged, riots and strikes paralysed Barcelona, Valencia and the railways. Peasants marched on Jerez and Cadiz. In January 1933 the hill town of Casas Viejas, an anarchist stronghold in the far south, near Gibraltar, heard, wrongly, that national libertarian Communism had been declared. Mostly tobacco smugglers and poachers, the people there had been fired by promises of land reform. Five hundred of them attacked the local Guardia headquarters and killed two men. Proclaiming independence, they started planning redistribution of the land. When the army arrived, dozens were killed, including sixteen prisoners whose bodies were thrown into the burnt remains of anarchist headquarters. When it became clear that the government, at least tacitly, had endorsed these bloody reprisals, the already tottering Republic slipped a little further towards disaster. Ominously, Hitler became Chancellor in the same month. But in the spring of 1933 Acin unexpectedly wrote to tell Buñuel he had won 100,000 pesetas in the lottery, and was ready, over the objections of his anarchist comrades, to offer 20,000 pesetas towards the film that would become *Las Hurdes*.

Las Hurdes is a mountainous district in western Spain near the Portuguese border. The lowlands, Las Hurdes Bajas, were lush and prosperous, but the flinty uplands behind them, Las Hurdes Altas, were among the most deprived areas in Spain. The peasants, many descended from bandits, smugglers and renegade Jews who had fled compulsory conversion, lived in medieval conditions, ravaged by malnutrition, malaria and in-breeding, and almost without a culture. 'I didn't find a single drawing, nor a song, nor a firearm,' Buñuel said.* 'At the same time they don't make bread. It was an almost neolithic culture, without folklore, nor artistic manifestation of any sort. The sole tool which they possessed was the plough.'

Even before the Republic, Las Hurdes had been considered a case history of isolation and neglect. Until the sixteenth century it was reputedly haunted. Miguel de Unamuno wrote about it at length in his 1922 book *Andanzas y Visiones Españolas*. In 1925 Gregorio Maranon, the doctor and writer who would later become a Republican politician and administrator of Las Hurdes, persuaded King Alfonso to pay a visit. The King was so struck by the poverty that he ordered the first road to be built into the area. Work went slowly, however. Spain seemed almost to prefer Las Hurdes in its primitive state. Maranon, a bullfight *aficionado* and cultural traditionalist, regarded it as Spain in its purest form, and even Unamuno suggested that in its misery something of the nation's ancient soul and dignity was revealed.

Whatever Buñuel said later, the idea of a documentary about Las Hurdes did not originate with him. In 1931 Yves Allegret had gone to Spain with his wife Renée and the young Rumanian cameraman Eli Lotar, with the idea of making a film. Lotar had migrated into movies from still photography, where he had won a reputation for unsparing depictions of Paris's *bas fonds*. His 1929 series *Abattoir* showed slaughtered animals lying under blood-soaked sacks on the footpath, and the flayed forelegs of calves lined up in dozens against a wall, neat as umbrellas. He had already shot documentaries for Joris Ivens and was, like Allegret and Ivens, a committed Trotskyist.

---

* It is interesting that he should place guns on the same level as music and art.

They intended to film the anarcho-syndicalist communities of the far south, soon to explode in the rebellion of Casas Viejas, but in Carmona, near Seville, they were arrested. Renée was allowed to return to Paris, where she pulled every string to get her husband and Lotar released, but they still spent weeks in jail. *Persona non grata* in Spain, Allegret made a film on Tenerife instead. Lotar retained the camera equipment, and the idea.

Lotar and Allegret may not have known Ramon Acin but he was a prominent regional organizer (he and his wife were executed in 1936), and the anarchist leadership was sufficiently small for news of a possible film to get around. The story of Acin's lottery win, despite its Surrealist overtones of chance, sounds thin. The anarchists had much to gain from a film which highlighted conditions among the rural poor, where most of their power lay. They almost certainly supported and funded the film, via Acin.*

There was little or no market for documentary, so Buñuel had nothing to gain from making one. The fact that, initially, *Las Hurdes* had no sound track suggests rather that it was intended for public meetings where a lecturer would read Unik's didactic commentary and answer questions afterwards. In the late 1970s Buñuel admitted: 'We're talking about a tendentious film. Such poverty [as one sees in *Las Hurdes*] doesn't exist in Las Hurdes Bajas [. . .] I photographed Las Hurdes Bajas in passing, but almost the entire film occurs in Las Hurdes Altas.' In case anyone should doubt where his sympathies lay, Buñuel made them clear on the first day of filming. 'Do you see this wonderful valley?' he asked the crew. 'Well, this is where hell begins.'

In the Spanish Bookshop in Paris Buñuel found *Les Jurdes: Etude de Géographie Humaine*, written in 1927 by Maurice Legendre as a doctoral thesis for the School for Advanced Spanish Studies. Buñuel knew Legendre, then director of the French Institute of Madrid, through his daughter Aliette, who was an *escudero* of the Order of Toledo. Legendre's facts and the poetic style of Unanumo, some of whose phrases turned up in the commentary for Buñuel's film, provided the basis for *Las Hurdes*, known outside Spain as *Land Without Bread*.

Buñuel's team had all the hallmarks of a Communist cell. Lotar shot it, Unik wrote the commentary (*Vogue* also commissioned a three-part article on his experiences), and Sanchez Ventura and Ramon Acin were assistant directors. There was no shortage of helpers behind the scenes. In a revolution led not by politicians but by writers and journalists,

---

* Buñuel always called the 20,000 an 'investment', and paid it back to Acin's daughters after the war.

Buñuel was bound to know many of the hierarchy personally. Gregorio Maranon had been at the Resi; it was he who declared Buñuel's youthful torso 'perfect'. Juan Negrin, Finance Minister and eventual Prime Minister of the Republic, had been his professor of physiology. Luis Araquistain, right-hand man of Civil War Prime Minister Largo Caballero and his ambassador to France, was an ex-art critic who had belonged to the Ultraista *peña* in Madrid. Health Secretary Marcelino Pascua, later the Republic's ambassador to Moscow and Paris, was in the Order of Toledo, and Luis's old friend Pepe Moreno Villa, with whom Jeanne had once flirted, was director of the Royal Library.

Buñuel used his connections. Pascua gave him a letter of introduction to the authorities, as did Ricardo Urueta, Director of Fine Arts. Lorca and Ugarte were also unwittingly recruited. The Barraca planned a Holy Week tour to the north-west, taking in Salamanca, the university town only 100 kilometres from Las Hurdes, so the crew travelled that far with them in an old Fiat Luis bought for 4000 pesetas.

From there they headed for Las Batuecas, the largest town of Las Hurdes Bajas, arriving on 20 April. After a week of research, they shot their first material on the 28th. For the next three weeks they would drive two hours into the mountains every day, then hump the camera equipment over mountain tracks to their location. Luis, already a keen mechanic, repaired the car when it broke down. By 22 May, after only one quick trip back to Madrid by Buñuel, they were finished.

From its opening, *Las Hurdes* wears its political heart on its sleeve. A map shows the area's closeness to Salamanca, 'the centre of high culture'. The Church, traditionally the source of education and social services, has abandoned Las Hurdes. All that remains are roofless churches and abbeys, including the Carmelite convent built in 1599 to drive away the area's evil spirits. In some churches, remarks the commentary, the bell is still rung every day at noon.

The Republic is even less in evidence, although the importance of education to new Spain is represented by the schoolteacher in the tiny village on which the film focuses. He is the only source of enlightenment, symbolized by the bread he hands to the children every day. Lotar's camera lingers on young/old faces ravaged by starvation and sickness as they watch a boy write on the blackboard, 'Respect the property of others', then tilts up to the incongruous print of a girl in a crinoline, an irony underlined in Unik's commentary.

Without religion, the *hurdaños* have reverted to more primitive traditions. The first major scene in *Las Hurdes* is a wedding in the village of La Alberca where the men participate in an ancient sacrificial game. A live chicken is suspended from a cord across the street and riders compete to tear off its head. In the village, a dead baby, there being no priest, is buried by the villagers without religious ceremony. In the absence of electricity, Lotar had to light the interiors of the windowless stone cottages with burning brands, the smoke of which adds to the medieval atmosphere.

Apart from the few terraced fields by the rivers, agriculture was unknown in Las Hurdes Altas. Since the locals superstitiously refused to kill the wild goats, eating them only if one fell to its death, everyone lived on pork, encouraging deficiency diseases. The only export was a bitter local honey that had to be hauled out by donkey. During the long trip the primitive containers sometimes broke, drawing bees from miles around. Doused with honey, the pack animal was stung to death. Lotar filmed such an episode, showing first the donkey twitching under attack, then its head crawling with bees and finally the body torn by a dog. Resonances of the donkey in *Un Chien Andalou* and the hand crawling with ants are unmistakable.

Buñuel is silent on whether he engineered this sequence, although he did fake the scene of a goat falling from a cliff. A puff of smoke is visible at the corner of the frame, and Luis admitted that he shot the donkey with his pistol. In fact someone else probably shot it. For a man who could watch the pain of animals with unconcern, Buñuel was extremely squeamish about killing them himself. On *The Young One*, when a rabbit needed to be shot, it was his son Juan Luis who fired. Years later, the obvious use of a rubber rat in a trap for a scene for *That Obscure Object of Desire* where a real one would have been more convincing earned him a citation from the French equivalent of the RSPCA. Buñuel was pleased, but Juan Luis and his cousin Pedro Christian, Conchita's son, compiled a list of the animals and insects slaughtered in his films. It made a respectable menagerie.

In Madrid, since there were no Moviolas, Buñuel edited his footage on a kitchen table with a razor blade and magnifying glass. Lotar complained of his penny-pinching insistence on conserving film, but the main problem seems to have been that some footage, possibly because of a camera malfunction, is out of focus. Two shots in the completed film, both looking down a cliff, are still badly blurred, and Buñuel said that he rejected many much worse, leaving four reels of offcuts.

He would always insist that *Las Hurdes* was essentially Surrealist, and although he meant the argument to counter accusations of propaganda, it is true that, even when trying to make a didactic film, he could not deny his nature. Its cut-aways to snakes, toads and insects, the cruelty to animals and the morbidity implicit in shots of dead or dying children manifest Buñuel's lifelong preoccupations. Nor did politics blind him to bourgeois pleasures. In Las Bajas Hurdes the team stayed in the deconsecrated Carmelite convent which now operated as an inn. Set in a leafy valley, with nineteen chapels, beds for twenty people, superb orchards and a mineral spring, the place so impressed Buñuel that he tried to buy it. The owner only wanted 150,000 pesetas, which Luis hoped his mother would advance, but war broke out before they could close a deal. This was just as well, since property owners were among the first victims of the death squads.

Buñuel finished *Las Hurdes* quickly, but not quickly enough. In the 1933 elections, the right won a majority. Militant Fascist groups mushroomed, soon to coalesce into a powerful force. On 28 November Ugarte wrote to Lorca, who was in Argentina, that the Barraca was having trouble getting its grant from the new administration. The following year it was halved. The right-wing press stigmatized the troupe as homosexual intellectuals perverting the peasantry with 'corrupt foreign-inspired customs', displays of 'shameful promiscuity' and 'Jewish Marxism' – rhetoric almost identical to that used against *L'Age d'Or*. The tide was running against the Republican cause and its propaganda.

Not waiting for a censorship certificate, which would have almost certainly been refused, Buñuel held an invitation screening of *Las Hurdes* at the same Cine de la Prensa where *L'Age d'Or* had its Spanish premiere. There was no sound system, so he read the commentary, with Brahms's 4th Symphony for background. The response was as cool and muted as the music. Not only was *Las Hurdes* less audacious than *L'Age d'Or*; its anarchist tone made many viewers uneasy.

Still hoping for censor clearance, Acin persuaded Buñuel to show the film to Gregorio Maranon. This was a miscalculation. Harried by accusations that the Republicans were trying to undermine the 'real' Spain with foreign trash, the man who first drew attention to the *Hurdaños'* plight told Luis that his film was negative and pessimistic. Why had he not shown the regional dances with their seventeenth-century costumes? As for a land without bread, he insisted he had seen cartloads of wheat on the roads there. Buñuel accepted this response with his usual irony, and continued to show *Las Hurdes* to workers' groups, though it would be decades before it was screened theatrically in Spain.

16

'All around the barren hills of Aragon
Announce our testing has begun.
Here what the Seventh Congress said,
If true, if false, is live or dead,
Speaks in the Oviedo Mauser's tone.'
– John Cornford, *Full Moon at Trierz: Before the Storming of Huesca.*

Although it had not been screened publicly, *Las Hurdes* had the effect of lumping Buñuel with the anarchists. He soon broke with them, however, alarmed by their fanaticism and unpredictability. Ramon Acin described how his comrades, when the Communists offered them evidence of three police informers in their ranks, refused to act. 'We prefer stoolies to Communists,' they said. Buñuel severed his connections in 1934 but he was in no hurry publicly to endorse Communism. When Antonio Roces urged him to join the Spanish Party, he excused himself, saying he belonged to the French Party and could not switch without its permission. He did, however, as insurance, coax from the novelist Ramon Sender an ID card for the UGT, least militant of the Communist unions.

Even fifty years later, Buñuel remained evasive about his political stance at the time. Asked if he actively fought for the Republic, he admitted: 'Very little. I did do something, but I prefer not to deal with it here.' In fact he stayed on the fence. Intellectually he supported the left, but his family and education, not to mention the growing excesses of the Republic, inclined him to the moderates. There were professional reasons as well for remaining unaligned. In what became known as the 'Two Black Years' from December 1933 to February 1936, the new government of Alejandro Lerroux and José Maria Gil Robles, by encouraging private enterprise and making covert alliances with the Army, the Church and the Fascists, reversed much of Azana's socialization and, in doing so, encouraged Spain's struggling film industry.

*

Since Luis's return from America, Jeanne had continued to work at the Spanish Bookshop, studying shorthand and typing in her spare time. Almost resigned to their celibate relationship, she was astonished when, in January 1934, Luis announced that they would marry. However, he insisted that the wedding must take place entirely on his terms. It would be a civil ceremony, without guests or reception, and must remain a secret even from her parents. Dutifully Jeanne kept her mouth shut, but as French law requires banns to be posted outside the local *mairie*, her father quickly found out. He went straight to a bistro for a few drinks before breaking the news to his wife who, like him, had dreamed of a white wedding and the customary banquet.

Luis told Jeanne he could spend only one day in Paris. From the station he went straight to the *mairie* of the 20th *arrondissement* where they were married with Hernando and Loulou Viñes and a passing stranger as witnesses. Jeanne insisted they stop at a Photomaton for pictures. The snaps show her as delighted, Luis sullen. After lunch at the Cochon de Lait near the Odéon Theatre, Luis left to meet Aragon and Sadoul, then caught the night train. Next day, Jeanne bought her own wedding ring, since Luis did not hold with such bourgeois trifles.

One would like to think that Luis had some pressing reason for marrying with what was, for Jeanne and her family, humiliating speed, but he invalidated the obvious one, a desire to avoid meeting the Surrealists or the Communists, by calling on Aragon and Sadoul. Offhandedness, even cruelty, characterized most of his early married life, but he may have acted from his conception of principle; the Permanent Revolutionary, loyal to a Higher Cause. Perhaps his formal nature simply rebelled at the thought of a French wedding reception. The sweating crowd, the baffling introductions to scores of cousins and aunts, the drunken toasts with children chasing one another underfoot may have seemed unendurable.

The larger question, of why he got married at all, remains unanswerable. Friends insist that Luis and Jeanne were a life-long happy couple. But Jeanne's own reminiscences suggest a stormier relationship, strained by Luis's long absences and sexual eccentricities. Buñuel himself gave no reason for his change of heart about marriage. He may simply have acted, not for the first time, on impulse.

Jeanne spent a month in Paris getting a new passport in her married name, then followed Luis to Madrid. Her disillusion with marriage intensified when she found they would be living at the Residencia.

She endured its undergraduate atmosphere for three months, sitting through the post-lunch and post-dinner *peñas* and looking interested, even though all-male society bored her and she understood almost no

Spanish. She took to slipping away for long periods on the pretext of going to the toilet, until Lorca commented rudely, 'If you had to get married, Luis, why did you have to marry a pisser?'

She also got to know her mother-in-law and sisters-in-law. Doña Maria asked directly if she and Luis had slept together before they were married, and was surprised that they had not. She expected more from Paris, and her son. She gave Jeanne a *diamanté* watch, the traditional gift to a new wife, and some useful advice. 'Always tell Luis "Yes", then do what *you* want. This what I used to do with Don Leonardo and we were very happy.'

Meanwhile, Buñuel had found a job. Sound cinema had finally arrived in Spain after an embarrassing delay. At the first screening of *The Jazz Singer* Ramon Gómez de la Serna had come on stage in blackface to explain that Hollywood's first partial talkie would be projected silent; nobody had yet installed sound equipment. But in 1932 Fox and Warner Brothers had begun dubbing in Madrid, and Warners hired Luis as supervisor. He stayed with them for ten months, well paid but underemployed.

Meanwhile, Ricardo Urgoiti's chain of independent cinemas was foundering. New Spain wanted escapism, not foreign art, and he survived on Disney cartoons. Buñuel suggested more commercial features.

'Impossible,' said Urgoiti. 'The Hollywood studios have the business sewn up.'

'Then make your own!' Madrid was littered with bankrupt studios, hundreds of actors were unemployed, and cheap comedies and melodramas were thick on the ground.

'Where does the money come from?' Urgoiti asked. Exasperated, Buñuel offered to coax 150,000 pesetas, half the budget of the first feature, out of Doña Maria. 'And so I became a producer,' he said. 'A demanding and sometimes shady one.'

For years Buñuel refused to acknowledge the four examples of what he called '*cine nefando*' ('abominable cinema') he made for Filmofono, as Urgoiti christened his company. This was not a retroactive decision, based on their low quality; from the start, it had been agreed his name would be kept off the films. Buñuel's usual self-effacement came into it, but he was also intent on proving something both to the Spaniards and to himself on the purely professional level. 'While in Hollywood,' speculates John Hopewell, probably accurately, 'Buñuel became fascinated by American work methods . . . [He] wanted to play at Hollywood in Madrid. Filmofono [. . .] was an experiment in production; punctuality, eight-hour days, lunch breaks, rehearsals before shooting, one take per scene, and all power to the producer.'

At the end of the summer Sadoul came to Spain and Buñuel took him to Toledo. Sadoul immediately noticed Buñuel's almost mystical attitude to the city. Garaging his car in a Spanish/Moorish ruin like some medieval pilgrim, he led him on one of his midnight pub-crawls in search of unquiet spirits.

Jeanne did not accompany them. In July Luis had sent her back to Paris to close his apartment. With no money for helpers, she shifted the heavy furniture herself. After she felt a sharp pain while straining at a large wardrobe, her doctor confirmed she was pregnant and warned that more hard work might lose her the baby. She spent the next five months in bed at her parents' house; plenty of time to study Luis's list of acceptable names for the child, all of them female, since girls ran in both families. In the event he had wasted his time because the child born on 9 November was a boy, whom Jeanne, in a rare moment of independence, christened in a combination of both their names, Juan Luis.

For the first Filmofono production, Eduardo Ugarte suggested *Don Quintin el Amargao (Don Quintin the Bitter)*, a play by his father-in-law Carlos Arniches y Barrera, which he had adapted with Jose Estremerain into a *zarzuela*, a melodrama with songs. It had been a hit in Margarita Xirgu's stage production with Alfonso Munoz, whom they hired to star.

Don Quintin is a struggling middle-aged salesman who leaves his young wife and baby girl in the city to check out a provincial job located by his best friend. The train is stopped by a landslide and he returns home unexpectedly to find the helpful friend in bed with his wife. In the resulting brawl she tells Quintin he isn't the father of little Maria, so he kidnaps the child, abandoning her at random on the doorstep of a fisherman's cottage. The owners bring her up with their own daughter, Jovita, a talented singer and dancer. Meanwhile Don Quintin, embittered, has opened a cabaret, to which Jovita and inevitably Maria find their way for a tearful reconciliation.

With its romantic sub-plots and the wife's death-bed revelation that Quintin is indeed the father of his baby girl, *Don Quintin* gave the *Madrileño* audience just the diversion and reassurance it needed, while the nihilism of Don Quintin's character and the celebration of chance and coincidence harmonized with Buñuel's cynicism. Years later he remade the story in Mexico, virtually unchanged.

As he trawled Spain for competent technicians and actors, Luis realized that assembling a Hollywood-style team in Madrid would take months. Those he did recruit, mostly old friends of himself and Ugarte, were Communists. Jose Maria Beltran, who shot all four Filmofono films, had worked for years with Carlos Velo, the left-wing documentarist who had arranged the special ants for *Un Chien Andalou*. He brought with him Velo's sound-men Leon Lucas de la Pena and Antonio Roces, the latter a high-ranking Party cadre.

It was harder to find a director. *Don Quintin* is credited to Luis Marquina, an assistant sound-man who found himself promoted to director at a salary of 1000 pesetas. A poem by Marquina's father Eduardo, a now-forgotten verse dramatist, had driven Buñuel to wreck Tono's Christmas tree in Hollywood, but Marquina senior was artistic adviser to a number of star/producers, most notably Margarita Xirgu, who created the starring roles in Lorca's *Yerma* and *Blood Wedding*, so Buñuel buried his resentment and employed the son.

Because of Marquina's incompetence, Luis was increasingly pressed into the role of producer/director/writer. Beltran maintained that Buñuel 'did everything: contracts, casting, script (in collaboration with Ugarte), rehearsals, lighting corrections, camera angles and, naturally, direction and editing. We were no more than humble students.' While this is an exaggeration, Buñuel was often on the set. He showed Marquina how to light the whole set and pan with action in the Hollywood B-movie style rather than waste time relighting new set-ups. His lead actress Ana-Maria Custodio, a close friend and member of the Order of Toledo, was also ordered to drop her ladylike style and ham it up.

It would have cost only a few pesetas more to retake shots where sound was inaudible, the actors fumbled a line, or where Jose Maria Torres's admittedly impressive city street sets rocked or boomed hollowly, but Buñuel was unrelenting. 'He counted up every fraction of every minute,' Urgoiti recalled, 'every metre of raw film. I stayed in my office, waiting for him to come and ask for more money. Instead, after three weeks, he came in with the finished film and part of the money I had given him. "Take the change," he said. "Keep it for the next one."'

For Buñuel, bringing the film in on time and under budget had been an act of will. To someone who had thumbed his nose at the mighty MGM, anything should be possible. But he paid a high cost in physical terms. Long hours and heavy lifting brought on the sciatica that would plague him for the rest of his life.

By Hollywood standards these films are raw, showing the technical problems Buñuel faced in the cramped and primitive CEA and Roptence studios, his three-week shooting schedule and penny-pinching technique. Audiences, however, were so delighted to see Spanish stories and *Madrileño* actors on the screen, rather than American comedies remade by Frenchmen with Mexican actors, that the first two were as successful on film as on stage. Buñuel made enough from *Don Quintin* alone to buy himself a couple of acres outside the city and to move into a decent seven-room apartment.

The space was needed because Jeanne had finally brought Juan Luis home. Her arrival was as fraught as the marriage in general. The moment he heard about the birth of his son, Luis had badgered Jeanne to return but, despite repeated cables and postcards, she refused to travel in the winter with a small baby. She also wanted to spend her birthday with her parents who, cheated of a wedding, suggested a gala christening. Luis angrily vetoed this. Juan Luis was not to be baptized. 'No son of mine is going to be brought up a Catholic! I don't want his head filled with devils and hells.'

It was not until 10 March 1935 that Jeanne reluctantly boarded the train to Spain, instructing Georgette to cable Luis they were on their way. Arriving in Madrid, she was first surprised, then alarmed, not to see him on the platform. Surrounded by suitcases, she waited for hours, helpless without the address of the new apartment. Fortunately she remembered Conchita's address and took a cab there. 'Woman, this is an apparition!' said Conchita. She and her husband, Pedro Garcia de Orcasitas, put Jeanne in a taxi. Luis was astonished to see her. He had seen no wire from Georgette, he said – perhaps not surprisingly, given the spasmodic strikes that affected public services in Republican Spain.

Luis was moved to see his boy, but the marriage immediately resumed its customary distance. Jeanne, exhausted, wanted to lie down. Luis took her through the large apartment and indicated a door. 'This is your room,' he told her. 'I have the one opposite.' Throughout their marriage they never shared a bedroom.

'This is the way our married life started,' Jeanne wrote later. 'Luis was making movies and seeing his friends. From time to time he would go out at night – with whom? I was in the house with my son, adapting myself to my new life.'

The 'with whom?' was rhetorical. Within a few months of arriving in Madrid, Jeanne found traces of lipstick on Luis's clothes. Casting the second Filmofono movie, *La Hija de Juan Simon (The Daughter of Juan Simon)*, another comedy with music adapted with Ugarte from a traditional stage play, he had fallen for an eighteen-year-old he called 'Pepita'.

Right. Luis (right) as a baby with his mother and sister.

Below: Buñuel, seven years old, in the uniform of the Jesuit College, Zaragoza.

Centre, right: Buñuel (left) aged twelve, Zaragoza, 1912.

Bottom, left: Don Leonardo Buñuel, c. 1918.

Bottom, right: Buñuel (left) spars with an unidentified friend on the Residencia exercise track, 1918.

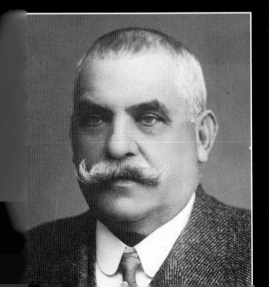

Left: Buñuel in costume for Jacques Feyder's *Carmen*, Paris, 1920.
Below: Buñuel and Federico Garcia Lorca in a carnival plane at the San Antonio de la Florida fair, Madrid, 1923.
(BFI Stills, Posters and Designs)
Opposite, top: The Order of Toledo, 1924. Left to right: Pepin Bello, Juan Moreno Villa, Maria Luisa Buñuel, Luis Buñuel, Salvador Dali and José Maria Hinojosa.
Opposite, middle: Buñuel (left) dressed as a nun, with Jeanne and Georgette Rucar and Juan Vicens de la Slave, Paris, 1925.
Opposite, bottom: Buñuel (second from right) with Josephine Baker and cast and crew of *La Sirène des Tropiques*, August 1927.

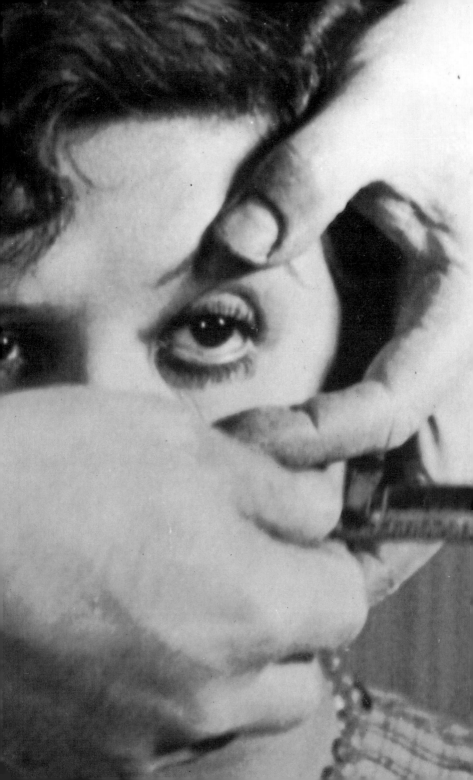

Un Chien Andalou, 1929
Opposite: The razor's edge.
(Museum of Modern Art Stills Archive
Left: Buñuel clowns with Salvador Dali and
Dali's sister, Ana Maria, during the writing
of the film, Figueras, February, 1929.
Above: Buñuel acting in the film. *(MMASA*
Below: The ass in the piano. *(MMASA)*

Previous spread: Dalí by Buñuel and vice versa at Cadaques, August 1929, during the scripting of *L'Age d'Or.* (Cinemathèque Française)

Left: On the set of *L'Age d'Or,* March 1930. Standing, from left: Gaston Modot, Lya Lys, Jacques Brunius. Seated, from left: Claude Heymann, Buñuel, Jeanne Rucar.
Centre, left: Buñuel with Georges Auric (left and Charles de Noailles, Hyères, 1930.
Bottom, left: Salvador Dali and Gala Eluard at Cadaques, August 1930, shortly after they met for the first time.
Below: Buñuel and Jeanne on holiday in Santander, 1930.

Right: René Crevel, Pierre Unik and Buñuel, Paris, c. 1933.
Below: Luis and Jeanne on their wedding day, 1934.
Bottom, left: Buñuel, a harassed young father, with his sons during a New York heatwave, 1940.
Bottom right: Buñuel shows off the quarry of the hunt at the home of MoMA head Alfred. E. Barr, c. 1940. *(MMASA)*

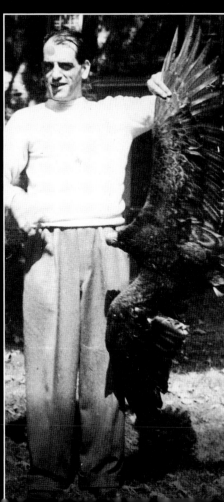

Left: Bunuel at the Museum of Modern Art, New York, early 1940s. *(BFI)*

Below, left: Salvador Dali in the Jardin du Luxembourg, Paris, 1954.

Below, right: Luis Buñuel and his mother, reunited in Pau, 1954. *(Cinemathèque Française)*

Bottom: Buñuel on the set of *The Criminal Life of Archibaldo de la Cruz*, 1955 with (left to right) unidentified, Jeanne Buñuel, the dummy of Miroslava Stern, Miroslava herself, Jose Ignacio Mantecon, Rafael Buñuel and (seated right) Eduardo Ugarte. *(MMASA)*

Above: Fernando Rey contemplates the shoes of his dead wife in *Viridiana*. *(MMASA)*
Below: Silvia Pinal in *Viridiana*. *(MMASA)*

Above: Beggars assume the pose of The Last Supper in the most sacrilegious scene of *Viridiana*, 1961. *(MMASA)*

Simon of the Desert, 1965

Left: Silvia Pinal as the hermaphrodite Christ. *(MMASA)*
Below: Simon (Claudio Brook) and the herdsman (Jesus Fernandez). *(MMASA)*
Opposite, top: Silvia Pinal tempts Simon.

Opposite, bottom: Auguste Carrière as the Jansenist nun in *The Milky Way,* 1968. *(MMASA)*

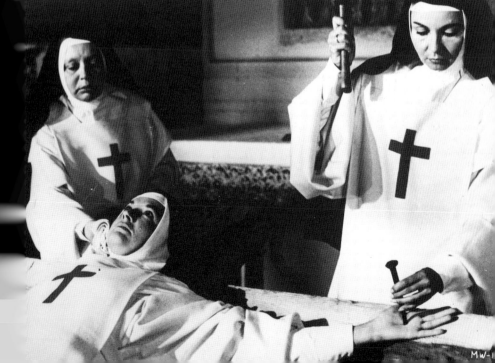

MW-1

 Above: Directing *Belle de Jour*, 1967.
Below: Buñuel directs the rape of Severine (Catherine Deneuve). *(M M A S A)*

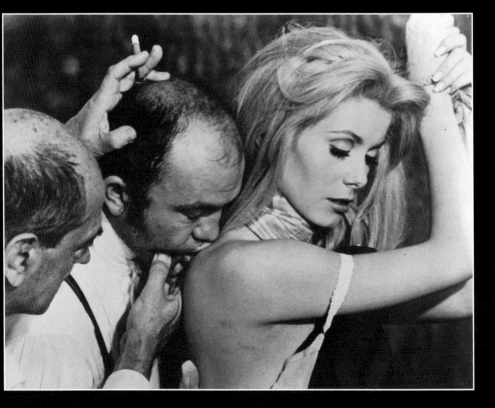

Above: Jeanne holds a toy pistol to Buñuel's head at the end of an obviously alcoholic lunch, Mexico City, late 1970s.
Below: President Miguel de la Madrid (left) with Jeanne Buñuel and Fr Julian Pablo, February 1983.

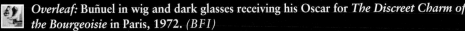

Overleaf: Buñuel in wig and dark glasses receiving his Oscar for *The Discreet Charm of the Bourgeoisie* in Paris, 1972. *(BFI)*

The affair took place mostly in the countryside, away from the rumour mill of Madrid. Luis arranged a mountain picnic and they danced in a café at Bombilla, but although he held her hand, kissed her cheek, even hugged her, his upbringing made it impossible to consummate the relationship. The idyll ended when a friend told him that, throughout the romance, he had been sleeping with Pepita himself. Tormented by jealousy, Luis took her on a drive and, as a test, proposed she become his exclusive mistress for 2000 pesetas a month. She agreed, and they finally lay down naked together, but Luis remained impotent. They went dancing out of town at Puerta de Hierro, where Luis abruptly announced he knew about her double life and left her by the road. He never saw her again.

Jeanne packed a bag and kept it hidden in her room, telling herself she could leave any time, but in reality, penniless, alone and saddled with a baby, she was powerless. Even in the new Spain, women remained second-class citizens. Every day, as Luis and his friends argued politics over lunch, Jeanne was told to go to her room or to the kitchen.

She saw her mother-in-law once a week and became friendly with Luis's brother Leonardo but when she tried to call on Conchita, Orcasitas, a mentally unstable doctor, made it clear she was not welcome. Among other things, he resented the fact that Juan Luis was more robust than his own children. Conchita and her four sons could see Jeanne and Juan Luis only in Madrid's main park, the Retiro, when they went walking in the afternoons, but Jeanne was forbidden to visit their house, nor could Conchita call on her.

Through Conchita, Jeanne met a French girl and went to her home for coffee, but when she asked Luis if she could visit them at home, he angrily refused. Even their maid revealed hidden antagonisms. Jeanne surprised her slapping Juan Luis. When she demanded an explanation, the maid snapped, 'Because he's a pig of a bourgeois, like you.' In microcosm Jeanne was experiencing the enmities and jealousies that would explode in Civil War.

In June, Doña Maria phoned Jeanne and told her to get Juan Luis ready for a promenade, and sent a car. Instead of going to her mother-in-law's house, however, the driver took them to a church where she was waiting with a priest. Jeanne protested, but Doña Maria was adamant.

'Girl, be quiet! Luis has nothing to do with this. The baby must be baptized. I'm the grandmother and I'm responsible before God.'

Juan Luis was baptized with Doña Maria as the godmother and the priest as godfather. Jeanne dreaded having to break the news to Luis, but that evening Doña Maria rang and told him herself. His reaction was predictable. 'He insulted his mother on the telephone,' said Jeanne, 'and

I can't tell you the words, because they were horrible. After that he turned his rage on me.'

For months he refused to talk to her. He relented only when she woke in pain one night and discovered an ominous lump in her stomach. For the first time he showed some compassion. 'Poor little thing,' he said. 'Tomorrow we'll go to the doctor.' By then, the lump had disappeared. However, Luis never really forgave what he regarded as a far greater betrayal of their marriage than his love affairs.

Despite working in a political minefield, Buñuel was blossoming as a producer. A Communist film company devoted to quick money-makers was less of a contradiction in the Spain of 1934 than it might have been at any other time and place. The crew instantly organized itself on Marxist/Leninist lines, with which, fortunately, Buñuel's political credentials and policy of equal salaries accorded totally. Nevertheless some propaganda crept into even these escapist productions. Hammers and sickles and anti-Azana graffiti are scratched on the walls of a prison in *La Hija de Juan Simon*, and Buñuel himself makes a brief appearance as one of the convicts harmonizing on Angelillo's song yearning for his freedom.

Enrique Herreros, the studio publicist, cheekily advertised the film as 'like the music of de Falla and the Gypsy Romances of Garcia Lorca – the triumph of the popular roots of culture'. In a roundabout way, this was true. Iberia had a long literary tradition of novels and plays which traded on torture, witchcraft, gypsy curses, crumbling castles, randy monks and dishonoured nuns. Half the British four-volume novels of the Gothic period were set in this phoney Spain, and so-called *españolada* plays which exploited this ambience, though usually written for foreign audiences, had a large local following, especially in times of national stress.

Buñuel, though he agreed that *La Hija de Juan Simon* was 'horrendous', had already betrayed in his Toledo shenanigans a taste for antique fantasy, the more irrational the better. Again, it was a style he would return to in his Mexican films, particularly his version of *Wuthering Heights*, *Abysses of Passion*, and in his unfilmed *The Monk*. In the 1940s Buñuel praised ghost movies like William Dieterile's *Portrait of Jenny* and the British anthology *Dead of Night*, where atmosphere has the ascendancy over sense.

Juan Simon, a gravedigger, opens the film, digging a grave in a picturesquely gloomy cemetery and singing the show's most popular song, the lugubrious *Milonga*, in which he laments that he buries his own heart in the earth.

His daughter Carmela is lured away to Madrid by a suave seducer, takes a job in a café and becomes pregnant. Just as she is about to slide into damnation, Juan Simon and Carmela's faithful boyhood admirer Angel (played by the Communist flamenco dancer Angelillo) save her, Angel by winning fame for his flamenco and Juan Simon by bamboozling everyone with a machine he is supposed to have invented that will register the 'Sixth Sense' of characters and foretell the future. It is actually a movie projector.

As a theatre piece, *La Hija de Juan Simon* had collected subplots and setpieces along the way until the text bore as little discernible relation to its original as a contemporary British pantomime *Aladdin* to *The Arabian Nights*. Architect and designer Nemesio Sobrevilla had mounted the most successful recent stage production, so Ugarte hired him to direct the film. It was a disastrous decision. His design borrowed from German Expressionism – the graveyard scene, though it is certain that Sobrevilla shot it, not Buñuel, might be a parody of *Chute de la Maison Usher* – and he staged musical numbers to match it, including a flamenco routine in a cabaret where the teenage Carmen Amaya, later an international star, makes an appearance. After a week's shooting he was well behind the tight schedule and Buñuel, having failed to bully him into a faster pace, declared him a madman and had Urgoiti fire him.

Ugarte directed a few scenes, then begged Buñuel to take over until they found a new 'front'. Though in agony again from sciatica, Luis agreed. He worked until José Luis Saenz de Heredia, a young director who had made his first feature the previous year, a comedy about the movies called *Patricio Miro a Una Estrella (Patricia Looked at a Star)*, heard there might be work at Filmofono.

Fernando Remacha, the musical director and one of the steering committee, asked how much experience he had.

'Very little,' Saenz de Heredia admitted. 'I've directed a film, but I don't know much.'

'Good,' Remacha said. 'I'll be frank with you. It is true that we need a director, but more in name than in fact. The man who is really going to make the film is Buñuel.'

'I just want to learn the job, that's all,' Saenz de Heredia said. 'Dealing with a talent like Buñuel will be all the better.'

Saenz de Heredia said he offered to work for nothing but since Buñuel insisted everyone be paid, he got 1500 pesetas and credit as director on this and the next Filmofono film; credentials that he built into a successful post-war career. The fact that he was the cousin of Primo de

Rivera, founder of the Spanish Fascist Party, didn't hurt, and probably had something to do with his Filmofono hiring.

On 6 May 1935 the right revealed its hand when Gil Robles became Minister of War and appointed Francisco Franco his chief of staff. All over Spain the liberal arts were stifled. In the summer the Barraca's funding stopped altogether. Filmofono, however, continued to work. Hurriedly Buñuel and Ugarte put together a script for *Quien Me Quiere a Mi? (Who Loves Me?)*. Saenz de Heredia was by then skilful enough to direct without help, but perhaps because the script was for the first time an original with a topical subject, divorce, which Azana had liberalized, the film was one of Buñuel's few commercial failures. As John Hopewell says, 'sensing that Spain was falling apart, Spanish audiences sought a cinema of national archetypes which were seemingly impervious to change and allowed Spanish spectators, through their identification with stock racial models, a sense of solidarity'. Nobody wanted to know about the real world, which was too visible all around them.

In December 1935 the government fell again. Mussolini had invaded Abyssinia and Hitler's power was growing. The right wing was coalescing in a National Front, and in response, on 15 January 1936, the left, excluding the anarchists, created a Popular Front. Nobody any longer doubted that the conflict could only be settled in blood.

Herreros had optimistically announced sixteen Filmofono productions for 1936/7. Buñuel would have revived *Wuthering Heights* and adapted *Fortunata y Jacinta* by the late nineteenth-century realist Benito Perez Galdos, whose *Nazarin* and *Tristana* he would later film. He also planned a version of Pio Baroja's trilogy *La Lucha por la Vida* about the Madrid slums which prefigures *Los Olvidados*, and Ramon de Valle-Inclan's *Tirano Banderas*. This ambitious and liberal programme was, however, to die with the whimper of *Centinela Alerta! (Sentinel, Alert!)*.

Ugarte and Buñuel went back to Arniches for their story, a parody of the military. Word had spread of Buñuel's private studio, and a trickle of Frenchmen got in touch. One was the young photographer Henri Cartier-Bresson, whom Luis had met in Paris and who fancied himself as a movie director. G.W. Pabst had already refused to apprentice him, and Buñuel did the same.

He was not so dismissive of Jean Gremillon, director of the critically acclaimed *Remorques*, offering him 15,000 francs to make *Centinela, Alerta!*, with the option not to have his name on it. Gremillon agreed and, since Buñuel, who shot a few scenes when Gremillon had toothache, did not care to sign the film either, it was simply released as

'Produccion Filmofono number 4'. When it opened, however, in August 1936, at the Avenida Cinema in Madrid, Buñuel's Spanish career was over and Filmofono already a memory. Civil War gripped the country. In September Buñuel would leave for Paris and an exile of twenty-five years.

17

' . . . But today the struggle.
Today the deliberate increase in the chances of death.
The conscious acceptance of guilt in the necessary murder.'
– W. H. Auden, 'Spain'

On 16 February 1936 Spain voted a narrow parliamentary majority to Azana, and the left, desperate to establish itself while its ebbing power remained, rushed even its most immoderate policies into law. Catalonia was given limited independence. The Institute of Agrarian Reform dismembered the big estates and threw the pieces to the peasants. Employers were required to rehire anyone they had fired. The imprisoned were set free: not only political detainees but convicts, mental patients, even lepers, though the inmates of the Fontilles leprosarium sensibly refused to leave.

Under the new order, a mere three hours' work a day earned every citizen the right to food, clothing, education, amusement, transport and medical attention. In his essay 'Barcelona', Cyril Connolly described how, in the Catalan capital, 'the [anarchist] initials, CNT and FAI, are everywhere. They have taken over all the hotels, restaurants, cafés, trains, taxis, and means of communication. Their first act was to abolish the tip as being incompatible with the dignity of those who receive it.'

Watching a workers' paradise in the throes of parturition moved Buñuel deeply. He and Elie Faure, the authority on Spanish painting, had stood at a hotel window a few weeks before and wept as they watched a peasant army with pitchforks and sickles march by. But when law and order collapsed under an avalanche of ill-considered reform and simple revenge, and deputy Margarita Nelken called for a revolution of 'huge flames which can be seen all over the world and waves of blood which turn the seas red', Buñuel and other moderates became apprehensive.

Within a month of the elections, seventeen churches and eleven convents, thirty-three right-wing clubs, ten newspapers and twenty-two other buildings were torched. Fifty people died and 200 were injured in factional fighting. In Calanda the CNT executed eighty-two landowners and Catholics, including the Dominican monks at the convent on the edge of town.

In an official report, anarchist propagandist Agustin Souchy proudly cited Calanda as a model community. 'What was once the church is now a food warehouse [. . .] The new meat market is in the annexe, hygienic and elegant, such as the village has never known. No purchases are made with money. The women receive meat in exchange for coupons without paying anything or rendering any service [. . .] Collectivists and individualists live peacefully side by side. There are two cafés in the village. One for the individualists, and the other for the collectivists. They can permit themselves the luxury of taking coffee every night [. . .] A splendid expression of the collective spirit is the communal barber shop, where the service is free. The peasants never used to shave. Now nearly all faces are well groomed. Everyone can have a shave twice a week [. . .] Wine is served at the rate of five quarts a week. Food is not lacking.'

To Buñuel it seemed his home town had become a sort of Cockaigne, where peasants lived not in dignity and equality but as surrogate *señoritos*, being shaved and loafing in cafés. He scoffed in particular at the declaration by the town crier that free love now prevailed. Puzzled locals hardly knew what it meant.

Lorca was heard everywhere, both in person and through his work. Alberti and his wife were also militant Popular Front supporters. But life in Madrid was hazardous. 'Politics and the arts had [. . .] become inextricably mixed,' says Ian Gibson, 'and political significance was given to the least word or most apparently trivial action on the part of writers, painters and thinkers.' Identity cards gave one's profession and tax bracket, and anyone with a university degree or earning more than 100,000 pesetas risked being imprisoned or summarily executed. As a hereditary landowner and a film producer, Buñuel was equally at risk from the anarchists, Communists and the right wing, which opened a dossier on him, apparently picturing him as a drug addict, and tagging him for execution. Scared after being caught in a skirmish on the Plaza de la Independencia, he borrowed a rifle but, in an absurdist moment, realized he didn't know which side to shoot at. In embarrassment and confusion he returned the gun and, late in June, alarmed now, sent Jeanne to Paris with Juan Luis.

Saenz de Heredia, who, as Primo de Rivera's cousin, was a prime target for the death squads, had been sleeping in the park rather than risk going home. When the left arrested him, Buñuel went to the Roptence studios and petitioned the workers' soviet to help. The technicians had no grudge against Saenz de Heredia, and with the help of a studio delegate, Buñuel was able to free him. A few days later, to Luis's embarrassment, the director slipped out of Spain and declared himself a Falangist. In 1941, he directed *Raza, El Espiritu de Franco (Race, the Spirit of Franco)*, his own adaptation of a propagandist novel by 'Jaime de Andrade' – actually Franco himself.

Violence continued into the summer. An attempt was made to blow up the home of left-wing leader Francisco Largo Caballero. De Rivera was jailed for the crime and on 13 July two Guardia Civil took Calvo Sotelo, leader of the right, from his home, shot him twice in the back of the head and dumped the body at Madrid's East Cemetery. Three days later Buñuel woke to explosions. A Republican plane was bombing the Army barracks at Montana; Franco had launched a carefully planned military uprising.

In one day his troops seized all of Spanish Morocco and began a march across Spain. 'Black Squads' fanned out through the country, exterminating known Communists and anarchists. Each morning, their night's work littered the shady lanes at Casa Campo, the park on the outskirts of Madrid.

Early in August Ugarte and Buñuel spent a few days with Lorca, camping in sleeping bags at the monastery at El Pauler. Lorca announced he had decided to go back to Granada. Knowing that he would be more vulnerable there than in Madrid, Buñuel tried to talk him out of it. Dali had already tried to persuade Lorca to go to Italy, but he refused both suggestions. On 19 August, in a village near Granada, Lorca was murdered with dozens of other Communists. His body would never be found.

Dali was supposed to have shouted 'Olé!' when he heard the news. Lorca had not been killed for his politics, he said, but 'for reasons of personality, and, like myself, Lorca had personality to spare'. Dali also implied he might have been shot because of his homosexuality. His killer was said to have boasted, 'I put two bullets in his arse for being a queer.' Buñuel was furious at Dali's 'ignoble' suggestion, all the more so because of his own feelings about Lorca. 'The news of his death was a terrific shock,' he wrote in *My Last Breath*. 'Of all the human beings I have known, Federico was the finest. I don't mean his plays or his poetry; I mean him personally. He was his own masterpiece. Whether sitting at the piano imitating Chopin, improvising a pantomime, or acting out a scene from a play, he was irresistible. He read beautifully, and he had passion, youth and joy. When I first met him, at the Residencia, I was an unpolished rustic, interested primarily in sports. He transformed me, introduced me to a wholly different world. He was like a flame.'

Buñuel knew it was only a matter of time before he was picked up. He was saved, he says, by a call early in September from Julio Alvarez del Vayo, foreign minister in the coalition government just formed by Largo Caballero to fight the Fascists. Although officially socialist, Largo Caballero had been forced to cede so much power to the left in return for its support that his administration was essentially Communist. Fortunately for Buñuel, this brought some old acquaintances to power. Pascua was ambassador to Moscow and Luis Araquistain became ambassador to France. Alvarez del Vayo, Buñuel said, simply told him to go to Geneva and take instructions from the embassy there. He immediately caught a train to Port Bou.

At Barcelona, an old friend, José 'Pepe' Bergamin, a writer who contrived to be both Catholic and Republican, boarded the train with an eighteen-year-old militant student, Ricardo Muñoz Suay. Both were on their way to a conference in Geneva. At this point the stories diverge. Muñoz Suay told Max Aub that, over lunch in the dining car, Luis took out a jewelled necklace and said, 'This thing belonged to a countess, a marquise, a bourgeoise, a capitalist, whom I've robbed (or killed) in Madrid.' While Muñoz Suay goggled, Buñuel went on, 'I'm going to Paris. I don't have any money, so I need to sell the collar.' He held it out to Bergamin. 'Would you like to buy it?' Bergamin declined and they went on chatting until they reached the border. An astonished Muñoz Suay attributed the incident to straight-faced Surrealist humour, but never forgot it.

This is perhaps the place to say something about Buñuel's sense of humour.

Michel Piccoli once asked, 'How is Jeanne?'

Buñuel replied, 'She's fine. She has a lover.'

Piccoli laughed, but Buñuel did not, so he stopped. 'And you know him?'

'Yes. It's a priest.'

Piccoli laughed again, but Buñuel just stared. 'There's no need to laugh,' he said, 'because these things happen.'

Fairly sure he was having his leg pulled, Piccoli asked Buñuel the next time he saw him, 'How's your wife's lover?'

Still expressionless, Luis said, 'That's all over. My wife is dead.'

Later, Piccoli visited Buñuel is his Paris apartment at the Hotel l'Aiglon. On the floor was a rug in fake leopard skin.

'Well, there's success for you,' Piccoli said. 'A suite in Paris and a panther skin.'

Buñuel said, 'That's for the little actresses. When I receive them, I make them lie on the floor. Then I cut the carpet around them and they leave with half a coat. That way, they have to come back for the other half.'

Piccoli had never seen Luis so much as flirt with one of his actresses, but his icy calm still made it hard to know if he was joking.

The murdered countess probably belongs to the same imaginary world as Jeanne's lover and the actresses in leopard-skin coats, but Buñuel's tales often had some tenuous connection with fact. He *had* slept with actresses, and the possibility of a romance between Jeanne and a young composer in Mexico was to drive him to threats of murder. It is unlikely that he killed any countesses but quite possible that, far from heading to Geneva on a diplomatic mission, he was simply on the run, having grabbed what portable wealth he could, perhaps from his mother. It is hard to find any other motive for him to be carrying jewels of any kind.

His experience at the border supports this theory. Bergamin and Muñoz Suay, though only representatives of a Barcelona student union, had diplomatic passports with AFI and CNT stamps. Had Buñuel been on an official mission he should have had the same. Instead he carried only his normal passport, which, Bergamin warned, would never satisfy the anarchist border guards. Versions of what happened at Port Bou again differ. Muñoz Suay said Buñuel just breezed through, explaining later that he had snarled, 'I shit on God', and the guards, convinced of his fervent anarchism, passed him. Buñuel prefers a version in which he swore at the three so virulently that they were frightened to delay him. Either way, it is evident he did not carry the credentials one might have expected.

The alacrity with which Buñuel left Spain at the outbreak of war should not be taken to mean that the conflict had little significance for him. On the contrary, no event in his life affected him so profoundly. For the next half-century he would discuss it continually, sharing most of his social life with veterans, fellow Republicans or Communists. It became the water in which he swam. Although he never addressed the war directly on screen, the treacheries it engendered were to become the subject of a dozen films where, as if the event itself were too horrible to regard directly, he viewed in an oblique light the moral decline and institutional evil of totalitarian Spain. Luis Buñuel was maimed by 1936 as much as any amputee.

In Geneva, the Republican ambassador passed him on to Paris. Georgette lent Luis and Jeanne an apartment in square Albin Cachot, not far from the Hôtel des Terrasses, and Luis reported to Araquistain. Paris festered with spies and agents for every Spanish faction, as well as for the British, American and especially the Russian governments. The embassy in rue de la Pépinière was as much part of the Republican front line as the trenches before Madrid. Though technically socialist, France's Popular Front government did not recognize Republican Spain. Money, however, spoke louder than diplomacy. At the start of the war, Spain had 710 metric tons of gold in its reserves. Two hundred tons were immediately shipped to French banks to purchase arms. Franco accused the Republicans of 'pillage' and formally advised France he would demand restitution. Wary of an international brawl and of stirring up his own Communists, Léon Blum closed the border to military traffic on 8 August, though 'non-military' oil from the United States were still let through. Finance minister Juan Negrin promptly shifted Spain's remaining gold to Russia which, once it became the Republic's primary arms supplier, took over large parts of the war effort.

For Araquistain, Buñuel became something between courier, cultural attaché, social secretary and press agent, doing a little spying on the side. Ostensibly he kept track of films made by the various factions, and helped film-makers wanting to shoot in Spain. André Malraux had championed the Loyalists, repeatedly touring the United States to raise funds, and Buñuel was responsible in part for the funding of *L'Espoir* (*Man's Hope*), his feature about fliers in Spain. When Joris Ivens launched Contemporary Historians with Hemingway, Lillian Hellman, Dorothy Parker, Herman Shumlin and Archibald MacLeish, Buñuel issued the permits for him and Hemingway to film *The Spanish Earth*. He also endorsed Ivor Montagu and Norman McLaren to cover the siege of Madrid, and John Dos Passos to research his book *Journey Between Wars*.

Every country had its own private agenda for Spain. Russian propagandists Roman Karmen and Boris Makaseyev were allowed to shoot all over the country on the understanding that they would submit the footage to Paris for vetting. When they, and most of their film, disappeared, Buñuel demanded an explanation from the Soviet ambassador, who told him someone had gone over his head. Almost certainly the Russians never intended clearing their film. Called *Spain* and edited by Esther Shub, an ace compiler of documentary footage, it was not released until 1939, too late to protest its distortions.

Buñuel was not entirely uncreative in these years. With money from the French Communist Party, he supervised the production of a thirty-five-minute documentary, *España 1936*, also known as *Espagne 1936*,

Madrid 1936 and *España Leal, En Armas!* This compilation of available footage, some of it Karmen's, covering the pre-war elections, the riots, parades and finally the war, exists in both French and Spanish versions. It lacks credits, but Jean-Paul Dreyfus claimed he assembled it under the *nom de guerre* 'Jean-Paul le Chanois'. In 1938 Buñuel testified before the Paris union tribunal that he and not Dreyfus produced and supervised the film, and co-authored the commentary with Pierre Unik. He was awarded the credit although, in the 1970s, reluctant to be too closely identified with what is frankly (and officially) Communist propaganda, he said, 'Some books have claimed this film as mine, but that is not the case.'

He was prouder of *Las Hurdes*, which Braunberger undertook to distribute if music and a commentary were added. Araquistain paid, aware that the film could be useful as propaganda. Communists in Britain were soon advertising 'The Film That Answers Franco. The General says there is no Agrarian Problem in Spain. See the truth – stark and horrible in *Land Without Bread*'. Sadoul too retroactively recruited it to the cause, calling it in 1936 'a love song for the living Spain, a cry of hate against the Francos who would like to transform the whole peninsula into an immense Las Hurdes'.* Braunberger did well with the film, but his old habits persisted, and Buñuel had to visit his office with a hammer in his hand and threaten to smash his secretary's typewriter to get even part of what was owed.

Secret Agent Buñuel travelled around Europe and five times to Spain with propaganda leaflets and sometimes large sums of money. When Juan Negrin came to Paris, Luis and the painter Luis Quintanilla were issued with pistols to act as bodyguards. His familiarity with Montparnasse's cafés made him an ideal person to eavesdrop on the *gauchepin* community, a riff-raff mostly of South Americans, some of them freelance assassins under contract to Franco or Stalin. One Colombian who, with Paris as his base, moved around Europe, bombing to order, even showed Buñuel some of his hardware and, for his own reasons, offered to betray his superior, but when Luis told the French police, they ignored it. As long as he only killed outside France, they were indifferent.

Too busy to socialize, Buñuel lost touch with old friends like the Noailles. Breton did call to ask about Péret, rumoured to have been purged as a POUM member, and Luis was able to establish his survival. From time to time rumours circulated of Buñuel's death. Sadoul took the opportunity of an October 1936 review of *Las Hurdes* in *Regards* to note: 'Many papers have announced that Luis Buñuel has been gravely

---

* In fact Franco admired the region and poured aid into it.

wounded on the Guadarrama front. We can refute this news. Buñuel, who struggles with all his strength for the defence of the Spanish Republic, is in excellent health.'

As a matter of business, Buñuel kept up with Communists like Sadoul and Jacques Prévert, who introduced him one day in Les Deux Magots to a dapper Russian on the fringes of movies named Oscar Dancigers. In his pearl-grey fedora and flannel suit, Dancigers did not look anything like a comrade, which was his greatest value to the movement. The meeting would prove useful to Buñuel a decade later, when Dancigers became his producer in Mexico.

Occasionally Luis met Dali, who tried to broker a deal with wealthy English collector Edward James (his lover at the time) to present the loyalists with a bomber. According to Dali, James wanted to swap the plane, then at a Czech airport, for some paintings from the Prado, which he would hold in London until the war ended. If the Republicans won, they would be returned. If not, the government in exile had a bargaining chip and a nest egg.

James remembers the incident differently. He said Dali introduced him to Buñuel in Paris in the second or third week of the Civil War and suggested James buy some planes to be delivered in Czechoslovakia. As security, James would get some El Grecos, to be exhibited at the Royal Academy for the Republican cause. Buñuel took up the matter with Madrid and James approached Kenneth Clark, director of the National Gallery, who said he needed to consult the Louvre, which had made a similar offer, but Alvarez del Vayo vetoed the idea anyway. If exporting Spanish gold was regarded as pillage, he reasoned, how would Spaniards react to mortgaging El Greco?

Luis enjoyed being a secret agent. Telling Jeanne he needed seclusion, he rented them an apartment in suburban Meudon. The house was surrounded with gardens, through which he would sneak each night, gun in hand, in case of ambush. Now that Juan Luis was old enough to shoot, he began training him with an air rifle. Georgette's generous hips offered a target which Luis was too weak to resist and, confident that her girdle was thick enough to protect her, he encouraged Juan Luis to use her as a target. She carried the bruise for weeks.

As Franco gained power, however, Buñuel felt his espionage efforts were increasingly futile. In the last of them he stood at Bayonne in the Basses-Pyrénées and floated leaflet-loaded balloons across the border, realizing glumly that only a fraction of them were likely to be read. Soon Negrin and other members of the government would flee to France. Calanda had been reoccupied and a hundred people shot. In Zaragoza, Conchita was arrested, but released after, Luis said, 'a close brush with execution'. He also heard (erroneously) that Rafael Sanchez Ventura was dead. A Lazarist priest who escaped, bringing with him Dali's portrait of Luis from the Residencia, warned him: 'Whatever you do, don't go back there!' Buñuel needed no urging. He had already made other plans.

18

'To those who sail the salt quotidian sea
The tempting syren sings across the flood,
But once plunged in, they find her out to be
A desert island with a coast of mud.'
– Charles Madge, 'Delusions'

'I saw Luis Buñuel for the last time before the war at a reception given by the Republican ambassador in Paris,' Sadoul recollected. 'An orchestra played in a garden. And the scene tragically evoked *L'Age d'Or*. Not long after, Buñuel was going to take the path of exile.'

Following the balloon débâcle, Luis asked Marcelino Pascua, who had replaced Araquistain, for more important work. As Luis remembers it, Pascua suggested he return to the United States and find a job as technical adviser in Hollywood. In this way he could eradicate errors in films about Spain and the war.

In 1936/7, while Spain dominated the headlines, many studios planned Civil War films, but in the end only two were shot; Paramount's *Last Train from Madrid*, a melodrama on the *Grand Hotel/Shanghai Express* model, set in a world closer to Ruritania and Zenda than Spain, and *Blockade*, a Henry Fonda/Madeleine Carroll action romance produced by maverick Walter Wanger and written by committed Communists Clifford Odets and John Howard Lawson.

Blockade, originally called *The River Is Blue*, was in trouble from the start. Joseph Breen, head of Hollywood's self-censorship office, urged Wanger to omit anything that 'could possibly be tied in with the actual events that have occurred or are occurring in Spain'. Wanger complied. Former Communist Granville Hicks recalled the left's disappointment. *Blockade* was 'going to strike a great blow for the Loyalist cause in Spain. But when the picture appeared, it did not even indicate on which side the hero was fighting.'

Even so, *Blockade* met with massive orchestrated protests, mainly from Catholics, when it opened in the United States in July 1938. They blocked its New York opening at Radio City Music Hall. Twentieth Century-Fox barred it from its theatre chain and promptly shelved its Civil War drama *Alcazar*, while Universal abandoned *Delay in the Sun*. *Blockade*'s wider release was halted while, Lawson claimed, 'copies of the script and the film itself were being sent to Paris and to London for consultation with important political figures there'. Some minor cuts followed. 'The film was not slashed and it was not censored heavily,' Lawson acknowledged, 'but it was changed to please the reactionary elements in Paris and London.'

Pascua and Buñuel may have seen *Blockade* or read the script but even so it seems a slim pretext to go to Hollywood where, as Buñuel must have known, the protests of one man, and a foreigner at that, would count for nothing. True, he could produce Frank Davis's letter politely hoping they would work together again, but such documents cut little ice. Anyway, where he might be listened to, in matters of background detail, the changes, politically, would not be worth making. He only ever quoted one error he might have corrected; Spanish peasants were shown drinking wine from giant biblical wineskins rather than small hard leather bottles.

Given the Hollywood situation, and taking into account the fact that Pascua offered only the flimsiest accreditation and did not even pay his fare, one is bound to look elsewhere for reasons why Luis hauled his young family halfway across the world. He may have feared for his life once Franco came to power. Many Republican agents were imprisoned or assassinated, even in Paris, and in Spain intellectuals were prime targets: thousands, especially teachers, were executed. It is more likely, however, that Buñuel was sick of France and wanted to get out, as many of his friends had done already. As the war turned against the Republic, the climate of acceptance for émigré Spaniards in Paris became more chilly. The winter of 1938 was bitter. Pipes burst. Cold drove many from their rooms, but the police warned foreigners not to let friends share their apartments without official permission. Those who took refuge in the cafés were harassed. Arturo Barea, another Republican exile, met a young Basque in the Dôme who had been asked three times that day for his papers. A gendarme had told him, 'It's high time we cleared France of all those Reds.' The police also queried the Republican passports of Barea and his companion, suggesting they surrender them and register as refugees. When they stood on their rights as Spanish citizens, the police shrugged: 'You'll soon be refugees anyhow, whether you like it or not.'

Barea moved to England. Buñuel, married to a French national and with a child, could be more confident of being allowed to remain, but he was not yet naturalized, which made his residency insecure. Ugarte, Dali,

Gustavo Duran and Federico Garcia Lorca's younger brother Francisco were all in the United States, as were Juan Negrin's son Juanito and his actress wife Rosita. Urgoiti, Beltran and Angelillo had gone to Argentina, where they made two films together, and Velo and Oscar Dancigers were doing well in Mexico. The Americas began to look more and more attractive.

Luis's friends knew how much he had lost by remaining in France while so many others headed for the sun and money. In particular Dali's success rankled. Sadoul said: 'We saw Buñuel again in Paris in 1937, [serving] the Republican cause, while his old friend, Salvador Dali, was in New York, organizing masked balls for millionaires and consenting to paint the portrait of the French ambassador.'

Dali's visits to the United States turned him into an international celebrity. *Time* put him on its cover and on New Year's Day 1937 his first big US show opened at the Julien Levy Gallery in New York. In January he and Gala went to Hollywood, staying at the Garden of Allah, meeting the Marx Brothers, for whom he wrote a short screenplay, *The Surrealist Woman*, and Cecil B. DeMille.

The DeMille rendezvous was engineered by George Antheil, then working with Boris Morros on the score of *The Plainsman*. Immediately they entered DeMille's Pope-like presence, Dali kissed his hand.

'Ah, Mr DeMille!' he cried in a repetition of his first meeting with Picasso. 'I have met you at last, you, the greatest Surrealist on earth.'

'Surrealism is a new European art movement,' Antheil explained hurriedly to a puzzled DeMille, 'a kind of realism, but more real than realism – "super-realism", so to speak.'

DeMille, flattered, asked to hear more. Next day, all Hollywood knew that Dali and Surrealism had CB's seal of approval. Morros, until then sceptical, was suddenly eager to help. Deciding Dali would be ideal to design sets and dream sequences for Paramount, he suggested showing the studio brass and DeMille *Un Chien Andalou*, which he had not seen but had heard was a masterpiece.

'I've seen it,' Antheil enthused, 'and it *is* terrific. It's wonderful! It's beautiful!'

The screening, however, was disastrous.

'The first thing that happened,' Antheil recalled in his autobiography, 'was that one of the biggest producers on the lot got violently ill. He had to leave very suddenly. The rest were nailed to their seats as if hypnotized by a king cobra. Boris turned to me and hissed "I thought you said this was the most beautiful picture you ever saw!" Cecil B. DeMille, king of the Surrealists (American branch), was a pale green when the lights went up. He got up and left without a word. So did the others, when they recovered.'

Dali, shrewd enough to realize that there is no such thing as bad publicity, rang Gala and told her delightedly: 'It was the *greatest* success imaginable. They were *speechless!*'

As his New York show drew baffled but copious press coverage, Paramount had second thoughts about rejecting Dali. Antheil was asked to bring him in to discuss a contract as design consultant, but Salvador, knowing he had milked Hollywood of everything he could use for the moment, insisted he wanted work as a screenwriter, not a designer, and swept back to New York, where the Four Hundred were waiting to lionize him.

To Buñuel, unable to get even the most pedestrian film work, Dali's posturing was intolerable. Jeanne confirmed that a major motive for his leaving France was simple ambition. 'Los Angeles was the place for movie-makers,' she said. 'There were techniques, money, opportunities. Someone told Luis: "Go to the United States. There are lots of chances there." He was pleased with the idea.' He fired off dozens of postcards. One went to Frank Davis at MGM. Davis confirmed he did have a Civil War project in development, an original Laurence Kirk story about a shipful of Spanish refugee mothers and children *en route* to the USSR from Bilbao. It was called *A Cargo of Innocence*.

Buñuel decided to gamble on this slim chance, and set about borrowing the money he needed. Sanchez Ventura advanced 800 dollars and Luis Quintanilla's mistress Ione Robinson, who also happened to be sleeping with the financial comptroller at the American Embassy, contributed as well, but on 9 September Buñuel wrote for the first time in years to Charles de Noailles, explaining that he was leaving on 'a so-called "official" mission' that would keep him in the United States for some months, and asking for the loan of 425 dollars to take Jeanne and Juan Luis. Charles responded with his usual generosity, asking only in what form Luis wanted it; a cheque in French francs, a draft on his New York account, or cash?

The Buñuels went to London, then took the ten-day transatlantic trip, most of which Jeanne spent in her bunk, sea-sick. She roused herself only to protest when well-meaning passengers fed Juan Luis a cold, green, gelatinous, plainly pernicious dessert: Jello.

They spent their first week in America at Princeton with ex-Residencista Augusto Centeno. Knowing he would need a car in Los Angeles, Luis quixotically decided to buy one in New York and drive to California, a trial even in the freeway era but in the days of two-lane blacktop an

eight-day ordeal. They took Route 66, through Missouri and Oklahoma, then following the *Grapes of Wrath* Okies across New Mexico
and Arizona. Travel for Luis was always just a means to an end, to be got
through as quickly as possible, usually in a stupor. But Jeanne was
fascinated, in particular by the desert, the vastness and, even in autumn,
the heat. Somewhere in Oklahoma they ran into a brush fire but Luis just
floored the pedal. Juan Luis got out to piss and had his first experience of
cactus when he kicked an interesting fuzzy green ball with his French
sandals. At an Arizona gas station, two women drew up in a big car with
a panting dog which gorged itself on ice water and fell dead. Jeanne,
always superstitious, saw bad omens.

In Hollywood, they found a small apartment at 5672 Fountain
Avenue and Luis checked in at MGM where, to his relief, Frank Davis
put him on the *Cargo of Innocence* payroll, though more out of
friendship and political solidarity than need. The Spanish war (or any
other foreign political situation) never interested Hollywood beyond its
utility as exotic background. Even Fascism was handled gingerly until
well after Hitler began devouring Europe, nobody wishing to jeopardize
the continental market. Washington was equally diffident. FDR invited
Hemingway to screen *The Spanish Earth* at the White House but, after
sympathizing, explained he was powerless before an isolationist Congress and a pro-Franco Catholic lobby. Liberal film-makers contributed
thousands of dollars for ambulances at private screenings of *The Spanish
Earth* but none would do anything to find it a release or make more like
it.

Buñuel was still reading the screenplay when *Cargo of Innocence* was
suspended. He remembers a Motion Picture Producers' Association
order forbidding all Spanish Civil War films. There is no record of any
such blanket prohibition, but *Blockade* had made all the studios wary,
not least MGM, which regarded itself as the voice of morality and
consensus. In one of his Pat Hobby stories, Scott Fitzgerald's burnt-out
hack writer is handed a script and told: 'Clean up the stuff about Spain.
The guy who wrote it was a Red and he's got all the Spanish officers with
ants in their pants. Fix that up.'

For four years *Cargo of Innocence* would wander in Re-development
Hell. Adapted by R.C. Sherriff, author of *Journey's End*, as a Royal
Navy story and possible Robert Donat vehicle, it was re-Americanized
by US Navy Captain Harvey Haislip when Donat refused. After Pearl
Harbor, veterans Herman Mankiewicz and John L. Balderston turned
it into a USN version of *In Which We Serve*, with an American destroyer
on convoy duty rescuing a boatload of mothers and babies, no longer
Spaniards but one-size-fits-all Europeans. It was shot in 1942, with

Robert Taylor heading a cast of old reliables, including Charles Laughton as an admiral who trumps Noël Coward's stiff-upper-lip heroics by reciting the Declaration of Independence. Robert Z. Leonard directed and co-produced. Released in the United States in 1942 as *Stand by for Action*, it sank with all hands. In the *New York Times* Bosley Crowther snorted that it displayed 'the sort of mock heroics which insults our fighting men'. If Buñuel saw the film or even knew of its existence, he never said so.

1938 and 1939, bumper years for Hollywood, were lean for Luis. Thanks to well-placed colleagues or refugee groups like the American Committee of Aid to Intellectuals or the Hollywood Anti-Nazi League, the cream of Europe's artists – Reinhardt, Schoenberg, Stravinsky, Delaunay, Huxley, Brecht, Heinrich and Thomas Mann – were either already in Hollywood or on their way. A mere Spanish experimentalist living with his wife and small child attracted no interest.

The passport to Hollywood acceptance was contempt; if they thought you didn't want them, they had to have you. Some of Dali's arrogance would not have gone amiss, but Buñuel lacked that flair. He and Antheil gloomily discussed Salvador. 'Inasmuch as [Buñuel], his wife and his little boy seemed to be such absolutely normal, solid persons,' said the composer, 'as totally un-Surrealist in the Dali tradition as one could possibly imagine, I asked him whether Dali "puts it on".'

'Yes,' Luis told him. 'He puts it on. It's good business.'

Each mail brought a new irony. The Noailles wrote to ask if he could give Aldous Huxley a hand, when the novelist was working at MGM on *Madame Curie* and being fêted by Chaplin, Garbo and Krishnamurti. Another letter informed Luis he had been drafted into the Spanish Army. Fortunately the ambassador in Washington told him to stay put, so he did not risk the fate of Breton, who in September found himself back in uniform as medical instructor at a flying school in Poitiers.

He tried selling jokes to Chaplin, but Charlie, never charitable, would not see him. He also resurrected his Goya treatment, retitled *Goya and the Duchess of Alba* and augmented with some new and more quirky details. A relative of Charles IV is shown as a foot fetishist, with a closet filled with stolen shoes, and Buñuel, whose hearing was increasingly poor, builds up the detail of Goya's deafness. He showed the treatment around Paramount, but nobody could visualize a swashbuckler whose hero painted.

In desperation, Luis borrowed another 1000 dollars from Sanchez Ventura, and resignedly turned to his old standby, dubbing, while Jeanne did translations into French from her fumbling English, which was still so bad that, to order three lamb chops from the butcher, she had to point to her side, hold up three fingers and baa like a sheep. With money running out, she tried borrowing from her family, but help was grudging. A package finally arrived from the Rucars via a friend, but it contained only a large print of Dali's portrait of Luis. Completely broke, the Buñuel's were saved by a 20-dollar money order from Georgette.

Another expatriate, Michel Weber, came to their rescue. Weber had been working, uncredited, on Reinhardt's *A Midsummer Night's Dream* at Warners, part of the fallout from which was a large house at 8802 Ashcroft Avenue in West Hollywood, a quiet street a few blocks south of Melrose, where Weber and his family lived rent-free. 'Come and live with us,' they offered. 'One day we'll buy the food and the next day you can do it.'

The house had a library, a billiard room and seven bedrooms but almost no furniture. Luis and Jeanne were already installed when Franco marched into Madrid on 28 March 1939. Weber and Luis looked for work, joined sometimes by the composer Edgard Varèse. Other members of the Spanish community helped out. Janet, the American wife of the Spanish writer Luis Alcoriza who, as 'Raquel Rojas', had earned a living as a flamenco dancer in Spain, sent Luis to her father, who worked in the music department of a Hollywood studio. He got them occasional jobs.

As a last gesture Luis composed a twenty-one-page 'autobiography' which Jeanne typed, with copious corrections and notional spelling. Intended to sell him to independent producers, it summarized his life and career, ending with pages of enthusiastic quotes about *Un Chien Andalou* and *L'Age d'Or*.

Under 'MY PRESENT PLANS' he wrote: 'I should like the making of documental films of a psychological nature', and outlined two subjects, *The Primitive Man* and *Psycho-Pathology*. These synopses are the first evidence that Surrealism, Communism, the Civil War and perhaps, too, the enforced leisure of California and that state's famous acceptance of eccentricity had fundamentally changed Buñuel's point of view.

He had reverted to his adolescent fascination with the blind instinct of insects. People no longer seemed quirky and individual but almost absurdly predictable. In *The Primitive Man* Buñuel argues that our higher impulses – religion, love, patriotism – can be traced back to the moments when man discovered language and fire. The film would show 'the terrible struggle of primitive man against a hostile universe, how the world appeared, *how they saw it*, what ideas they had on love, on death, on fraternity, how and why religion is born'.

Psycho-Pathology aimed to 'expose the origin and development of different psychopathic diseases [. . .] The spectator could see for himself the world in which a schizophrenic lives, or realize of what the paranoiac's interpretation of reality consists. [. . .] I intuitively feel that such a documental film, apart from its great scientific interest, could depict on the screen a *New Form of Terror* or its synonym *Humour* and at certain times a strange poetry, not presented to date, a product of those two sentiments.' Buñuel never got beyond these vague notes but in them he discloses for the first time those themes that were to dominate his career.

His new detachment also influenced his future choice of actors and subjects. He had always been casual about performers but now he would become more so, accepting almost any actor since, after all, they were simply experimental animals and therefore interchangeable. As for subjects, he would take on even the most trivial. A musical or domestic farce would do as well as anything to demonstrate the blind working of chance and those irrational drives that control our lives, just as they control the scorpion and the ant.

Nobody, however, showed any interest, and Luis realized the futility of remaining in Los Angeles. Jeanne was pregnant again, and he needed work, as did Nino Weber, so while Jeanne and Juan Luis remained with Weber's wife, the two men headed east at the end of 1939. Luis's autobiographical note had ended: 'As I could legally remain in the United States, I plan to stay here indefinitely, intensely attracted by the American naturalness and sociability', and, whatever the effort, he was determined to act on it.

19

'New York, skyscraper champion of the world, where the slickers and know-it-alls peddle gold bricks to each other, and Truth, crushed to earth, rises more phony than a glass eye.'
– Ben Hecht, *Nothing Sacred*

Events in Europe were decimating Buñuel's generation. Of the Surrealists, Aragon, Eluard, Tzara and Thirion would stay in France with the Communist resistance. Robert Desnos was to die just after his release from Theresienstadt, the Nazi 'show camp', Fondane in Auschwitz and Pierre Unik in Silesia, apparently in 1944, although his body was never found. On 21 August 1940, in Mexico City, Stalin's agents caught up with Trotsky. Many friends fled Paris on 25 June 1940, the day after the start of the Nazi occupation. René Clair, Jean Renoir and Antoine de St Exupéry arrived in New York on 31 December to swell a French community which already included Hélène and Pierre Lazareff, André Maurois and Jules Romains.

Breton followed, as did Yves Tanguy, who had married an Italian princess and was trying with her help to stop drinking. Max Ernst's unstable ex-wife, the painter Leonora Carrington, arrived with her new husband, Mexican poet Renato Leduc, followed by Ernst and his second wife, Peggy Guggenheim, the millionaire art patron. Péret, having ransomed himself from the Nazis, paused *en route* to Mexico. Joan Miró, André Masson, Marcel Duchamp and Fernand Léger also passed through at various times. 'The French are like herrings,' said Renoir. 'They travel in shoals.'

Unlike Los Angeles, New York could be hospitable to artists on their uppers. For every Ferenc Molnar getting rich in a Plaza suite selling what would eventually become *Carousel*, there was a penniless Bela Bartók in a tiny apartment transcribing Armenian folksongs, a make-work project invented by Elliot Carter.

Buñuel might also have benefited from this largesse but he was hampered by his reserve, which alcohol, deafness and his sometimes alarming first impression magnified into what many took for rudeness. Anaïs Nin, who knew him from Paris, bumped into him in April 1941 at a party at the Manhattan home of Mercedes Matter, daughter of the painter Arthur Carles. Isamu Noguchi and Pierre Matisse were there too, but it was Buñuel who made the impression. Nin noted in her diary his 'thyroid eyes' and the moles on his chin, but conceded that 'he has a fierce, sharp humour, a bitter sarcasm and at the same time towards women a gentle, special smile'. Leonora Carrington was less flattering. She told him: 'You look so much like the orderly I had at the mental institution at Santander.' Luis was amused rather than offended. A Carrington painting would become one of the fixtures of his house in Mexico City.

Delphine Seyrig, later to star in *The Discreet Charm of the Bourgeoisie*, but at that time eight or nine and in transit with her parents from Lebanon to Paris, may also have met Buñuel. In *My Last Breath* he recalls her reminiscing about sitting on his knee and being frightened by his bulging eyes. But Seyrig has said: 'Not only do I not remember this – I don't remember *saying* this. Don Luis's hearing wasn't good, and he may have misheard something I said: "Imagine. We might have met. You might even have held me on your knee", or something like that.'

Despairing of finding work in the arts, Buñuel was ready to do almost anything to survive. A fellow Catalan named Gali told him he had danced in hotels when he first arrived. He sent Luis to a man named Untel, another Catalan with connections in the hotel workers' union, who might place him as kitchen help. Fortunately, before he was forced to become a *plongeur* like Orwell, Buñuel ran into George Antheil, who introduced him to Iris Barry.*

Forceful, vivacious and opinionated, with violet eyes, an Eton crop haircut and a ringing laugh, Barry, a convinced Communist with a taste for high-quality alcohol and low-quality men, had worked her way from the north of England to New York through sheer force of will. The daughter of a gypsy fortune-teller (or so she told her friend Elsa Lanchester), she had been the mistress of, among others, dancer Paul Draper and writer Wyndham Lewis, by whom she had two children, before marrying the head of a large British film company. As passionate about cinema as everything else, she helped launch the London Film Society and was film critic of the *Spectator* and the *Daily Mail*.

* Buñuel later told Max Aub he had already known her in London, but this seems unlikely.

In the early 1930s she had gone to New York with a new husband, an inoffensive and deaf Vassar English professor, Alan Porter. Trapped in this dead-end marriage, Barry deteriorated. 'Iris used to get so drunk on bathtub gin,' recalled Lanchester, 'that she'd fall across the bed and you couldn't move her. She smelled like a polecat. The gin was coming out of her skin.' Installing Lanchester and her husband Charles Laughton in their hotel on their first trip to America, Barry warned Lanchester tipsily: 'Now you're in America, Towser, don't trust anyone – even your own mother. And don't forget, the only thing that counts is the dollar.'

A new husband, John 'Dick' Abbott, and a new project straightened Barry out. Alfred Barr, head of the Museum of Modern Art, decided it needed a film library to conserve classic films and distribute copies to schools and film societies. In 1934, he persuaded the Rockefeller family and John Hay 'Jock' Whitney to fund it. Barry was in charge though, because the trustees were sceptical of a woman and a foreigner, Abbott had formal control.

Barry joined MoMA in 1932 and was curator of the collection until 1947, although her methods did not satisfy everyone. She refused to circulate Pearl White's serial, *The Perils of Pauline*, finding it 'dull', and even Mervyn LeRoy was moved to protest about the abysmal MoMA print of his *I Am a Fugitive from a Chain Gang*. A borrower raged at Barry's 'superficial realization of her responsibilities [and] abysmal ignorance of the American film's worth and import. [. . .] Personal reaction, or the lack thereof, seems by the results to be the only yardstick with which the curator is capable of evaluating values. This and the preposterous printed forewords with which the classics of the screen are defaced above Miss Barry's bold signature have rightly won her in civilized circles the title of "The Attila of Films".'

Barry, who had arranged the 1933 New York screening of *L'Age d'Or*, put Luis up in her Turtle Bay house while he looked for work, and introduced him to the sculptor Alexander Calder and his wife. A large and genial man who loved children, Calder generously offered the Buñuels part of his large apartment. A grateful Luis sent for Jeanne and Juan Luis, who arrived at Grand Central on 2 January 1940. This time Luis managed to meet the train.

They lived with Calder until the baby arrived in May. Certain of a girl this time, Luis urged friends to 'think pink' with their gifts, but it was a boy again, whom they named Rafael, after Sanchez Ventura. The two families got on well. Calder was a surrogate uncle to Juan Luis, who himself later became a sculptor, working first in wire, as Calder did in his mobiles. Juan Luis recalls 'Sandy [. . .] making beautiful things for me out of corks and bits of wire, while he was talking to my parents. I liked watching him make them. I'd throw them away so he'd make me another.'

When Calder moved to Connecticut the Buñuels took over his lease. Juan Luis was enrolled in the Dalton School, where classes were in English. He spoke no Spanish until the family moved to Mexico in 1945, and he is still known to most people in private as 'John'. Luis, sensing his deficiencies as a father, took classes in English and baby-care, but in both cases his patience quickly wore out, though he did soften sufficiently to allow Rafael to be christened, with the Negrins as godparents.

Iris Barry taught a film history course at Columbia and invited Buñuel to discuss *Un Chien Andalou* and *Las Hurdes* at the Museum of Modern Art on 10 June. Both films, obtained from Braunberger, had been censored, putting Luis in a bad mood, which the students' incomprehension exacerbated. One compared *Las Hurdes* to *Lost Horizon*; fortunately Luis had not seen Capra's Utopian fantasy. As the questions petered out, Barry remarked: 'We seem to have been struck dumb. One might say your razor has also cut out our tongues.'

Another MoMA presentation of *Las Hurdes* in June 1941 elicited the same reaction in a more extreme form. 'Each spectator had to pay 10 dollars,' said Eric Bromberger.* 'Ten minutes after the first turn of the reel there was nobody in the cinema and the manager asked [Buñuel] sharply to leave.' Anaïs Nin in general corroborates this account. Buñuel had been asked to choose some films from the Museum's collection to accompany *Las Hurdes*. 'He walks up and down the aisles, rubbing his hands,' recalled Nin, 'saying: "It is a slightly morbid program." Morbid! A Spanish village dying of goitre. A film taken inside Bellevue [Mental Hospital]. An island where people are dying of leprosy. Flesh disintegrating, rotting before actual death. People began to leave. At the end the hall was almost empty. Buñuel loves to shock, to frighten, to horrify. Buñuel with his popping eyes and a mole on the tip of his nose revelling in showing a leper praying with his stump, or a leper without lips playing a flute.'

Barry, whom Buñuel credits with 'a diabolical flair', had ambitions beyond managing MoMA's film library. During the Depression, the federal government had funded some important socialist documentaries through instrumentalities such as the Tennessee Valley Authority. Films like Pare Lorentz's *The Plough that Broke the Plains* were milestones of

* Bromberger believes the screening – of, he says erroneously, *L'Age d'Or* and *Un Chien Andalou* – was arranged by 'the intelligentsia and great publishers of New York in [Buñuel's] honour'. This is probably an error, though Barry may have hoped that publicity would encourage someone to employ Luis.

agitprop, and Barry, in common with many other left-wingers, lamented the fact that, with the war, funds for such films had dried up.

Looking for other potential sources of funding, Barry targeted the Office of the Co-ordinator of Inter-American Affairs. The OIAA was gorged with money, earmarked for propaganda in South America, where many nations, particularly Argentina, were potentially Fascist. Germany was already busy there. With the Spanish film industry at a standstill, Berlin had started producing features in Spanish, while continuing to distribute propaganda via its embassies and Brown House social centres.

To woo South America, Roosevelt launched the Good Neighbour Policy, a propaganda offensive with Hollywood supplying the shock troops. Studios were glad to co-operate. Foreign revenue had sunk since the loss of Europe, but they hoped that audiences south of the border might yet save them. Orson Welles went to Brazil to make *It's All True*, and Walt Disney led an animation team to South America to research *Saludos Amigos* and *Three Caballeros*. *Down Argentina Way*, *Weekend in Havana* and *That Night in Rio* launched stars like Carmen Miranda and Olga San Juan, and Cesar Romero was seldom out of work. Less obtrusively, Washington choked off the Argentinian cinema with an embargo on film stock, while helping Mexico, which joined the Allies in 1942.

Fortunately for Barry, the Co-ordinator of Inter-American Affairs was MoMA's richest patron, dashing young millionaire Nelson Rockefeller. She found him sympathetic to the suggestion that the Museum should be involved in some way in the OIAA's work. Rockefeller, however, had his own hidden agenda. He saw the OIAA as a stepping-stone to the White House. It was a classic case of one hand washing the other, and Rockefeller acted quickly. Arguing that Hollywood had neglected the vital short film area in its Hispanic propaganda, he allocated funds to MoMA to revoice existing documentaries in Spanish.

On 28 February 1941 the OIAA granted MoMA a 125,000 dollar contract to '(a) establish and maintain a film catalogue, (b) gather desirable films from all sources, (c) review such films, (d) edit them, (e) sound-track the final negative in Spanish and Portuguese, (f) arrange for the production of new 16mm films, (g) arrange for the safekeeping of all negatives and prints, (h) ship finished prints to Latin-America, (i) and maintain records of the showing of films in Latin-America and of audience response.' The films would mostly be distributed through American embassies. Barry was confident that, once she had proved herself with dubbing, independent production would follow.

She assembled a small production team. She had to proceed carefully. 'Nobody was ever more cowardly in the world than Nelson, you know,' Orson Welles told Barbara Leaming. 'He didn't want to be near anything that was under any kind of shadow.' Barry knew she was taking a risk hiring Soviet documentarist and historian Jay Leyda, and another with Buñuel. She gingerly introduced Luis at a reception to Jock Whitney, who had been deputed to make sure nothing compromised Rockefeller. He and Luis retired to the Plaza bar where Whitney asked directly if he was a Communist.

'I am a Republican,' Buñuel said.

If Whitney understood the ideological gulf between Spanish socialism and the GOP, he did not press it, and Luis was allowed formally to offer his services to MoMA on 14 January 1941. A month later, when the first OIAA contract came on line, he moved into its West 53rd Street offices as chief editor and head of the writer's department at 270.88 dollars a fortnight. He never mentioned *España 1936*, the only film which could directly link him with the Party, and until the 1970s it remained forgotten. He did, however, detail some of his political affiliations on a visa questionnaire, and this, along with his support of anti-Franco publications like *España Libre*, would backfire a decade later.

In April 1939, Franco put all art in Spain under government control. Indigenous languages like Catalan, Basque and Galician were outlawed, as were foreign names for hotels, shops and cinemas. All films had to be dubbed into Spanish, and their content brought into line with Falangist law and Church dogma. For the next thirty years, down-beat foreign films would be given up-beat endings, and illicit relationships retrospectively sanctified. The married couple of John Ford's *Mogambo* became brother and sister to excuse Grace Kelly's affair with Clark Gable. *The Virgin Spring*, *The Seventh Seal* and *Bicycle Thieves* blossomed with new messages of hope and holy redemption.

Scores of Spanish intellectuals who had hung on, hoping to live and work under the Falange, headed for New York. Many drifted into Buñuel's pool of freelance translators and speakers. It soon included Eduardo and Paulo Ugarte, Paul Duarte, Francisco Garcia Lorca and Gustavo Duran. Most were veterans of the Civil War and almost by definition Communists, with tormented personal lives that more than accorded with those of Buñuel and Barry.

Duran was among those closest to Buñuel. Since working with Luis at Paramount in Paris, he had commanded a division in Spain, been wounded twice and captured, only to be released by an old friend and smuggled to Marseille. Hearing of his arrest and assumed death, his father cut his throat. Bitter at having lost his family, musical career, country, language and culture, Duran refused to talk about the war. He never returned to Spain. After six months with Buñuel he joined Rockefeller's OIAA staff, then spent the rest of the war in Havana running Ernest Hemingway's bumbling private espionage service, the 'Crook Factory'. After the war he became a US Presidential adviser on Latin American affairs, at the price of informing on his old Communist colleagues.

Anguished or not, Buñuel's team did dub scores of short films. The young composer Gustavo Pittaluga supplied music where needed. Buñuel never claimed much merit for these films. It was Pittaluga who, thirty years later, originated the legend of 'maybe 2000 remarkable works'. According to him, 'we were sent anodyne documentaries, often extremely feeble primary materials, which the Museum team turned into marvellous films [. . .] Through his reconstruction of the material, cutting or extending scenes, creating dialogue and sound track, [Buñuel] would create a good documentary through editing.'

Buñuel made no such claims. Far from being a skilled editor, he had almost no cutting-room technique when he joined MoMA. He had never laid sound nor used a Moviola. When a student asked about 'opticals' in *Un Chien Andalou*, Barry had to explain the term. Of the forty-two films handled in his first year, the majority were US Air Force training films and promotional shorts for Greyhound and General Electric, plus some newsreels of a US archbishop's Mexican visit and the annual Santa Barbara Spanish-American festival; no masterpieces there, except perhaps Joseph Losey's *A Child Went Forth*, about progressive schools, one of the few independent films Buñuel bought.

The cottage industry tone of MoMA's operation changed after December 1941. With America at war, documentary was suddenly big business. The forces demanded training films. Washington wanted patriotic shorts.

Cultivation of the Hispanic market had paid off handsomely. Even with the Brazilian and Mexican cinema both booming as Hollywood films became weighed down with propaganda, studios owed 14 per cent of their foreign revenue to South America. 1941 was a golden year, with gross income up 35 million dollars on 1939. Columbia doubled its profits. Warners made 5.5 million dollars and MGM 11.5 million.

Success, however, merely sharpened Hollywood resentment that

MoMA should enjoy a slice of this lucrative market. MoMA's contract, which had been renewed annually, was unprecedented. With it, the government effectively went into competition with Hollywood. At the time the studios, happy to support any overture towards new markets, had not made an issue of it, but now that serious money was involved, they became less tolerant.

A campaign was launched to destroy the MoMA film unit. The first salvoes were fired early in 1942 in the pages of the *Motion Picture Herald*, the industry's most prestigious trade paper. Since it was edited in New York, only a few blocks from MoMA, editor Terry Ramsaye could easily keep an eye on what was happening there. Slighting references to 'the Nelson Rockefeller – John Hay Whitney Museum of Modern Art' began to appear. In February 1942, Ramsaye sneered that MoMA, 'engaged in spreading things cultural, has started a campaign of its own to furnish our soldiers in camp with books – on ART!' In June it mentioned Leyda's presence on the staff, describing him as 'among the editors of the leftist quarterly *films*, and technical consultant on the staff of Artkino, motion picture outlet for the US of Russia's pictures-of-message'.

In August, on the pretext of a report that the War Production Board was to ration film stock, Ramsaye suggested that this step 'will be received by the motion picture industry with considerably more equanimity if the subsequent councils on the subject should indicate that the prodigal consumption of material by the many and assorted government bureaus and departments not directly related to the war is to be curbed adequately'. In December it announced that employees of the 'Rockefeller–Whitney endowed' MoMA and 'Rockefeller-directed' Office of Inter-American Affairs were being asked to join the federal payroll. Government control, it implied, would straighten out these arty left-wingers.

Barry, refusing to surrender without a fight, decided to show Hollywood what American propaganda was up against. Many German films had been seized when Hitler declared war, including negatives of Leni Riefenstahl's *Triumph des Willens (Triumph of the Will)* and Hans Bertram's documentary on the invasion of Poland, *Feldzug in Polen*. Under Buñuel, the MoMA team cut Riefenstahl's two hours to forty-three minutes which, if anything, amplified the film's impact. Rockefeller arranged for a White House screening, after which, on 30 January 1943, Barry and Abbott hosted 'Two Evenings of German Propaganda Films 1934–1941' at the Film Arts cinema in Hollywood for a celebrity invited audience. Although Chaplin giggled so much at the posturing of Hitler and his minions that he fell out of his seat, most of the 900 guests –

many more waited outside – were shocked. René Clair spoke for most of Hollywood when he urged Barry never to let the American public see the films. 'If you do, we're lost.' The MoMA unit won a brief reprieve.

Anticipating that MoMA would eventually come under federal control, Buñuel applied for American citizenship. On 18 June 1942 he appeared before a Washington tribunal of representatives from the Departments of State, Labor and Justice, and the Navy, Army and FBI. They cleared him to file the preliminary papers.

He had begun to feel at home in New York. He spent hunting weekends at Alfred Barr's upstate retreat. MoMA's collection allowed him to improve his film education. He had a taste for horror films, and he screened programmes of them for other enthusiasts on the staff, occasionally adding *Un Chien Andalou*. When Margaretta Akermark squealed at its first scene, Buñuel reassured her: 'Don't worry. It's only a cow.'

He often brought home other Spaniards, including Gustavo Pittaluga, who caught Jeanne's eye. They never had an affair, though she does admit to flirting. The Buñuels became closer to Pittaluga and his mistress Ana-Maria Custodio during the next decade, though Luis's jealousy would strain the relationship.

America had sexually liberated Jeanne, or at least her imagination, but Luis remained inhibited. She fantasized about sleeping with other men, not because she didn't love Luis but simply to explore her sexuality. When she discussed it with him, he was horrified. She also scandalized a Hollywood dinner party with her fantasy of bearing a black son. All of this fed Luis's growing jealousy. Despite his taste for group sex, he was haunted by a fear of being observed while making love. In dreams, he imagined people watching him through windows. No matter how often he changed rooms or even houses in the dream, the phantom watchers followed. Sometimes, when he was finally alone with his fantasy partner, he found her vagina sewn up. Under the shadow of these fears, Luis and Jeanne made love only at night, and always with furniture leaning against the door, blocking the keyhole. If there were guests, Luis invented pretexts to get them out of the house.

Obsessive punctuality made Luis a bad guest and a worse host. He often had friends to dinner as an excuse to show off his favourite paella. With its mixture of seafood and chicken, all of which had to be prepared separately before being added to the saffron rice, paella demanded to be eaten as soon as it was ready. Guests were expected to be punctual and Luis was furious when they were not. On one occasion in New York, the lateness of some guests so incensed him that, when they finally turned up, he opened the door with the big dish in his hand, put it on the floor and stamped in it, shouting, 'Here's the paella you wanted!'

In February 1943 the studios brought their campaign against MoMA into the open. The *Motion Picture Herald* urged that all OIAA films henceforth be made in Hollywood. It even nominated two experienced producers to supervise: Mervyn LeRoy, who had his own reasons for disliking Barry, and Jack Chertok, head of MGM's short subject department. The same month, Jock Whitney discreetly resigned from the OIAA to become Public Relations Director of the 8th Army Air Force, with the rank of Lieutenant Colonel and an office in London. In May the Office of War Information took control of all raw film stock, with the right to limit supplies to those who might waste it. Ramsaye headlined the report 'SENATE UNIT TO WEED OUT MEDDLERS IN US FILMS'. Nobody was in any doubt that Barry's operation was doomed.

Her enemies seized any pretext to attack MoMA. *The Secret Life of Salvador Dali*, published by Dial late in 1942, was a gift in this respect. Salvador's confession of incestuous longings, homosexual leanings, masturbatory fantasies and excremental transports of delight left reviewers goggling. Tired of badgering Luis for shared credit on the film, Dali used the book to disown *L'Age d'Or*, which was, he said, 'no more than a caricature of my ideas'. Accusing Buñuel of having 'attacked Catholicism in a primitive manner', he described one of the more anti-clerical scenes, adding piously: 'I accepted the responsibility for the sacrilege, even though it was not my intention.' He went on even more damagingly to charge that, by creating the shortened *In the Icy Waters of Egoist Calculation*, 'Buñuel expunged his most frenetic passages [. . .] with the goal of adapting it to Marxist ideology.' This might have passed without comment, but some Hollywood PR man, aware of the premium on anti-MoMA items, picked it up. A Catholic lobbyist named Prendergast protested to the State Department, and New York's Cardinal Francis Spellman supposedly visited Barry and demanded to know why she was harbouring the Anti-Christ. The tale relates that Barry, in tears, called Buñuel in and fired him. This is mostly invention. Barry seldom wept, at least not when sober, and Spellman never made house calls, although Monsignor John J. McClafferty, editor of the *Catholic Herald*, did convey His Eminence's displeasure. In 1962, Luis would nominate as the three most repugnant men of the century President Harry Truman, German Chancellor Konrad Adenauer and Spellman.

In fact, Barry wavered for a week. On 19 June MoMA presented, as 'Films and Reality', a hurriedly assembled programme of German propaganda, including *Triumph of the Will*, but it had none of the impact of the Hollywood screenings. On 26 June a *Motion Picture Herald* article, 'MUSEUM'S PACT WITH CO-ORDINATOR PENDS', announced that henceforth Hollywood would produce part of the OIAA's film needs. MoMA's film budget was cut by 66 per cent. When even the truncated contract had not been signed late in June, the *MPH* made it clear the problem lay with MoMA's staff. Their particular target was Buñuel, although forty people would eventually leave the OIAA and MoMA in this covert political purge.

Alfred Barr urged Luis to stay, but he decided to resign, and a grateful Barry leaked the news. He had not even submitted his resignation when the *MPH* reported it on 27 June. '[Buñuel] has been a storm centre of submerged inquiries and discussions for more than a year,' Ramsaye said, 'growing out of his left-wing and Surrealist film activities in France some years ago. It will be remembered that he was associated with the making of *L'Age d'Or* in collaboration with Salvador Dali, famed Surrealist artist, under the patronage of Etienne Beaumont, [sic] Vicomte de Noailles, in Paris. The picture was ultimately suppressed in France.'

On 30 June 1943 Buñuel wrote to Barry: 'In view of the continued references made in the *Motion Picture Herald* of a prejudicial nature to me, and in consequence of my conversation with you of this date, I feel I have no alternative but to resign [. . .] It seems evident to me that some person or a group of persons is determined to stir up trouble about me, presumably with the intention of embarrassing or discrediting the Co-ordinator [of Inter-American Affairs] and the work of his film division, using for that purpose the tendencies represented in one of my pictures, made in 1930 in Paris, and entitled *The Golden Age*.

'As you are one of the few persons in this country who have seen this film, you will understand, no doubt, that it could never be regarded as an anti-religious picture. Certainly, are in it symbolized the obstacles which religion, as well as society, oppose to the attainment of love. The film was a surrealistic poem.' To counter the accusations of 'left-wing feelings', Luis quoted the tribunal who had approved him for the first level of citizenship the previous June.

Since Buñuel's English was hardly equal to such phrasing, Barry probably composed the letter. Luis must have seethed at the need to repudiate both his Communism and anti-clericalism, but it was the least he could do to protect Barry and her unit. He ended by assuring her that he would carry with him 'the pleasantest memories. I have always found here a spirit of sincere cooperation for my work, together with the greatest comprehension and cordiality in our relations.' Barry's reply on

30 June left no doubt where the real blame lay. 'That your resignation, too, is a consequence of your interest in the success of the Co-ordinator's film work I also realize, and I can only say that I deplore the existence of a situation which made it seem advisable.' Margaretta Akermark and the rest of his staff scribbled their best wishes on the back of a publicity photograph of Buñuel posed with them on the Museum roof in happier times, but Luis was off the premises before the ink was dry. His departure was so hurried that carbons of screenplay treatments remained in his desk.

20

'A collection of shacks at the end of a poisoned rainbow.'
Micheál MacLiammóir on Hollywood

In time, Buñuel would see his resignation from MoMA as fortuitous, but in June 1944 it was a catastrophe. He had only 300 dollars in the bank and little prospect of earning more. Smeared now as politically unreliable, he could kiss US citizenship goodbye. Even his visitor's visa was threatened, and until the 1970s, when he hired an Immigration lawyer to clear his name, he would be subjected to interrogation and surveillance every time he entered the United States.

The author of his downfall was staying at the Sherry Netherland, and Luis went to see him. They met in the bar. Dali was unrepentant. Any loyalty to the Surrealists had died once Breton began calling him 'Avida Dollars'. Luis told him what damage the book had done. Behind his curved waxed moustaches Dali smiled his small, closed-mouth cat smile and said, 'The book has nothing to do with you. I wrote it to make *myself* a star.' (Jeanne remembers it differently. According to her, Dali said, 'I did it just to amuse myself.') Luis also asked him for the loan of 50 dollars to tide him over. Dali replied with a long letter in which he sanctimoniously counselled against borrowing from friends, adding that he was glad Franco had won the Civil War. Luis was incensed. Though Dali proposed reconciliations for the next forty years, he always refused.

Buñuel (and history) blamed Dali exclusively for losing him his job but the revelations of *My Secret Life* merely hastened it. Maliciously or not, Dali articulated truths which Buñuel himself had acknowledged often enough. Given the political climate of the mid-1940s, exposure was inevitable, if not through Dali then from a Party list or an informer. As another Communist intellectual, Donald Ogden Stewart, said of his own blacklisting, 'I wasn't so much caught as caught up with.'

The Buñuels moved into a one-bedroom apartment in the Washington Building at 244 E. 86th Street. Even here, Luis maintained his distance from Jeanne, sleeping on the couch while she and the boys shared the bedroom. The firmer sofa helped his back, and for the rest of his life he would sleep on hard mattresses or on the floor. But he also felt more secure in seclusion.

With no money for a baby-sitter, Jeanne seldom left the apartment. Even with much mending, her clothes became threadbare, but she refused to spend much-needed money on replacing them. Luis finally ripped the most tattered dress from her back, then gave her 5 dollars and insisted she go out and buy another. A provident Jeanne stretched it to two. To make matters worse, Luis's sciatica reappeared. For weeks he could move only on crutches, and Jeanne had to bathe him. He would never again be entirely free of back problems.

When he could walk, Luis turned, first for company, then work, to émigré society. There was a silver lining to his troubles. Had he stayed at MoMA, he might easily, like others of the thirties' avant-garde, have drifted to teaching in some academic backwater, screening *Un Chien Andalou* and *L'Age d'Or* once a year to baffled freshmen. Exile and the company of exiles kept him lean, hungry and committed.

Breton's arrival in New York also rekindled Luis's interest in Surrealism. He joined the circle that met democratically at the apartments of various sympathizers and became the nucleus of the anti-Fascist magazine *VVV*. Exile had not dulled Breton's arrogance. When the group roosted with a rich dilettante who tried to join in the conversation, Breton (who, like St Exupéry, never learned English) snapped, '*Monsieur, vous nous emmerdez. Sortez d'ici.*' ('Sir, you're giving us the shits. Get out of here.') Meekly, the man left.

With no doctrinaire squabbles or prospective *scandales* to occupy their minds, Breton's New York circle had an almost playful atmosphere. If things lagged, Luis demonstrated one of his mesmerist party tricks. Leaving the room, he would invite Ernst, Tanguy or Duchamp to pick up an object while he was absent. When he returned, he could usually identify what had been touched and by whom.

The large secluded patio of one borrowed apartment also suggested a film project to the group, and Buñuel, Duchamp and Léger discussed making a pornographic movie there. Buñuel's sole experience of film porn was *Sister Vaseline*, a two-reeler involving a nun, a randy gardener and a friar, shown to him by Mauclaire. He had not particularly cared for it but at the time he and René Char had contemplated shocking a bourgeois audience by including it in an otherwise conventional programme, ideally when children were present. Since New York courts could impose ten-year jail sentences for producing porn, the project was quickly dropped.

Buñuel also joked again about opening a bar, this time with Juanito and Rosita Negrin. Speculating how revolution might be loosed on capitalist America, they invented a wildly expensive nightclub called the Cannonball. In French argot, a *coup de bambou* means a gross overcharge; a *coup de canon* would be an even more extravagant rip-off. At the Cannonball, where only the most exotic concoctions would be served, a cannon near the door would ritually fire every time a client's tab passed 1000 dollars. Out in the suburbs, poor workers would hear, and hopefully, be moved to rise in their wrath.

The only significant remnant of Luis's New York career is a twenty-two page outline he wrote with the exiled poet Juan Larrea of the latter's lost novel, *Illegible, Son of Flute*.* A fable he later dismissed as 'a bit of a throwback to Surrealism; a few good ideas clustered about the old chestnut of a dead Europe and the new life flowering in Latin America', it follows its hero, Villa-Lobos, through a series of dream-like incidents that take him from Finisterre, the literary end of the earth, to the idyllic paradise Columbia, 'the country of the pigeon, of the winged being, where the creative imagination spreads its poetic wings'.

In an introduction to the treatment, Buñuel complained that realism preoccupied the cinema. 'Moving pictures merely repeat what we have been told for centuries by novels and plays. Thus, a marvellous instrument for the expression of poetry and dreams (the subconscious world) is reduced to the role of simple REPEATER of stories expressed by other art forms.' The narrative, with its train- and ship-wrecks, conversations carried out in lantern slides, and repeated invocation of mother, religion, eternal renewal and *l'amour fou*, has the comic-book jerkiness of much twenties' Surrealism. It falls as flat as the final poem which, aiming at the profound, barely achieves the banal.

> What is life? Madness.
> What is life? Illusion.
> The dreams of a shadow.
> Even the greatest good is little:
> All life is a dream.
> And dreams are dreams.

There was as yet no formal anti-Communist blacklist in America, so Buñuel could work. Through screenwriter Vladimir Pozner, he recorded commentaries in New York for what he remembers as fifteen or twenty training films about artillery and bombing made for the Corps of Engineers by MGM.

---

* Buñuel said he did not start work on this until he arrived in Mexico in 1947, but a copy of the treatment, titled simply *Illegible*, was found in his desk at MoMA after he left.

It was almost a year before he found a steady job. Still on crutches, he hobbled into Warner Brothers' New York Office, to be offered a twenty-six week contract as Spanish Dubbing Producer in Hollywood at 200 dollars a week. Under the deal signed on 15 May 1944, Warners advanced him 750 dollars, paid for the family's train tickets to Los Angeles, and bought up for 160 dollars the balance of the lease on his apartment signed on 30 June the previous year. It also agreed he could continue to work on private projects.

Buñuel has said that he expected to produce features for Warners, then supposedly thinking of repeating their 1930 experiment of foreign versions for the Spanish market, but the files do not bear this out. He was hired for dubbing alone, and with no great enthusiasm on Warners' part. One senses some vigorous string-pulling from a friend of Buñuel's in the New York bureau behind the LA office's grudging wire to its Foreign Versions Department: 'AGREEABLE WORK WITH HIM IN FREE-LANCE BASIS UNTIL SUCH TIME AS HE MAY FIND A SOLID SPANISH LEADING MAN IN CALIFORNIA.'

Still barely able to walk, Luis spent most of the train trip to Los Angeles on his back. He and Jeanne found a small bungalow on Fulton Avenue, one of the quiet, wide, tree-lined streets that cross the San Fernando Valley, and for eighteen months he drove every morning to the Warners lot to supervise the revoicing of films for Latin America. His first completed job was *My Reputation* with Barbara Stanwyck and George Brent, which became *El Que Diran*. Warners were proud enough of the result to announce it in the trade press. Buñuel later claimed he had thirty-four employees, but he probably meant the freelance 'stock company of more than forty experienced Latin American artists' that Warners mentioned in its press release. In November Buñuel's salary was raised to 225 dollars a week, so obviously he gave satisfaction, but his heart was not in the work. He made a negligible personal impression. Rudi Fehr, long-time head of Warners' editing department and usually a mine of reminiscence, does not remember him at all.

Life in Los Angeles was agreeable enough. Jeanne loved the beach. Luis preferred expeditions into the countryside, on which he acquainted himself with the animals and especially the insects of California. 'My first recollection of my father,' says Juan Luis Buñuel, 'is going out in the country and looking under rocks for ants and spiders and such. I've done the same with my children and I'm sure his father did the same with him.' Luis drove up into the high desert around Llano and Antelope Valley where he could enjoy his growing collection of hand-guns. A few years later, asked by a French magazine to name his hobbies, he nominated 'Ballistics' and his collection as 'Modern arms'.

Since Californian public schools were so poor, Juan Luis went to the Sacred Heart school on Sunset Boulevard, continuing an education which Luis ensured was almost totally American. In deference to Doña Maria, Luis did agree to his son receiving his First Communion when he was eleven. The evening before, the priest sent all the communicants home for their fathers' blessings. When Juan Luis asked Luis to comply, he lifted him by the lapels of his white suit and snarled: 'If you tell my friends about this, I'll kill you.' He never got the blessing. Both sons continued their education in the United States, Juan Luis graduating from Oberlin, Rafael from the University of New Mexico.

Buñuel continued to find his friends among the émigrés. As well as the Spanish contingent, he socialized with René Clair and Erich von Stroheim. Often they met at the home of Albert Lewin, who had left MGM to direct his own films, and whose modernist Santa Monica house was filled with contemporary art, some of it Surrealist. Man Ray, another friend of Lewin's, had also returned to the United States and was flirting with working as a movie cameraman to eke out his photography income. Buñuel's imagination was caught by a huge garbage dump outside LA, a wasteland of debris: 'everything from orange peels to grand pianos and whole houses [. . .] inhabited by real people'. He and Ray wrote a treatment for *The Sewers of Los Angeles*, a von Stroheim-esque drama set there, but, not surprisingly, had no luck in finding funding. With the young Spanish writer José Rubia Barcia, an authority on Valle-Inclan who taught at UCLA, Buñuel also collaborated on the treatment for a thriller, *The Midnight Bride*, about a girl's mysterious disappearance, but aroused no interest.

Robert Florey had come to Hollywood from Paris in the 1920s as a gangling young assistant director, and quickly appointed himself Hollywood's unofficial French cultural consul. Relentlessly gregarious, he took it upon himself to show new arrivals around Hollywood, introduce them to the community, lend them French books. He had met Buñuel and seen some of his films – without, according to his biographer, particularly liking them.

In 1945 Florey, like Buñuel, was under contract to Warners, and contemplating without relish a Curt Siodmak screenplay called *The Beast with Five Fingers*, based on a story by William Fryer Harvey about a famous pianist who, incapacitated by a stroke, lurches around his Gothic mansion attended by a sinister secretary to whom he has promised to bequeath his library of occult books. When he leaves everything to a niece, the secretary sets out to dispose of her, until hallucinations of the pianist's severed hand, scuttling across the tiled floors like a white spider, drive him crazy.

Warners wanted the secretary to be played by Peter Lorre, to cash in on his success a decade before in Karl Freund's *Mad Love*, where he had played a sinister surgeon who grafts a murderer's hands on to those of a pianist. Florey did not want to do the film, and had already sat out a six-month suspension for refusing to make it. Having finally acquiesced, however, the director, Buñuel claimed, asked him to work on the script.

Time and speculation have embedded the legend of *The Beast with Five Fingers* in Buñuel scholarship. Some sources claim that Buñuel planned the entire severed hand sequence, but that producer William Jacobs vetoed the result as too florid. Buñuel himself insisted that his ideas were the entire basis of the script.

Though Florey never referred to him in connection with the 1947 film and Buñuel is mentioned nowhere in Warners' files on the production, there are good reasons to think he worked on it in some capacity. He misremembered dates and confused chronology but he seldom lied, and never in such factual detail. As for the film itself, the severed hand, its Hispanic setting and morbid humour (the hand solos on a Bach chaconne for the left hand), the fruity performances by Lorre and Victor Francen, the latter a precursor of the suave bearded aesthetes played by Fernando Rey in late Buñuel, all argue for Luis's involvement. But there is no denying that the original already contained the ambulant severed hand.

A clue may lie in Buñuel's request in 1945 that Braunberger reassign to him the rights in *Un Chien Andalou*. The producer grudgingly agreed, retaining *Las Hurdes*, and noted that Luis later made distribution deals on the film in the United States. Perhaps he intended selling *Un Chien Andalou* to Warners, via Florey, to protect itself from charges of plagiarism. Had he sued Warners as he contemplated, the issue would be clearer, but friends advised him that the studio lawyers would mangle him in court. Though Buñuel dropped the matter, it always rankled with him.

By the time *The Beast with Five Fingers* was released, Luis had left both Warners and the United States. In the summer of 1945, another old friend had appeared in Hollywood. After Pierre Batcheff's suicide, Denise married Roland Tual and, as she had always intended, became a producer. Probably with the idea of remaking it, MGM bought her production of Robert Bresson's *Les Anges du Péché*, a melodrama about the relationship between a delinquent girl and a novice nun, and Denise arrived in April 1945 to discuss it with Louis B. Mayer. She had a reunion with René Clair and Luis, who lamented the frustrations of working in Hollywood. Later, lunching with Mayer, she mentioned Buñuel.

Mayer cupped his hand over his ear. 'Who's that?'

'Buñuel.'

Mayer turned to an assistant. 'Who's he?'

The assistant did not know, so Denise filled him in, concluding, 'He's a great director.'

'If he was,' LB snorted, 'I would know.'

Tual pressed on. If Mayer would just reserve a corner of the huge MGM lot for a sort of laboratory studio where directors like Buñuel, Clair and Renoir could work on new ideas, new ways of making films . . . Mayer looked aghast. What right had a foreigner and, worse, a woman to advise him? 'If Hollywood needs to change its way of making films one day,' he snapped, 'it'll happen, and quickly. We don't need a laboratory for that!' Tual soon found herself out on her ear, and MGM's interest in *Les Anges du Péché* cooled rapidly.

With the war over, Hollywood was worried, without reason, that markets would collapse. Salary cuts were in the air, and it was always messengers, janitors and contract staff who went first. Buñuel was not asked to go, but he made no effort to stay.

Hollywood's political climate was turning against the left. He had felt the first chill in 1944 when he was told that he would have to register his guns; only American citizens could hold weapons. A Communist friend named Payne, secretary to the Governor of California, arranged things, but at the same time warned Luis that the state assembly's Fact-Finding Committee on Un-American Activities under Senator Jack B. Tenney was determined to expose Communism in Los Angeles. He himself was getting rid of all his Marxist books.

On 17 November Luis's contract expired. He was uncertain of his next move, until Denise Tual suggested a new avenue. 'Puffed up with the success of *Anges du Péché* in France,' she says, 'I was full of audacity, and of ideas.' If Hollywood didn't want her, she would go to Mexico. She decided to film *The House of Bernarda Alba*, Lorca's 1936 play about the women of a tyrannized provincial household. Its all-female cast made it a natural step from the largely feminine *Anges du Péché*.

She proposed the project to Buñuel. 'I hadn't time to finish my phrase,' Tual said. 'It was a subject he loved, which reunited him with his youth, his friend Lorca, with Spain. He didn't need another argument to follow me to Mexico.'

In fact, Buñuel was lying. He still had his doubts about Lorca's flowery language, and could not see how it could be adapted to the screen. For the next thirty years producers would propose that he film *Bernarda Alba*. He always refused. However, he could see some logic in Tual's suggestion of a Mexican film, and agreed to go with her to explore it.

The trip began disastrously. Luis, who hated flying and could only endure the experience when drunk, dragged his feet to such an extent that they left on separate planes. As Tual prepared to take off in a craft that looked to her like some dilapidated toy, Immigration officers piled in a repatriated Mexican family, including a squalling baby with infected ears.

The plane was stifling, and the trip was made no less unpleasant by a night landing in the desert to refuel after most of the gas leaked out. As they landed in Mexico City, a steward sprayed the cabin with DDT. Dizzy and sick from the journey, the fumes, the heat and the altitude, Tual still managed to correct her make-up and straighten her Paris *tailleur*, having noticed a gang of pressmen and a mariachi band on the tarmac. But they were waiting for Shirley Temple, who had been expected on the same flight. To round off the trip, Mexican Immigration judged her visa 'irregular' and locked her up until Buñuel arrived to talk (and bribe) her out.

Initially, Mexico City, with its eighteenth-century houses built from volcanic stone the colour of dried blood, did not impress either Denise or Luis. The office blocks erupting next to ancient churches knocked crooked by earthquakes were like a metaphor for the violence implicit in Mexican society. The spirit of dictator Porfirio Diaz, ousted in 1918, still hung over the country, as did more ancient dispositions to feuding and ritual magic. On their first morning Buñuel called Tual to read her the list of the previous day's crimes from the morning paper; eight assassinations, two rapes, a dozen kidnaps. 'You know,' he told her, 'the Mexicans must have their publicity. If there were no more assassinations, kidnaps or rapes, there wouldn't be any more American tourists. They're cultivating their legend.'

Buñuel too was cultivating his legend, though more publicly than he would have liked. Raoul Levy, a young French screenwriter and eventual producer who would be responsible for the French version of *The Adventures of Robinson Crusoe*, but who committed suicide in 1966 over his unrequited love of Jeanne Moreau, was astonished to run into him one morning leaving the Penitenciaria de Mexico, where Trotsky's assassin was held. Buñuel told Levy he had slept there, in the spare bed in the killer's cell. 'It was the best night I've passed in Mexico,' he said.

Even allowing for the possibility of a deadpan Buñuel joke, there is a mystery here. In 1945 the true identity of Trotsky's killer was still obscure. His victim knew him as Mornard, lover of his secretary Sylvia Agelof, whom he had met and seduced in Paris. He entered Mexico on a doctored passport taken from the body of a Canadian named Babich, killed fighting Franco. The OGPU changed the name to 'Jacson', not realising the spelling was odd, but nobody in Mexico questioned it.

Since Mexico had no death penalty, he was sentenced to 19½ years in 1943. The government, no friends of Trotsky, made sure he served it in comfort, installing him in a large cell with a patio and, since he was frightened of being poisoned, allowing his girlfriend, a nightclub dancer, to visit him daily with meals, champagne and other home comforts. Members of the Mexican Communist Party also kept him supplied with luxuries, in return for which he gave frequent interviews praising Stalin.

It was not until the early 1950s that Jacson/Mornard was identified as Jaime Ramon Mercader del Rio, born in Barcelona in 1913, the son of a wealthy Catalan. Mercader's Cuban mother Caridad ran off to Paris with her four sons and daughter, and became an active Party member and lover of some prominent cadres. In 1936 she and her children went to Spain to fight for the anarchists. Her eldest son was killed, and Caridad, wounded, returned to Paris in 1938. Ramon, the oldest surviving son, who had fought with the anarcho-syndicalist guerrillas, went to Moscow with his sister, where he was recruited as an agent to work in Mexico.

It strains credulity that Buñuel should have visited Mercader without knowing he was Spanish. Given Luis's *entrée* to Communist circles in Paris and Barcelona and his position at the Paris Embassy, it is likely he met Mercader/Mornard there, or at least knew of Caridad and the family. Luis was also friendly with David Alfaro Siqueiros, the Stalinist painter who led earlier attacks on the Trotsky compound, and Diego Rivera, who rented the villa to him. The incident underlines that intimacy with the Party which Luis was always at pains to deny.

In four years in Mexico, the urbane Oscar Dancigers had created a reputation both for his wily manipulation of the film market and for his gambling, which ate up all his profits and sent him searching desperately for new sources of income. Mostly his Aguila Films acted for American companies shooting south of the border. The Good Neighbour policy had been a goldmine to the Mexican bureaucracy, which could make life hell for a Hollywood unit if the correct graft was not paid. The problems of Fox's *The Captain from Castile* were held up as a horrible example.

'There are ways of getting things done in Mexico,' said John Steinbeck, a film of whose story *The Pearl* was shot there in 1945, 'and they are not the same as our ways. Any American company which gets into Mexico and tries to use our methods is going to find itself very royally taken.' The shooting of *The Pearl* had convinced him that 'everybody in Mexico up to the president himself could be bought'.

The man doing the buying on *The Pearl* had been its producer, Dancigers. 'He is a man of great integrity, enormous experience, and honesty,' Steinbeck wrote in a memo to the producers of *Viva Zapata!*. '[. . .] He knows how to do everything in Mexico. He knows not only Mexican law, but the laws of the unions, which are equally important, and a violation of any of them will bring your production to a standstill. He knows, further, how to keep costs to a minimum.' Dancigers exhibited, he said, 'all the cunning a refugee has had to acquire in order to survive'. He was 'a master of the *mordida*' – literally 'the bite'; appropriately, since the producer bore a striking resemblance to *Dracula* star Bela Lugosi.

Luis arranged a meeting with Dancigers, and Denise poured out her enthusiasm for the Lorca project. After only a minute, however, the producer made a *moue* of disdain; it was not his sort of film. Denise shrugged off his refusal; she would simply make it in France. Meanwhile, Buñuel had contacted Paquito Lorca in New York about the rights. Leaving Luis in Mexico City, Denise flew there, to a chilly reception. 'The man is little; a thin mouth, piercing eyes, not very polite,' she remembered. 'My arguments didn't reach him. It was like doing business with a Martian.' Lorca asked, not unreasonably, that Denise at least buy an option on the play but, without a financier, she refused. They agreed she would go back to Paris and look for money there. Buñuel later rang Lorca, who told him he had had a better offer from a British company. If this was so, nothing came of it. The first screen version of the play was a French TV production in 1960. Meanwhile, Luis, waiting to hear from Denise, had an unexpected call from Dancigers. 'I just might have something for you,' the producer said. 'But would you mind staying in Mexico?'

21

'South is not an American direction.'
– J.G. Ballard, *Hello America*

The post-war haemorrhaging of left-wing film-makers from Hollywood, of which Buñuel was part, received far less publicity than the Washington HUAC hearings and the imprisonment of the Hollywood Ten. Many slipped away to London or Paris, but the writers Albert Maltz, Hugo Butler and his wife Jean, Gordon Kahn, John Bright, Dalton Trumbo, Ring Lardner, Ian McLellan Hunter and many others less significant moved to Mexico, establishing communities in Mexico City and Cuernavaca where they lived for periods ranging from a few months to years, funnelling screenplays into the studios under aliases and through 'fronts'.

Their status with the Mexican government was always ambiguous. Maltz warned Herbert Biberman of the 'campaign here directed against those North American politicals who are at the moment in Mexico'. The pro-Catholic, pro-United States paper *Excelsior* campaigned against them. In 1952, *Saturday Evening Post* journalist Richard English would charge that 'American Commies have been feeding anti-US propaganda for use behind the Iron Curtain out of Mexico via Havana'. He also claimed 'the Mexican FBI keeps up a complete file on [the exiles] down to the last peso on their current bar bills'.

The even larger number of Spanish Communists in Mexico seemed to arouse less curiosity, but Buñuel still wondered how he would be received. Fortunately Fernando Benitez, secretary to the Minister of the Interior, introduced him to his boss, Hector Perez Martinez, well known as a friend of Spanish émigrés. He promised to fix a visa. Buñuel went back to the United States to sell up and wait for the call from Dancigers. When Jay Leyda, himself about to return to Europe, visited him in Los Angeles, Buñuel insisted that despite some reservations, he looked forward to Mexico. 'I shall find *something* to do there,' he said. Leyda felt he was whistling in the dark.

Francisco Aranda believes Buñuel would have found his way to Mexico sooner or later in any case. 'Not only the idiom and the race but the physical types, the dry and dusty landscape, the impassioned speech, the attitudes to life and death, the religious problem, the social structure which he attacked, all combined to restore him to conditions in which he could be himself.'

It is an inviting theory, but Buñuel was genuinely indifferent to where he lived. 'I'm not a great traveller,' he told *Cahiers du Cinéma* in 1967. 'Any unknown district disturbs me. I prefer to go back to those places I already know. For me, they are all like one another: London, New York, Moscow, Paris. I know nothing of Andalusia. I know nothing of Castile or Aragon. And if it wasn't for my films, I wouldn't know Mexico either. I don't know any of the other areas where I've shot. Next door to the horrible parched desert that you see on the screen, I've always found a remarkable hotel. Five minutes from the forest I show on the screen there are air-conditioned places. I like less and less to move myself, as the cinema demands, with an army of people. I look more and more to work in a comfortable ambience without too many complications. To be happy, it's enough for me to have some oaks.'

Certainly Buñuel was less out of his element in Mexico than he might have been in, say, England, a country for which he had a typically French artificial nostalgia, probably traceable to his *señorito* snobbery; there is no lord like an milord. (At one point he contemplated shooting *The Exterminating Angel* in London, or at least with a British cast.) Obviously he enjoyed speaking Spanish again. Also, even though President Cardenas had just announced, to an uproar from the old revolutionaries, 'I am a believer', anti-clericalism still flourished there. But Buñuel was a man at home nowhere. He would live in Mexico as he had in Paris, in a world of his own which ran to his schedule and obeyed his rules. The British critic Michael Wood is right in saying that Mexico 'above all [allowed] Buñuel to practise being *no one*, like Odysseus, and nourished his secret personality and his ability to be everywhere'.

Until 1945, film production in Mexico had soared as the United States obligingly choked off supplies to Argentina, its greatest rival. Mexico produced seventy films in 1943 alone. With producers queueing to use the three main studios, CLASA, Azteca and Mexico-Films, entrepreneurs had hurriedly updated facilities and built new ones. The Tepeyac studios were refurbished, and American businessman Harry Wright constructed a new complex between Azteca and CLASA in the suburb of Churubusco. Denise Tual toured its fourteen sound stages and modern post-production facilities, and agreed they were impressive. In September 1943, even before Churubusco was finished, two RKO executives arrived in Mexico City to buy a controlling interest. They also offered to distribute the entire output of CLASA/Film Mundiales, particularly the films by their biggest star, the comic Cantinflas.

Internationally, Mexican cinema seemed to have arrived. Raoul de Ande, head of the producers' organization, announced that the existing hand-to-mouth system of turning out single films cheaply for Mexico alone was a thing of the past. A new legal structure categorized films as Class A (1 million pesos),*B (600,000 pesos) and C (300,000 pesos). The government offered some assistance, but A and B productions got the lion's share. C films were expected to survive on what they could earn in the market. De Ande wanted companies with continuity of production who could mount programmes of films with export potential. The implications to small operators like Dancigers were clear. This Hollywood-style Mexican industry would marginalize them.

Dancigers would have preferred to continue as a well-paid middleman for foreign companies on location, but his Communism, an advantage in negotiating with Mexico's biggest film union, the Sindicato de Trabajadores de la Industria Cinematografo (STIC), which was rigidly Marxist, did not sit well with Hollywood. When Steinbeck and Elia Kazan suggested shooting *Viva Zapata!* in Mexico with Dancigers as co-producer, Twentieth Century-Fox's legal department tabled a 107-page State Department file fingering him as a Party veteran and one-time active agent.

At Mexico City airport the Buñuels were met by Luis's most influential friends, José Ignacio and Conchita Mantecon. As Governor General of Aragon under the Republic, Mantecon, officially socialist but secretly Communist, had fought the excesses of the anarchists. He had ordered the CNT to break up its collective farms and return confiscated goods, and once made a speech from the window of the Buñuel house in Calanda urging the people to forget free love and get on with their lives. At the end of the war he fled to Mexico and a frugal exile. In 1948 he would reveal his sympathies and join the Party, but for the moment he was another of the covert Communists who surrounded Luis almost all his life.

Jeanne was glad of a support group. The Mantecons, with Ugarte, Luis and Janet Alcoriza, and Ana-Maria Custodio, Luis's star from the first

---

* 100,000 US dollars at the 1946 rate. A Hollywood B-picture cost around 125,000 dollars, a cheap Western 85,000 dollars. Most of Buñuel's Mexican films were made on the budget of a Blondie and Dagwood comedy or a programmer like *Think Fast, Mr Moto*.

Filmofono production, now married to Gustavo Pittaluga, assisted in finding an apartment and domestic help. She would rely on them increasingly as Luis became more deeply involved in film-making. Juan Luis enrolled in the American School, joined the Boy Scouts and began to enjoy life in a country where the air was still unpolluted and the company congenial. Jeanne was less happy. Social occasions assumed a numbing sameness. After dinner, almost always with exiled Republicans, the men would retire to smoke and talk while the women played canasta.

Once they were settled in, Buñuel started discussing projects with Dancigers. He showed him the *Wuthering Heights* and *Illegible* treatments but the producer brushed them away. Perhaps later, he said, when business had improved. What he needed right now was Class C films with export potential. Buñuel cobbled together screenable prints of some Filmofono productions from the battered copies that survived Mexico's haphazard projectionists and ran them for Dancigers. The fact that he had not actually directed them did not arise, although it was soon to prove embarrassingly obvious that, though able to lecture others on Hollywood technique, he was less skilful at employing it himself.

Dancigers had hired two stars who were big in the Latin American market, Argentinian tango singer Libertad Lamarque and Jorge Negrete, Mexico's most popular cowboy vocalist. Though running to fat, Negrete, who affected the full *charro* costume, including pistols, and never appeared without his groom, had a huge following. '[He] towers over the colourfully clad extras who surround him,' wrote a puzzled British critic of the time, 'and, like Frank Sinatra in the States, makes women swoon with his songs. He is the embodiment of the "he-man", the bad boy who wins the girl with tears and by knowing when to use his revolver, which is far too often.' His appeal went beyond the box office. Negrete had been instrumental in forming STPC, a breakaway union opposed to STIC. When STIC threatened to strike, he and other actors had turned out with guns to frighten off the pickets. His presence in the film was useful insurance.

Resourcefully Buñuel found a plot in a novel by his friend Michel Weber about gold prospectors, which he shifted to the rowdy coastal oilfields of Tampico before their 1938 nationalization. Edmund Baez and one of Mexico's most prolific screenwriters and novelists, Mauricio Magdaleno, wrote the script, initially called *In Old Tampico* but changed to *Gran Casino*. To rewrite it, Luis checked into the spa of San José Purua in Michoacán, partly for peace and partly for its hot sulphur springs, which helped his sciatica. It became his favourite hideaway. He would work there on twenty more screenplays. In the bar of its hotel, overlooking a canyon filled with vegetation and with a giant *ziranda* tree almost touching the window, encouraging him to imagine its branches filled with birds, snakes, even naked women, Luis could relax and fantasize at leisure.

Buñuel started shooting on 26 November 1945. Negrete and Libertad competed vigorously for the spotlight during the musical numbers, but although Buñuel described the shoot as a duel of egos between them, the five songs, average for a cheap musical, are among its more interesting sequences. Buñuel had not been behind a camera for ten years and even then was less than adept technically. Sensing his insecurity, cameraman Jack Draper was unhelpful. Their problems show in the film's hit-or-miss style, with odd cuts from extreme close-up to long shot, and jarring appearances by the Los Calaveras singing trio. Dancigers, as part of a sponsorship deal with the distillers, also insisted on a bottle of Fundador brandy being prominently displayed at every opportunity.

The only Buñuelian touch comes during a moonlit love scene on an oil-field. As Negrete and Libertad share their first kiss, the camera tilts down to the muddy ground which he idly pokes with a stick. He lifts out the stick, dripping, and the camera tilts back to their faces as the kiss ends. The connotation of sex with mud, first seen in *L'Age d'Or*, would be repeated periodically in Buñuel's films, culminating in Séverine fouled in *Belle de Jour*.

Despite, or perhaps because of, its occasional virtuosity, *Gran Casino* flopped. For two years after it, Buñuel did not work at all. The family survived on loans from the long-suffering Doña Maria. He had to stop repaying Sanchez Ventura, who complained to their Paris friends that Buñuel was buying champagne with his money. A surly Luis responded that it was not champagne, but whisky. The two men became estranged for some years. Buñuel was also embarrassed when Benjamin Péret turned up on the set of *Gran Casino* and asked for work. Driven out of Brazil for his Communism, he had arrived broke in Mexico City and moved in with the Surrealist painter Remedios Varo. Luis, with almost no money to support his own family, could do little to help him.

All the same, life in Mexico City was more comfortable and cheaper than California. Buñuel applied for residency in 1948. He saw plenty of his adoptive country in those years. Tourism demeaned a *señorito*, but Luis enjoyed the aristocratic rituals of the camping trip and the hunt, although he hated actually killing anything. Fortunately plenty of Mexicans were ready to join him in a weekend of shooting at nothing in particular.

The revolutionary tradition still flourished in Mexico, especially in regions like Guerrero, on the south coast, where guns were respected and used. Luis revelled in tales, however apocryphal, of vendettas, manhunts and backlands revenge. The reasoned cruelty and sanctioned violence of Mexico widened his sadistic streak.

Like most compact machines, the pistol had a special appeal for the Surrealists. Breton had posited as 'the simplest Surrealist gesture' simply shooting at random into a crowd. Even in Spain nobody pushed the nihilism and randomness of Surrealism that far, but in Mexico Buñuel was to see Diego Rivera do something very like it, taking potshots with his revolver from his car.

Negrete was not alone in carrying a gun on the set. Directors like Chano Urueta routinely packed a .45. 'You never know what might happen,' he told Luis. Pedro Armendariz, the lead in Buñuel's *El Bruto*, also went armed, and blew out his brains in a hospital in 1963 when diagnosed as suffering from cancer. The most notorious *pistolero* in the film business was director Emilio Fernandez, nicknamed 'El Indio' ('The Indian'). Vicious and hysterical, with an effeminate voice that belied his taste for violence, he killed four men, including an extra on one of his films, and was jailed for shooting a journalist in a trivial argument over a Cannes Festival prize. Dancigers loathed and feared him, ever since Fernandez had slapped him in some film wrangle.

Buñuel had brought from Los Angeles the nucleus of a respectable arsenal. Even as a child he had been fascinated by pistols. At fourteen he stole a small Browning from his father's armoury and carried it until his mother became suspicious. When two boys threatened him with a bloody banderilla, he took out the pistol and aimed it at them. Later he apologized, but his pleasure at the power conferred by this elegant little instrument remained with him all his life. In Mexico he became an adept fast-draw *pistolero*, practising every weekend at a nearby gun club. For the 1968 Mexico City Olympic Games, he was invited to captain the Mexican shooting team – an emeritus position which, nevertheless, he turned down. Like all his enthusiasms, that for firearms was essentially private.

'He regularly cleans and polishes shotguns and Winchester carbines, rare Mausers and Lugers, Smith and Wessons, little Astras and ancient duelling pistols as dainty as greyhounds,' commented a visitor, who also noticed 'his little crucible, [where], with the ritual gestures of Crusoe, he moulds lead shot'. Always a tinkerer who carried a tool kit everywhere and enjoyed doing small repairs, Buñuel learned to fill his own cartridges, experimenting with new kinds of powder and larger loads. He would try these out in the house, if necessary, often with his sons as a fascinated audience.

'His ideal was to judge the powder in a bullet so accurately', recalls Juan Luis, 'that he could shoot a bullet into his hand. One day he called me and said, "That's it. I've got it. The narrowness of the barrel, so many grains of powder; it's perfect." But, just in case, he put a book, a small pillow and a piece of paper on the floor. "The bullet shouldn't go through the piece of paper." Bang! The bullet went through the paper, the pillow, the book *and* made a hole in the floor!'

In Cleveland in the 1960s, Juan Luis found the perfect gift for his father. The Bullet Trap was an armoured box, the interior steel spiral of which would stop anything up to a .38. Buñuel used it to practise indoors, which further damaged his hearing. Already totally deaf in his left ear, he continued to shoot, even though, a few years before, participating in a Zaragoza gun competition held in a tunnel, he had been agonized by the noise. By the mid-1950s he needed an electronic aid. Juanito Negrin, an ear and brain specialist, told him in the 1970s that he could clear the ossification surgically, but Buñuel refused. 'He was too scared,' says Juan Luis.

Dancigers was not idle while Buñuel was out hunting. He released features in both 1947 and 1948, then made two films in quick succession with the actor Fernando Soler. A fixture of Mexican stage and screen, Soler was an improbable leading man on the lines of character actor Cecil Kellaway but, despite his paunch, comic moustache and baldness, which he disguised with artful recombing, Mexican audiences liked him. He specialized in roles as the tyrannical father trying to control disobedient children, which critics saw as evidence of a subconscious yearning for the more certain days of Diaz.

Protective of his image, Soler directed himself in the Dancigers movies, so there was no work for Buñuel. Instead, Luis began collaborating with Janet and Luis Alcoriza. They were a gaudily theatrical couple. In Spain, Alcoriza's family had run a travelling theatre. He acted in it, but he was more playboy than artist, a life-style he retained even when he fled to Mexico. Needing money to support his fast cars, all-night parties and flagrant infidelities, he began writing scripts with the tolerant Janet. Buñuel took a paternal interest in both of them. With the couple, he wrote *Si Usted no Puede . . . Yo Si (If You Can't . . . I Can)*, a script which the Alcorizas adapted for Julian Soler to direct in 1950.

Dancigers urged them to keep working, and suggested a story about street kids, a subject going through one of its periodic vogues. Anonymous in overalls and a straw hat, Buñuel toured the back streets of Mexico City in search of material. Often alone but sometimes with set designer Edward Fitzgerald, he prowled through the *ciudades perdidas*, the 'lost quarters' of Nonoalco, the Romita Plaza and the slums of Tacubaya, observing the markets, street kids and mutilated beggars, but, above all, the poverty and superstition that debilitated the city even as the gimcrack skyscrapers of the economic boom rose above the slums. Social workers at the Juvenile Court had plenty of stories about street gang warfare and murdered children. They fuelled Buñuel's Jansenist conviction that, for all the pietistic bromides of Hollywood fantasies about slum-kid redemption like *Boy's Town*, some social ills, especially those contracted when young, could not be cured. Perhaps it was even sacrilegious to try. If God had not wanted them shorn, he would not have made them sheep.

The experience produced plenty of story ideas. One followed the lottery ticket sellers who pestered people to buy what they insisted was their last ticket or '*huerfanito*' (orphan). He roughed out *Mi Huerfanito, Jefe! (My Orphan, Boss!)* and with the Alcorizas, another treatment, more bleak and unsparing, called *La Manzana Podrida (The Rotten Apple)*, based on a news story about the corpse of a twelve-year-old found on a city dump. With contributions from Juan Larrea and Max Aub, another Spanish émigré who had written Malraux's *L'Espoir*, this became *Los Olvidados* (literally, 'The Forgotten Ones').

Soler was happy with his two Dancigers films and agreed to let Buñuel 'help out' on the next, *El Gran Calavera (The Great Madcap)*, which the Alcorizas adapted from a Spanish play by Adolfo Torrado. A grateful Buñuel started shooting at Tepeyac on 9 June 1949. The comedy of the rich and spoilt discovering new values when they lose their money and have to fend for themselves was a Hollywood perennial. It would come as no surprise to see the plot of *El Gran Calavera* used for a Tyrone Power/Priscilla Lane romantic comedy with a 'character drunk' like Leon Errol in the Soler role, although the chalky lighting and banal shooting are more reminiscent of other regional imitations of Hollywood, like the thirties comedies of Australian Ken G. Hall.

Soler plays Don Ramiro, a wealthy businessman who has started to hit the bottle since the death of his wife. His family and staff exploit him until his brother Gregorio persuades them to play along in a charade. When Ramiro wakes up from a drugged sleep he finds himself in a mean flat in a poor suburb with his brother Ladislao, sister-in-law, son and daughter Virginia. They tell him he has been in a coma for a year since his firm went broke.

They expect the lesson to last only a day or two, but Ramiro discovers the deception and turns the tables, convincing the family he really is ruined. They are forced to live like the poor for months. Ladislao becomes a carpenter, his wife takes in laundry, the son shines shoes, the daughter keeps house. Inevitably, it is the making of them. Their health and temper improve, and Virginia falls for Pablo, an electrician who cruises the streets advertising Sin of Syria face cream and Sigh of Venus stockings over a loud-speaker on top of his car. Inadvertently their first love scene is broadcast for the neighbourhood. Forced by the snobbish family of her fiancé Alfredo into an unwanted marriage, Virginia is rescued by Pablo, who drives his car up to the church and drowns out the service with advertisements. As the lovers flee, Ramiro fends off the guests with a large cross.

Some critics later detected Surrealist wit and subversion in *Gran Casino* and *El Gran Calavera*, but Buñuel was the first to admit that both were mediocre in technique and banal in content. However, the working-class setting of the latter let him include some of the detail he had seen on his walks about Mexico City. He had fun, too, with the anti-clerical climax, which he would echo in *The Exterminating Angel*. Soler was too familiar with his character to need much direction, and the men got on well enough to work together in two more films. Soler even agreed to an improvised opening scene. The soles of six pairs of shoes sticking into the camera resolve themselves into a heap of sleeping drunks sobering up on the floor of a police cell, the smartest footwear among the miscellany of dirty sneakers and sandals belonging to Ramiro. The men disentangle themselves and, after formal expressions of mutual regard that parody Mexico's lumpen provincial etiquette, wander off into the morning streets.

Gran Casino had demonstrated to an alarmed Buñuel that B-movie technique, all medium long shots and simple pans, had its limitations. Worried about his technical shortcomings, he worked out the shooting of *El Gran Calavera* in more detail beforehand, and used the film to brush up. He was tested by the ambitious first-act interiors, including a reception for Virginia's engagement to the gold-digging Alfredo (played by Luis Alcoriza) which Ramiro drunkenly disrupts, calling Alfredo's mother 'Señor' because of her moustache.

Determined never again to be faced with technical challenges he could not solve Luis evolved a technique that was to become the envy of every technician, and the delight of penny-pinching producers. Each of his films had about 125 shots, which he planned in detail beforehand at home, complete with measurements and durations. 'He prepared a film with a stop-watch,' said Gabriel Figueroa. 'He'd arrive with a plan of work already made, and would move an armchair half a centimetre, a table a metre; cut the beginning and end [off a script], remove anything decorative, and you'd have his work plan almost exactly.' He seldom needed more than two takes of a shot, and never covered himself with additional shooting. On a typical feature he would expose only 20,000 metres of film, against the 80,000 of most directors. He never looked at rushes. Pierre Lary, his assistant on his last films, nervously called it 'working without a net' but admitted that it worked. Editing also took only a week or two, since it simply involved assembling the footage. Not for the first time, Luis had discovered that will and persistence would solve the most intractable problem.

El Gran Calavera opened on 25 November 1949. Its modest box-office success made Buñuel ambitious. Since Dancigers was preoccupied with potboilers, he began discussions with an independent producer, Pancho Cabrera. From his old Filmofono schedule, he proposed a book by Benito Perez Galdos. It should not be difficult to replicate his nineteenth-century Spanish settings in Mexico, and his Zola-esque realism could well appeal to the Latin American audience. Cabrera was tempted. An international star like Dolores del Rio might well agree to play in such a film. With Cabrera's money, Buñuel acquired from Maria Perez Galdos, the writer's daughter, the rights to two novels, *Doña Perfecta* (1876), about a young man stifled by the overbearingly clerical society of a small town, and *Nazarin* (1895), the story of Don Nazario Zaharin, a saintly priest who tries to replicate the humility, poverty and chastity of Christ, and is, naturally, hounded and criticized for it. The more embittered tone of *Nazarin*, written late in Perez Galdos's life, when the writer was already going blind, appealed to Buñuel. If anything, he took the point of view of the mob and the state rather than that of the writer. Don Nazario, however well-meaning, seemed to him absurdly unrealistic, fatally misled. How might a man fall into such a trap? Could he escape from his delusions and come to some accommodation with his fellow men? Robinson Crusoe, as isolated on his island as Nazario is in his system of belief, would attract Buñuel for the same reason.

Assuming Cabrera had got his message, Luis gave him *Nazarin* to adapt. The result appalled him. Cabrera not only swallowed Perez Galdos's piety whole, but augmented it, so that the priest was now a plaster saint. When he turned to *Doña Perfecta*, the news was even worse. One morning, Buñuel read in the trade papers that Cabrera would produce the film with Dolores del Rio, but with Roberto Gavaldon directing. When Buñuel confronted him, the producer explained casually that del Rio preferred to work with the man who made her two last films. Furious, Luis demanded the rights to the book, which he finally won after union arbitration. But it would be years before he found anyone ready to make it the way he wanted.

Dancigers, meanwhile, had launched his plush new company, Ultramar, and was ready to back Buñuel, though only in films he felt would sell. The two men settled on a compromise. For every two or three commercial projects, Buñuel could make a more personal film. Dancigers, however, hedged his bets. There must be no expensive stars or sets, and Buñuel would draw only a basic salary. As for Luis's technical problems, the producer covered himself on the first film, *Los Olvidados*, by hiring the country's most prestigious, stubborn and fast-working director of photography, Gabriel Figueroa.

Handsome, with a strong profile and a dramatic moustache, Figueroa might have made an actor but for his shortness. Roaring around Mexico City in his Mustang, he was the acknowledged star among Mexican technicians. After starting out as a studio portraitist, he had come under the influence of Eduard Tissé's epic compositions for Eisenstein's uncompleted *Qui Viva Mexico!* and the agitprop murals of Siquieros and Rivera. In 1935/6 he studied in Hollywood with Gregg Toland, who lit *Citizen Kane* and *The Grapes of Wrath*. Toland convinced him that painterly pictorialism best rendered Mexico's harsh light and massive cloudscapes. By 1950 his visual signature was well established and much imitated. Elia Kazan bemoaned his taste for groups of women in *rebozos* holding candles, and red-filtered shots of men massed in spotless *guyaberas* against cauliflowers of cumulus. He was bitter that, as head of Section 2, Tecnicos y Manuales (cameramen and technicians) of STIC, Figueroa alone had the power to clear *gringo* units to shoot in Mexico, often demanding a Marxist slant as the price of acceptance.

Dancigers cajoled Figueroa. He would almost certainly lose his last centavo on Buñuel's film, he told him, but he liked Luis very much and wanted to make him happy, so he was hiring only the greatest talents . . . Figueroa was not fooled, but as a favour to a couple of comrades, he took the job.

It is hard to imagine the stiff-necked pre-war Buñuel knuckling down to a collaboration with someone like Figueroa, but fifteen years in the intellectual wilderness had softened his character and taught him that film was a collaborative art. 'Until I came here, I made a film the way a writer makes a book, and on my friends' money at that,' he told the German critic Wilfried Berghahn in 1963. 'Here in Mexico I have become a professional in the film world.'

22

'In this life it is not difficult to die.
It is more difficult to live.'
– V. V. Mayakovsky

Buñuel invited fifty friends to a first screening of *Los Olvidados* on 9 November 1950. 'As they left, all of them were very polite. "Very good, Buñuel, very good", without any enthusiasm, and a severe expression. Then Bertha Gamboa, a Mexican, the wife of [the painter] Leon Felipe, came at me with nails sharpened, a furious air, a harpy, ready to tear out my eyes. I was frightened, I couldn't step back. She screamed at me: "Worthless! Trash! Dirty beast! Those children aren't Mexicans! I'm going to have you arrested. Hooligan!" She's beside herself. And Lupe Rivera, daughter of the painter Diego Rivera, was next to her, stiff as a statue. [David] Siqueiros, who was on my right, and who had already congratulated me with enthusiasm, said to me: "Pay no attention".'

But Buñuel couldn't get over it. These people were friends and, in many cases, political allies. Most had dined with him and Jeanne. They were, however, mostly Mexicans, and, as such, provincial and chauvinistic. It was a jolting reminder that Paris did not have a monopoly on prejudice. His discouragement increased when *Los Olvidados* was attacked by the same patriotic and moral factions that had forced *L'Age d'Or* off the screen. In Mexico City they stopped short of closing the cinema, but Pedro di Urdimalas, who had advised Buñuel on Mexico City slang, asked to have his name taken off the film, and Jorge Negrete, meeting Luis in the Tepeyac cafeteria not long afterwards, told him: 'You made that *Olvidados* thing? If I'd been in Mexico at the time, I'd have made sure it was never shown.' Others demanded his Mexican residency be revoked.

There was a certain naiveté in Buñuel's surprise. He knew *Los Olvidados* was not only unlike any film he had ever made; it was unlike any other made in Mexico. People who noted his theme and cast of unknowns expected something in the semi-documentary Neo-realist tradition pioneered by Zavattini and Rossellini. They were not prepared for a film that leapfrogged Neo-realism entirely, taking them into areas of Freudian obsession and Surrealist dream imagery.

Buñuel met Zavattini later, and tried to explain to him his reasons for rejecting Neo-realism. 'We were having lunch together, and the first example I could think of was the glass of wine which I was drinking. To a Neo-realist, I said to him, a glass is a glass and nothing else [. . .] But that same glass, seen by different men, can be a thousand different things [. . .] and none sees it the way it really is, but the way his desires and his mood want to see it. I strive for a cinema that will make me see those types of glasses, because that cinema will give me an integral vision of reality; it will increase my knowledge of things and beings, and will open to me the marvellous world of the unknown.'

Los Olvidados follows a few weeks in the lives of half a dozen Mexico City pre-teen street kids. In that time, one boy, Pedro, dies and another, Ojitos (Big-Eyes), abandoned by his father, joins. Too lazy and ill-organized to be called a gang, the group hangs about the markets and building sites, gossiping, bumming cigarettes and playing at bullfights.

They're aroused to action and violence by the reappearance of Jaibo, an older, taller boy who's just escaped from a reformatory and is looking for revenge on the informer who put him there. Sexually mature, socially empowered, as thin, sinewy and pale as one of El Greco's androgynous Christs, Jaibo propagates sex and murder through his total immorality. Hoping to touch him with the magic of a disease traditionally associated with mysticism and prophecy, Luis also made him an epileptic, but played it down in the final version.

Jaibo tracks down the informer Julian and, on a piece of waste ground with the skeleton of a growing skyscraper in the background, and watched by a horrified Pedro, smashes his skull in.

Pedro's still attractive mother Marta becomes a prize for whom the two compete. She has no time for her son. The more he begs for love, the more she fobs him off. But Jaibo's muscles, his frank admiration of her breasts and thighs as he watches her stooping and squatting at her housework and, most provocatively of all, his sentimental reminiscences about his own mother excite her, and she lets herself be seduced. In one of the film's most mysterious scenes, which owes something to both Surrealism and von Stroheim's *Greed*, Pedro dreams of finding Julian's body under his bed. As he turns from the corpse, Marta wakes. He demands meat from her. She advances on him, offering a raw chunk of flesh, but Jaibo rises from beneath the bed and wrestles it from him.

Jaibo has Pedro framed and sent to the reformatory, then beats him to death with an iron bar, but is himself shot down by police. Embarrassed to find Pedro's corpse in their hen-house, friends pile it on a donkey, carry it to the city dump and roll it down into the refuse; the real-life incident that inspired the original story.

In counterpoint to the background freeways and high-rises, the world of *Los Olvidados* is almost medieval. The tiny shacks with four or five beds to a room are just annexes to barns filled with hens, sheep or donkeys. Magic rules in these gimcrack byres and cribs. In particular, their owners aspire to the purity symbolized by the natural whiteness of their beasts. The blind musician works his sympathetic magic on Marta, stroking her naked back with a white dove to draw out pain, and is paid is asses' milk. Ojitos sucks from a ewe's udder, and an adolescent girl, Meche, bathes her arms and legs in milk to make the skin more creamy. At moments of threat a black cock appears to crow at the peasants' doom. Pedro, seen caressing and cooing at chicks early in the film, ultimately comprehends the deception in their whiteness and smashes the reformatory's chickens to pulp, but at his death a white cock sits triumphantly on his chest.

Although *Los Olvidados* seamlessly weaves the ethereal with the corporeal, Buñuel wanted it even less naturalistic. He shot Pedro's dream in slow motion, with lightning flaring inside the tiny bedroom. Only technical problems stopped him from having it rain as well. He also toyed with having Marta, preparing a meal, move aside a silk top hat standing incongruously on a shelf in the middle of the squalor. In the fight between Jaibo and Julian he wanted a full orchestra perched and playing in the high-rise behind them, but Dancigers, understandably, vetoed the idea.

Buñuel had called in his old Aragonian friends to help on the screenplay. Max Aub did some drafts. So did Juan Larrea, and Julio Alejandro, later to become his regular collaborator. None received credit. Early drafts began with the street kids digging through the junk heap and finding the portrait of a Spanish *hidalgo*, whom they recognize as one of the city's beggars. Pedro di Urdimalas, who, like many Mexicans, revered the old order and especially Spain, made Buñuel drop the scene. Luis managed a few subversive references by giving them to the malevolent blind musician and magician who nostalgically sings songs of Diaz and swears that, under his regime, the street kids who harry him would have been killed.

Los Olvidados was cheap, even for Mexico. Buñuel shot it in eighteen days during February 1950 for 450,000 pesos; somewhere between a C and a B budget. His fee was the equivalent of 2000 dollars, with no percentage of the profits. Months were spent in casting. An open call at the Tepeyac Studios for twelve- to eighteen-year-olds with a grade school education produced 300 applicants; without the educational restriction they would have been overwhelmed. One of those who auditioned was José de la Colina. 'The camera made less of an impression on me,' he wrote, 'than the gaze of that robust man with the demeanor of a boxer or a teamster, the head of an excavated statue (as Ramon Gómez de la Serna said), and a strong voice with an Aragonese accent. He seemed like a hunter stealthily observing his prey.' He did not get the role but later became a leading film critic and writer on Buñuel, and his friend.

Dancigers insisted on paying lip service to Neo-realism by inserting an opening credit claiming many of the actors were amateurs: despite the cattle-call auditions, however, this was not true. Mario Ramirez, who played Ojitos, was a genuine peasant but Roberto Cobo (Jaibo) was a chorus boy with some stage experience who went on to a long career in films. A well-educated and blonde ten-year-old from a middle-class background, Alma Delia Fuentes, was chosen to play Meche. Stella Inda, who played Marta, was well known, and Miguel Inclan, the blind musician, a famous screen villain. After the film was released, Buñuel was accused, rightly, of casting non-Mexican types. What he had looked for was not local authenticity but a sense of the universal.

Initially Figueroa did not enjoy working with Buñuel. Luis had no use for epic landscapes and, after a few days, the cameraman protested to Dancigers that any newsreel hack could do what he was doing. The producer mollified him. Figueroa grudgingly kept at it, only to fall out with Luis again, this time over framing. For a track across a piece of waste ground where the kids play, Buñuel asked him to cut them off below the knees. Influenced by Toland, an admirer of Vermeer who lit his pictures by Old Master rules, Figueroa protested that this transgressed the fundamental rules of art. He offered 1000 pesos if Buñuel could find a painter who framed his pictures like that. A few days later Luis came on the set with a magazine reproduction of a Van Dyck that used his framing. Figueroa was impressed that a director cared enough to think out a question rather than, like most of the people he worked with, simply order something done. He gave in gracefully, and became in time a friend and one of Buñuel's greatest admirers.

After a struggle with the unions, who tried to impose a Mexican composer and a conventional score, Buñuel commissioned Gustavo Pittaluga to underline the film's subtext in music, though to mollify STIC the music is credited to Alfredo Halffter 'from themes' by Pittaluga. Even so, Halffter was threatened with expulsion for letting his name be used.

The lack of any concession to optimism in *Los Olvidados* alarmed everyone. Like *Las Hurdes*, it was worse than cruel; it was pitiless. As André Bazin wrote in an admiring and influential review, 'it never refers to moral categories. There is no Manichaeanism in the characters. Their guilt is purely fortuitous, the temporary conjunction of different destinies which meet in them like crossed swords. [Jaibo], though he is vicious and sadistic, cruel and treacherous, does not inspire repugnance but only a kind of horror which is by no means incompatible with love. One is reminded of the heroes of Genet.' Or of Sade. As Buñuel told Bazin, 'to see and think out a situation from a Sadique or a Sadist point of view – rather than, shall we way, a Neo-realist or mystical one', came naturally to him.

Arturo Ripstein, the young Mexican director who became a protégé of Buñuel, believes his greatest sin in Mexican eyes was to examine reality without resort to myth. No matter how miserable their lives, Mexicans had always had the refuge of fantasy – that the desert would eventually bloom, that a lost general like Emilio Zapata would return one day, that the worst delinquent had some good in him. 'Buñuel looked at things clearly and plainly,' says Ripstein, 'without mythologizing them. That made him fair game for the intellectuals.' However highly Buñuel was praised, he would never be embraced by Mexico. He remained, as he preferred to be, an outsider.

Dancigers brooded on *Los Olvidados*, and delayed releasing it. Clearly it was a commercial disaster. He berated himself for ever agreeing to back it. Buñuel saw his career once again fading away. Fortunately Fernando Soler had been sufficiently impressed with *El Gran Calavera* to offer Luis a project for producer Sergio Kogan, who had commissioned a story from Manuel Reachi as a showcase for his voluptuous wife, Rosita Quintana. She is a runaway reformatory girl who takes refuge in Soler's hacienda and overturns its calm life with her sexuality. Resignedly, Buñuel wrote a script with Jaime Salvador, and Rodolfo Usigli, the novelist whose *Ensayo de un Crimen* he would film later. Between them they amplified the theme of sexual destruction which Buñuel had foreshadowed in *Los Olvidados* and would readdress in many later films. By August, he was shooting *Susana*, later variously known as *Demonio y Carne (The Devil and the Flesh)* or *Susana the Perverse*.

Buñuel shot *Susana* in twenty days, and it looks like it. There is none of the style of *Los Olvidados*. Except for the flamboyant jail opening in which Susana, terrorized by rats and spiders, cowers from sadistic warders in her cell, it is lit with bland, bright professionalism by José

Ortiz Ramos and staged on sets that belong in a Gene Autry singing western. Flouncing, pouting and smouldering sensuously whether the pretext presented itself or not, Quintana, whose peasant blouse, when it is not plastered to her by water or mud, slips off her shoulders every few seconds, excited Buñuel with her heavy breasts and meaty legs, which he enjoyed displaying as much as she did. He also had fun setting up a scene where broken eggs run down Susana's legs after Don Guadalupe's son Alberto accosts her on her way back from the hen-house and crushes her basket, and a feast of voyeurism where, as she undresses against a conveniently lit window, her three lovers, each unknown to the others, spy on her. But he delivered the film to a grateful Kogan knowing it was the nadir of his work as a director.

While Buñuel shot *Susana*, Dancigers had been hard at work trying to sanitize *Los Olvidados*. He inserted an introduction which, over stock shots of Paris, New York, London and the ritzier tourist streets of Mexico City, claimed that the film aired an international social problem from which Mexico City, 'a great and modern city', suffered as much as anyone. Despite this, it opened on a Thursday in November at the Cine Mexico with its pungency largely unimpaired. The public reaction was as hostile as that at the private preview. Dancigers stayed away. Buñuel was left to face alone the hundred people who showed up. By Saturday Dancigers had decided to pull the film.

Los Olvidados might have stayed on the shelf had the Cannes Festival not accepted it for screening in May 1951. A Mexican film was a novelty for a festival that prided itself on internationalism, and its director's reputation was sufficient to guarantee interest. Buñuel in 1951 was, as British critic Penelope Houston said, 'little more than a name in the cinema text-books, a film-maker who had not been heard from in more than a decade, a survivor from the remote enthusiasms of Surrealism'. His reappearance, and from Mexico of all places, seemed almost miraculous. For that alone he deserved some sort of prize. The jury acknowledged this personal triumph by giving him the Palme d'Or for Best Direction. The film also won the prize given by FIPRESCI, the international critics' organization. French and American distributors snapped it up, and Dancigers, elated, re-released it in Mexico City, where it ran for six weeks at the Prado to hostile but respectful reviews. Like most provincial cinemas, Mexico's was naively impressed by foreign success.

European distributors, no less horrified than Dancigers by the film's bleakness, renamed it in a more conciliatory way. In France, to Luis's scorn, it was called, *Pitié Pour Eux/Pity for Them*. Jacques Prévert wrote a poem that tried to soften its message, or lack of it.

> Los Olvidados.
> Children too soon adolescents.
> Children forgotten, discarded, wishing for nothing.
> Los Olvidados.

The poem's false compassion convinced no one. For once American distributors were closer to the mark when they chose to call *Los Olvidados The Young and the Damned*.

23

'Beyond the pale of morality and law, incapable of pity, an unredeemed mass of human energy and loneliness, of instinctive, tragic will, as a blind man pictures in his mind, dark and formless, the world outside, so Don Mariano pictured the world of sentiment, legality and normal human relations. What other notion could he have of the world if, around him, the word "right" had always been suffocated by violence, and the wind of the world had merely changed the word into a stagnant and putrid reality?'
– Leonard Sciascia, *Il Giorno della Civetta* (translated by Archibald Colquhoun and Arthur Oliver)

The influence of *Los Olvidados* was enormous. It ran for months in both Paris and London. A generation of Hollywood film-makers who never saw the film benefited from the way in which it heightened acceptance of anarchy's glamour and eroticism. Young directors in Eastern Europe, many of whom had been diffident about their innate nihilism, were, like Roman Polanski, 'bowled over [by] the violence, the realism, the unambiguous appeal to the emotions'. (Buñuel reciprocated by admiring *Repulsion*, the most Buñuelesque of all Polanski's films.) Andrej Wajda's *Ashes and Diamonds* and *Kanal* likewise might have been made by Buñuel. Its success, however, was not an unmixed blessing. On the strength of it, Kogan sold *Susana* to Europe. Critics viewing it wondered whether it had been made by another Luis Buñuel entirely.

His enthusiasm revived, Dancigers pushed Luis to make another commercial film. Eduardo Ugarte, who had now left Argentina for Mexico, still owned the rights to *Don Quintin el Amargao*, which Buñuel sensed would be a good vehicle for Fernando Soler. With Ugarte, Alcoriza, Mantecon and Pepe Moreno Villa he screened the country's sole surviving print. The *Madrileño* vividness of its accent and gesture startled and saddened all of them. It was a reminder to Luis of the country they had all lost, apparently forever.

For the remake, the Alcorizas simply Mexicanized the argot and setting. Gangsters pull guns more readily than in the Spanish version, and Quintin's club, Al Infierno, with its giant sidewalk *papier mâché* devil, is as provincially crude as the tunes performed by Lily Aclemar's busty Jovita, but since almost every scene is an urban interior, it takes a scholar of Spanish to tell the two versions apart. To Buñuel's disgust, Kogan released the film in August 1951 as *La Hija del Engano (Daughter of Deceit)*. The unfamiliar title meant it had to wait until 1973 for a release in Spain, where the original *Don Quintin el Amargao* was famous. It was not a film Luis looked back on with much pleasure. In 1968, when a French cinema showed it as part of a Buñuel retrospective, he saw the poster and burst out laughing: 'That's a dreadful film,' he told Jacques Fraenkel. 'I pity the poor spectators who have to sit through it.'

After the success of *Susana*, Kogan was an enthusiast for Buñuel. In April, Luis had started shooting his *Una Mujer Sin Amor (A Woman Without Love)*. An ill-advised transposition of André Cayatte's *Pierre et Jean* of 1943, based on Maupassant's story, it explored the same formula of tyrannical father/outcast child/deathbed resolution as *Don Quintin*. An old antique dealer drives away his son, who takes refuge with an engineer. His wife follows, to become the engineer's mistress and bear him a son too. The boys grow up together, then find themselves rivals for the inheritance of their two fathers. Buñuel shot it in twenty days in the CLASA studios, and edited it in three. Later, he counted it the worst film he ever made.

He started a new and better one in August. The idea came from Malagan poet and editor Manuel Altolaguirre, a Residencista, and friend and publisher of Lorca, who had settled in Mexico with his wife Maria Luisa Gomez Mena. He described to Buñuel a bus trip he had made along the Guerrero coast from Acapulco to Zihuatanejo, where each twist of the mountain road offered some fantastic event. It would make a good comedy, he thought, and was ready, indeed eager to co-produce with his wife if Luis would direct.

Buñuel liked Altolaguirre's enthusiasm. Driving around Mexico City, car window open and arm stuck out to grip the roof, the poet would exult: 'Me, a film producer! Can you believe it?' His wife was less cordial. The first time Luis and Jeanne visited them, she took one look and shouted over her shoulder: 'Monolo! He's nowhere near as ugly as you said.' Sniffing Jeanne's armpits as she took off her coat, she said, 'I like that. You smell clean. Not like Monolo's balls.' Luis was dubious about working with this eccentric pair, but he needed the money.

Subida al Cielo, literally 'Heaven's Gate' or 'Ascent into Heaven', is a beauty spot through which the film's bus passes during the trip and where the most important romantic incident takes place, but the film became better known under the more prosaic *Mexican Bus Ride*. It could well have been a disaster. Buñuel didn't like comedies and initially could not imagine making one. Fortunately, in moral twilight, irony is easily mistaken for humour, and since Buñuel had irony to spare, he enjoyed the idea of the nightmare bus journey undertaken by the film's hero, Oliviero, as much as his stern nature allowed. He was hampered by a zero budget for special effects (the model shots of the bus on mountain roads are risible) and the fumbling Esteban Marquez as Oliviero. A movie-struck boy who worked in a flower shop, Marquez faked his way on to the film by claiming to have studied with the teacher and director Seki Sano. Until it was too late, Buñuel mistook incompetence for Method technique. The boy's ignorance emerged when Luis, as a joke on the prevalence of *mordida*, called the actors together and told them solemnly that they would have to pay him 100 pesos for every close-up. Marquez offered to buy as much as Buñuel could squeeze in.

For all its problems, however, *Subida al Cielo* is a goldmine of references to Luis's sexual preoccupations. The scene where Lilia Prado, the young dancer who plays the beautiful Raquel, boards the bus, showing off her fine calves and feet in ankle-strap stilettos, so turned him on that he repeated it in the 1953 *La Ilusion Viaja en Tranvia (Illusion Travels by Streetcar)*. Oliviero making love with Raquel by a lake during a thunderstorm also evokes Luis's taste for aquatic sex. 'Both my sons are children of the water,' Jeanne has said. 'Juan Luis was conceived in the bathtub in Paris and Rafael in the shower.'

Though his salary remained paltry, Luis was aware that producers were beginning to see him as a director of more than usual competence and sophistication. This was confirmed when Kogan offered him a film with Pedro Armendariz, the country's most highly regarded dramatic actor. Alcoriza came up with a bleak script called *El Bruto* about a slaughterhouse worker lured into becoming enforcer for a property owner. As Raymond Durgnat notes, 'Buñuel has a special feeling, as many left-wing thinkers do, for the workers' sons who become agents of the bourgeoisie; the gamekeepers in *L'Age d'Or* and *The Young One*, the major-domo in *El Angel Exterminador*, the policeman, the strong-arm men. In one sense, they are traitors to their class. In another sense, they represent the constant pull of self-interest in every member of the proletariat. Or again, they can be seen as victims of the "confusionism" spread by the reigning culture.'

There were plenty of resonances between *El Bruto* and *Los Olvidados*, from the low-life tenement setting, the innocent girl ('Meche' again), and the main character Pedro, the brute of the title, unregenerate, pure in his violence, hunted down by the police. *El Bruto* 'could have been good', Buñuel said later, but with only eighteen days to shoot it, he could not hope for the same degree of detail. The best he could do was to humanize Pedro, showing him supporting a gaggle of grasping relatives, and play on his delicacy in details like his careful extinguishing of a candle with wet fingers.

Shooting in Mexico City's abattoirs, the Rastro, Buñuel was amused to see the Virgin of Guadulupe looking down benignly on the slaughter. Kogan made him cut the blood, though the Virgin remained. As well, he tried to dress Armendariz in the white T-shirts he had seen on men at the Rastro, but the actor announced they were the sure mark of a homosexual. Ordinary shirts with rolled sleeves replaced them. Armendariz also changed the dialogue where he is chased in the slaughterhouse. He was supposed to order Meche: 'Pull out [the knife]. There. Behind.' 'Behind' had gay overtones, he decided, so that too had to go.

Buñuel was consoled for the failure of *El Bruto* by the success of *Subida al Cielo* at Cannes in 1952, where it won an unexpected and probably undeserved special critics' prize for Best Avant-Garde film, given mainly in acknowledgement of his earlier work. Buñuel, who hated prize givings and flying equally, did not go to Cannes, but Altolaguirre was more than ready to accept the award for him.

Buñuel's optimism about his career began to cool after *El Bruto*. By the start of 1952, Mexico's film industry, its independence already cooling, was heading into the winter of all national cinemas which defy the Hollywood machine. Hoped-for overseas sales had not materialized, and local films, unpopular with Mexican audiences, were increasingly shelved in favour of those from the United States. Unions demanded more government investment and a limit on imports; aims they were ready, even eager to strike for. Unless he could break into the European or, better still, American market, he would find himself, after seven years in Mexico, back where he started.

Through the early 1950s the image of a world swept by plague preoccupied Buñuel. Like Sade, he often entertained visions of the millennium and man's final apocalyptic self-destruction, the ultimate murder. He signed petitions against nuclear proliferation and, after trying to evoke the bomb in *Subida al Cielo*, worked it into the end of *Simon of the Desert*, where the world rocks towards Apocalypse to a dance called 'The Radioactive Flesh'.

Rachel Carson's *Silent Spring* (1962) would convince Buñuel we must eventually stifle in our own wastes. 'I never saw him so depressed,' Jean-

Claude Carrière said of his reaction to the anti-pollution jeremiad. He liked Jean Giono's novel *The Hussar on the Roof* (1951) about a France ravaged by pestilence. Giono offered to adapt it to Mexico but, for Buñuel, catastrophe demanded a culture ripe with achievement and price. Defoe's *A Journal of the Plague Year*, a documentary reconstruction of the Black Death sweeping London, was the most promising subject, but Luis could not convince Dancigers it would make a film. Talk of Defoe attracted the attention of George Pepper and Hugo Butler, who had fled to Mexico from Hollywood after being named in the 1947 Californian UnAmerican Activities hearings. Pepper, a violinist, had been a musicians' union organizer. In Mexico he turned to producing, using the ironical pseudonym 'George P. Werker'. Butler was a seasoned screenwriter, with credits on *The Adventures of Huckleberry Finn*, *Edison the Man*, *Young Tom Edison* and *Lassie Come Home*. He also adapted *The Southerner* for Renoir, and worked on the leftist dramas *He Ran All the Way* and *The Prowler*.

Pepper and Butler offered Buñuel and Dancigers the script that was to become *The Adventures of Robinson Crusoe*. Initially Buñuel was not interested. Though ideal for Mexico's limitless jungle and clean, empty beaches, the story of young Crusoe, spoilt son of a rich merchant marooned for twenty-eight years on a remote island, did not address the Millennium. On the other hand, some of its concerns were his, and Sade's; loneliness, sexual abstinence and fantasy, the nature of the self, and of God. Dancigers badgered him to accept. Here at last was a film that might crack the tough international market.

From his first loss of faith, the concept of deity continued to intrigue Buñuel, as it had Sade. Isolated on an island where, by virtue of technology and intelligence, he enjoyed almost infinite control over the insects, animals, neighbouring cannibals and passing pirates, Crusoe assumed god-like powers. Does deity, then, reside simply in power? In the film, Buñuel would put into Friday's mouth Sade's famous question: 'If God is all-powerful, why doesn't he kill the Devil?' Robinson cannot answer, although by the end of the film, when he maroons the pirates who have tried to kill him, counselling them that they will survive only if, like him, they learn compassion and the ability to live in harmony, he seems to have rejected deity as an empty concept, preferring a humanist/ anarchist vision of life. Salvation is to be found only in the Self.

After reworking Butler's script, which would be credited to him and 'Philip Ansel Roll', Buñuel agreed to do it, though he was well aware of the logistical problems he was taking on. Shooting for the international market meant colour, English and Spanish language versions, and an American star. Combined with expensive location shooting and a longer schedule than the standard twenty-four days, these demands pushed the cost of *The Adventures of Robinson Crusoe* to a stratospheric (for Mexico) 300,000 dollars,*some of which Dancigers raised from Californian businessman Henry F. Ehrlich.

The Technicolor Corporation and its three-strip process had a near-stranglehold on colour cinematography in Hollywood. Independents were forced to employ an 'official' Technicolor cameraman and pay the company owner as 'Color Consultant'. Rushes were delivered in black and white, and one had to wait for weeks to see the final result. This often meant expensive retakes. Dancigers decided to bypass them in favour of the new Eastman Kodak film. Based on a single-strip process developed in Germany, it was cheaper and more flexible, and would soon supplant Technicolor. Since this was the first Eastman film shot outside the United States, however, each day's shooting still had to be flown to Los Angeles for processing.**

Pepper and Buñuel combed low-budget independent films in search of a cheap American leading man. Pepper knew Orson Welles from Hollywood. He had done work for the Hollywood Democratic Committee, which Pepper chaired. Thinking he might help out former comrades by playing Crusoe, they screened his 1948 Republic production of *Macbeth*, shot in three weeks on a budget of 800,000 dollars. Pepper pointed out to Buñuel that Welles wore furs and a heavy beard, just as Robinson would need to. A prima donna like Welles, however, was the last thing Luis wanted, especially given his notorious tendency to hijack films in which he acted. Instead, he indicated Dan O'Herlihy, the slim young Irish actor who played Macduff, and said, 'I'll take him.'

Even O'Herlihy acknowledges he was an odd choice. He had never played the lead in a film, know nothing of Buñuel, could not speak Spanish, nor swim. Furthermore, he did not have the build for such a physical role. In *Macbeth*, Welles had padded his costume to give him some muscles.

Signing the contract for 300 dollars a week, O'Herlihy was sworn to secrecy. Hollywood had filmed *Robinson Crusoe* repeatedly over the years, and MGM was rumoured to be planning a new version. A cover story was prepared. If anyone asked, he was to claim he was working on another lost-man-in-the-jungle subject, Conrad's *Heart of Darkness*.

---

* Buñuel later revised this to 150,000 dollars. The higher figure may cover both Spanish and English versions.
** The film is supposedly shot in 'Pathécolor' but, like 'Warnercolor' and Twentieth Century-Fox's 'Deluxe Color', this was just an individual label for the Eastman Kodak process.

In Mexico, Buñuel was filling the role of Friday. Jaime Fernandez, the director Emilio's younger brother, who had been an extra in *El Bruto*, heard while working on a Ricardo Montaban movie that Dancigers and Buñuel were casting. He hurried to the Ultramar offices in a rainstorm and arrived late. Five actors had been chosen for screen tests, but when Luis saw Jaime, he made it six, and finally gave him the role.

Had he recognized the brother of 'El Indio' and selected him just to irritate Dancigers? If so, he succeeded. The producer was furious, though Buñuel talked him round, and even persuaded him to increase Fernandez's salary. This still meant he was paid far less than the standard rate, as was everyone on the film. Luis's own fee was a meagre 10,000 dollars.

Buñuel started shooting interiors at Tepeyac. The technical demands of colour put him in poor humour from the start. His cameraman, Alex Phillips, a Canadian, had worked in Mexico since the early 1930s but had never shot colour. He was determined to get it right, even if it meant spending hours lighting. 'He was the only man who ever ignored Buñuel,' said O'Herlihy. Shooting in both English and Spanish presented problems as well. Few Latinos knew Defoe's book. The plot had to be set up, with much preliminary story-telling. (The Spanish version runs 140 minutes, against the English film's slim eighty-nine minutes.)

With O'Herlihy, Buñuel maintained his customary distance. 'He pretended not to talk English,' O'Herlihy said. 'He didn't communicate with anyone until after one o'clock. He behaved as if he had a hell of a hangover. He would mutter to the assistant, and the assistant would tell me: "He wants you to come in, pick that up, put it down and walk out that way." But after lunch he opened up and was genial and there was communication. He would still have his instructions translated but they'd be directed to me, not via the assistant.'

The meagre advice Buñuel gave O'Herlihy on motivation was the same as he gave to Catherine Deneuve fifteen years later. 'To make a film you must never work with effect in mind. *Never effect*.' O'Herlihy resisted, particularly in the scene where Robinson, maudlin drunk in his cave, imagines the shouts and songs of his lost drinking friends. 'He wants to emphasize the alone-ness,' said O'Herlihy, 'so he's up at the far end of this very large stage with the camera on a crane up against the roof at a distance, and I said: "Señor!" and he called back, in Spanish: "Yes, what is it?" And I shouted: "I thought you said; nothing for effect".'

The nearest coastline suitable for Crusoe's island was due west, at Manzanillo, on the Pacific coast, near Colima. For someone like Buñuel, who loathed being far from the comforts of home, and who would choose the first location he came to rather than search further afield for a better one, the very thought of such an odyssey was anathema. The unit, including Hugo Butler, flew down in a DC3 that stopped at every tiny airport to deliver mail. Buñuel, as usual, numbed himself with alcohol for the flight, and dozed throughout. Their route took them over Paracutin, the active volcano. 'The pilot, to show off, flew down into the maw of the volcano and circled,' O'Herlihy recalled. 'And I leaned forward and tapped Buñuel on the shoulder and said, "Señor, we are landing." He said, "Thank God", then looked out the window and screamed. When we landed he actually presaged the action of John Paul II and kissed the ground.'

Complications increased on the remote location. Scorpions abounded. The unit doctor reassured everyone they were not *that* poisonous, and anyway he had plenty of anti-venene. Under close questioning, however, he admitted that he was the second doctor on the production. The first had died – of a scorpion bite. For the scene where he runs down a hillside thick with undergrowth, O'Herlihy insisted that two grips in heavy boots pound along the same track two or three times before each take.

Buñuel perspired furiously in the jungle humidity, drinking enormous quantities of water as well as his nightly cocktails and bottle of wine. His drinking, which he made no attempt to hide, had assumed legendary proportions. A visiting critic described his taste for Hungarian red and his habit of nipping, on set and off, from a pocket flask. Luis did nothing to dispel the impression, but he normally kept such *ad hoc* tippling to a minimum. 'Drinking for him wasn't drinking,' said Joyce Buñuel. 'It was a ceremony. He loved ceremonies.'

Dancigers spent some time on location, and Jeanne and Juan Luis paid a brief visit, but Luis, slumped in his chair or wandering under the trees of the coastal forest, seemed more immured than usual in a private world. He would not discuss their roles with either actor. Even the crew seemed to be ostracizing them and, since the nearest town was kilometres away, they felt increasingly alienated.

After three weeks, Fernandez told Dancigers that, if Buñuel was unhappy, he would understand if he wanted him replaced. Next day, Buñuel beckoned him over and explained that the crew were under orders to ignore them, to help their performances. 'It was killing him,' says Fernandez of O'Herlihy, and, despite his lack of English, he tried to befriend the increasingly troubled star.

Gradually the atmosphere thawed as actors and director found a common wavelength. Towards the end of the six weeks' location they began to see that, although the incidents of Crusoe's life might appear banal, they (and particularly those Luis had interpolated into Butler's script), represented Buñuel's personal meditation on Defoe's story. Some effects were obvious, like Crusoe's stab of desire as he watches the wind stir the woman's dress he has hung up as a scarecrow, and when Friday carelessly puts on a gown. Others were more complex. By placing two ant-eating beetles on a pile of sand and, as they burrow in, supplying them with a passing bug as their first meal, Crusoe played out his realization of his growing likeness to a God and, conversely, the obvious derivation of God's image from the human. 'He saw symbols in things,' says Fernandez. This realization gave the actors the confidence they had lacked, and they began to join in the game.

The dog who played Crusoe's supposedly beloved Rex took an instant dislike to O'Herlihy, and he to it. For the scene where he is supposed to weep at its death, O'Herlihy could not work up the emotion. He suggested instead that Luis shoot his back, shaking with sobs. Buñuel incorporated the idea, so O'Herlihy offered a more complex one for the fever dream in which Robinson, desperately thirsty, is visited by his father (also O'Herlihy) who, babbling about living in the best of all possible worlds, tantalizingly offers him water, then breaks the jug and even wastes gallons washing down a huge bristly hog. 'I suggested that, at the end, instead of his just saying the words and disappearing, he should be seen floating on a nearby lake and, as he says the words, he grins and submerges. Buñuel said, "This is Buñuel!" And that's how we did it.'

As the shooting continued, Luis showed his hand more and more. Even his morning silences came to seem less like bad temper, distance or hangover and more like the discomfort of a shy man. To O'Herlihy this came as a kind of revelation. 'In the mornings he wasn't cold. He was just miserable.'

The actors also caught some of the unexpressed tension between Buñuel and Butler, who continued to defend the little documentary realism remaining in his script. For a scene where Robinson demonstrates his gun by shooting a duck, Buñuel told the assistant that he wanted gaudy plumage: red, green and blue, even if it meant painting the bird to achieve it.

Butler protested at the unlikelihood of this. Buñuel said, 'This is an island. Who knows what sort of animals are here?'

'How are we supposed to react to it?' O'Herlihy asked when he was alone with Buñuel. 'With surprise?'

'If people even notice the duck and not you,' Buñuel said, 'then you're not doing your job.'

In the event, the duck they used was a quotidian yellow, but a point had been made about the film's balance of reality against fantasy.

Butler's politics took a further battering when the papers carried reports of a new decree by Stalin that all art must serve socialist realism. Butler loyally defended it, and O'Herlihy attacked him. Buñuel would not be drawn into the argument, but later, when O'Herlihy asked him where he'd prefer to work, Hollywood or Moscow, he said dismissively, 'A pox on both.'

The argument broke down some final barrier, however. A few evenings later O'Herlihy, trying to flag a cab to take him into Manzanillo, was surprised when Buñuel joined him. 'We were seven miles or something from the peninsula where the village was. A couple of taxis passed and didn't stop. I got out and stood in the road and waved. One of them stopped, but there was a passenger in the back. He opened the door and I said, "Are you going to Manzanillo?" The man slammed the door and said something very rude. Buñuel opened the door and stepped in. I stepped in with him, and I saw Buñuel had a gun. "Take us to Manzanillo," he said. And the driver said, "*Si, señor*".' O'Herlihy left the film Luis's passionate lifetime supporter. 'I loved him because I thought: "This is an absolutely straight, honest human being, and a creator." That's a wonderful combination.'

24

'The big room he walked in,
Over the smooth floor,
Under the sky light,
Was his own brain.
– Geoffrey Grigson, 'Before a Fall'

For years, the Buñuels rented apartments, but in 1952 Luis commissioned a two-storey house on Cerrada de Felix Cuevas in Colonia del Valle, in those days a quiet suburb halfway between Mexico City and the film studios. Emilio Fernandez and other film people lived nearby, though more ostentatiously.

Luis ignored the prevailing taste for Latino arte moderne – Orozco and Frida Kahlo side by side with Mayan statuary and pre-Columbian pots – and elected for a modest French-style suburban family home. The only concession to Mexico City was some facing in volcanic stone. At the Residencia he had often fantasized to Bello about living as a feudal lord in a remote valley in the Sierra de Guadarrama, cut off from the world, safe with his courtiers and soldiers in his castle. The two-metre high wall of the new house with a single red steel gate was as close as he could come in real life.

To his Mexican friends, Buñuel always seemed to hover between two worlds. He did not share the country's taste for festivals, fairs and public gatherings. 'Buñuel lived like an old Spanish gentleman, and according to strict rules,' says Arturo Ripstein, whose producer father Alfredo was one of Luis's hunting friends. 'Within his house the rules were hard, and his wife and sons had a hard time.'

Juan Luis insists, 'I never recall him smacking us or punishing us severely,' but most people who observed the Buñuels at home sensed an almost Victorian inflexibility. 'Each day was the same,' recalled Silvia Pinal, his favourite star in the early 1960s. '12 o'clock, drink. 1 o'clock, dinner. All the time the same. He was like Hitler in his house. Like Othello.' A teenage Juan Luis told a journalist, 'My father is Mexico's leading square. He goes to bed at nine o'clock and rises at dawn, and his idea of the perfect life is to stay home.' Joyce remembered the sameness of the routine. 'He would have his coffee alone in the kitchen at five o'clock in the morning, fairly often. Feed the dogs. Take a walk with his cane, very early. A long walk. Come back, have another breakfast, and usually go up to his study and read. Later in life, when his eyes were getting bad, he got very nervous because he couldn't read any more. That was isolating him from everything he cared about. Then, at twelve o'clock, bingo, on the nose, he was down in the bar starting to mix a martini.'

His insistence on the whole house following his regime was absolute. When Conchita visited them from Spain, she ignored his rules, especially in the matter of getting up early, though she sometimes did so to let out Luis's dog, Tristana if it scratched and whined enough. Pinal, hearing dog sounds late one morning when she'd called to meet Conchita, looked out to see Luis on his knees at Conchita's door, pretending to be Tristana.

Garcia Ascot remarked, 'There is something of the monk in Buñuel. A solitary house, a monastic room, scorn for the superficial or decorative aesthetic. He is only exacting about eating and drinking – but even then, simple food, wine and good whisky. That is all. In his library are three main sections: Galdos, some Surrealists and precursors, and Fabre's *Souvenirs Entomologiques*.'

While Luis lacked sociability, other aspects of his personality harmonized all too readily with the Mexican temperament. 'He was very egoist,' said Pinal. ' "Don't touch this. It is mine." A real *macho Mexicano*.' Jeanne, albeit affectionately, agreed. 'It seems to me the reason why Luis always kept me out of his intimate conversations with his friends and his intellectual life was because he was a *macho*. Luis was a jealous *macho*. His wife must be a kind of child bride who wouldn't grow up. He never told me about his projects, his dreams, his problems, of the way he took care of money, of politics, of religion. He decided everything; where to live, the time to eat, where we would go out, the education of our sons, my relationships, my friends.' Jaime Fernandez concurs: 'He always said he didn't understand *machismo* as the word is understood in Mexico, but deep down he had many of its characteristics. He was very jealous, for example. Very possessive. He didn't permit his wife to have a lot of friends.'

Sexual jealousy plagued Luis. Even with Jeanne in purdah, he remained obsessively suspicious, especially of her relationship with Gustavo Pittaluga and Ana-Maria Custodio. Not long after they moved to Mexico, Jeanne became pregnant again. She was delighted, hoping for a girl, but Luis's instant hostility shocked her. 'I would have liked to have a daughter,' Luis later admitted, then went on, startlingly, 'but with a father so jealous she would have ended as a prostitute or a nun.' He persuaded Jeanne to have an abortion, ostensibly because they could not afford another child. Ana-Maria, not Luis, took her to the doctor, and stayed with her afterwards. Forlorn, Jeanne asked about the sex of the foetus. The doctor could not or would not confirm it was female, but the phantom daughter was to become an increasingly real presence in Jeanne's life. 'If I had had her, I wouldn't have been so lonely,' she said in old age. After the abortion, Luis decreed no more children.

Jeanne remained close to the Pittalugas but Gustavo found Luis increasingly difficult. Matters came to a head shortly after *Subida al Cielo*, for which Pittaluga supplied the music. Jeanne dropped in on Ana-Maria but found only Gustavo. They chatted and, back home, Jeanne casually told Luis of her few moments alone with the composer. Furious, he accused her of having an affair. He went to his room, took a gun and rang to tell Pittaluga he was on his way to kill him. Jeanne and Gustavo talked him out of it but Luis did not work with Pittaluga again for more than a decade.

Release of *The Adventures of Robinson Crusoe* was delayed by additional shooting to shore up a characterization which Luis's pursuit of the intellectual had left a little threadbare. He had already shown Robinson in despair, stumbling into the surf with a torch in his hand, begging for help from a non-existent God, then quenching the flame in the foam, like his hopes. Now he brought O'Herlihy back to Mexico and, rather than go on dreaded location again, shot some pick-ups in a Mexico City park, framing out passing traffic. For the longer scenes he took him to San José Purua and had him assert his humanity and independence by bawling the 23rd Psalm from the terrace of the hotel, looking out over the wooded valley that had given Buñuel so much inspiration. Robinson gets, as he expects, only an echo in return. It became one of the film's most moving moments.

Dancigers was keen to keep up production, particularly since the long-awaited strike now looked imminent. Buñuel did not protest. He was, as usual, broke. When Butler and Pepper found out how little he had been paid for *Robinson Crusoe*, they offered him 20 per cent of their own share. Luis refused, perhaps from pride, but more probably because he knew they would not be seeing real money for a long time.

They proposed another script, *El Cadillac*, but he turned it down, preferring to adapt Mercedes Pinto's novel, *Pensamientos*. Pinto based the book on her own life with a dangerously paranoid husband, but Buñuel changed the title to *El*, the male definite article, and added some details from the behaviour of Conchita's husband, Pedro Garcia de

Orcasitas. Since his jealous outbursts against Juan Luis in Madrid, his brother-in-law had become increasingly unstable. On one occasion he imagined he saw Buñuel on the street, poking faces and making 'evil eye' gestures. When he went home to get his gun, his family were able to convince him that Luis was in Zaragoza.

For years Buñuel denied any other personal significance in his choice of *El*. 'I did what I did with most of my Mexican films,' he said. 'They proposed a subject to me and instead of it, I made a counter-offer which, though still commercial, seemed more propitious for examining the things that interested me.' Years later, Buñuel was still complaining of how fast he had to shoot *El*, and hoping to remake it. His only satisfaction appeared to be that Jacques Lacan showed it in his classes as a classic example of paranoia.

Yet *El* is one of Buñuel's most personal films and, given his psychology while it was being made, deeply revealing. But it would years before he would admit it. Eventually in 1977, he acknowledged, 'It may be the film I put the most of myself into. There is something of me in the protagonist.' As an emblem of his involvement, he put on a habit to play his hero in the last shot, weaving crazily along the paths of the monastery where he's incarcerated.

Always on the lookout for low-priced international talent, Dancigers hired Arturo de Cordova, a Yucatan-born Mexican who had enjoyed a minor Hollywood career as a swashbuckler in films like *Frenchman's Creek* and *The Adventures of Casanova*. De Cordova's matinée idol profile and hairline moustache were in demand while leading men were scarce, but since both his talent and intelligence were limited, and he spoke English with a Bronx accent, peace-time forced him back to Mexico. Luis cast him as Don Francisco Galvan, a wealthy middle-aged property owner from an old family, and a model of the repressed, obsessive and fanatically jealous Hispanic male.

In the absence of any direction from Buñuel, de Cordova, dimly sensing some sexual dysfunction in the character, decided from an innocuous scene where he visits the butler in his bedroom that Francisco was a closet homosexual. Luis convinced him the incident had no significance and, to kill any lingering eroticism, placed an upended bicycle with a half-mended tyre beside the servant's bed. Absurdities like this, piled on Galvan's bizarre behaviour and de Cordova's accent, were too much for Mexico City audiences, which laughed through the film. Even the preview audience giggled, and Dancigers walked out when it hooted at the heavy rope Francisco carried as he tried to mutilate his wife Gloria by sewing up her vagina, an image from his own dreams, and from Sade. To top off the disaster, the Mexican film industry finally went on strike just after *El* was released and Buñuel, instead of working on a new film, joined the picket line.

Tony Richardson, not yet a film-maker but still directing on stage and for TV in London, visited Buñuel six weeks into the strike. He was nervous about the meeting. 'I had heard stories, of the terror of airplanes, the wild drinking, the smashing of dishes he had cooked, in fury at the late arrival of guests, the horror film shows organized at the Museum of Modern Art. The setting of our first meeting, the offices of Ultramar Films in Mexico City, could not have been more different. They are at the end of the Avenida de la Reforma, Maximilian's great boulevard. At the cinema next door *El* had just opened. Inside, in a large central office partitioned with open desks and lined with pearl glass offices, hippy secretaries giggled over a box of marshmallows, and thin young men with slickly pressed suits and plastered hair joked in passing [. . .] The outer door opened again and Buñuel came or rather burst in; loose jacket, uncreased trousers, shaggy woollen open-necked shirt, middle height, broad, muscular, a square and deeply lined face, huge dark eyes [. . .] The suggestion of a capacity both for riot and for discipline was the most emphatic of my impressions.'

While the strike dragged on, *El* was shown at Cannes in May 1953. Buñuel did not attend, but he was told that the screening had gone badly, having taken place on a day reserved for honouring war veterans. In Hollywood Ehrlich and O'Herlihy were preparing the US version of *The Adventures of Robinson Crusoe*. Word of the film had got around, and MGM asked to see it. Afterwards, they offered Ehrlich 1 million dollars for the rights. 'Of course, you know they only want to keep it out of circulation,' O'Herlihy said. Ehrlich agreed. By then he had found out MGM's plans. They saw *Robinson Crusoe* as a romantic comedy for new British action star Stewart Granger. Friday would be swim queen Esther Williams. Fortunately Granger refused to sign the long-term contract MGM demanded and their project was shelved.

Elsewhere, audiences were tuning into a recognizable 'Buñuel touch'. His name became a synonym for cruelty, indifference, ingratitude and casual sacrilege. Luis did nothing to encourage acceptance or court popularity, either from critics or film-goers. The irritation he had felt at Breton's disinclination to burn the Prado, or at those who praised the artistic achievement of *Un Chien Andalou* and *L'Age d'Or* rather than surging into the streets and loosing anarchy, had solidified into indifference about what anyone thought of his films. The meat was in their intellectual argument. As to what people made of the packaging, he was as uninterested as Graham Greene might be in the binding of his new novel or Picasso in the way a picture was hung. 'Buñuel doesn't make full contact with us,' *New Yorker* critic Pauline Kael says, 'and the distance can be fun; it can result in the pleasure of irony, though it can also result in the dissatisfaction of feeling excluded. His indifference to whether we understand him or not can seem insolent, and yet this is part of what makes him fascinating. Indifference can be tantalizing in art, as in romance.'

Buñuel's habit of planning every film beforehand modulated into a strategy to neutralize interference. If the cast wanted direction, he would simply feign deafness or ill-temper as he had with O'Herlihy. Sometimes, Silvia Pinal noticed, he would turn off his hearing aid entirely on the set. 'Why do you do that?' she asked. Luis waved at the people around him and said, 'Why should I want to listen to all this stupidity? I prefer my own thoughts.' When a performer pressed, like de Cordova, he bluffed. For a scene in *El* where Don Francisco beats a wild tattoo on the staircase with a stair rod, the actor proposed that, instead of banging the treads, he run upstairs, rattling the rod against the banisters like a small boy on a fence. Buñuel told him solemnly, 'That's how a schizophrenic would behave. Don Francisco is a paranoiac.'

For someone who scorned gratuitous effect, *Wuthering Heights* was an odd choice for a film, and Buñuel's reason for making his adaptation after *El* provides one of the puzzles in his career. He blames Dancigers, who, he says, pleaded that he had hired Jorge Mistral, Ernesto Alonso, Irasema Dilian and Lilia Prado for a musical and desperately needed a vehicle for them. But Prado, the seductress from *Subida al Cielo*, was the only singer in this group. Spanish-born Mistral, with his Farley Granger good looks, specialized in seducers, while Dilian was a Pole, and hardly prime material for a Mexican musical. Yet it is equally unlikely that Buñuel, even with his indifference to actors, would have chosen such a cast to film a project about which he was truly enthusiastic.

Luis had nursed his ambition to film *Wuthering Heights* for twenty years. It had become such an article of faith that he never thought to re-read the script or question its worth as an idea. Having finally pushed Dancigers into funding it, however, he found that the project no longer interested him. In 1934, the doomed love of the déclassé Heathcliff for the genteel Cathy, and its survival even after her death, had echoed his preoccupations. 'I've always liked the story of *Wuthering Heights*,' he said, 'in which love is also enmity and destruction.' But the anonymous *frottage* of the Bal Bullier, his whorehouse debauches, the urge to overpower his women by hypnosis or drugs, all belonged in the past. A different Luis picked up the old Unik/Sadoul screenplay late in 1952, and found it sadly wanting.

Through the end of the year he reworked the script with two new writers, Arduino Mauri and Julio Alejandro. Mauri came on board because he was married to Irasema Dilian, who played Catalina/Cathy. Alejandro, who would become his co-writer for the next decade, was a more typical Buñuel collaborator. He fought in the Republican navy, then in World War II, during which, as a prisoner of the Japanese in the Philippines, he had been ferociously tortured. Spanish, Communist, subtly maimed, he fitted the model of Luis's colleagues at MoMA.

Alejandro confirms that Buñuel changed his mind about *Wuthering Heights*. 'Everything was already prepared for the shooting when he re-read the book and, a curious thing, that second reading impressed him less than the first. But he was already completely involved and had to make it.'

Buñuel shot the film in March 1953, at the *hacienda* of San Francisco de Quadra in the barren uplands of Guerrero, near Taxco. Critics noticed immediately that this was mighty odd country. Thunderstorms crash and flare each night, but dawn reveals a land as parched and bare as the slopes of Paracutin. Most of the trees are dead, but Eduardo, the effete Hindley character, still finds plenty of butterflies and insects for his collection. Given the solidity of its walls, the main house, a near-fortress of fieldstone in a Neo-brutalist style somewhere between Frank Lloyd Wright and medieval mead hall, has remarkably flimsy doors and windows. Half the film's entrances, particularly by Alejandro/Heath-cliff, are made by kicking down or smashing one or another, always to the accompaniment of thunder, lightning and a gust of rain.

Even Emily Brontë would have flinched at the film's cruelty, especially towards animals. A pig is noisily stuck, to the horror of Isabel, and in his first scene Eduardo selects a live butterfly from a jar, impales it and leaves it to flutter and die. A servant tosses a live frog on to hot coals, then carries the smouldering carcass through the house. Ricardo takes time out from brutalizing his young son to snatch a moth out of the air and feed it to a spider that lurks inside a grotesque splatter of gummy filiments, like a giant gob of spit.

'One of the things [Luis] demanded,' says Julio Alejandro, 'was that I didn't put any love scenes into the film. Myself, I found it difficult to make a script of *Wuthering Heights* without love scenes. But Luis put it like this: he had understood immediately that it wasn't a novel of love, but of hate. And that was the whole merit of the film.' In fact *Wuthering Heights* does not quite lack love scenes, but the few there are seem infected with the same savagery as the humans' relationship with nature.

Kisses are never given on the lips but always on the neck, like vampire bites, and, in the film's most famous image, Alejandro and Caterina embrace on a raw hillside of what looks like volcanic ash, next to a dead tree.

Through the film, the 'Liebestod' from *Tristan and Isolde* rumbles and mutters. Although the choice of Wagner echoes the style and reminds us he used the same music in *Un Chien Andalou*, Buñuel repudiated the track, claiming the music was added while he was absent in Europe. But he would not go back to Europe until April 1954, well after the film's music was mixed. *Wuthering Heights*, variously called, in a literal translation of Brontë, *Cumbres Borrascosas* or, as Dancigers retitled it, *Abismos de Pasion (Abysses of Passion)*, is, for better or worse, with its cruelty, its nihilistic view of sexual relationships and its Wagner, representative of Buñuel's truculent state of mind at the time.

25

'Among the Spaniard's many defects is that of improvisation, which arises from the belief that he knows everything.'
– Luis Buñuel

From 1945 to 1953 Buñuel had almost no contact with the world outside Mexico. He did not leave the country, wrote few letters and saw almost no strangers except for the rare adventurous critic who made the pilgrimage to Mexico City.

World cinema was drifting in a trough between the tidal wave of Neo-realism and the equally traumatic impact of the *nouvelle vague*, but few directors of substance noticed or cared less than he. He saw fewer than half a dozen films a year and liked almost none of them. He approved of *La Strada*, but turned against Fellini after the self-psychoanalysis of *Eight and a Half*, while *Juliet of the Spirits* would drive him to angry denunciation. The Neo-realists were no more ready to welcome him. When Vittorio de Sica came to Mexico in the 1960s with the idea of making Oscar Lewis's *The Children of Sanchez*,* he saw *Viridiana* and was horrified by its cynicism. 'What has society done to you?' he demanded. 'Have you suffered so much?' As he left, he asked Jeanne conspiratorially, 'Does your husband beat you?' Luis repaid the compliment by suggesting de Sica star as the crushed and servile old lover in a version of Pierre Louÿs' *La Femme et le Pantin (The Lady and the Puppet)* which a Franco/Italian company asked him to make in 1956.

Filmgoing for Buñuel was complicated by his deteriorating hearing: the gunfire damage, exacerbated by the onset of Ménière's Syndrome, was gradually ossifying the bones of his ear. People got used to him cupping his right hand to his ear, or wearing a pair of black spectacles with a built-in hearing aid. Within a few years he used an aid constantly.

---

* The project was cancelled when Figueroa refused his political blessing.

The cinema strike had petered out with few gains to the film-makers. Having failed to expel Hollywood by industrial action, Mexican cinema was fighting to retain its remaining independence. The new enemies were the exhibitors William O. Jenkins and Gabriel Alarcon, who had absorbed most of the nation's cinemas and built dozens more. Overwhelmingly they screened imported films. In 1953 the director of the Banco Cinematografico, Eduardo Garduno, attacked Jenkins's business, charging 'the monopoly hangs heavily over the nation and, in addition, prevents the healthy development of production'.

In 1947 the Banco had put up 200,000 pesos to launch Peliculas Nacionales S.A. to compete with Jenkins. Among the companies participating was CLASA/Films Mundiales, the privatized vestiges of the partly state-owned studio floated in the 1930s. CLASA needed to produce films recognizably different from the dubbed Hollywood product. They asked Luis to submit some ideas.

With José Bergamin, Buñuel had developed a notion from his days in New York, of a group of bourgeois who become trapped in their elegant home after a dinner party. *Los Naufragos de la Calle Providencia (The Castaways of Calle Providencia)*, as he called it, was never made, though it would become the basis of *The Exterminating Angel*. He also proposed Perez Galdos's *Tristana*, with Alonso and Pinal, but CLASA shivered at its anti-clericalism and passed.

They compromised on a Mexico City comedy by Mauricio de la Serna and José Revueltas, *La Ilusion Viaja en Tranvia*. As Luis Alcoriza and Buñuel rewrote the slight story of two tramcar employees sentimentally attached to their decrepit vehicle, it began to develop the rambling *tertulia*-like stringing of anecdote that Luis would perfect in *The Discreet Charm of the Bourgeoisie* and *The Phantom of Liberty*. It also acquired an ingenious and unexpected leftist political subtext which CLASA were only too happy to bring on board.

Buñuel was always offhand about *La Ilusion*, perhaps because its politics, more than appropriate to Mexico at the time and to its film industry, not to mention his own pre-war ideals, were more genial than the cynical side of his character would like. He preferred to stress the film's Surrealistic contrivance. When the Latin American Film Institute asked him to present a programme of extracts from his films, he included the sequence where slaughtermen's flayed carcasses and severed pigs' heads being transported across town by the old No. 133 sway above the heads of the passengers. He compared the scene to the collages of Max Ernst, which also juxtaposed grotesque heads with mundane bodies, inserting startling events into the prosaic daily life of Paris.

Among the film's other fantastic elements was the *pastorela*, a naive devotional playlet, traditionally performed by amateurs on religious holidays. Although he never enjoyed working on stage, he had been coaxed into producing Moral's *Don Juan de Tenorio* for the Day of the Dead, and enjoyed the experience. The *pastorela* of *La Ilusion* is authentic, its crêpe-bearded God, horned Devil, and Adam and Eve in baggy leopard skins based on characters and costumes Luis had seen in *pastorelas* near his own home.

Buñuel finished shooting *La Ilusion* on 28 September 1953. In January 1954 he was on location in a stifling Santa Cruz to start a second film for CLASA, *El Rio y la Morte (The River and Death)*. Miguel Alvarez Acosta, a career diplomat and friend of Luis who was then ambassador to France, had written the novel *Muro Blanco sobre Roca Negra (White Walls on Black Rocks)*, and pulled strings so that Buñuel could direct the film version.

A story of a Guerrero feud spanning generations, it swings between western, soap opera and ironic comedy. Buñuel and Alcoriza rewrote much of the novel's rambling narrative, but Acosta insisted that the point of his story, an argument for the civilizing effect of higher education, should not be compromised, and 'corrected' their version. Luis was scornful of Acosta's premise that, if everyone went to university, blood feuds would disappear. Hadn't university graduates killed one another during the war in Spain? He wanted to end the film tragically, with the two modern representatives of the feud turning from their rapprochement to reaffirm the traditional slaughter. 'There are so many social problems,' Buñuel told Jaime Fernandez, who played one of them, 'that it can never end. The vendetta must continue.' But Acosta overruled him.

Luis had to content himself with subversive editorial comments, like the moment where some visitors condole with the parish priest about the amount of violence in his district. He agrees, then shows the gun he carries under his own soutane, grinning, 'I'm not stupid, you know.' He also unearthed a Guerrero ritual where the victim of a feud is paraded through the streets in his coffin. At each corner the mourners invite neighbours for a last drink, after which the corpse is carried to the house of his killer, where his relatives demand the assassin come out and pay for his death. In such cases, however, the killer is usually safe on the other side of the river, where victims, like dead Hurdaños, are rowed to be buried.

Early in 1954, Buñuel made his first trip to Europe in almost a decade. Conchita had written that Doña Maria was losing her memory, and Luis wanted to see her again while she was still alert. The Cannes Festival had invited him to serve on the jury in May, under Cocteau as Chairman, and *El* was due to open in Paris in June (as *Tourments*). Against Luis's better judgement, CLASA sent *The River and Death* to the Venice Festival with a Mexican delegation, including Jaime Fernandez. He refused to accompany them. He would have preferred to be represented by *Robinson Crusoe* but, to his amusement, most people seemed to regard it as a film for children, which helped commercial success in the United States but undercut its intellectual impact. When it had its American première in August, an Academy membership which clearly had not understood the film nominated Dan O'Herlihy for the Best Actor.

Luis's trip began badly and got worse. Alvarez Acosta was flying to Paris as well, so the two men travelled on the same plane. At New York airport, on their way to have a coffee before boarding their Air France flight, an official demanded Buñuel's passport. Acosta went on, but Luis was locked in an interrogation room, under guard.

Taking out his pocket flask, he politely offered his minder a sip. The man drained it. Deprived of even a drink, Luis fumed for twenty minutes until a policeman appeared with a file.

'Mr Gustavo Duran?' he asked.

A surprised Luis said, 'No, Mr Buñuel.'

The man looked at the file again, said hurriedly, 'Oh, yes. Sorry', and left.

Twenty minutes later Luis was escorted to the plane, which everyone else had boarded. Only then was his passport returned.

When he returned to Mexico, Luis confronted Duran and accused him of having informed on him to the US government. Duran admitted it. 'Yes, old man, I denounced you. You have no idea . . . The hours I spent with those CIA types. Six months. I told them everything they wanted.'

Barred from entering Spain, Luis arranged to meet his mother and the rest of the family in Pau, in southern France. There, in the Café Aragon, with the snow-capped Pyrenees in the background, they had a poignant reunion. It was to be his last glimpse of Doña Maria in a rational state. She already had trouble remembering which country she was in, and senile dementia would increasingly erode her mind. Within a few years she lost all short-term memory. Luis would watch fascinated as she paged slowly through a magazine, only to turn at the end to the first page and go through it again. Juan Luis and his cousins played jokes on her. 'We'd knock on the door. She'd open it: "Hello! How *are* you? Come in." A few moments later we'd slip out and knock again. She'd welcome us in again. "How *are* you . . . ?" Black Spanish humour.'

*

Luis did not enjoy Cannes. It was crowded and noisy. In the middle of an official dinner he would get up abruptly and leave. Jaime Fernandez noticed him alone at a table in the Hôtel Martinez and offered to buy him a drink. After that, they met every day for champagne and a powerful cocktail of Luis's devising called the Buñueloni, a version of the Negroni, mixing Caprano and sweet Cinzano with his favourite Beefeater gin.* Buñuel joked with Fernandez: 'If you drink four of these, I'll give you a film when we get back to Mexico.' The most Fernandez could manage was two.

Buñuel loathed his service on the jury. The members were deadlocked between uncommercial European films and the pressure of Hollywood, which was lobbying for Fred Zinnemann's anodyne *From Here to Eternity*. Cocteau proposed a compromise choice, René Clément's *Monsieur Ripois*, a Gérard Philipe romance, shot mostly in Oxford. Buñuel refused to vote for it. When the awards were announced, the Japanese *Gate of Hell* had won Best Film, but Clément received Best Director, and *From Here to Eternity* an Out of Competition Prize. Furious, Buñuel stormed out of the closing ceremony, walked to the beach and threw his dinner jacket into the Mediterranean.

At Venice, *The River and Death* did not impress critics but went down well with the public, which recognized affinities between Guerrero's feuds and the classic Sicilian vendetta. Buñuel was not consoled. Cannes, for all its petty wrangling, had reminded him of the range and variety of world cinema, its writers and performers. To have access to these, however, he must relocate in Europe. That had its problems, however. To work in Europe was to re-enter the political cockpit he had been glad to escape.

After Cannes, he returned to Paris, and wept as he walked the familiar streets. Politically, however, the occasion was less sentimental, and led to a definitive break with the official arms of both Communism and Surrealism.

The Party, now heavily Stalinist, had criticisms of *Los Olvidados*, which an embarrassed Georges Sadoul was delegated to explain. In particular it objected to a scene where Pedro drifts to the richer parts of Mexico City. As he looks in a shop window a homosexual tries to pick him up, but a policeman scares him off. Later, in the reformatory, a liberal governor, to demonstrate his trust, sends him to buy cigarettes outside the gates.

'So?' Buñuel said.

Both sequences, said Sadoul, depicted bourgeois authority figures in

* Serge Silberman offers an alternative recipe: 60 per cent gin, 25 per cent red vermouth, 15 per cent Punt e Mes port, plenty of ice and a slice of orange. 'Explosive!' he declares.

an unacceptably flattering light. Buñuel wearily recalled Breton's question when he allowed Auriol to publish the screenplay of *Un Chien Andalou*: 'Are you with the police or with us?' On that occasion he had taken the criticism to heart. This time, conscious after almost twenty years that his own Communism would always be personal, even religious, a kind of inner commitment to a private conception of social justice, he ignored it.

He was in good company. Luchino Visconti made no secret of his Communism either, but he never actually joined the Party and often opposed it publicly, condemning, for instance the Soviet invasions of Hungary and Czechoslovakia. He also felt able to maintain his standing as the hereditary Duke of Milan, and to profess a belief in God. For him, and for Luis as well, Communism was, in Laurence Schifano's phrase, 'a lay religion'.

If Communism had not changed with the post-war world, neither had Surrealism. Most of the pre-war brotherhood were purged or dead. Breton's 1950 *Almanach Surréaliste du Demi-Siècle* included work by only one other pre-war member, the undeviatingly strict Péret, with a few De Chirico and Ernst illustrations, though Ernst too would be purged in 1955, dismissed by Breton as 'a money-grubbing art dealer', like Dali, for winning the Venice Biennale.

When Buñuel called on Breton, he found him preoccupied with doctrinal squabbles and his credentials as a pioneer. Dali's exploitation of Surrealism's decorative and playful aspects at the expense of the political and literary meant that the world regarded him and not Breton as the true pope of Surrealism. Worse, Dali had just announced his conversion to Catholicism, promising, 'My painting in future will be an amalgam of my Surrealist experience and the classicism of the Pre-Raphaelites and the Renaissance.'

In the lithograph *Sometimes I Spit for Pleasure on the Portrait of my Mother*, Dali had painted the words of the title over an outline of the Christ of the Sacred Heart. For the *Almanach*, Breton reproduced the picture with the addition of a newspaper report of Dali's conversion, and called the piece *L'Amalgame*. An apostasy that would once have stirred him to a furious pamphlet provoked no more than this amused shrug. As he lamented to Luis in 1955, 'It's sad, but it's no longer possible to scandalize anybody.'

Buñuel believed no such thing. It was not he who had abandoned Surrealist principles but Breton, and thereafter he regarded himself as pursuing a private Surrealist agenda. 'Having talked for hours and hours about Surrealism with Luis,' said Jean-Claude Carrière, '[I believe that] the real desire [of the movement] was not aesthetical but social;

revolutionary. It was a revolutionary movement. They were young – we must not forget that – and they really wanted to change the world, using scandal, provocation, poetry, dark explorations of the mind as weapons. Of course it was a chimera. It was a Utopia but that was the point. Of course they were artists; they were writers; they were photographers, painters, film-makers so they used the weapons they had, but basically what they shared at the beginning was that deep desire to change a world they couldn't stand after the First World War and the massacre of that war. And the reason why they separated, why they got so much divided was because of the faithfulness or not to this primitive desire.'

To that ideal Buñuel would be rigorously faithful. The failure to achieve it, and the decline of Surrealism into the decorative clichés of Magritte wall-paper and Dali dream sequences depressed him. 'Very much later, in the seventies,' Carrière recalled, 'I said to Buñuel: "Could we say that Surrealism has failed in the essential and succeeded in the superfluous and the secondary?" and he said "Yes".'

The European trip dramatically increased Buñuel's visibility. French film critics interviewed him at length, and in London *Sight and Sound* published Tony Richardson's account of his Mexico City visit and an exuberant survey of his films. It was the first major appreciation of Buñuel's work in English, and highly influential. Looking beyond the deficiencies of acting and his nonsensical plots, Richardson, using with relish such words as 'relentless' and 'gloating', evoked Buñuel's austerity, cynicism and, above all, humour; qualities that would recommend him to the emerging generation of European artists.

Producers were quick to approach Buñuel with projects. A Swiss financier suggested an adaptation of *Thérèse Etienne* by German novelist John Knittel. A Franco/Italian company wanted him to make an original called *Dolores* or, alternatively Pierre Louys' *La Femme et le Pantin*. As usual, however, Buñuel found more inspiration in writers along what Robert Browning called 'the dangerous edge of things'. He read *Celà s'Appelle l'Aurore (They Call It Dawn)*, a novel by Emmanuel Robles, a working-class Spaniard from North Africa, discovered by Camus in 1937. Robles wrote about a situation that was increasingly to preoccupy Buñuel; a closed community, in this case the island of Corsica, where infidelity, disease and betrayal echo the political unrest just below the surface. Robles took his title from Jean Giraudoux's *Electre*, where the heroine Narsès asks a beggar: 'Is there a name for the moment when the day breaks, as today, when everything is ruined, ravaged, yet the air is still fresh, and when one has lost everything, and the city burns, and the innocent slaughter one another, but the guilty lie dying in a corner of the new day?'

'It has a beautiful name, Narsès,' says the Beggar. 'It is called "dawn".'

Not only did Robles evoke the atmosphere of the Spain both he and Buñuel had lost; he did so with a political edge that Luis responded to. He would film *Celà s'Appelle l'Aurore* in 1955.

Thinking about *La Femme et le Pantin*, Buñuel began to play with the theme of a stiff Spanish military officer reduced to a fawning puppet by a manipulative woman, and wrote a script, which the producer rejected. 'I asked for an adaptation of the Pierre Louys novel,' he complained, 'and he turned me in something that was pure Buñuel from start to finish.' Buñuel maliciously suggested Vittorio de Sica as the ageing lover, but the producer saw it more as a vehicle for Cary Grant and Brigitte Bardot. Julien Duvivier eventually made the film, with Bardot but without Grant. Buñuel shelved his script until 1977, when it was transformed into *That Obscure Object of Desire*.

The Mexican cinema was in a slightly healthier state when Buñuel returned. Garduno had forced through a law limiting foreign movies to 150 a year (the total for 1954 was 346). It never reached this target, but between 1954 and 1958, distribution of Hollywood movies in Mexico sagged and local production soared, from twenty-two features in 1954 to 230 in 1956. Film-makers like Luis should have flourished. Instead, comedy westerns, soap operas and musicals proliferated. Half the films made in 1954 were domestic melodramas. Of the remainder, thirty exploited that year's dance fad, the cha-cha.

Ernesto Alonso, who played Eduardo in *Abismos de Pasion*, had formed a co-operative to film *Ensayo de un Crimen (Rehearsal for a Crime)*, a novel by Rudolfo Usigli, who had worked with Buñuel on the dialogue of *Susana*, and asked him to direct. Usigli's novel, based on a real case history, tried to analyse the intellectual processes by which a man decides to commit murder. Buñuel did not find this particularly interesting but, as with *El*, he was intrigued to enter the mind of a paranoid for whom daily reality was flooded with sinister significance. As he said, 'The cinema seems to have been invented to express subconscious life.'

Like Francisco in *El*, Usigli's hero was a prosperous and apparently upright citizen. Buñuel made an instant connection with the sort of men who had kept Franco in power. As if he had appointed himself the bad conscience of the regime, for the rest of his career he would use his films to target prosperous landlords and professional men, minor landed gentry, upper-middle-class snobs living on private incomes, and particularly jacks-in-office (usually with military rank) who administered corrupt governments. The fact that he was himself a product of the same class seemed only to add spice. Surrealism thrived on such ironies, and what Buñuel proposed to do was revive Surrealism's old revolutionary spirit, even if he had to do so alone.

He worked with Usigli for a fortnight, but the writer resigned over the liberties Buñuel was taking. Ugarte replaced him. He and Buñuel changed the character's name and that of the story (to *The Criminal Life of Archibaldo de la Cruz*), and Luis got on with what G. Cabrera Infante called 'exercis[ing] those gifts sequestered from his days as a Surrealist. Namely, masochistic surprise and the sadism of objects.'

In Luis's version, Archibaldo (Alonso) is a bourgeois marked for life by a random childhood event. Fascinated by a music box his mother has given him and the accompanying fable that a king once used it to make enemies disappear, young Archibaldo dresses in her clothes and dances in imitation of the ballerina on top. His nanny catches him but, while he's being scolded, a stray bullet from the revolution taking place in the street kills her. To his delight, blood dribbles down the silk-stockinged legs revealed in her fall. Archibaldo grows up to become a potter and ceramicist, but he's unstable and suggestible. Even the blood of a shaving cut reminds him of the maid's legs. In an antique shop he finds a music box identical to his mother's, and imagines it confers on him the ability to kill people, particularly women, simply by willing it. As coincidence involves him in a series of grotesque deaths of women, including one acted out in his home workshop, where he burns a wax dummy of his fiancée in a kiln, his twisted imagination convinces him the power is real.

While Buñuel was shooting *Archibaldo* in January, a handsome, actorish man named Gustavo Alatriste, the lover (and later husband) of Ariadne Walter, who played Archibaldo's fiancée Carlota in the film, often dropped in to see her. Luis got to know him. An entrepreneur whose taste for actresses led him into the movies, he had told Buñuel he was thinking of going into production. Luis did not discourage him. Eventually Alatriste would marry another actress, Silvia Pinal, produce *Viridiana*, *The Exterminating Angel* and *Simon of the Desert* for her to star in, and weave through much of Buñuel's later career, not always to his advantage. *Archibaldo* was also to have its uncanny parallel in real life. Miroslava Stern, who played Lavinia, committed suicide shortly after the film was shot – and was cremated, the fate planned for her by Archibaldo.

26

In 1955 Buñuel still held the Communist belief in radical change and
permanent revolution, but tempered now by self-interest and his ironic
view of history. He had seen the socialist future in Mexico, and it didn't
work. Approvingly he quoted a Chilean refugee who said, 'Mexico's
fascistic, but it's a country where fascism has been softened by
corruption.' The same was true of Spain. Battering the Fascist sword
against the intractable Spanish character had blunted it into a plough-
share. The country had never been so prosperous. Buñuel could now
imagine going back some day, and even working there.

That he should be hostile to Franco and at the same time want to live
again in Spain was not contradictory. Buñuel had seen enough of the
Civil War to realize that its excesses were mostly manifestations of
Spain's endemic cruelty, vindictiveness and hypocrisy. That both sides
were guilty of atrocities moderated his anger at those committed by
Franco. 'I've never been one of Franco's fanatical adversaries,' he wrote
in *My Last Breath*. 'As far as I'm concerned, he wasn't the Devil
personified. I'm even ready to believe that he kept our exhausted country
from being invaded by the Nazis. Yes, even in Franco's case there's room
for some ambiguity.'

To Buñuel, the worst betrayals of the Civil War were personal. It was
easier to accept treachery on the national scale than the duplicity of Dali
or Duran. And he was interested to talk to Lucia Bosè, his star in *Celà
s'Appelle l'Aurore*, and her lover, the matador Luis Dominguin, who
haunted the set and rang up constantly to make sure Bosè was not seeing
too much of her co-star Georges Marchal. These were intelligent people
who had made an accommodation with Franco and, however much
Buñuel disapproved, he could not help finding their choice intriguing,

though when confronted, in the case of *Viridiana*, with a chance to conciliate, he would elect to remain a subversive.

Jean-Claude Carrière believes that Buñuel's evolving acceptance of Franco had a significant effect on the climate of opinion in Spain. 'With his incontestable authority in the Spanish world, Buñuel could say what no Republican would have said, that Franco had helped save the Jews. His famous phrase about Franco – "I am even prepared to believe that he kept Spain out of World War II" – that phrase was like a bomb in Spain; that Buñuel [. . .] could say that [in 1983], that contributed to the national reconciliation in Spain, and had considerable importance for the success of the Socialists in the election [. . .] He was like the father long in exile who remains nevertheless a force in Spain. You know, Buñuel is clearly a greater man than Picasso. You have to go all the way back to Goya to find a figure of that importance.'

Celà s'Appelle l'Aurore, which Buñuel made in Corsica and around Nice from August to October 1955 for a Franco/Italian consortium, was a useful vehicle to pay old scores but also to explore his ambivalence about Spain. The main character, Valerio (Marchal), is a doctor who has worked in Africa but sold out to a Corsican company run by Gorzone (Jean-Jacques Delbo). By controlling Valerio, the priest and the police commissioner, Fasaro (Julien Bertheau), Gorzone rules the island.

Buñuel enjoyed characterizing Gorzone and Fasaro as the sort of well-meaning *bourgeoisie* who backed the Falange and went on to prop up Franco. Neither, however, is a monster. Like Crusoe, they grapple with the problems of being God and, superficially at least, behave no worse than he (or God) did. Early in the film Fasaro stops his men beating up a prisoner, though a few scenes later he casually smashes an old rapist's hand: the Lord giveth . . .

What Gorzone and Fasaro lack and what Valerio discovers in himself is what Crusoe lacked at the start of his time on the island: the moral worth conferred by compassionate interaction with others. Buñuel's sly and skilful manipulation of details dramatizes this. It seems only fair that Gorzone should refuse to reinstate his dismissed gardener at the cost of sacking the man hired to replace him – but the new man is Gaston Modot, the love-crazed hero of *L'Age d'Or*. Buñuel might as well have cast Boris Karloff, so negative is the impression he conveys. Fasaro seems pious and cultivated. There is a Crucifixion on his wall and a book of poetry on his desk. But the Crucifixion is by Dali, and the book, pointedly juxtaposed with a pair of hand-cuffs, is the collected works of right-wing Catholic poet and playwright Paul Claudel, a *bête noire* of the Surrealists. Fasaro knows portions of Claudel by heart, and recites some to Valerio as they drive across the island. Again, Buñuel poisons the character by subtle association.*

Luis seems never to have read Graham Greene, but there is an affinity between the work of the two men at this period. Both were remote, ascetic, misanthropic, Catholic/atheist. Greene's protagonists in *The Heart of the Matter* and *The Comedians*, lonely men drifting along the edges of empire, troubled by moral doubts, losing themselves in casual infidelities but obsessed always with the lack of meaning in their lives, are interchangeable with Valerio and his equivalents in *Death in the Jungle* and *Fever Mounts at El Pão*, except that social justice rather than God saves Buñuel's men. The films are scattered with quasi-devotional fetish objects that Greene might have relished, like Valerio's photograph of a cement statue of Christ which World War II engineers in Africa had pressed into service as a telegraph pole, so that insulators branched from his face like exotic flowers.**

Catholics in general took the film badly. Buñuel was widely quoted as having joked, 'Thank God I'm still an atheist,' and though this was hardly original – on 17 October 1927, Paris-based avant-garde publisher Harry Crosby (he of the tattooed Crucifixion on the sole of his left foot) wrote to his mother, 'Thank Christ I am not a Christian' – it gained added venom coming from the mouth of so unregenerate an enemy of the Church. Some sticklers also complained about Luis showing a priest socializing with a dictator.

François Truffaut, then writing for *Cahiers du Cinéma*, said dismissively, 'I dislike *Celà s'Appelle l'Aurore* because it's badly acted; that's all there is to it.' In general, however, he liked Buñuel's work, and did his best to push it in *Cahiers*, behind the back of the editor, Jacques Doniol-Valcroze. His enthusiasm was not shared by Eric Rohmer, then so right-wing and Catholic that colleagues like Ado Kyrou called him Fascist. 'The film is just one cliché after another,' Rohmer wrote of *Celà s'Appelle l'Aurore*, 'a huge ado about nothing. I hope that Buñuel has not said his last word. For the time being anyway, he only occupies a small niche in the history of the cinema, as Dali's collaborator on *Un*

---

* Julien Bertheau felt uncomfortable mocking Claudel; he had played in *The Annunciation of Mary*, from which Buñuel took his quote. Luis told him it wasn't necessary to send up the text, but Claudel's daughter protested the slur.
** And what an amusing film, in the light of *The Criminal Life of Archibaldo de la Cruz*, Buñuel might have made from *Our Man in Havana*, compared to Carol Reed's stolid transcription.

Chien Andalou and *L'Age d'Or*, and as Mexico's virtually only director; all in all, a pretty small niche.' This incensed even Buñuel. When he was introduced to Rohmer at *Cahiers du Cinéma*, he said politely, 'I'm glad to meet a Fascist.' Rohmer looked startled. 'Well, that's what I've been told,' he said. As Rohmer stood red-faced, he walked out.

Buñuel had few reasons to hurry back to Mexico after *Celà s'Appelle l'Aurore*. Juan Luis had gone off to college in 1953, and Rafael would soon leave home as well. Doña Maria's declining health was also on his mind. Professionally, Mexico was depressing. In France there was growing interest in his work, though *Archibaldo de la Cruz* still had not had a French release, so in November Buñuel introduced a screening for psychologists and psychiatrists of the Circle Psyche du Cinéma at the Musée de l'Homme.

A number of French producers and actors wanted to work with him. Shooting *Interdit de Séjour (Forbidden to Stay)*, the young actor Michel Piccoli badgered assistant director Marcel Camus who, he knew, had been Buñuel's assistant (along with Jacques Deray) on *Celà s'Appelle l'Aurore*, for an introduction. In the end Piccoli wrote to Buñuel directly, inviting him to one of his stage performances. Luis wrote that he would like to come, cabled to say he couldn't make it on the night agreed, then rang to make sure Piccoli had got the cable. Puzzled by this elaborate courtesy, Piccoli nominated another night. Luis came, but slipped away when he saw Jean Renoir in the door of Piccoli's dressing room, presenting his own compliments. He apologized next day. 'I have a horror of socialites, but I very much liked the show – one piece in particular, *Les Reliques* by André de Richaud, an author that I have a passion for. I've come close to filming one of his texts, *La Barrette Rouge* or *La Fontaine des Lunatiques*. Could you introduce me?' Piccoli arranged the introduction, and he and Luis became good friends – good enough for Piccoli to become the butt of his deadpan tale about Jeanne and her priestly lover.

Just as Buñuel's options were running out in France, independent producer David Mage offered him José André Lacour's *Death in the Garden*, a novel set in the diamond fields of some unnamed Latin American country. Dancigers would co-produce, and the film would be shot in Mexico. Reluctantly, Buñuel accepted.

Mage intended to cash in on *The Wages of Fear*, Henri-Georges Clouzot's hit film about drifters in a South American country hauling nitro-glycerine to an oil-well fire in return for a ticket back to Paris. He wanted Yves Montand, star of *The Wages of Fear*, for the hero, Chark, but the actor was committed to a film in Italy. He compromised by hiring

Vanel from the original cast and casting Montand's wife Simone Signoret opposite Georges Marchal's Chark.

Superficially, *Death in the Garden* is a conventional south-of-the-border Western, though at 145 minutes in Mexico (107 elsewhere, where the title was also changed to *Diamond Hunters*), it is long for its slim story. But Freddy Buache sees it as typically Buñuel. 'Nothing either begins or ends in this film. Everything is transitory. Good is but a transitory aspect of evil, and evil a fleeting guise of good, and it is no good referring to the tenets of classical morality. What may seem to be a crime can turn out to be a good deed, and vice versa. It is a film about ambiguity.' This might explain why Mage commissioned a script from, of all people, Jean Genet, but the author of *The Thief's Journal* took the money and did not deliver.

Buñuel spent some time at the Montands' country home at Autheuil discussing the contract. The first morning, they were woken at dawn by shots. Luis was practising marksmanship in the garden, 'to calm his nerves', he said.

Signoret, who had seldom been separated from Montand, repented of the deal even before she left. With Vanel, Marchal, Piccoli and Michèle Girardon, she flew out of Paris on 23 March 1956. As the actors passed through New York airport Vanel was alarmed to see, ill-concealed in Signoret's papers, a Communist tract. She hoped that this, with her passport and its many admission stamps to socialist countries, would get her sent back to France and Montand, but, to her irritation, the Americans took no notice.

Buñuel was envious. Washington's curiosity about him had, if anything, increased. On his way back from France, he had been detained and interrogated about his subscription to the anti-Franco *España Libre* and his name on an anti-bomb petition. He now required a special authorization each time he wanted to visit the United States, and as long as he stayed there two FBI agents tailed him from the door of his hotel. When Juan Luis applied for his visa to go to college, the Mexico City embassy hauled out a massive FBI file marked 'Buñuel' and began quizzing him. He pointed out that, when his father was attending Communist meetings with Aragon and Triolet, he had not yet been born.

Luis found the FBI's games more amusing than offensive. He and Juan Luis cooked up some gags to play on the Immigration and Customs Service. Arriving at a US airport, one of them would nervously pat a pocket.

'What have you got there?' the customs officer would demand.

'Uh, nothing.' Finally he would hand over a pack of cigarettes. Carefully peeling one apart, the customs man would find a rolled slip of paper saying: 'The person reading this is an asshole.'

The writers who worked on *Death in the Garden* were almost as rag-tag as the cast. After Genet, the Surrealist humourist Raymond Queneau tried his hand. Buñuel liked his ideas, but most were too gag-like to suit the violent plot. One showed Djin, the local prostitute, buying soap. 'One cake,' she tells the shop-keeper. As she is about to pay, a contingent of soldiers rides in. 'Better make that six,' she says, anticipating a sharp rise in trade. Gabriel Arout, Alcoriza and Buñuel himself revised it extensively, rising at 4 a.m. every day during the shoot to rewrite the day's work. Buñuel enjoyed playing with the ambiguities, but the story never looked like achieving the power of *The Wages of Fear*.

When Buñuel cabled Michel Piccoli, offering him the role of the priest, Lizzardi, 'forty-five years old and plump', the actor, who was thirty, tall and thin, suspected a gag. After finding that some older, plumper, more pious performers had also been offered the part, he turned it down, only to be bombarded with cables: 'Scheduled for role of priest Stop Send your response please', 'Send Piccoli for the role of priest.' Piccoli acquiesced and flew to Mexico City. Buñuel met him at the airport. 'I'm glad to see you,' he said, 'but what are you doing here? You're not at all like the priest.' Mockery, Piccoli decided, was a working tool for Luis. 'You are artists. Very good,' he told the cast. 'I detest artists. But you,' he said, singling out Piccoli, 'you're a *great* artist.' Praise or insult? With Buñuel, one never knew.

Nobody liked the location shooting near Lake Catemaco, where they were accommodated in huts built near large mango trees. Fruit thumped noisily on to the corrugated iron roofs, raining bugs down on the inhabitants. Perhaps taking a cue from Buñuel, the cast approached the production with bantering belligerence. 'He found us unruly,' Vanel admits. Signoret seemed to invite discord simply by her presence. Noticing the chasuble around Piccoli's neck, she joked, 'Are you cold? You've brought your muffler.' Piccolo threw one end over his shoulder as Parisians wear their scarves, and Buñuel had to warn him, 'You can't joke like that with all these Mexicans here. They are great believers.'

A few days later, Luis invited his stars to dinner for his famous paella. Afterwards, Luis Alcoriza, in the sort of black joke Luis knew and understood, moaned loudly about what he said was a terrible meal. Missing the humour, the French actors took it for a dire insult on Buñuel. When Alcoriza invited them to his place the following week, the guests waited until the plates were set down, then opened bags and produced their own canned food and bottles of wine, which they proceeded to eat instead of his meal. No amount of protests from Alcoriza could convince them it had been a joke.

Luis was amused when he heard this, but less when Signoret interfered with shooting, lecturing him on technique, and bullying cameraman Jorge Stahl Jr into changing set-ups. After a few days, Luis had a cord strung around the camera with 'Actors Forbidden to Enter This Area'. However, even Signoret was easier to deal with than Michèle Girardon. An amateur pushed on the production by parents who wanted a movie career for her, she was inept, her husky Ingrid Bergman jollity absurdly at odds with the setting and her dusky *métèque* make-up. Obviously someone liked her, however, since she played another jungle ingénue in Howard Hawks' *Hatari!*

Stories of revolution in isolated communities would preoccupy Buñuel for at least one more film, but in the meantime he fell in with a new and younger producer, more ambitious than most others working in Mexico. Manuel Barbachano Ponce had started in newsreels, then moved on to directing, and to producing features by Juan Antonio Bardem, Jaime Humberto Hermosillo and, in particular, Carlos Velo, Buñuel's old comrade who became Barbachano Ponce's production supervisor, editor and house director. *The House of Bernarda Alba* came up again as a possible subject, but Buñuel couldn't find any more enthusiasm for the play than when Denise Tual had suggested it. They got further with Alejo Carpentier's novel *El Acoso (The Pursuit)*, but Luis finally persuaded him to film his failed project of two decades before, Perez Galdos's *Nazarin*.

Nazarin, the film that decisively relaunched Buñuel on the international scene and became the foundation of the second and richest part of his career, started shooting at Churubusco on 14 July 1958. Luis and Julio Alejandro changed the setting to Mexico under Diaz, though the fields and villages through which Nazarin passes could belong to half a dozen centuries and countries. Figueroa again lit the film, gritting his teeth as Buñuel excluded all dramatic skyscapes and picturesque groupings. Luis imported young Spanish actor Francisco 'Paco' Rabal to play Nazarin, part of a more than usually interesting cast for a Buñuel film. Rita Macedo from *The Criminal Life of Archibaldo de la Cruz* is the prostitute Andara, his first disciple; Pilar Pellicer and Rosenda Monteros, the latter destined to become a minor international star, have small roles. Buñuel also cast Jesús Fernandez, the first of many dwarfs in his films. He found them fascinating, a combination of child and lover, with satyr-like associations. He particularly relished the fact that

Fernandez, whom he would use again in *Simon of the Desert*, had two full-sized mistresses in Mexico City, and alternated between them.

Nazarin was finished at the end of 1958 but Barbachano Ponce, aware he had a controversy on his hands, dragged his feet about releasing it. The film did not show publicly until June 1959. Meanwhile, John Huston, who was shooting *The Unforgiven* in Durango, was so impressed that he spent a morning ringing Europe, arranging its showing at the 1959 Cannes Festival. To independents like Huston who had fought Hollywood for decades and mostly lost, Buñuel was a touch-stone, an emblem of independence, and proof that personal cinema could exist. 'You can [. . .] say he likes feet and all that,' Orson Welles told Peter Bogdanovich. 'Jesus, it's all true. He's that kind of intellectual and that kind of Catholic [. . .] A superb kind of person he must be. Everybody loves him.'

Films were never discussed at the Buñuel home, and his sons knew little of his work. Luis preferred it that way. He disliked acolytes, assistants or admirers. After seeing *Nazarin*, eighteen-year-old Arturo Ripstein nervously called on him to say he wanted to be a director just like him. Luis slammed the door in his face. Admitting him at last, he remained angry. 'People don't come and say they want to do what you do,' he said. 'This is not something people say to one another.' He sat Ripstein down in the living room and screened *Un Chien Andalou*, without comment. '*This* is what I do,' he told him curtly.

After graduation, Juan Luis had no ambition to go into movies but Oscar Dancigers asked if he would translate for Orson Welles, whom Juan Luis knew only as the radio producer who terrified America with *The War of the Worlds*. Having set up the thriller *Touch of Evil*, Welles had conceived a wild idea to film *Don Quixote* in Mexico. The plan collapsed, though he did shoot some footage for a film on which he would work desultorily over the years in half a dozen countries but never finish. Juan Luis metamorphosed from translator into assistant, and by the time Welles started to shoot *Touch of Evil* was ready to go into the film business.

27

'I shall resume my Numidian flight, skirting the inalienable
sea . . .'
– Saint-John Perse (translated by Denis Devlin)

'Why did you agree to make this film?' Buñuel asked Gérard Philipe
partway through location shooting in Cuernavaca for *Fever Mounts at
El Pāo*.

'I don't know,' said the pale, languid star, famous for his stage roles in
classics like *Le Cid*. 'And you?'

'I don't know either,' Luis said morosely.

The Franco-Mexican co-production, based on a successful 1955 novel
by Henri Castillou, did nothing for the careers of anyone associated with it.

'We were both weak,' Buñuel told Derek Prouse. 'There were certain
political and social elements I liked in the story, but they finally got lost
in the melodrama.'

There were any number of literary adaptations Buñuel would rather
have been working on. Between 1958 and 1960 he contemplated eight
or nine, including Berthe Grimault's novel *Beau Clown* and André
Gide's *The Prisoners of Poitiers*. He also liked Henry James's oblique
ghost story *The Turn of the Screw*. The Freudian analysis in Edmund
Wilson's *Seven Types of Ambiguity* had exposed its minefield of sexual
innuendo, and Buñuel was attracted to putting this on film. William
Golding's *Lord of the Flies*, a fable of stranded schoolboys reverting to
savagery on a remote island and constructing their own theology,
intrigued him as *Robinson Crusoe* had done for its revelations of man's
urge to create a god in his own image. The Gothic flamboyance of
Lewis's *The Monk* also appealed, and he discussed it with Philipe, who
would have been interesting casting. 'We worked for months on the
script,' sighed Luis, 'then Philipe went cold on the idea.'

He was even more drawn to *The Loved One*, the short, malicious
novel about Hollywood that Evelyn Waugh wrote after a 1949 visit.

The Loved One combined satire of the funeral industry with an even more sarcastic view of the British expatriate film colony. Waugh's agent A.D. Peters wanted £10,000 for the film rights, but since Buñuel was the only bidder, he was able to option the book for little money. '[Peters] sold [*The Loved One*] years ago to a mad Mexican for a paltry sum,' Waugh told Nancy Mitford, the book's dedicatee, in a letter, 'with the assurance that it would never be produced, but that Alec Guinness (who was to star) and I might have an agreeable jaunt together to Mexico.' Hugo Butler wrote a script and Buñuel retained his option until the early sixties but the project eventually passed to MGM, who financed Tony Richardson's 1965 version, dismissed by Waugh (and everyone else) as 'an elaborate travesty'.

Having done little with the rights to *Un Chien Andalou* he had regained almost twenty years before, Buñuel agreed in 1960 to a reissue of the film with a sound track that duplicated the records he had played to accompany it on the first screening. The Argentinian composer Mauricio Kagel also approached him to write an original score. Whether Buñuel ever agreed is debatable, and he is unlikely to have enjoyed the result, a *misterioso* piece for small orchestra, garnished with eerie canine howls. Kagel didn't reveal its existence until after Buñuel's death, when it was used on a Swiss TV broadcast of the film.

Around this time, a mineral-water company approached Buñuel to make a commercial for its product, which was under threat from foreign imports. He suggested a Crucifixion scene. Christ says: 'I thirst', a centurion offers him a bottle. He shakes his head . . . So did the agency.

Luis should have shaken his head to *La Fièvre Monte à El Pão*, also known as *Los Ambiscos/The Ambitious Ones*, its first release title in the United States, and *Republic of Sin*, but unsuccessful under all its aliases. Another of Dancigers' co-productions, it began shooting in May 1959 with French principals but a mostly Mexican cast. Buñuel had worked with Alcoriza on Charles Dorat's adaptation of the novel, but it remained unregenerately stodgy, its political intricacies leaving no room for sexual eccentricity.

Shot by Figueroa, *Fever Mounts at El Pão* is one of the most technically polished of Luis's Mexican movies, but the very gloss, particularly in the *Good Housekeeping* decor of the governor's mansion, with its venetian blinds and potted plants, undercuts what little moral point the story can stir up. Helpless, Luis acquiesced to the setting in Cortez's palace at Cuernavaca, and Maria Felix's glamour. Her strip for Jean Servais's decadent governor Gual belongs in a *Playboy* centrefold, with long legs slipping out of black stockings in the gloom, half obscured by a giant rubber plant.

Ines was the sort of vamp Felix played as a matter of course, but the rueful good humour of Philipe is wrong for Vasquez, the liberal security chief doing his feeble best to fight a corrupt administration. He looks pale and ill at ease, his thin body swimming in the obligatory white linen suits. After the shooting, Philipe, a committed socialist, visited Cuba where, in a gesture that conveyed some of his distaste for the film, he gave part of his fee to the Cuban Film School. During shooting he had complained of fatigue, which Luis put down to the heat. It was only when he returned to France that liver cancer was diagnosed. He died in 1959. *Fever Mounts at El Pão* was the last film of a distinguished career, and among his weakest.

Despite its tropical setting, Buñuel meant the island of Ojeda, like Corsica in *Celà s'Appelle l'Aurore* and the unnamed country of *Death in the Garden*, to serve for Spain, and its endemic corruption for the evils of Franco's regime. Here, however, the moral imperatives are less clear. Where Valerio and Chark attack the system, Vasquez vacillates. He co-operates in order to achieve better conditions for the convicts and accepts Ines's corrupt favours, but both Gual's death and that of Ines are none of his doing. The rebels kill Gual and Ines is shot foolishly trying to crash a border post. A few years before, Buñuel would have been scathing about such compromises, which mirrored those of the New Left in Spain, more ready to collaborate with Franco than Luis's generation had been. Instead, he found himself unconcerned. At sixty, his anger, like his sexuality, was mellowing.

In October 1959 Buñuel went back to New York for the first time, except for airport stop-overs, since 1944. He was casting a new film. *Nazarin* won a special jury prize at Cannes in May and had begun to make a little money, so George Pepper, now incarnated as Olmec Pictures, had offered Luis another Hugo Butler script, based on Peter Matthiessen's short story, *Travellin' Man*. Pepper had hopes of shooting the story where Matthiessen set it, off his native Virginia Tidewater country, but with almost everyone involved still under a political cloud, there was little hope of that. In the end Pepper retained his 'George P. Werker' alias, and Butler signed the script 'Hugo Mozo'* which he later changed to 'H.B. Addis' after the brand of pencil with which he wrote it.

Matthiessen's racist parable was relatively uneventful, only subliminally betraying his left-wing politics. A black man lands on an island reserved for white hunters and is outwitted and killed by one of them. The black, Traver, and his white antagonist Miller are the story's only

---

* A *mozo* is the lowest form of domestic servant; a janitor.

characters, but Butler, with Luis's encouragement, developed an entirely new and exotic plot.

In his version, Miller is a game warden who shares the island with thirteen-year-old Evie and her dying grandfather Pee-Wee. Traver, a musician on the run from a false rape charge, arrives while Miller is visiting the mainland for supplies. Intrigued by the innocently sensual Evie, he stays too long. Pee-Wee dies, and Miller helps Evie bury him.

Death co-exists comfortably with life in this Eden with its nymphet Evie. The starving Traver bites into a live crab, a skinned rabbit hangs waiting for the pot, a badger kills Evie's hens, and the whole island is dedicated to the hunt, but in the middle of it all Evie, the primal innocent, goes on tending her bees among the flowers.

With Pee-Wee's death, Evie no longer has a protector, and Miller seduces her, a crime against both God and the State, even in this primitive community. Next morning, Jackson and the Reverend Fleetwood arrive from the mainland. Traver hides in the woods. Hearing he's accused of raping a white woman, Miller, sensitive about his own transgression with Evie and sensing that Fleetwood has guessed the truth, helps Jackson hunt him down.

Fleetwood suggests a secret compromise to Miller. In return for his silence about having deflowered the more-than-willing Evie, Miller will marry her and free Traver. Evie and Fleetwood leave for the mainland with Jackson, who swears to return with the law. Evie says she'll be back to see Miller on Saturday, but neither is sure of that; awakened now, she's eager for experience. After they've gone, Miller, his racism eroded, and feeling more equal than master, tells Traver courteously: 'Your canoe is ready', and watches him sail away.

Luis enjoyed himself in New York. Richard Nason, interviewing him for the *New York Times*, was impressed by his 'gala red-and-blue striped jacket with brass buttons [shining] in bright contrast to his leathery features'. But he could not pin him down about the film's plot or even its 'moral'. 'Oh, you are right, there is a moral,' Buñuel conceded, 'but it is up to you to provide it. I do not like to make cheap philosophy. Besides, I would be very happy if you didn't publish anything. I hate publicity. It is false. It makes the good things, the human things disappear. It is enough you know me, I know you. I care only what my friends think. And money?' He shrugged. 'If I made too much, I might stop working.'

He chose two near-unknowns, Bernie Hamilton, brother of jazz drummer Chico Hamilton, for Traver, and fifteen-year-old Lynn Loring as Evie. When Loring dropped out, Buñuel returned for a second trip with Juan Luis and selected an amateur, Key

Meersman.*Claudio Brook, a tall, thin Mexican who spoke perfect English and would appear in a number of Luis's films, played the Reverend Fleetwood, but the larger role of Miller remained open, until Zachary Scott filled it.

Scott was another of the ailing left-wing talents Buñuel seemed to attract. Hugo Butler knew him from Renoir's *The Southerner*, which he had adapted to the screen. After the war, Scott escaped from lounge-lizard roles in films like *Mildred Pierce* to his first love, the theatre, where he and his wife Ruth Ford devoted themselves to Faulkner's plays. In January 1959 Tony Richardson's successful London production of *Requiem for a Nun* opened on Broadway. Scott and Ford anticipated a long run. Instead, it closed after forty-three performances, and Scott became available.

The Young One was shot at Churubusco and on location south of Acapulco in January 1960. The shoot attracted more than the usual number of onlookers, including a friend of Gabriel Figueroa, a monosyllabic little man with an accent, whom Juan Luis later discovered to be B. Traven, reclusive author of *The Treasure of Sierra Madre*.

With as skilled an actor as Scott to work with, Buñuel had visualized a calm, measured film, but the less experienced members of his cast quickly sank this hope. Hamilton got so carried away that he had to be pulled off Graham Denton in the fight scene, and even Ruth Ford's intensive coaching could not coax a performance from Meersman. Bowing to the inevitable, Buñuel asked Scott to abandon Faulknerian understatement, and overplay. Meersman learned from the experience, since she had a success in her only other film, Damiano Damiani's *Arturo's Island* (1962). 'And finally,' Luis said, 'I'd still prefer to work with someone like her than with any star. The chances of capturing something real are so much greater.'

For Scott, the experience of Mexico was congenial. He hired a trolley car, fitted it with a bar and a *mariachi* band, and cruised Mexico City, offering free rides and a drink to passing strangers – *La Ilusion Viaja en Tranvia* brought surprisingly to real life.

In May 1960 *The Young One* was shown at the Cannes Festival. Buñuel went with it, and met the young Spanish critics and directors who would lure him back to Spain to make *Viridiana*. Although he shot two more films in Mexico, his career there was effectively over. From now until his death he would be considered, as he had always considered himself, a European film-maker.

---

* Often misspelt 'Kay'. Meersman was distantly related to Francis Scott Key, composer of 'The Star-Spangled Banner', and used his name.

28

'So, in the end, nothing explains anything.'
– Christian in *The Exterminating Angel*

Viridiana repositioned Buñuel at the centre of the cinema world. He never said so, but this had probably been his plan from the moment the film was proposed. Scandal, after all, had worked well with *Un Chien Andalou*. By 1962, he had relocated in Europe. Although he returned to Mexico to make his next film and continued to live there for part of the year, he increasingly spent long periods in Paris or Madrid, preparing and shooting.

Jeanne went back briefly with Luis to France and an emotional reunion with what remained of her family. Within a few days of her return, Georgette died. In Spain, she spent some time with the Buñuels, and with the Pittalugas, who had just moved back after decades in exile. As his fires cooled, Luis forgot the jealousy of earlier years and was reconciled with his old friend. He would even ask him to select the extracts from Handel's *Messiah* and Beethoven's Ninth Symphony used as background music for *Viridiana*.

Since *Viridiana* was a Mexican production, Spain could not stop its international distribution. It did the next best thing, sequestering the original negative and banning all Buñuel films. However, all the copies needed of *Viridiana* could be generated from the duplicate negative smuggled to Paris by Juan Luis. Inevitably the scandal sharpened interest. Even before *Viridiana*'s French release, the critic Freddy Buache was asked to arrange a screening in a private Champs-Elysées cinema. Guests included Georges Franju, Jean-Paul Sartre and Simone de Beauvoir.

Franco, who responded to the Church's anger rather than the film's content, did not himself see *Viridiana* for years. Afterwards he is said to have remarked, 'I can't understand the fuss.' But, as Buñuel commented, how can you shock a man who has committed so many atrocities? Meanwhile, tour operators in Barcelona offered day trips to cities in southern France like Perpignan and Biarritz. The fare included a morning's shopping and an afternoon screening of *Viridiana*. But it would not open publicly in Spain until 1977.

The General's mild reaction suggests the respect in which, despite the fact that he had hoodwinked the nation, Buñuel was still held. Even after *Viridiana*, it would have been delighted to have him back – on its terms. 'The main problem with Buñuel for Franco's regime,' says John Hopewell, ' [. . .] was that he had the personality and the genius to found a school of film-making in Spain. A country whose moral standards were set by the Church could hardly have its film standards set by its most famous atheist.' Spain and Buñuel were to fence for the next five years, with Buñuel trying to set up films there, especially Perez Galdos's *Tristana*, and Franco at first welcoming the overtures, then rebuffing them on a technicality. But it was already evident that nothing could keep Buñuel out. As José Bergamin told him in a letter, he seemed like Antaeus, Gaea's gigantic son; wrestled by Ulysses, he regained his strength every time he was thrown to earth.

Viridiana continued to encounter problems in Catholic countries. Italy, still smarting from Fellini's *La Dolce Vita*, did not show it until 1963, when it was banned and Buñuel sentenced *in absentia* to a year in prison. In Belgium, where the Union of Film Critics awarded it their Grand Prix, copies were seized and mutilated. Even the Swiss loathed it. At the same time, more thoughtful Catholic critics were finding much to praise.

Buñuel, begging the question of whether the depiction of the damage wrought on the will by belief can properly be called 'religious', always argued that the film was essentially devout, 'because in every scene there is an underlying sense of sin. The old man cannot violate his niece because of this.' Gabriel Figueroa too believed that Buñuel was only 'irreverent; not against Catholicism. The irony is that even though his films are labelled anti-religious and anti-Catholic, Buñuel is actually preparing for his next life, trying to come nearer to God all the time. He is one of the most religious of men.' Luis would have his final satisfaction in 1977, when an aged Dominican approached him during the shooting of *That Obscure Object of Desire*. He introduced himself as Father Fierro, who had begun the anti-*Viridiana* furore, and asked forgiveness. Buñuel threw him off the set.

Although Buñuel did not like working with stars, *Viridiana* was an agreeable reintroduction to actors who, unlike some of those forced on him in Mexico, took a professional approach to their work. In particular Fernando Rey, who played Don Jaime, became a favourite performer and friend. In him, Buñuel found the embodiment of *señorito* suavity and good-natured vanity. Rey had fought Franco and later made a living as a dubbing voice, so they had much in common, but the actor, who mostly made a career of playing cardinals, grandees and kings, especially Philip II, contributed to Buñuel's films a quality Luis himself envied, the playful arrogance of the man of affairs who understands and enjoys power. Whether smuggling heroin as the corrupt ambassador in *The Discreet Charm of the Bourgeoisie* or being humiliated by beautiful tormenters in *Tristana* or *That Obscure Object of Desire*, Rey never lost his urbanity nor the melancholy *gravitas* that implied hidden depths of decadence and disappointment. The actor's self-satisfaction was as unshakeable off screen as on. Buñuel once paid a group of children to come up one by one and ask for his autograph, but ignore Rey sitting beside him. After the first couple, Rey burst out laughing. It was inconceivable that people should not recognize him, so Luis had to be playing a joke.

Jokes like this, directed as often against Luis as members of the cast, were a feature of Buñuel's sets. Luis and Max Aub were dining in a large Mexico City restaurant with a group of Mexican and Spanish intellectuals shortly after wrapping *Fever Mounts at El Pão* when, after the meal, most of the staff came up and asked for Luis's autograph. When he asked why he was so popular, one explained, 'For a hundred autographs like yours, we can get one of Maria Felix.' It dawned on him then that the gag had been set up by Aub.

Although Franco had ordered UNINCI to be closed down as a punishment for *Viridiana*, on paper the consortium was still functioning and, more important, solvent. Funds from the film's distribution were supposed to be deposited in a Swiss bank until ownership could be settled, but Alatriste was adept at eluding such barriers. Immediately after *Viridiana*, he offered to fund Buñuel in another Mexican film and asked him to suggest a title.

The offer tempted Luis. Alatriste was unreliable, paying fees late, if at all, hiding in his office bathroom to avoid process-servers and even offering bribes to an Immigration official to let him out of the country when some creditor had issued a court order to keep him in Mexico. He was no intellectual either, having admitted that it took him three screenings to understand *Viridiana*.

None of these characteristics put Buñuel off. Alatriste would never interfere in a film at the script stage; he simply would not know or care what the film was about. Luis also recognized in him a mixture of 'wiliness and innocence' not unlike his own. No saint in real life, Alatriste could unselfconsciously attend Mass to pray for the answer to a financial problem. He was capable of generous gestures, like taking over a whole restaurant because he knew it embarrassed Luis to dine in noisy places where his deafness was more evident, but his naiveté in anything but business was profound. He once asked Luis if one could tell simply from their appearance whether a person was a marquis, a duke or a baron.

Never short of projects, some of them with completed scripts attached, Buñuel suggested a film he had in mind since 1940, when the experience of New York and his re-encounter with Surrealism triggered a surge of creative dream imagery that also produced the story of *Simon of the Desert* and an anecdote of a little girl who becomes invisible to her parents which he used in *The Phantom of Liberty*.

With the shell of the old Spanish empire increasingly stifling to new visions, the image of a group of the bourgeoisie prevented by some dread from leaving a house occurred to many Latin American writers at almost the same time: Julio Cortazar, Alejo Carpentier, Jorge-Luis Borges, Carlos Fuentes and Gabriel Garcia Marquez, some of them Buñuel's friends and admirers, all played with tales of empty mansions, derelict churches or cities inhabited by the remnants of a ruling class who cowered in rags among the ruins.

Buñuel first used the idea in the unproduced short, *The Castaways of Calle Providencia*, written with Alcoriza, though it could be traced back to *L'Age d'Or*, where a cart rumbles unremarked through a drawing-room *soirée* and a formal concert is enlivened (but not interrupted) by violent death and sexual delirium. Now he and Alcoriza fleshed it out into *The Exterminating Angel*.

The title is José Bergamin's. He mentioned it at a *peña* in Madrid during pre-production for *Viridiana*, and Luis liked it enough to buy it. Bergamin claimed the phrase was biblical, specifically from the Book of Revelations. Yet although that collection of visionary ravings has no shortage of destroying, rampaging and warning angels, none is described as 'exterminating'.

Buñuel was indifferent to provenance. His Sadeian taste for the apocalyptic was tickled by the vision of an omnipotent power visiting death on mankind like a farmer spraying insecticide on locusts. Over the years he gave various other sources for the name: the motto of a Spanish religious group, the Mormons' Angel Moroni, and a Valdes Leal painting of an angel with a six-thronged whip scourging a penitent before the throne of God, an image Buñuel liked so much that it was used on the film's poster. In fact the quote is from 2 Samuel 24:16, where God sends an angel to punish David. 'And when the angel stretched out his hand upon Jerusalem to destroy it, the Lord repented him of the evil, and said to the angel that destroyed the people, it is enough.' The French

Bible translates this as: '*L'Ange étendit sa main vers Jerusalem pour l'exterminer: mais Iohve se repentit du mal et dit à l'Ange exterminateur de la population: "Assez!"*' Nobody has satisfactorily explained its relevance to the film. Raymond Durgnat's suggestion that the 'angel' is 'the spiritual climate of bourgeois conformism, drawn to its (desired) conclusion of inner paralysis' is as good – or as bad – as any.

Until the 1960s, it was usual for fantasy in anything but a horror film to be given a realistic framing story, and for the transition to be clearly marked. As the image dissolved, electronic music invaded the sound track and a voice intoned: 'I dreamed I was in a big house . . . ' This was Dali's vision of dream reality, something between the fantasies he designed for Hitchcock's *Spellbound* and a Saks Fifth Avenue window.

However, *Last Year in Marienbad* had shown that some audiences would accept fantasy without narrative justification, an insight that influenced *The Exterminating Angel* more than Buñuel was prepared to acknowledge. In both films, bored bourgeois in formal clothes go through repetitive gestures, playing games, chatting coolly to cover up passionate relationships that may or may not have existed in another time and another place. Both films repeat scenes, apparently without reason. The guests in *Angel* enter the salon twice, meet or are introduced three times; the same toast is given twice, and their isolation begins and ends with them arranged in the same positions while the identical piece of music is played. 'In life, as in film,' Buñuel wrote, 'I have always been fascinated by repetition', but he never explored it on film before *Angel*, and when he first did so it was in terms that Resnais had pioneered in *Marienbad*.

Whatever force keeps Edmundo and Lucia Nobile and their guests in the drawing room of their house after a post-opera supper has no rational explanation. The guests loiter in the room for days, deteriorating physically and mentally but most of all socially. One dies, two lovers commit suicide, another has a dream in which a severed hand pursues her around the room. A hole is broken through the wall to reach a water pipe, and some sheep, props in an elaborate practical joke, frightened into the room by a bear acquired for the same reason, are slaughtered for food. Urns become lavatories. At a certain moment, one guest, Letitia (Silvia Pinal), notices that the group has re-formed exactly as it was when they first entered. Another, Bianca, is badgered into playing the Paridisi piece she was performing at the time and, the spell broken, Letitia leads the guests outside.

Buñuel had originally intended a revolutionary bomb to blow them up as they stepped into the street, but on second thoughts he devised a more ironic conclusion. Next morning, they all attend Mass in the crowded cathedral but, as it ends, the congregation and three priests find it impossible to leave. Outside, a riot erupts. As police shoot down demonstrators, a flock of sheep surges across the square and into the cathedral.

Buñuel finished shooting in January 1962. The film was shown at Cannes in May. 'It literally mystified Cannes' Cartesian public,' Robert Benayoun wrote in *Positif*. Buñuel would have had wider appreciation outside the Hispanic world if he had catered to those who wanted a key to What the Film Really Meant. He never obliged. 'Was there an explanation,' demanded Benayoun rhetorically, 'a key to this delirious, irrational film, made up of *non sequiturs* and hallucinating visions?' If there was, Buñuel wasn't telling. ' "Why the bear?" the festival-goers feverishly demanded,' Benayoun wrote delightedly, 'like the spectators of *L'Age d'Or* demanded: "Why the cow?" ' Juan Luis, who translated at the press conference, said simply: 'Because my father likes bears.' Luis refused the tempting suggestion from Communist critics that the bear scaring the sheep into the starving guests represented Russia feeding the poor, or that the final revolution symbolised the start of World War III. Even the Surrealist agenda didn't fit. Returning from the primitive lavatory, guests remark that, looking down into the urns, they'd seen an eagle far below, and that a cold wind blew leaves on their faces, but Luis explained this as simply a memory of the mountain town of Cuenca, where the privies were holes cut in a shelf of rock overhanging the abyss.

In a letter of 16 August 1963 to critic Herman G. Weinberg, Juan Luis summarized the film's sub-text, or lack of it, on his father's behalf. 'There is not much to explain,' he said. 'The *Angel* is probably just a repetition of themes which he has used in all his films [. . .] *obsessions* would be the correct word. As to symbolic interpretations, I think there are none [. . .] As to the repetition of events [this] is just an idea he had. He says: "In everyday life we repeat ourselves every day [. . .]." '

'As to the ending, there is really no logical explanation. *The Exterminating Angel* is like a plague; first it starts with a small group of people, then with a whole church full, then on to the rest of society [. . .] Has it to do with the menace of atomic war? I personally think that it is not that direct but that it is that *feeling* or an abstracted statement that he has felt about the situation of modern man [. . .]' And the sheep stampeding into the church? 'What is more logical,' he asks, 'than to have some thirty sheep enter the church because there are a greater number of people to be fed? Three sheep for twenty people, thirty sheep for 300 persons.'

This was not what a professor of Cinema Studies 101 wanted to hear, and Buñuel's films were seldom in demand for film courses. There is, however, at least one specific political gibe in *The Exterminating Angel*. One of the cupboards in the film contains a cello, and the instrument turns up in a dream, where a saw cuts down a tree, slices the strings of a cello, and then attacks a hand. 'Buñuel couldn't stand American politics,' explained Jean-Claude Carrière, 'and in particular he disliked the American presidents. He was furious when Pablo Casals played at the White House. That's why he put the cello in.'

Critics like Robert Benayoun had been convinced that, for all its obscurity, *The Exterminating Angel* was a certainty for the Palme d'Or: 'From the moment the Buñuel was projected, the Festival of Cannes was already won,' he said confidently. He did not reckon, however, on Festival president Robert Favre le Bret who, having helped *Viridiana* win its Palme d'Or the previous year, now had other cabals to placate, specifically the Americans, who had entered Sidney Lumet's solemn, lengthy version of Eugene O'Neill's *Long Day's Journey into Night*, with Katharine Hepburn and Fredric March.

American distributors dominated Cannes in the 1960s. They favoured films which would have some US circulation, and for which a Palme d'Or would be a useful marketing tool. Buñuel was never going to appeal to the American public, nor even to people who frequented art house cinemas. He was too obscure, too intellectual, too kinky. Americans preferred *The Leopard*, *The Umbrellas of Cherbourg*, *A Man and A Woman* and *Blow-up* – all winners of the Palme d'Or for Best Film at the time Buñuel's *Diary of a Chambermaid* and *Tristana* went unrewarded.

The year's only serious contenders for Best Film at Cannes 1962 were *The Exterminating Angel* and Antonioni's *The Eclipse*, but after some furious pulling of strings behind the scenes by Favre le Bret, Lumet's film, while missing out on Best Direction (not awarded) or Best Film (won by the Brazilian Anselmo Duarte's unremarkable religious allegory, *The Word Given*), received a collective Best Acting Award. *The Eclipse* got a Special Jury Prize and *The Exterminating Angel* nothing, though the furious international critics' group FIPRESCI honoured it, as did the Film and TV Writers.

Buñuel was philosophical. Years of watching his films die in front of baffled Anglophone and Francophone audiences had convinced him that only Spaniards understood his work. Fernando Rey remarks how in France or Italy 'audiences would take a Buñuel film like they'd take a Beethoven symphony – with the solemnity that befits a work of high art.

But in Spain, the audiences appreciate all the savage little turns of black humour.' When Joyce Kaufman, who married Juan Luis, asked why the lovers in *The Exterminating Angel* killed themselves, Luis sighed: 'That's the kind of question only an American would ask.'

An added drawback to widespread distribution of Buñuel's films was the opposition among Catholics, for whom his name would always carry a whiff of sulphur. (The Catholic Film Office also gave an award at Cannes, but they preferred *The Eclipse*.) With his usual false naiveté, Luis professed to be surprised and a little hurt at their disapproval. 'There are always details in my films which give rise to [accusations of blasphemy],' he said. 'Some of these details I take from real life. For instance, in *The Exterminating Angel*, where the cancer victim says to the doctor that [. . .] she will go to Lourdes where she will buy a "washable plastic Virgin". Well, Virgins are sold at Lourdes with that description. I have one in my house in Mexico.'

He had friends in the priesthood who, he insisted, secretly approved of his films. 'You know that the Dominicans are not only in favour of *Nazarin*,' he told Francisco Aranda earnestly, 'but are also for *Viridiana*?' But he neutralized any good this acquaintance might have done by telling priest friends that Christ was 'an idiot'. 'How could you think that,' one asked, 'of a man who said things like "Love thy neighbour as thyself"?' Luis replied: 'Give me a pen and in fifteen minutes I'll write you ten sentences like that.' His sparring with the Church was like his skirmishes with Franco. In neither case was he interested in joining their club. Even if invited, he would remain disobedient of their rules and careless of their etiquette. However, just as he had had fun with his Republican friends by pretending to surrender to Franco with *Viridiana*, he enjoyed twitting the agnostics by threatening to call a priest to his bedside when he was dying. This final Buñuel gallows joke was to become unexpectedly true in real life.

Friends continued to propose plays and books for Buñuel to adapt. The sprawling dramas of Ramon del Valle-Inclan were going through one of their periodic revivals in the early 1960s. *Divinas Palabras (Divine Word)*, his eight-hour cycle about miscegenation, cruelty, rape and revolt in the Spanish hinterland, had the same appeal to Luis as *Wuthering Heights*, but he worried about the resemblances to *Viridiana*. *Tirano Banderas* and *Romance de Lobos* were turned down for the same reason. Perez Galdos's novel *Tristana*, too, had resonances with *Viridiana*. It also demanded being shot in Toledo, which put it well out of bounds.

Buñuel considered Dostoievsky's *The Eternal Husband*, Malcolm Lowry's *Under the Volcano*, Georges Charles Huysmans's *Là-Bas*, about a man finding his way to God via the experience of evil, and Octave Mirbeau's *Diary of a Chambermaid*. The Mirbeau had intrigued the Surrealists, and he felt Pinal would be ideal as the young woman who takes a job in a remote château in the hope of finding a rich husband, only to arouse the sexual passion of her employers and their murderous gamekeeper. On the other hand, Jean Renoir had filmed the novel in 1946 in Hollywood with Paulette Goddard, so he could expect comparisons.

He was also tempted by another Surrealist favourite, an obscure short novel of 1903, *La Gradiva*, by Austrian writer Wilhelm Jensen, about a young man in love with a bas relief of Gradiva, a Roman girl, and in particular her feet. He dreams of her and keeps a copy of the relief in his bedroom. Finally he goes to Pompeii to see the original, and meets her double, a girl named Zoë ('Life' in Greek). Freud wrote an elaborate analysis of its sexual subtext. Buñuel also thought of adapting something by younger Latin American writers like Fuentes or Cortazar, in particular the latter's *Las Menades*, in which a concert audience hysterically invades the stage and assaults the musicians.

Out of these musings came *Cuatro Misterios (Four Mysteries)*. Sketch films on fantasy themes, like *Boccaccio '70* and *Histoires Extraordinaires*, were in vogue and Alatriste suggested combining *La Gradiva*, *Las Menades*, Fuentes's *Aura* and one more story into such an anthology. For the fourth part, Luis suggested his own *Secuestro (Kidnapping)*, from an idea by Fernando Rey. Rey would have starred as a bourgeois Jew who enacts in real life one of the medieval anti-Semitic blood libels, that of kidnapping a gentile adolescent and crucifying her. Although Rey snatches the girl in full view of everyone and carries her past border guards and police, nobody thinks to stop him or even remonstrate.

The package idea tempted Buñuel, especially its elements of secret ceremony. He even considered throwing his and Larrea's *Illegible* into the pot, but his enthusiasm for the project quickly flagged, in part, because it would mean yet another involvement with Alatriste. Fancying himself a salesman, he liked to hold on to a product while the price rose. *The Exterminating Angel* opened in Paris in May 1963, a year after Cannes, but would not be shown in Mexico until July 1966, and in most other countries until 1968. The same would happen to Buñuel's third and last film for him, *Simon of the Desert*. When he was not directly affected by them, Luis viewed Alatriste's machinations with tolerant amusement. 'Lately in Madrid,' he told Max Aub, 'he met [director Luis Garcia] Berlanga and a guy, a screenwriter, and made an agreement with them to produce a film. Very nice to both of them. They came to an agreement on the price [. . .] and as an advance he offered five hundred thousand pesetas to one and a hundred thousand to the other. "Shit, I don't have my cheque book with me. I'll see you on Monday at the bank. Ten o'clock." At ten o'clock on the dot, the three of them meet at the bank. Alatriste signs a cheque for six hundred thousand pesetas. Berlanga goes to the teller. Alatriste doesn't have *ten* thousand pesetas in his account. "Oh, yes, shit I forgot. Really, with all the things I've had to pay . . . But don't you bother with that. Tomorrow I'm going to Mexico, and Monday you will have your money." And nothing came!'

Such stories did not affect Buñuel's personal loyalty to Alatriste, who could always charm him with an extravagant gesture. Years later, when Alatriste was trying to launch a decentralized film studio in Cuernavaca, complete with a town for technicians, he was still apologizing for him. 'Note that with me he has always been perfect,' he said. 'He paid me five hundred thousand pesos to make a film which pleased me very much at the time. And we didn't make it. That's why I made *Simon* for him for nothing. And now, he wants to give me a house in Cuernavaca.' Needless to say, neither the town nor the house ever materialized.

Fortunately Buñuel had friends as loyal to him as he was to Alatriste. Weary of arguing that he could only be harmed by the buccaneering cinema Alatriste represented, they nudged him towards more solid financiers. It was this impulse that led Paris *Variety* correspondent Gene Moskowitz, running into Serge Silberman on the Champs-Elysées late in 1962, to suggest he make a film with Buñuel. It was an inspired guess of the sort that distinguished Moskowitz, one of the most genial but at the same time shrewdest film journalists of the 1960s. Silberman's record was patchy but distinguished. He had co-produced films with Spaniards (Bardem's *Death of a Cyclist* and *Callé Mayor*) and with directors who worked in the same twilight zone between art and commerce as Buñuel, in particular Jacques Becker.

Then in a wobbly partnership with Michel Safra, Silberman was alert to independent opportunities. He had not produced anything since Becker's last film, *Le Trou (The Hole)* in 1960. That had been an unalloyed disaster. Not only had Becker died during post-production but the dour prison escape drama was uniformly loathed, even by the preview audience. Silberman had arranged a sumptuous dinner for fifty at a luxury restaurant to follow the première. Not a single person came – 'not even', remarked critic François Chalais cynically, 'an enemy.'

The more Silberman thought about Buñuel, the better the idea sounded. Finding that he had returned to Madrid in October, he asked Fernando Rey, a mutual friend, to set up a meeting. Meanwhile, he booked himself into a hotel in Madrid. When he arrived, he found a message confirming a 6 p.m. rendezvous with Buñuel at the hotel. Half an hour before, he went to a nearby store to stock up on whisky. As he returned, the door across the corridor opened, and Buñuel came out. Silberman had not only by coincidence booked into the Torre de Madrid, but into the room opposite Luis's.

The coincidence could only impress a Surrealist, but Luis was won over still further when he learned that Silberman produced *Le Trou*. 'That's a great Surrealist film,' he said.

'We drank the whisky,' Silberman recalls. 'I asked him what he'd like to film. He preferred that I make a proposition. We competed with one another in politeness. "You." "No, after you." Finally, he gave me a choice.'

'The first,' Luis told him, 'is unfilmable. It's an adaptation of *Under the Volcano*.'

Silberman agreed that Malcolm Lowry's novel, which took place entirely in the mind of an alcoholic diplomat in Mexico during the last day of his life, was unpromising.

'The second would be about Gilles de Rais, with a little bit of Sade, to widen it out. And the third, *Diary of a Chambermaid*.'

It was Silberman's second shock of the day. During *Le Trou*, Becker, walking with him in the Bois de Boulogne, had told him that, for his next film, he wanted to film Mirbeau's book.

Buñuel's pleasure in Silberman's interest diminished when he nominated Jeanne Moreau to star. He liked Moreau, whom he had seen in Louis Malle's *The Lovers*, but she was building an international reputation for forthrightness as well as for acting, and he anticipated problems. He preferred Pinal. And she spoke Spanish. Working with Moreau meant shooting in France, where he had not worked since *L'Age d'Or*. His deafness would hamper him directing in French. He also worried that, to adapt such a French subject, he would need a French co-writer. Silberman, who reminded Buñuel of Pierre Braunberger with his shortness and nervously hectoring manner, assured him crossly that Moreau would be fine, and that scenarists would queue to work with him. Even so, they parted with nothing settled.

*

Back in Mexico Alatriste had not given up on *Cuatro Misterios*. He had found a small Spanish production company, Epoca, ready to share costs, and confident of winning the Franco government's generous subsidy for approved film subjects. The Ministry of Culture had been overhauled, and the new men in charge seemed amenable to Luis working in Spain again. Alatriste submitted the script to Madrid. When it came to it, however, the censors insisted that *Secuestro* had to go.

Not surprised to find that Franco's bureaucrats were not as liberal as Alatriste, or they, thought, and unwilling to fight over a film to which he was not particularly committed, Buñuel suggested to Epoca that they switch to *Tristana*. As a novel, albeit minor, by an acknowledged Spanish master it might not encounter the same problems. Epoca agreed, and advanced him 30,000 dollars to start work on a script.

Buñuel and Alejandro wrote the *Tristana* screenplay over Christmas, updating the action from the late nineteenth century to the 1930s. In the spring of 1963 he returned to Spain and submitted it for censorship. This time, he was assured, there would be no problem. He assembled a crew and chose locations. He had wanted to shoot in Salamanca or Toledo, but agreed to compromise on the suburbs of Madrid. Filming was scheduled for the summer.

It all seemed too good to be true, which indeed it was. At the last minute, the Ministry of Culture rejected *Tristana*; Don Lope's enthusiasm for duelling supposedly contravened new laws against affairs of honour. The pretext was so trivial and flagrant that even Epoca were amused. Luis had spent their 30,000 dollars but they did not ask for return of the money, on the understanding that, if the film could be revived, he would pick up the reins again. Resignedly, he told Silberman in April that he was ready to make *Diary of a Chambermaid*.

They agreed to meet at the Cannes Festival, where Silberman roped in François Truffaut, who had helped make Moreau a star with *Jules et Jim*, to reassure Luis. Since Moreau had a house near St Tropez, Silberman suggested they have lunch with her. They set out to drive there.

'It was hot,' recalls Silberman. 'We stopped along the way for a drink. A Picon/beer. Very good.'

'She's going to talk to me about movies,' Luis said idly, 'and I'm going to talk to her about birds.'

Ten kilometres later, they stopped for another Picon/beer. They arrived at Moreau's place in a genial frame of mind. It was a good lunch. She reassured Luis that stardom did not interest her; she had turned down *Spartacus* and the Mrs Robinson role in *The Graduate*. If she had but known it, however, Luis was more appreciative of her legs and feet and swaying walk than her CV. He also admired her relish for food. 'She ordered something with lots of garlic and butter,' Juan Luis says, 'and afterwards she mopped up the sauce with bread. My father was impressed "The way she eats!" he told me.' By the end of the meal, she had been cast.

29

'Always the solitary will be first
Like a worm in a nut
To reappear along the convolutions
Of the freshest brain.'
– Paul Eluard, *Du Fond de l'Abîme* (translated by Stephen Spender and
Frances Cornford)

With Moreau settled as the star of *Diary of a Chambermaid*, Silberman
moved into high gear. Both he and Buñuel agreed the film must be shot in
autumn for the correct mood and, since a co-writer was needed,
Silberman ordered half a dozen candidates to Cannes for an audition.
The first was Jean-Claude Carrière, a thirty-two-year-old with ambition
but patchy film experience. He had novelized Jacques Tati's *Monsieur
Hulot's Holiday* and *Mon Oncle*, written a documentary about the sex
life of animals called *Bestiare d'Amour*, and two shorts and a feature for
the comic Pierre Etaix, one of which, *Happy Birthday*, won an Oscar in
1962.

Silberman told all the writers that Buñuel was preparing the Mirbeau
book, and mainly needed someone who knew the French countryside.
'That was the only requirement,' says Carrière. 'We were to meet
Buñuel, who would choose, instinctually, one of us.' He re-read the
novel and roughed out a structure for a screenplay.

Luis was staying at the old Hôtel Mont Fleury in the hills above
Cannes. Carrière's appointment was for 1 p.m. When he arrived, Luis
was on the terrace with friends. At one minute to one, he stood up, said
goodbye and walked into the lounge where Carrière was waiting. As he
sat down, he asked, 'Do you drink wine?'

'I felt it was more than a polite question,' Carrière says. 'Mundane,
but something deeper, coming from a different intention. Something
inquisitorial, almost.'

'I not only drink wine,' Carrière told him. 'I produce wine. I have my
own vineyard.'

Buñuel's face, recalls Carrière, became 'illuminated', and he ordered a bottle.

They chatted. Luis liked Carrière's deep voice, which he could hear easily. 'Carrière says silly things,' he said, 'but at least I understand them.' They discussed the book, and agreed on where it needed changing. Luis never saw the other candidates. Carrière wrote ten scripts with Buñuel and ghosted his memoirs, *My Last Breath*. He and Luis were obviously attuned, but Carrière left Cannes with the feeling that, had he been teetotal, he would not have got the job.

In July and August, Buñuel and Carrière met in Madrid to work on the screenplay. Carrière never realized that the collaboration almost collapsed before it got started. After a few days, Luis told Silberman, 'Serge, this boy is very intelligent, but I can't keep working with him. He agrees with everything I say.' Carrière quickly learned that, as Dali had done, it was essential to contradict Luis if the creative juices were to flow.

Mirbeau wrote *Le Journal d'Une Femme de Chambre* in 1900 and set it a few years earlier, at a time when the *ancien régime* was under pressure from the new socialists. Luis moved the time to 1928, when the same social conflicts had resurfaced, this time with working-class Fascists making common cause with the aristocracy.

Célestine, a sophisticated city girl, takes a job as maid at the country house of the Monteil family, classically enfeebled *haute bourgeoisie*. Ambitious for social standing, she is prepared to do what she must to find a rich husband, suppressing for the moment her essential carnality. 'From now on, no more love for Célestine,' she tells her diary.

A little girl is raped and murdered while gathering snails and berries in the woods nearby. Suspecting Joseph, the game-keeper, a Fascist sadist, Célestine offers herself to him in the hope he'll confess. Mirbeau's ending, where she's married to Joseph and running a bar with him, confessing to her diary that he 'holds me, possesses me like a demon. And I am happy to be with him', didn't satisfy Buñuel. He preferred that Célestine sacrifice the diabolical Joseph, with whose evil one feels she's instinctively in tune, to make her advantageous marriage.

In Luis's version, Célestine, instead of surrendering to Joseph, coaxes him into confessing the murder, reports him to the police, then leaves to marry the Monteil's slightly dotty neighbour, Captain Mauger. Joseph avoids jail and opens a bar in Cherbourg, from where he watches in approval as a Fascist crowd marches by, shouting: 'Vive Chiappe!' – Luis's final gibe at the Prefect who banned *L'Age d'Or*, but a rueful acknowledgement that the forces of bourgeois conformism always win in the end.

*

Buñuel was convinced that some personal erotic demon, an urge stronger than hunger, rules most of us, as it did him all his life. The sin of the Monteils is to deny this. Descending on the hapless under-maid, the head of the house tells her, 'I'm all for *l'amour fou*,' debasing what was for Luis almost a sacred concept. Madame Monteil spends hours locked in the bathroom with her unguents and gadgets. She complains to the priest that her husband demands sex twice a week. He agrees that is too much, but 'the thing is that *you* shouldn't get any pleasure out of it'. She looks down her nose: no risk of *that*.

Even Joseph refuses Célestine's calculated offer of her body, preferring to make her a business proposition, where she will marry him and ensure the success of his bar by flirting and, if necessary, sleeping with the clients. It is only when she agrees to think about it that he screws her, sealing the bargain.

Diary of a Chambermaid, like most of Buñuel's films with Carrière, has a very French sense of the erotic and sensual which he would never have achieved with a Hispanic co-writer. In particular, he felt freer with Carrière to explore the full palette of decadent imagery. Joseph is established as a monster. Since the meat of a goose is reputedly sweeter without the trauma of decapitation, he butchers them by thrusting a needle through the brain. The child he kills in the woods is found with her thighs crawling with snails, Luis returning to the oozing blood imagery of *The Criminal Life of Archibaldo de la Cruz*.*

Carrière did not suffer from the sexual disquiet and Republican indignation that burdened Alejandro and Alcoriza. What would have been in their hands an assault on the landed gentry became the more personal account of a young woman's manipulation of her weaker 'betters'. For the first time, a Buñuel heroine is not a dove, frightened of but eager for soiling. Instead, Célestine is a dainty bird of prey, coolly chasing her victims before settling on them with steely claws.

The film started shooting on 21 October 1963, with interiors at Billancourt. Piccoli was the son-in-law and Carrière played the small role of the priest but, after that, Buñuel had the anticipated problems with casting. For Marianne, Piccoli suggested a tiny, dumpy actress who called herself Muni. 'You're comical,' Luis told her, reminded of Jesús Fernandez. 'Yet I don't laugh,' she said wistfully. Buñuel took an instant liking to her. She appeared in three more of his films.

---

* On first release, censors cut this disturbing shot, but it is restored in most extant prints.

Buñuel worked with instinct, too, in casting the fetishist father. 'He felt he needed some sort of perversion in the actor to be able to approach the character,' says Carrière. He narrowed it down to two actors. 'Jean Ozenne was a homosexual. Luis didn't know it, but he felt something. The other was the same kind of distinguished and nice man, also with a secret, though nobody quite knew what. He had two photographs of the two actors, one in each pocket, and from time to time he'd take out a picture and have a look, and finally he chose Ozenne.'

After *Diary*, Moreau was publicly enthusiastic about Buñuel, and eager to work with him again. For his part, Luis called her 'the best actress I have worked with'. He proposed to Silberman the film he'd discussed with Gérard Philipe of Matthew Gregory Lewis's 1795 Gothic melodrama, *The Monk*. Its central character, Ambrosio, most resolute of the Inquisition's officers in Madrid, is cursed by a woman whom he has tortured and executed for adultery. The devil sends temptation in the person of Matilda, a sorceress, disguised as the handsome, admiring novice Rosario. The story spirals down into a welter of murder, torture and retribution.

He was less interested in the sensational plot than the forces that might drive a religious zealot to depravity. Visits to Spain had reminded him of the asceticism and self-denial of monastic life. Much as its calm drew him, he knew that sexual hallucination and sado-masochistic frenzy often festered in its isolation. With ill-concealed lubricity, he wrote: 'To prepare *The Monk* I consulted many texts on the monastic life. One of them speaks of a Visigoth monk condemned to twenty lashes of the whip for having been late to dinner. *Viginti Flagela.*'

The Monk would have redressed the balance of *Diary*, showing sexual frenzy in full cry, unmediated by bourgeois good breeding. Silberman encouraged Buñuel and Carrière to start work on a script. David Selznick also wanted him to do a film with his wife Jennifer Jones. But the most pressing overtures were from Alatriste.

Back in Mexico City for Christmas, Buñuel visited his plush Camino al Desierto offices to hear about the new schemes. The first, and most attractive, was *Johnny Got His Gun*, from the novel by blacklisted writer Dalton Trumbo. A ferocious attack on militarism, *Johnny Got His Gun* shows an American boy turned into a deaf, dumb, blind and lifeless trunk by war. Interested, Luis got together with Trumbo who, in April 1964, presented him with a copy of the book inscribed 'For Luis Buñuel – who is going to bring this book to life. I thank him in advance. With deep respect.'

They worked on the script for a few months, Buñuel mostly talking and Trumbo taking notes. Since a good deal of drinking took place, the notes sometimes rambled, and work turned into something more convivial. Juan Luis remembers Trumbo in his cups expressing admiration for Jeanne's parrot, a vicious bird that only she could handle. 'Dalton said: "I love birds. Let me have him." My mother warned him, but he put out his hand, and the parrot jumped on it and bit it to the bone. He was so drunk he hardly noticed. He lifted the bird up to his mouth and tried to kiss it, and the bird sank his beak into his lip, twice. There was blood everywhere, but Dalton didn't care. My mother got it away from him. The last thing I remember seeing is Dalton waving from the back of a taxi, drunk, with blood down his chin and all over his shirt.'

Johnny Got His Gun drifted into the limbo of most courageous projects, but Alatriste had another to suggest. *Two Free Movies*, as he called it, revamped the anthology idea of *Cuatro Misterios*, but with two stories instead of four, two directors instead of just Buñuel, and a single star: inevitably, Silvia Pinal. At this point Luis should have thanked Alatriste politely and left, but the producer was uniquely capable of charming him. They began talking about Luis's possible contribution, based on episodes in the life of St Simon Stylites, the ascetic who lived on top of a column in the Syrian desert existing on a diet of lettuce and inspiring the ancient world with his piety.

Events, too, combined to force Buñuel into accepting. In April David Selznick suffered a heart attack. Silberman also wrote to say he was breaking up with Michel Safra and had no money to start *The Monk*. Worst of all, *Diary of a Chambermaid* opened in Paris in March to tepid reviews. 'The novel is execrable, and the film is not good,' wrote Claude Mauriac in *Le Figaro Littéraire*. 'How is it [. . .] that one feels not only disappointed but embarrassed?' Moreau's beauty and Roger Fellous's photography of the wintry countryside struck critics as exhibiting a 'good taste' inappropriate to a director from whom they expected amusingly corrupted nuns and monks, and the rough melodramatic Spanishness they enjoyed in Rivera, rioja and flamenco. Pauline Kael spoke for many when she dismissed *Diary* as 'revoltingly "beautiful"'. Instead of returning to Spain in the spring, Luis went to New York and started researching *Simon of the Desert*.

A Surrealistic coincidence seemed to endorse Buñuel's decision when, at the New York Public Library on 42nd Street, he discovered that the best book on Simon, by Father Fostugières, was being used. As he turned from the catalogue, he found the man next to him with the entry card in his hand. Back in Mexico, Luis wrote the screenplay with Alejandro, transposing the Fostugières history and some descriptions by a priest named Delhaye.

Simon (Claudio Brook) has been on the column for six years and six weeks when the film starts. Watched by a mob, including a dwarf goatherder (Jesús Fernandez), he's about to descend, but only to transfer to a higher column provided by a wealthy and pious merchant.

His mother settles nearby in a hut, looking after his needs and dealing with the many visitors: soldiers, monks and a succession of supplicants. The devil, played by Pinal in a variety of disguises, decides to pull Simon down. Having failed to tempt him physically as a provocative *fin de siècle* schoolgirl in black stockings and garters, she incites Trifon, a monk, to plant wine, cheese and fruit in the bag that carries his lettuce. She appears again as a hermaphrodite Christ with a beard, carrying a lamb. Her appeal this time is intellectual. How can he truly worship God, she asks, if he has not given full satisfaction to the flesh? Simon spots the heresy and cries: '*Vade retro!*' ('Get thee behind me, Satan!') Furious, the devil, this time manifested as a coffin that snakes across the desert in jerky stop motion, transports him into the future, showing him the inevitable end of the world; a New York disco doing the 'Radioactive Flesh', not just the 'latest dance' but 'the last dance', to a group called The Sinners.

When he began shooting, Buñuel confidently imagined he was making a feature. Alatriste had budgeted *Simon of the Desert* at 120,000 dollars, half of which he had raised on a distribution guarantee. Since the producer was broke, however, that was all the money Luis would see. The shortage meant he had to stop at forty-two minutes.* 'I had to cut a full half of the film,' Luis complained. 'A meeting under the snow, some pilgrimage scenes, and a visit from the emperor of Byzantium all wound up literally on the cutting room floor, which explains why the ending seems somewhat abrupt. In the second part [. . .] Simon [. . .] is returned to his own time. He dies in a state of mortal sin after having succumbed to the temptations of the flesh.'

Buñuel filmed in the desert for eighteen days, with a couple of days interiors at Churubusco, where the cheapness of the production was shown up by the Hollywood-type luxury of Servando Gonzales's desert railroad adventure *Viento Negro (Black Wind)*, shooting at the same time. 'For the pilgrimage I needed five hundred extras,' Buñuel said. 'I couldn't get more than twenty-five, Indians for the most part, when what I needed were Syrians. I put them a long way from the camera so you

---

* Depending on the version, *Simon of the Desert* runs from forty-two to fifty minutes.

couldn't see their race.' He was so pressed for help that, when Juan Luis, who had just finished shooting his award-winning documentary *Calanda*, about the 1964 drumming, visited the set with Brazilian director Glauber Rocha, the hottest of Latin American film-makers as a result of his *Black God, White Devil*, Luis distractedly shook Rocha's hand, then put them both to work arranging extras.

Figueroa, who lit the film, chafed at the restrictions. 'You can see from the sky that we made many retakes,' he said. 'In the same scene you can see sometimes a clear sky, sometimes clouds. It's not obvious, thanks to some work in the laboratory, but I wasn't able to wait for a match.' Japanese critic Kenji Kanesaka visited the set on the last day of shooting at Churubusco. Figueroa had set up a back-projected cloudy sky for a retake with Claudio Brook, but Buñuel was not satisfied. 'Now I will have to show you the special Luis Buñuel-style back projection,' Figueroa said wearily, and led everyone into the back lot, where the scene was shot against a clear sky. It was obvious even then that it would not match, but Luis was past caring about such niceties – if indeed he had ever cared in the first place.

Now that he had the first part of *Two Free Movies*, Alatriste pursued a director for the second half with typical eccentricity. According to Buñuel, he approached both Stanley Kubrick and Vittorio de Sica. Alatriste himself mentions Federico Fellini, Jules Dassin and Akira Kurosawa. According to Pinal, Dassin and Fellini agreed, but only if they could star their own wives, Melina Mercouri and Giulietta Masina. Buñuel would later say, 'the only person whom I believe capable of making something to complete *Simon* is Fellini,' but there is no record that Fellini ever heard of the film.

Alatriste also met Orson Welles in Madrid, and offered to back him in a feature in return for making the second half of *Two Free Movies*. Welles agreed, nominating *Don Quixote* as the feature, and asked to see *Simon*. There was no copy in Madrid, so Alatriste flew him to Rome. On the flight back they struck a deal: 20,000 dollars down, then 180,000 dollars during the five weeks of shooting. 'You make what you like,' Alatriste told Welles. 'When you're ready, send me a telegram and I'll send you the money.' Some time later Welles wired Alatriste that he was ready to start. Alatriste never answered.

Buñuel brought *Simon* to its premature conclusion on 21 December 1964. Over Luis's objections Alatriste entered it in Venice the following year. In August it won the FIPRESCI prize and some lesser honours there. Plenty of producers were prepared to release *Simon*, but Alatriste hung on to the film for years. 'With *Simon of the Desert* he has done things which appear incomprehensible,' Buñuel told Max Aub in 1972. 'He has not given up that film until now. And now there are some English who are saying that they've heard of it and want to buy it [. . .] They have offered him $10,000 cash, plus forty per cent of the box office. That's an adequate offer. He has responded: "I have received your friendly proposition. I'm sorry, but for that money all I can offer you is a party here, in my home. I invite you, if you will come to Mexico, and I promise you that will not cost me less than 10,000 dollars." Pure lies, though he is like that, a good salesman.'

It would be years before *Simon of the Desert* reached every country. Alatriste did open it in Mexico City in February 1970, at his own cinema, which he christened the Buñuel. Luis was flattered, but wearily so. Despite Alatriste's blandishments, he would never work in Mexico again.

30

'Listen, I've had enough of the picturesque, of colours and charm.
I love love, its tenderness and its cruelty.'
– Robert Desnos, *Non, L'Amour N'Est Pas Mort* (translated by Bill Zavatsky)

Just before Buñuel shot *Simon of the Desert*, Luis's old friend, the artist Alberto Isaac, directed his first film, a comedy called *En Este Pueblo No Hay Ladrones (There Are No Thieves In This Town)*, based on a story by Gabriel Garcia Marquez. A small-town tearaway steals the billiard balls from the local bar, then realizes he has sentenced his friends to a life of unutterable tedium, since there is nothing else to do in town but play billiards. Returning the balls, he is caught. Luis played a priest in a celebrity cast that included Arturo Ripstein, Leonora Carrington and Marquez.

Dancigers was co-producing *Viva Maria!*, a comedy about two French girls involved in the Mexican revolution. Scouting locations, its director, Louis Malle, met Buñuel, who recommended Jean-Claude Carrière to him. Carrière eventually wrote the film, which starred Jeanne Moreau and Brigitte Bardot, both of whom made the now-ritual call on Buñuel at home. Pierre Braunberger, after a gap of decades, also wrote to Buñuel, suggesting a film of Fernando de Rojas's blood-boltered fifteenth-century romance, *Celestina*. This tale of aristocratic greed, lust and murder had interested Luis as a student but, as he wrote to Braunberger in September, turning him down, he now felt too old for it, besides which, he preferred to work with the people who were becoming his professional 'family'.

At Christmas 1965, Juan Luis, who was living in New York and making a reputation as a sculptor while also working in films, announced that he was going to marry Joyce Kaufman, a nineteen-year-old New Yorker of Russian extraction from Brooklyn with whom he had been living for three months. *En route* to Paris, Luis stopped off in New York to meet her. A Political Science major with no interest in films, Joyce was to discover only gradually that her prospective father-in-law was a legendary director and not, as she had imagined from her fiancé's off-hand comments about him being 'in the film business', a cinema manager or projectionist.

Buñuel made an instant impression on her. 'He was the kind of person you would never lie to. His eyes were never immodest but they were piercing.' This may have had something to do with the fact that his son's fiancée was dramatically beautiful: a journalist compared her to 'a mightily improved version of Liza Minnelli'. 'There was something about him that demanded your respect immediately,' Joyce went on. 'Somehow you felt he could see right through you, so there was no point in pretending. Either you said nothing or you said what was on your mind – and quickly. He wasn't interested in chatter. He *was* very interested in the well-being of his family, and of his sons and his wife. I sensed that he was worried that I would be disappointed at being married to someone who was in the movies, because it was a difficult life.'

Joyce's knowledge of Latin American and South American history impressed Luis. 'He said someone was a cardinal and I knew he was an archbishop. I told him so. "These Americans," he said. "When they know something they really know it, down to the bottom".' He was even more surprised to find that her father, a union organizer, had enlisted in the volunteer Lincoln Brigade and been badly wounded in the Spanish Civil War.

Juan Luis and Joyce shared a tiny apartment on Second Avenue and Seventh Street. The area did not impress Luis, and the problem of where they were to live joined the others on his mind as he left for Europe. Shortly after, Juan Luis got a job on a film in Indonesia and insisted on marrying Joyce before he left. In an echo of his parents' wedding, he left the day after, but not before insisting that Joyce move in with her mother in Far Rockaway, a two-hour train trip out of New York. Joyce insists she was put into a kind of Spanish *macho* purdah. Juan Luis argues economy: they could not afford to keep up the Second Avenue apartment. With time on her hands, Joyce signed up for film courses under Herman G. Weinberg at City College, the foundation of her own career as a director.

Still hoping to set up *Tristana*, Luis went to Spain for Christmas. Carlos Saura was making *Llanto por un Bandido (Time for a Bandit)* with Rabal, and asked him to play a cameo. He appears as the state executioner who throttles people with Spain's instrument of official murder, the garotte. For their continued opposition to *Tristana* he would cheerfully have placed the necks of certain of Franco's officials within its black iron ring, but instead he returned to Paris and began to review offers for films in France.

A few of the old Surrealists still loitered around Paris, living relics of the days of *scandale* and schism. Typically, Dali and Gala had turned a suite at the luxury Hôtel Meurice, decorated in eighteenth-century style and overlooking the Tuileries, into their Paris home-from-home. In October Dali attended the Paris première of Fellini's *Juliet of the Spirits*. Luis saw the film too, though not at the same screening, and felt impelled by Salvador's implied endorsement to condemn it as 'worthless. Neither true nor false Surrealism [. . .] Technical trickery, nothing but technical trickery.'

Until *La Dolce Vita*, Fellini had been a favourite film-maker of Buñuel's, although Luis, like Fellini himself, saw too few movies to make meaningful comparisons. He liked *Roma* for the anti-clerical relish of its ecclesiastical fashion show, and wired his congratulations, at the same time joking to his assistant director Pierre Lary: 'What have I done? He'll never stop ringing me up and writing to me.' Fellini was flattered, and responded by including *The Discreet Charm of the Bourgeoisie* in his all-time 'ten best' list. In general, both Buñuel and Fellini shared the great directors' discomfort at seeing the work of their competition. Juan Luis once lured Luis to an Ingmar Bergman film in New York. 'Max von Sydow was thinking about something or other, very seriously. My father went to sleep, and when he woke up, von Sydow was still thinking. He muttered and went to sleep again, and when he woke next time he said, "He's not still at it, is he? Let's go and have a drink".'

Dali was a rare survivor from his earlier days in Paris. Most of the people he had known in the 1930s were dead. Vicens de la Slave had died in Peking just after the war, Eluard followed in 1952, Tanguy in 1955, Péret in 1959, Cocteau in 1963, Tzara in January 1964, Thorez in July of the same year, Arp and Giacometti in 1966. In September 1966, it was the turn of André Breton.

By then, Buñuel was preparing *Belle de Jour*. Since Luis had been sarcastic about Breton in conversation, his production manager, Jacques Fraenkel, the nephew of Theodore Fraenkel, the Surrealist doctor who had attended Pierre Batcheff, was surprised when he asked him to drive him to the Batignolles Cemetery for the funeral. Untypically, Luis wore a large black hat and the bow tie that he always carried in his pocket in case he needed to attend a formal function.

The sparseness of the ceremony surprised him. 'Isn't anybody going to carry the coffin on their shoulders?' he muttered to Fraenkel, who explained that was not the French way. Nor was there an oration. Fraenkel expected a kind of reunion with those of the group who were left, but Luis stood for a moment at the grave, then slipped away. His disguise was effective; nobody recognized him. 'He was very, very moved,' Fraenkel says. Shortly after, Luis confided to him his horror of dying in France, alone and unmourned, like Breton. If he should fall ill, he was to be sent back to Mexico, no matter what the cost or his state of health.

Throughout the 1960s, whenever he was in Paris, Luis lived at the Hôtel l'Aiglon in Montparnasse, on the busy corner of boulevard Raspail and boulevard Edgar Quinet. In size and in its white stucco Art Deco exterior, it resembled the Hôtel des Terrasses where he had stayed in the 1920s. Its upper floors were divided into tiny apartments, one of which became his Paris *pied-à-terre*. He met people in the cafés of Boulevard Montparnasse, but preferred to drink his coffee, prepare his simple meals and mix his martinis and Buñuelonis at home. Sartre lived on Boulevard Raspail and they often took morning coffee in the same café, but seldom spoke. For a time Sartre's mother lived in the room next to Luis, irritating him by feeding pigeons which then defecated on his window-sill. From the window, he could look down at the calm of the Montparnasse Cemetery. He was at the heart of things but, as he always preferred, alone.

In Mexico, Buñuel's Paris agent had sent him Joseph Kessel's 1928 novel, *Belle de Jour*, asking if he would be interested in directing it for Robert and Raymond Hakim, with Catherine Deneuve. Luis had doubts, mostly about the producers. Since the 1930s, the Egyptian-born Hakims had specialized in discreetly salacious films by directors who, though well-established, were out of the mainstream. They had produced Duvivier's *Pepe Le Moko*, Renoir's *La Bête Humaine*, Becker's *Casque d'Or*, Chabrol's *A Double Tour* and Losey's *Eve* – which, notoriously, they recut and dubbed into a version so bad Losey disowned it. Their last film before *Belle de Jour* was, characteristically, Roger Vadim's oh-so-naughty remake of *La Ronde*. The Hakims were known never to send a franc until it was unavoidable, nor pay salaries except as a last resort. In *Belle de Jour*, Luis needled them by having Marcel and Hippolyte steal the payroll from 79 Champs-Elysées, the Hakims' own office.

In May 1966 Kessel sold *Belle de Jour* to the Hakims for 26 million old francs; a bargain, since for forty years nobody had imagined the book, scandalous in its day, could ever be filmed.*The deal was not closed until the producers were certain of Buñuel, whom they also got for a rock-bottom price, knowing, as Juan Luis frankly confessed later, that he 'hadn't a sou'.

The fact that he needed money did not diminish Buñuel's intransigence. If there was any difficulty about finance or any attempt to interfere with the film, he told the Hakims, he would walk off it. By July, he and Carrière had finished the script. Carrière, a good sketch artist, also made thirty drawings which the Hakims used to sell the project to distributors. Luis went to Zaragoza to see Doña Maria, and Carrière joined him in Madrid for a rewrite, but, by the start of autumn, cameras were turning.

Buñuel never hid the fact that he disliked Kessel's novel and was not particularly interested in filming it. It is difficult to see why. The story of Séverine, a beautiful bourgeoise, wife of a successful surgeon, who moonlights in a brothel to satisfy her masochistic impulses, might have been diagrammed for his obsessions. Although he updated it to the Paris of Yves Saint Laurent and the Citroën Déesse, the book also returned Luis to his youth, and the brothel culture he knew well.

Luis asked Fraenkel to find a location for the brothel around the Hôtel des Terrasses. Not knowing what to look for, Fraenkel read a newspaper report about the closing of a brothel near Porte Champerret and went to have a look. The building was nothing out of the ordinary. At a loss, he turned to Luis, who nominated a building at 1 square Albin Cachot, near where he had lived when he returned to Paris from Spain. in 1936.

Everyone assumed a man as priapic in his films as Luis must have mistresses in every capital, but any infidelities were mainly in his fantasies. 'I remember once,' recalled Carrière, 'the Hakim brothers told him, "Look, Luis, you can't stay like this all the time. You're not an old man. You're sixty-two, sixty-three, sixty-four. Why don't you come tonight to Régine's and we find some nice girl for you?" They told him this several times, but he never went. He wouldn't have liked it at all. He was deaf. Going to Régine's, a discotheque, was a sort of nightmare to him. He couldn't have stood it.'

During preparation in Madrid for *Belle de Jour*, Carrière and Francisco Rabal, who plays a petty criminal and client of Madame Anaïs's establishment where Séverine works, visited some brothels to gather local colour. 'Buñuel himself [. . .] came with Paco Rabal and myself,' said Carrière, 'and two or three times after the talk Paco and I went with girls. But Buñuel never went. Buñuel would go back to his room.'

---

* It was not even published in the United States until 1962.

Middle age had moderated Buñuel's youthful sex drive. Carrière dismisses the idea that Luis might have persisted with his infidelities into middle age. 'I think he was unfaithful to his wife only twice, and very briefly. As far as I know, the story between Jeanne and Buñuel was a fantastic love story from the very beginning. A long one. Maybe Jeanne says now in [*Woman Without a Piano*], half seriously, half jokingly, that he was brutal, but she would never have said the same when he was alive.

'They were all the time kissing each other; from time to time he would speak in a loud voice to her but I've been there hundreds of times eating with them in their house in Mexico and I loved her as my mother, and they were very well together, and making love until the last moment, as one of his sons told me. He was unfaithful, he told me, once or twice, briefly, with whores, but you can't call them . . . well, it doesn't count, you know. But he never had any other love story. *Never*. I was there all the time. We spent months and months together, and I never saw him with another woman. Months together, in Spain, in France, going to Venice . . . never, never.'

Jacques Fraenkel, however was a witness to at least one mildly compromising occasion. He had noticed that Luis was, unusually, taking an interest in a young actress on *Belle de Jour* and, a few days later, in a restaurant near the studio, he found them having dinner together. Unsure of the etiquette, he went over to their table and said hello.

'You remember M. Fraenkel,' Luis said, deadpan as ever. 'What you probably don't know is that he's very important in the Fascist movement. In fact he's the secretary general of the Anti-Jewish League.' Fraenkel retreated in confusion.

Buñuel packed *Belle de Jour* with old friends, and even appeared twice himself as an extra, in conversation with one of the Hakims in the café scene where Séverine meets the Duc, and as a pedestrian in the robbery sequence on the Champs-Elysées. Muni is Pallas, the brothel's maid, and Georges Marchal the ageing Duc (Luis insisted he wear no make-up; he looks deathly) who hires Séverine to impersonate his dead daughter in 'a very moving religious ceremony' redolent of incest and necrophilia, watched over by Grünewald's anguished Christ. Piccoli is Husson, the man-about-town who discovers her secret when he visits the brothel, Paco Rabal the Bolivian petty criminal who introduces her to Marcel (Pierre Clementi), a gawky thug with metal teeth and a sword cane, for whom she falls ecstatically.

For Séverine's straight-arrow husband Pierre, the Hakims recommended Jean Sorel, a darkly handsome young man who had just appeared in *La Ronde*. Buñuel accepted him with the shrug he reserved for leading men, and promptly treated him to some of his trade-mark deadpan. 'The first thing he ever said to me,' says Sorel, 'the very first thing, was "Why did you take this role?" Before I could answer, he said, "I'm only doing it to buy an apartment for my son".'*While Sorel pondered how to respond to this, Buñuel went on: 'You know, you'd better not ever go to Mexico after you make this film. Mexicans don't like cuckolds.' Later, during shooting, Sorel presumed on this imagined amity to rewrite his dialogue for the opening carriage scene. Buñuel quickly made it clear that his job was to deliver the lines which, in this case, had been written to appear naive and anodyne, like a cheap novelette. 'He spoke a very approximate French,' Sorel says sniffily.

It took time for Buñuel to warm to Catherine Deneuve. He felt, with some justice, that she had been foisted on him, first by the Hakims, then by her lover of the time, François Truffaut. 'Deneuve was pushed on him by Truffaut,' says Juan Luis. 'They were together at the time, and he wrote letters to my father, and suggested her.' Buñuel was always offhand about his star, and some of his team downright dismissive. Jacques Fraenkel said, 'She didn't understand the character.' Juan Luis agrees. 'She didn't know what she was doing.'

Buñuel invited Deneuve to dinner in his apartment, but she left with little more than an impression that he disliked actors in general and was reserving his decision about her. The only advice he offered was the advice he had always given actors: 'Don't do anything. And above all, don't . . . *perform*.' She remembered mainly the cemetery below his window, an appropriately melancholy background. Nevertheless she had the intelligence to put herself totally into his hands and 'after the film', recalls Fraenkel, 'he said to me, "She's really a very good actress".'

Until *Belle de Jour*, Deneuve's sensational personal reputation had never made it to the screen. She had mostly played girlish, affectionate ingénues. Buñuel was the first director to uncover the erotic fire beneath her crisp Saint Laurent tailoring, and she was grateful. Asked if roles like *Belle de Jour* offended her, she said, 'Well, strangely, the excessive things seem to be less difficult [. . .] I have much more difficulty when it's a question of a realistic and modern character, because [with erotic scenes] I don't feel too much involved myself [. . .] Physical scenes don't bother me; on the contrary, they help me to overcome my withdrawn side, to get out of myself.'

Buñuel's working methods remained as meticulous and spartan as ever. He always came to the set by Métro. Once, Piccoli offered to pick

---

* Luis did buy a small Paris apartment for Juan Luis and Joyce shortly after.

him up in the chauffeured car provided as part of his contract. Buñuel refused, then compromised: if Piccoli liked, he could collect him at the Métro station nearest the studio. He was as ferocious as ever about punctuality. Shooting began at 10 a.m. and ended at precisely 7.30 p.m. each day. French crews were not used to such discipline; *Belle de Jour*'s scheduled ten-week shoot took eight.

Buñuel did not get on with cameraman Sacha Vierny and his operator Philippe Brun, nor they with him. Famous for their films with Resnais, *Hiroshima Mon Amour* (which Buñuel particularly admired), *Last Year in Marienbad* and *Muriel, ou Les Temps d'un Retour*, they were used to collaborating with the director rather than simply doing as they were told. Buñuel's B-movie style irritated them as much as their *nouvelle vague* improvisation grated on him. 'He photographed in a very cold way,' says Fraenkel of Buñuel. 'Very anonymous. Very cold. Very icy.' Divisions in the unit quickly became formalized. At four o'clock every afternoon, Luis ordered a camera change, and while Vierny and his team were resetting the lights, Fraenkel, continuity girl Suzanne Durrenberger and first assistant Pierre Lary would retire to Buñuel's room for a 'script conference'. Lary brought the wine, Durrenberger the cheese.

Many people who knew Buñuel superficially in his last years thought him remote, but Michel Piccoli for one saw the compassion beneath his aloofness. 'That apparent severity hid an extreme attention to other people. "If they're late, they may have slept badly, and why did they sleep badly? They must be unhappy." When a friend divorced, or was living with someone else, Luis was shocked, but he was also bowled over, profoundly moved.'

He demonstrated this most intensely with his sons. When Rafael came to visit him on the set of *Simon of the Desert* after a long separation, members of the crew saw Buñuel in tears for the first time. Fraenkel remembers the boys calling on their father at the château where they were shooting *Belle de Jour*. Rafael was 6 feet 5 inches, tall and burly, and Juan Luis much the same. 'It was very cold, Buñuel came out, and here are these two colossi. And Buñuel wraps their scarves around the throats of each, to make sure they don't catch cold!'

Later, Rafael decided to tour Europe by motor-cycle. Luis insisted he keep in touch via a weekly postcard. One week, none arrived. Luis summoned Juan Luis and Joyce. In his hand was the contract for a new Silberman film, *The Milky Way*. Dramatically he tore it up.

'Rafael's overdue,' he said. 'Joyce, you're going to Munich. Juan Luis, you go to Athens. I'm going to Rome.'

Juan Luis said: 'To look for Rafael?'

'Yes.'

'But . . . once I get to Athens, what do I do?'

After a moment, Luis reluctantly agreed that the plan was not well thought out. Next day, Juan Luis had a postcard from his brother, telling him that he would be arriving at the l'Aiglon about seven that night. 'We were all to meet there for dinner,' says Juan Luis. 'I happened to drive by the l'Aiglon about five that day, and he was in front, walking up and down, very worried.'

Truffaut paid one of the most perceptive tributes to Buñuel in 1973, in a letter to Jean-Luc Godard. Excoriating Godard as 'the Ursula Andress of militancy [who makes] a brief appearance, just enough time for the cameras to flash, [delivers] two or three duly startling remarks and then [. . .] disappears again, trailing clouds of self-serving mystery', he contrasted him with 'the *small* men, from Bazin to Edmond Maire and taking in Sartre, Buñuel, Queneau, Mendès-France, Rohmer and Audiberti, who ask others how they're getting on, who help them fill out a social security form, who reply to their letters – what they have in common is the capacity to think of others rather than themselves and above all to be more interested in what they do than in what they are and in what they appear to be.'

Given the tensions on the set, it is astonishing that *Belle de Jour* is a masterpiece. In it, Jean-Luc Godard remarked, Buñuel seemed to be playing the cinema the way Bach played the organ. Rare among erotic films, it both analyses and evokes sexual obsession. The book gives Séverine no fantasy life, but in the film her head seethes with dreams, all redolent of a masochism that likewise is not mentioned in the book. Although the first scene where, out in the autumn woods in a landau with Pierre, she is dragged from the carriage at his direction, half-stripped, whipped and raped by coachmen, is as much about Buñuel's fantasies as Kessel's book, Luis uses it to make frankly visible Séverine's pleasure in what she does. In one of her most erotic sequences – another Buñuel addition – the maid finds her sprawled naked on the bed after satisfying a burly Asian who has arrived with an ominously buzzing sex-aid in a box. Sympathetically, Pallas says, 'That man frightens me. It must be hard sometimes.' Séverine looks into the camera with drowsy content and murmurs, 'What do you know about it, Pallas?'

While the humiliation and befouling experienced in her dreams is satisfying to Séverine, it is also, for Buñuel, a necessary and deserved punishment for her pleasure. In one such fantasy, she is tied to a post on a marshy plain while Pierre and Husson stir a pot nearby. Bulls bellow in the background.

Pierre asks: 'Do they give names to bulls as they do to cats?'

'Yes,' Husson replies, 'Most of those are called Remorse but the last one is called Expiation.' He and Pierre then pelt a calm, even exalted Séverine with mud. Buñuel was in his element as never before.

31

'Tangle with the Prince of Peace and you'll find a knife in
your back.'
– Joe Orton, *Funeral Games*

Buñuel worked more extensively than usual on the post-production of
Belle de Jour, enriching the sound track in particular with the near-
subliminal use of bells and animal sounds. So dense was its texture, in
fact, that he was convinced the film would elude most audiences
completely.

He also cut and shortened a number of sequences in expectation of
censorship. Even so, the film ran into immediate trouble. The authorities
demanded the religious overtones of Séverine's visit to the chateau of the
necrophilic Duc, with a mass being said in the background, be removed.
Two appearances of blood were also cut; one where Mathilde thrashes
the gynaecologist Professor's buttocks, and a second where, as Séverine
lies satiated after the Asian, Pallas picks up a blood-stained towel.

More would have been cut or modified had not André Malraux, then
Minister of Culture, been persuaded to intervene by his old friend Kessel,
who, after he got over Buñuel's slurs on the novel, liked the film. 'I was
nervous about going to this screening,' he wrote a friend. 'I came out of it
filled with gratitude. Buñuel's genius has surpassed all that I could have
hoped. It is at one and the same time the book and not the book. We are
in another dimension; that of the subconscious, of dreams and secret
instincts suddenly laid bare. And what formal beauty in the images! And
beneath the severity, the most contained and most moving pity.'

The critics disagreed. Released in Paris in May 1967, *Belle de Jour* was
almost as universally disliked by them as it was accepted by the public. In
a notoriously patronizing notice in *Le Monde*, Léon Baroncelli sneered:
'One can't believe that such bad dreams could go on inside Catherine
Deneuve's pretty head.' Henri Chapier, a Cocteauesque exquisite among
Paris's film critics, maintained: 'Upper middle-class Parisian women are
no longer restrained by sexual taboos, and we could only believe such a

story if it were taking place in Spain [. . .] or at the most in Bordeaux or Rouen.' Cannes refused it in competition, but the film would win the Leone d'Or at Venice in August and run for months in most European capitals.

Buñuel went with *Belle de Jour* to Venice, where Carrière witnessed a revealing flashback to the younger, more tentative Luis. 'One day we were invited with Jean-Paul Sartre and some other people to a drink somewhere, and Fritz Lang was there. I said to Buñuel, "Fritz Lang is over there. Would you like to meet him?" Because I knew how much he admired his work. But Buñuel was very shy, like a college boy, which was extraordinary. He asked me, "Where?" I pointed him out, and Buñuel, wrestling, struggling against this desire to go over, said, "What, this disgusting old man?"'

All Catholic children giggle secretly over the absurdities of their religion. At school and in the Residencia Luis had been as titillated as anyone by the contrast between the plaster images of Christ, Mary and the saints, and the physical functions they must have shared with ordinary men and women. The anarchists' all-purpose curse 'I shit on God' exhibits the same schoolboy scatological glee.

It was a short step from this to pointing out the absurdity of much Catholic dogma. Buñuel had been amused by the interminable internecine war fought by the Church against heresy. Every few generations, some ingenious sceptic seized on an improbability of Church teaching and, in suggesting an alternative, attracted followers but also, inevitably, the wrath of Rome.

From the early 1960s he had toyed with turning this recital of scepticism into a film and, in the process, affirming a lifetime's atheism. Silberman was willing to finance it, so in the autumn of 1967 Buñuel met Carrière in Spain, at the Parador Cazorla, a remote hotel in the Guadarrama mountains of Andalusia used mainly by hunters, to write a script. The road ended at the door of the hotel, and from the window they could watch men with guns hauling back the day's kill of ibex, a suitably unecclesiastical background for their work.

Winnowing Church histories, they compiled a list of apostasies and their repression, as grisly as it was comic. Most heresies, they found, sprang from six areas of doubt.

(1) The double nature of Christ. Was he God or man? God *and* man? God pretending to be man? Man pretending to be God? (2) The Trinity; how can three natures co-exist in the same entity? (3) The Immaculate Conception. Mary, a virgin, was nevertheless Christ's mother. (4) Transubstantiation. Can bread literally become the body of Christ? Is

this just a metaphor? (5) The problems of God's omnipotence (which Sade propounded and Buñuel restated in *The Adventures of Robinson Crusoe*). Is God all-powerful? If so, do we enjoy free will? (6) Evil. Did God create evil? Does its co-existence with good prove that the Devil can also create?

The list suggested no obvious structure, so they simply dramatized incidents illustrating the heresies, linking them with a pair of wandering modern pilgrims. From childhood holidays at Santander and San Sebastian, Buñuel remembered the tradition of a pilgrimage to the shrine of St James of Compostela at Santiago in the same far northwestern corner of Spain, only 50 kilometres from the Atlantic. The route from northern Europe was known as the Milky Way, because in AD 813 a hermit was supposed to have followed that field of stars (*campus stellas*) to the body of St James (Santiago in Spanish), hidden there for centuries.* The fact that James, who reputedly hacked off the heads of 10,000 Muslims, had been a favourite saint of the Falange also appealed to Buñuel. His vision of the Church undermined by its own internal disagreements would stand as a metaphor for the enfeebled Franco regime. There were resonances, too, with Surrealism, and Breton's habit of purging anyone who defied him.

For his cast, Buñuel rounded up the members of what was almost a stock company: Muni, Clementi, Claudio Brook, Georges Marchal, Piccoli and Carrière. He gave the role of a prostitute to Delphine Seyrig, to whom Carrière reintroduced him. Silberman was delighted to have Christian Matras to light the film, but the man who shot *La Grande Illusion* and Ophuls's *La Ronde* did not get on any better with Luis than had Vierny. On one occasion, while Buñuel was off set, Matras changed his camera position by 10 centimetres. When Luis returned, he noticed and demanded it be replaced.

Buñuel had hoped to start shooting in May 1968, but history intervened. France was paralysed as a flash-fire of strikes and sit-ins swept across the country and, subsequently, the world. The firing of Henri Langlois from his position in charge of the Cinematheque Française provoked Jean-Luc Godard and François Truffaut into hijacking the Cannes Festival, hanging on to the curtain to stop films from being shown. Production on *The Milky Way* was closed down for the duration of hostilities.

---

* Modern scholars believe the name more probably derives from the graveyard (*campostela*) on which the city was built, but Buñuel preferred his version, which he retold in an opening sequence of *The Milky Way*, complete with an antique map *à la The Adventures of Robinson Crusoe*.

Buñuel was astonished and amused by the fervour of the French dissidents Godard christened 'the children of Marx and Coca Cola'. In Mexico, an insurrection like this would have been, and, shortly after was, put down by the Army in a bloodbath. For his French friends, however, especially those in the movies, it was a glorious spectacle. Inspired, Jacques Fraenkel decided to join the Communist Party. 'Good idea,' Luis told him. 'At your age I would do the same thing.' Smiling, he went on, 'But one thing I can be sure of is: I'll never be your age again.' None the less he asked him to give his regards to some of the high Communist cadres, including Thirion and Vaillant-Couturier.

Godard and Claude Lelouch were on the barricades with cameras. Louis Malle formed his own flying squad, for which he tried to co-opt Juan Luis. 'He knew I had a .22,' says Juan Luis, 'and he told me to get up on the barricades and fire at the army when they advanced. "Where will you be?" I asked. Malle said, "We'll be fighting elsewhere."' Juan Luis prudently stayed at home.

The centre of student resistance in Paris was rue Gay-Lussac, which had been barricaded with banks of paving stones and smashed cars. At 2 a.m. on the morning of Saturday, 11 May, the CRS security militia attacked the students holding it. Later in the day, Luis asked Fraenkel to drive him there. Within a few metres of the Spanish Bookshop where Jeanne had worked in the 1920s, people carrying their morning *baguettes* walked wonderingly between the carcasses of eighty burnt-out and overturned cars that littered the road, and clambered over piles of paving stones. Everywhere, spray-painted on the walls, were slogans from the Surrealist days: 'All Power To the Imagination' and 'It is Forbidden to Forbid'. Here was everything Buñuel had hoped to see in 1930, when he urged the burning of the Prado. It gave him a bitter satisfaction.

In August, Buñuel started shooting *The Milky Way*. Although he would never admit it, his imagination had been refreshed by the revolutionary energy still crackling around the world. He had also obviously been watching some of the new movies that year. He never acknowledged seeing Godard's *Weekend*, any more than he confessed to having seen *Last Year in Marienbad*, which had such an influence on *The Exterminating Angel*, but *The Milky Way* is unarguably reminiscent of Godard's anti-bourgeois nightmare of the freeways. Godard also pioneered, in *Made in USA* (1966), the trick of drowning out political statements or sexual confessions with a siren, a passing plane or obtrusive music, an effect Buñuel used in *Discreet Charm of the Bourgeoisie*.

As the two shabby pilgrims (Paul Frankeur and Laurent Terzieff) pan-handle and hitch-hike along the freeways and back-roads of France and Spain *en route* to Santiago, the history of Catholicism unrolls behind them like a comic strip, surrealistically switching subjects from panel to panel. Occasionally they enter the action but more often they stare with dazed amusement while 2000 years of self-delusion, self-deception, nit-picking and hair-splitting ripple and flutter around them like a gaudy cyclorama.

Buñuel skates the line between farce and horror with effortless skill. A restaurateur discussing transubstantiation with a passing priest suggests that the change from bread into flesh can be explained by comparison with a hare pâté, both hare and pâté at the same time, only to hear chillingly that the Pateliers were burned for this grievous error, just as Albigensians and Calvinists were slaughtered for suggesting that the bread was a metaphor for Christ's body rather than the thing itself.

Buñuel finds it both appalling and comic that men should be condemned simply for pointing out that Purgatory, Confirmation and Extreme Unction were later embellishments of the Church, never mentioned by Christ. His heretics in general blaze as beacons of logic in a fog of sophistry.

He often seems more disapproving of the pious laity than the Church. Claudio Brook incinerating the corpse of a colleague retrospectively condemned for heresy has more dignity than the modern-day maître d' of a smart restaurant who leaves off lecturing his staff on apologetics to send the pilgrims packing without even a piece of bread. Interrupted by clients, he politely explains that they have been discussing why, with so many religious demagogues abroad in first-century Palestine, Christ alone should be remembered. 'Well, because he was Christ, of course,' the woman replies. 'Quite so, madame,' says the maitre d'. 'Some nice fresh oysters to start?'

The effrontery of the Church's confidence trick earns Buñuel's grudging admiration. Watching a more thoughtful monk faced down by his superior for daring to suggest that it is pointless to burn heretics, we recognize that, in the same situation, we would probably bow our heads as well. And perhaps so monstrous a lie as that of the Church achieves in the end something like the dignity of truth. Buñuel gives to a minor character a line that might almost be his: 'My hatred of science and my horror of technology will finally bring me round to this absurd belief in God.' In *The Milky Way*, what Pauline Kael calls Buñuel's 'Spanish schoolboy's view of life joined to an adult atheist's disbelief in redemption' is clearly on display.

Despite the commercial success of *Belle de Jour*, distributors did not stampede to screen *The Milky Way*. Those to whom Silberman showed it told him that the most they could hope for was 50,000 admissions in Paris and almost none elsewhere. He finally found a supporter in Boris Gourevitch, who owned a small chain of nine cinemas, one of them a porno house just off the Champs-Elysées. 'I don't understand any of it,' Gourevitch said of the film, 'but it's very beautiful. I'm going to help you.' He converted his porn cinema, changed its façade and opened the film there in March 1969 for a highly successful run. 210,000 people finally saw *The Milky Way* in Paris alone.

To Buñuel's embarrassment, *The Milky Way* was well received by the Church, sections of which were thawing in the liberalism of the Second Vatican Council. Rome even took in good part the fake execution of a recognizable Pope John Paul by Spanish anarchists, and when the Italian censor banned the film it intervened to reverse the decision. Despite protests from a few priest critics, the Spanish government also refused to ban it. The Festival of Cinema of Religious and Human Values in Valladolid invited the film, and the US National Catholic Film Office belatedly gave *Nazarin* an award as well. Embarrassed, Buñuel refused to attend the American ceremony and made much of the fact that he had also been presented with the prize of the Chevalier de la Barre, named in honour of an atheist precursor of Sade, but his stock among his free-thinking friends took a battering. After a Paris screening of *The Milky Way* for Fuentes, Cortazar, and Hernando and Loulou Viñes, Cortazar pointedly left without anything more than polite thanks. Later, he told Fuentes that he believed Vatican money had gone into the film. Buñuel laughed at this, but he must have realized at last the truth of Breton's jaded remark: you really couldn't scandalize people any more, not even the Church.

There was worse to come. Having been accepted by the Church, Buñuel was now welcomed back by Spain. While he was spending Christmas with his family in Mexico City, the principals of Epoca, the small company that had advanced him 30,000 dollars for *Tristana*, turned up with the news that they now believed it could be relaunched. Buñuel put on a cantankerous show. He was far more interested in *The Monk*, he told them, for which he and Carrière had written a screenplay. Silberman was now ready to finance it, and they even had the cast lined up: Jeanne Moreau, Peter O'Toole and Omar Sharif. To revive *Tristana*, he would need to look at the script again and almost certainly revise it. 'Why more films?' he demanded rhetorically. 'There are enough already.' Besides, he went on, they were 'as big a nuisance to make as they are to see'.

*

Overriding his complaints, Epoca, who had found Italian and French co-venturers to help finance the film, put up more money for rewrites (the script Buñuel used was the fourth version) and promised him the newly built Siena studios in Madrid, and locations in Toledo, as he had always planned.

Buñuel accepted Catherine Deneuve to play Tristana and the Italians' suggestion of current heart-throb Franco Nero as her young lover, but drew the line at their proposal to hire Fellini's and Visconti's cinematographer, Giuseppe Rotunno. He preferred the pedestrian José Fernandez Aguayo, although, more worried than ever about his hearing, he suggested that, if the Italians wanted to be helpful, they might send an ace sound recordist.

His Ménière's Syndrome had entered a new and dangerous phase. Driving home along the Insurgentes in Mexico City, he had pulled into the side of the road, overcome with dizziness. Jaime Fernandez found him and helped him home.

Buñuel arrived in Madrid in the spring of 1969 to find *Tristana* bogged down yet again. It lagged through the summer with nothing shot while Epoca wrangled over trifles with the Franco bureaucracy. In 1962 the notorious Arias Salgado had been replaced as Minister of Information by the more liberal Fraga Iribarne. The cabinet in general, however, remained dominated by Opus Dei, the shadowy Church pressure group to which Franco had handed near-control of the country in 1957 when he installed twelve members or sympathizers as ministers.

Iribane, remembering the double-dealing of *Viridiana*, told Luis: 'I have read your scenario. I have no comment to make. I want only that you will agree to film that scenario, no more, no less.' Buñuel refused. 'The scenario is a working tool, that's all. I won't promise something that I know I can't do.' Casting around for a way to break the deadlock, Luis remembered that he and Iribane, who had been a professor of political science at Madrid University, had a mutual friend in Rafael Mendez. 'Everything in Spain,' Dionisio Ridruejo has written, 'a telephone, a business connection, a flat, the most insignificant bureaucratic favour, is obtained because you have a friend.' Luis rang Mendez, who flew to Madrid and persuaded Iribane to relent.

Buñuel was determined that *Tristana* should mark his official and triumphant return to Spain. For *Viridiana* he had entered the country as he had during the Civil War, under false pretences, and with an ulterior motive. Now that he was being formally welcomed home, he was determined to enjoy the experience to the hilt. Typically, he refused to acknowledge his pleasure at being back. Toledo, he complained to journalists, was not the city he remembered. 'It's old, and stinks of piss.' They dutifully wrote this down, though anyone who knew Buñuel could see he was delighted to be in the old town once more.

Doña Maria died in Zaragoza on 29 June. Luis mourned, but the dead were dead. When he went back to Mexico after *Tristana* he brought one of Don Leonardo's rings which his mother had bequeathed him. Jeanne was touched when he gave it to her. It made up a little for the fact that she had never been given a wedding band. But a few days later, after Luis had had it appraised, he told her urgently, 'It's worth a fortune, Jeanne,' and persuaded her to sell it. With some of the money, he bought her a smaller ring.

Filming finally started in September, in a burst of New Age enthusiasm. Franco Nero's companion Vanessa Redgrave, just messily divorced from Tony Richardson, naming Jeanne Moreau as co-respondent, arrived with their son and set up hippie housekeeping next to the set. Nero was understandably distracted from a role that, like Jean Sorel's in *Belle de Jour*, gave him little or nothing to do.

Tristana was near enough in plot to *Viridiana* for the later film to seem like a remake. Don Lope (Rey) is an irascible *señorito* in 1920s' Toledo (updated from Perez Galdos's 1890s). He becomes the guardian of a meek young niece, Tristana, whom he seduces. Initially innocent, she agrees to be his mistress, though Don Lope continues to treat her like a schoolgirl, forbidding her to go out except with the maid Saturna. No amount of protection, however, can discourage Tristana from exploring her essentially perverse nature. Even crippled by an amputated leg, she is more than a match for any man, and sufficiently attractive even for Saturna's compulsively masturbating son, for whom she exposes her nude, mutilated body.

Though Deneuve is its putative heroine, *Tristana* is essentially Fernando Rey's film. The splendidly seigneurial Don Lope, who at the same time is a practical free-thinker, is Buñuel's tribute to the señoritos, and, one senses, to his own father.

By comparison, Tristana's schoolgirl innocence is trivial. Luis based some of this on his early memories of Conchita, his favourite sister. Don Lope rightly ridicules her belief, which Conchita had shared, that aesthetic and emotional choices are possible between everything in life: the best route for a walk, the most attractive column in a church, even the better of two peas. Far from being subject to logic and reason, Lope (and Buñuel) insist, life is a game of random chance where morality is irrelevant and the strong prevail. At the end of the film Tristana embraces this conclusion, and graduates from Don Lope's college of one by killing the professor. Buñuel never had a heroine in whom he invested more of himself and his beliefs.

32

'That is what I have all my life wanted to attack, to fight; sentimentality, the values of the bourgeois.'
– Luis Buñuel to Tony Richardson, 1953

The atmosphere of the Buñuel house on Cerrada de Felix Cuevas was more genial and welcoming than it had been in the 1950s, even though what had once been a sleepy neighbourhood on the edge of the city was now noisy and congested with traffic. The reddish brick had weathered into a pale pink and the red metal gate had been repainted white. There were no signs that one of the world's greatest film-makers lived here.

Inside, life had settled into a comfortable routine, at least for Luis. 'I am an anchorite now,' he said at the time of *Simon of the Desert*. 'I live a very isolated life. I never go to parties, theatres, pictures.' On the wall of the bar was a map of the Paris Métro. The living room was dominated by Dali's portrait of him from the Residencia. 'Thirty-five years is too long for a fight,' he told Penelope Gilliatt.

Joyce Buñuel recalled that 'he hardly spoke on the phone to anyone. Hated the phone. Couldn't hear, I guess. I think he couldn't bear it when I was in the house because of the phone. All my girlfriends calling; I could be on the phone for hours.

'After lunch he'd take his coffee up to his room, then he'd lie down for a siesta. Probably get up again about three-thirty and browse around, very often in the house. Dinner was at quarter to seven and he'd go to bed at eight-thirty. And that was it.'

Jeanne was resigned to this millpond existence. She was waiting for her grandchildren, the next milestone in any Frenchwoman's life. Until then, she played cards with the other Spanish wives. Though never a great drinker, she had discovered the consolation of tequila, and enjoyed a few glasses at noon and six, like Luis. And she sewed, unremittingly. Everyone remembers the sound of a Singer whirring in an upstairs room. Like the cards, it kept her hands busy. She had learnt that much from

Luis; his tinkering with his little tool kit, his fussy smoking of unfiltered Gitanes. When Luis cut his cigarettes to two a day, he found that the pleasure of smoking was mainly in its physical movements. Jean-Claude Carrière says: 'He told me that, if someone would take out a Gitane for him, open the box of matches, strike one, light it and bring it to his lips, all the pleasure of smoking would be gone.'

Juan Luis and Joyce, expecting their first child, Juliette, came to live in Mexico City in 1965 and stayed there, on and off, until the early 1970s, by which time Juan Luis was established as a director. Joyce too had begun winning a reputation as a screen-writer and film-maker. The family saw less and less of Rafael. After graduating from college he wrote a little for theatre, then went into television, after which he moved to Los Angeles and took up sculpture, like his brother. 'He had a real antipathy for the movie world,' says Joyce. 'I don't think it was easy for Rafael. It's difficult to be the-son-of. Then he was the-brother-of, and the brother-in-law-of. There were a lot of big personalities in the family, and I'm not sure that everyone was always listening. People have to be listened to.'

Luis had fewer and fewer visitors, except for old Republicans like the Mantecons and Antonio Galan, the treasurer of the Spanish Republic who had moved in next door. An exception was Luis Alcoriza. 'He was everything Luis was not,' says Joyce. 'He was a skirt chaser with a great smile. He drove a red-hot Mustang and was always out to parties until four a.m. It was a father-and-son relationship, though later Alcoriza was bitter that his career hadn't taken off as Luis's had. Luis didn't mind. Nothing that Alcoriza said bothered him.'

Occasionally Luis fantasized elaborate practical jokes designed to deflate the hard-playing Alcoriza, although he never inflicted them. In one, he invented a hunting trip in which he would point out a large eagle on the far side of a river, knowing that Alcoriza would not be able to resist shooting the bird. When he swam the river to retrieve it, however, he would find it was a stuffed one planted there by Luis. In another scheme, he would let Alcoriza pick up a beautiful girl in a restaurant where he and Luis were dining, only to find, later in bed, the words: 'With the compliments of Luis Buñuel' tattooed on her stomach.

'Luis hated to have people come to the door who were not invited,' says Joyce. 'There was no "dropping in". If you dropped in, you weren't received.' Most new people were foreign movie-makers making courtesy visits, like Joseph Losey, who called in July 1971 while preparing *The Assassination of Trotsky*, though Luis welcomed Joyce's father Rube when he came to Mexico City. 'He was an alcoholic,' Joyce says, 'and I told him: "Don't get drunk." He gargled with perfume to cover up his breath. Luis was very excited to meet him. My father brought his *mechero*, the cigarette lighter on a yellow cord they used in the trenches, and gave it to him. That was a very moving moment.'

Luis invited Galan and Mantecon to meet Kaufman. With Joyce and Juan Luis translating, he described being shot before Teruel and lying for four days while Franco's troops prowled the battlefield, bayonetting the wounded. Convalescing for months in the prison hospital in Madrid, he often dreamed of a skeleton bending over him to give 'the cold kiss of death'. Luis and the others were clearly moved, the more so because this was a war from which all of them had run.

Buñuel had announced that *Belle de Jour* would be his last film. He did the same for *The Milky Way*, though modifying the statement slightly to say it would be his last *narrative* film, which was close to the truth. The first hint that he might not be unalterably opposed to working again came in April 1969. Gene Moskowitz reported in *Variety* that Buñuel was about to film an 1895 play by Oscar Panizza called *Concile d'Amour (The Love Council)* which had just been performed in Paris for the first time. 'It shows heaven with a doddering God who hobbles around with a big crutch,' wrote Moskowitz, 'a Christ in his Crucifixion garb – weak, and always failing – a flirtatious, womanly Virgin Mary. Taking place in the fifteenth century at the time of a Pope given to orgies, it has God having the Devil help to punish him and mankind, and the Devil contracts venereal disease.' When the play had first been published, Panizza was jailed for a year.

Buñuel never acknowledged that he intended to film *Concile d'Amour*, if indeed he did. The report was probably leaked by Silberman, who saw nothing wrong in flying to Mexico City and pressuring Luis into a new project if he seemed to have been inactive too long. Later, *Variety* would remark: 'There have been some observers who have said Silberman exploits Buñuel and forces him out to make films. This is brushed off by Silberman who says when Buñuel is ready, he decides to work, but he has to be nudged a great deal.'

Silberman was disappointed that Buñuel had abandoned *The Monk* as he wandered from conventional narrative. The script was sold – 'for peanuts', says Silberman in disgust – to another producer who made a flat 1972 version with Ado Kyrou directing Franco Nero, Nathalie Delon and Nicol Williamson. Buñuel was still interested in Huysmans's *Là-Bas*, which he and Carrière would script later in the decade. Another project, a short film called *The Raising of a Communicant*, would have been combined with *Simon of the Desert* to bring it up to feature length. He liked two stories by the Italian Dino Buzzati, who had collaborated with Fellini on the unproduced *The Voyage of G. Mastorna*. One was his most famous novel, *The Desert of the Tartars*, about a desert garrison waiting decades for a threatened invasion that never arrives. The other, *The Sixth Floor*, dealt with a man who emerges from hospital after a routine operation convinced that he is dead.

Buñuel also thought about a short ghost story set in Guanajuato, the regional town where he filmed part of *El*. The main tourist attraction is the catacombs of mummies where, because of a peculiarity of the soil, corpses are preserved in startlingly good condition. In 1960, Buñuel had excitedly told Derek Prouse, 'an old woman of eighty can go and see her own grandmother looking younger than she is herself. It's marvellous. I'm hoping to shoot a scene there for my next film.' Buñuel would have shown a man and his little boy in Edwardian clothing touring modern Guanajuato and marvelling at the changes since their time. Only towards the end, as their clothes became more dusty and decaying, would their true nature be revealed, and the film would end with shots of their corpses, preserved and on display in the catacombs.

In 1970, Dalton Trumbo found backing to produce the script of *Johnny Got His Gun* which he and Luis had written together. He directed the film himself, and the screenplay had only his name on it. With typical chutzpah he cabled Luis in May 1971:

> Dear Luis, I took *Johnny Got His Gun* to Paris where it was unanimously accepted for Critics Week [at the Cannes Festival] stop Fauve [sic] LeBret said it was powerful but not the kind of film he thought people would want to see in the festival stop Several people in Europe are urging him to reconsider and allow it to enter in competition stop I am told the deadline for entrance is 48 hours hence stop If you can find an honorable way to cable him about accepting the film before you have seen it, I am told it would help us greatly stop If not I understand stop In the meanwhile you will see it the first of the week Salud Dalton.

Johnny Got His Gun made the Festival and shared a Special Jury Prize with Milos Forman's *Taking Off*. Buñuel found it too academic, but he dutifully turned up at the press conference and sat through the ritual of Trumbo's artistic Second Coming.

At Cannes, Luis also picked up the threads again with Carrière, who had co-written *Taking Off*. He confessed he was bored in Mexico City and wouldn't mind working again. Directors older than he were doing well. Luchino Visconti, who had taken over the Lido di Venezia for his lavish production of *Death in Venice*, had flatteringly remarked, when asked about revolutionary new directors, 'Luis Buñuel is the youngest revolutionary of all, and he's sixty-eight.'

However, it worried Buñuel that he seemed to be dealing repeatedly with the same subjects. 'They', he said (meaning Silberman), 'keep asking me to make another film, but all I am doing is telling the same stories.' Carrière reassured him that most great art is founded on re-examination. It drew them into a discussion of the theme of repetition itself which Buñuel had explored so amusingly in *The Exterminating Angel*. After Cannes, Buñuel went to Paris to see Silberman, who mentioned an embarrassing incident when he'd forgotten a dinner party he had arranged, and opened the door to find six puzzled, hungry friends. In Buñuel's imagination, the two ideas, of repetition and the non-occurring dinner party, clicked together. Silberman says, 'Luis said to me, "Serge, give me 2000 dollars. I have an idea for a script. I need to go to Spain to write it. If it takes longer, that'll be my responsibility." I gave him the money and he and Carrière went away. Three weeks later, I have a telegram: "The first draft is finished." I fly to Madrid and he hands me the script, as if I am the professor and he is the student. And of course it's wonderful. It is *Le Charme Discret*.'

Buñuel and Carrière delivered the screenplay in the summer of 1971 but in March 1972 they were still waiting for the green light on what was then known as *Bourgeois Enchantment*. In the meantime the Mexican Marco Polo production company had offered Buñuel *El Lugar Sin Limites (A Place Without Limits)*. A project of Roberto Cobo, who played Jaibo in *Los Olvidados*, the sub-Tennessee Williams drama was set in a village brothel run by the eccentric homosexual 'La Manuela' and his wife 'La Japonesita'. Fortunately Silberman came through with the money for *Bourgeois Enchantment* in April and Buñuel could pass on this ill-advised project, which Arturo Ripstein was to film in 1977.

The late-blooming creator is more common in film than many of the arts, but few have pulled off such a triumphant sunset conquest as Buñuel in *The Discreet Charm of the Bourgeoisie*. It was not only artistically his most fully realized work, but also his most financially successful, as well as the most critically acclaimed. At seventy-two, with only a decade to live, Buñuel finally came into his own.

The dimensions of his success were all the more striking for the fragility of the vehicle that brought it. *The Discreet Charm of the Bourgeoisie* is a stiletto heel of a film, relying so totally on balance that one mis-step might bring down the whole construction. Without perfect casting, it could easily have toppled, but by 1972 Luis's reputation was so assured that he could pick and choose his people, all of whom were prepared, for Buñuel, to work at scale, or even defer salaries.

Most of the cast, inevitably, were old friends. Buñuel signed Fernando

Rey, Delphine Seyrig, Paul Frankeur, Julien Bertheau, Michel Piccoli and Muni before he knew what roles they would play, although the moment he wrote the scene between the maid of a country house and the gardener, a polite and amiable man who also happens to be a bishop ('There are worker priests. Why not worker bishops?'), he could only think of Muni and Bertheau in the parts. Nor could Rey be anybody but the corrupt yet unfailingly courteous ambassador Rafael Acosta, named for Luis's old friend and antagonist, the one-time Mexican ambassador to France, Miguel Alvarez Acosta, author of *The River and Death*, but recalling also Rey's urbane drug smuggler in John Frankenheimer's *The French Connection*.

Delphine Seyrig was harder to place. In fact Buñuel had only the haziest ideas about which actresses might fill the three main roles, and his typical nervousness and diffidence about dealing with temperamental stars did not help. Silberman finally rang up the hottest actresses in France and asked if they were interested. Few were not. Candidates included Bulle Ogier and Stephane Audran, the beautiful wife of Claude Chabrol and star of his films.

'I'm not sure that he knew who I was,' says Audran. 'He was not very interested in actresses. Serge Silberman rang him up and asked if I could play a part in the film. And Buñuel said, "Why not?" I met him, just for fifteen minutes. He was very nice. He gave me the script. "There are two women," he said. "Take the one you prefer." It was the first time someone offered me this choice.

'Then I read the script. Well, it was hilarious. I told him that I wanted to be the one in the house, the hostess of the dinner party that never happens.' Buñuel acquiesced, and even wrote a new scene in which, overcome with lust as her guests approach, Mme Senechal slips into the bushes, hikes up her skirts and undoes her stockings and suspenders for a quickie with her husband. Audran, whom he always addressed punctiliously as 'Mme Chabrol', had the most beautiful legs in French cinema, and Buñuel wanted to show them off.

Seyrig became Mme Thevenot, and Bulle Ogier the third of the wives. To play Senechal, an agent sent Jean-Pierre Cassel. Despite being an accomplished *farceur*, Cassel was nervous as he stood in the mirrored waiting room in the Champs-Elysées to which he had been shown by Pierre Lary. 'When he finally arrived,' Cassel says, 'he looked at me, looked at Lary, said: "All right", and left.'

Cassel did not share Audran's amusement at the script. 'None of us knew what we were supposed to be doing in this film,' he said. 'The script was no help. Nothing but a lot of banal conversations, walking on the road . . . nothing *happened* in this script. But of course it just wasn't written.'

Luis had once joked with a Mexican producer, that if a film ran short, he could always insert one of his dreams. In *Charm* he gave in to the impulse and used three or four, including the nightmare of finding himself on stage during a play where he doesn't know his lines, and the dream recounted by the young sergeant, of meeting a dead relative (in Luis's case his cousin Rafael) on a dark street and following him into a house filled with cobwebs. Most poignantly of all, he re-created the recurring dream of seeing his parents sitting on the bed, staring at him with glowing (but in the film bleeding) eyes.

Buñuel started shooting on 15 May 1972 and finished two months later, well within his 800,000 dollar budget. As usual, he made almost no retakes and cut most of the film in the camera. He and Silberman had a continuingly friendly argument about how long it took him to edit the film. Buñuel said a day, Silberman a day and a half. Silberman had installed a new gadget to help Luis's sciatica and deafness; one of the first 'video splits' in Europe. Instead of standing for hours on the set, he could sit elsewhere in comfort, watching the action on a TV monitor and listening through amplified earphones. Luis inserted an end credit, 'Sound Effects by Luis Buñuel', a sly joke on his deafness.

As a result of this technical innovation, however, actors had even less direction than on other Buñuel movies. 'It was all technical,' says Cassel. ' "I want to see both your eyes" . . . "A little more to the left . . ." To me he said, "I need to see your hands all the time. Fix your tie. Touch your hair." He never said it, but later I realized he did this because we were all aristocrats, and gesture was very important. But he didn't tell the exact reason at the time. It was Fernando Rey who explained that to me. He said on *Tristana* he'd told him the same thing: "Always let me see your hands".

'Gradually he became very funny, and joked a lot. In the bedroom scenes, Stephane and I were supposed to be making love, but not really, and we didn't understand what was going on. He said, "Don't worry. You'll see, *Cahiers du Cinéma* will write a long piece about my style and my ideas about sex".' He was almost obsessively solicitous of the actors' comfort. He would not change a light if the cameraman asked him to, but would, and did, spend two hours relighting when a car had been parked too near a puddle of water and the actors would have had to wet their shoes to play the scene.

From the beginning, *The Discreet Charm of the Bourgeoisie* was a thunderous success. Not even a puzzling poster (Luis thought it stupid and offensive) of a giant bowler hat with bee-stung lips on spindly legs could mar the sense of a film that froze a generation and a class in amber.

Rather than wait for Cannes the next year, Silberman put the film on international release in time for the 1972 Oscars, where it was nominated for Best Foreign Film.

Buñuel was off-hand, even insulting, about an honour voted on by, as he put it, '2500 idiots, including for example the assistant dress designer of the studio'. When some Mexican journalists asked if he thought he would win, he said deadpan: 'I've already paid 25,000 dollars for it!' In the land of *mordida*, the joke was taken seriously. In April 1973 it duly won Best Foreign Film. Silberman collected the Oscar on Buñuel's behalf, but the Academy, notoriously thick-skinned, still wanted a photograph of him with the statuette for its files, so he let Silberman snap him, but disguised in dark glasses and a wig.

Late in 1972, Buñuel, Silberman and Carrière had been in the United States for the launch of *Discreet Charm*. Luis enjoyed checking out the restaurants and catching up on Californian wines. He did not turn up for his own press screening, and the few interviews he gave were unilluminating. *Newsweek* asked: 'Who are your favourite characters in the movie?' Buñuel responded: 'The cockroaches.'

When George Cukor called in Los Angeles, asking the three of them to have lunch with 'some friends', Luis did not realize an event was being planned in his honour. The 'friends' included most of Hollywood's greatest film-makers. Alfred Hitchcock, Billy Wilder, George Stevens, Rouben Mamoulian, John Ford and William Wyler were all eager to see Buñuel. As an added incentive, Cukor promised to invite the director whom Luis himself still really wanted to meet, Fritz Lang.

Given Luis's deafness and diffidence, the lunch was inevitably stiff, but Cukor's famous charm glossed over the awkward pauses. Hitchcock in particular was genial, chuckling to Buñuel about Tristana's artificial leg. But Ford was too ill to stay long – he died two months later – and, at the last minute Lang also cancelled, although, through Cukor, he invited Buñuel to his home the next day.

'The following day,' says Carrière, who remembered Luis's shy refusal to meet Lang at Venice, 'he came to my room – I swear – to ask me if he should wear a tie. A normal tie or a bow tie? Like a young boy going to a first rendezvous. So a car took him to Fritz Lang's. He came back at four o'clock in the afternoon, very merry, having drunk [a lot]. I said, "How was it?" and he said, "It was very nice. A wonderful man. Very interesting." He carried something under his arm. I asked him what it was. "Something he gave me," Buñuel said. "At the end, just before leaving, I couldn't resist asking him for an autograph." Buñuel was seventy-two and Lang about eighty! Lang was so eager and so happy to be asked that he went all over the house looking for an old picture of himself when he was thirty-five. He wrote a beautiful dedication – something like: "I am so happy to find that my work was the origin of one of the most original works in the history of the movies."

'He took this picture to Mexico, but you see, he was always fighting against his feelings. So when Arturo Ripstein [. . .] came one day to visit him and asked him, "What do you have there?" Buñuel said, "Oh, it's nothing. If you want it, take it." And Ripstein took [the picture] away.'

33

'A thought as of gold falls down with sad descent. The blinds have been drawn in the rooms in which the idylls are dead.'

– Léon-Paul Fargue (translated Wallace Stevens)

After the success of *The Discreet Charm of the Bourgeoisie* there was no possibility that Buñuel would not immediately make another film. *Charm* had not even been mixed before Silberman was pressing him. Luis was on holiday in Lausanne, at an inn famous for its hundred-year-old green Chartreuse. Silberman came down to see him, and they sampled the liqueur together. It put both men in reflective mood.

'Luis, it's curious,' Silberman said. 'You were born in Zaragoza, you're Catholic; you were brought up by the Jesuits. Me, I was born on the border of Poland and Russia; I was brought up by lay Jews, and yet look at us; we understand one another.'

Buñuel looked across the lake, speculating on an alternative reality. 'Imagine, Serge,' he said, 'during the war, we are in the same place, on the Swiss side of the lake. On the other side is occupied France. We take a boat and, just as we arrive on the other side, I tell you that you're Jewish.' Bunuel found this more amusing than Silberman did, but a few moments later he said, 'Serge, we're going to make a film about chance.'

'Chance governs all things,' Buñuel said in his memoirs. 'Necessity, which is far from having the same purity, comes only later. If I have a soft spot for any one of my movies, it would be for *The Phantom of Liberty*, because it tries to work out just this theme.'

At the end of 1973, he and Carrière were at work again in the mountains of Spain on a story. 'In the hands of a free spirit,' he had told an audience in 1953, 'the cinema is a magnificent and dangerous weapon.' Film directors use this sort of rhetoric all the time, but Buñuel believed it – and, more important, was prepared to put his belief to the test.

The *Phantom of Liberty* wanders with a deceptively cool lack of narrative coherence. Luis's first idea had been to observe a bourgeios couple waiting for a crucial telegram, then following the delivery man without revealing its contents. Finally the couple (Jean-Claude Brialy and Monica Vitti) become just the first links in a chain that joins dental nurse Milena Vukotic, masochist hatter Michel Lonsdale, terrorist poet Pierre Larf and a variety of other Buñuel regulars in a series of Surrealist encounters, the most memorable of which has some Parisian sophisti-cates sitting down on lavatories for a defecation party, then sneaking away one by one to a dining cubicle for a furtive meal.

The Phantom of Liberty became the sort of incitement to randomness and accident that Breton had always preached as one of Surrealism's most potent and significant acts. It thumbs its nose at the rational universe. Everything is chance, nothing is preordained. God cannot exist; no thinking creator could countenance the insane and random series of coincidences and eccentricities that constitute human existence.

The title Buñuel chose went over the heads of most Anglophones, since it rests on a divergent translation of a famous phrase. In English, Marx's *Communist Manifesto* begins with the ominous 'A spectre is haunting Europe.' Buñuel meant to suggest that the spectre conjured up by Surrealism, of free-will and chance, was likely to be even more disruptive. Unfortunately, since 'spectre' was usually translated as 'phantom' or 'ghost' in French and Spanish, the reference was lost to English audiences, and was obscured even more when translators sedulously included both definite articles, calling the film *The Phantom of the Liberty*, as if Buñuel meant a ship.

The film was enthusiastically received by critics but left audiences generally baffled. Again, Silberman acquiesced to a garish publicity campaign, building on that of *The Discreet Charm of the Bourgeoisie*. Instead of fat red lips with a bowler, its poster features purple buttocks surmounted by the statue of Liberty's crown and a hand holding her torch in a limp-dick droop – images which imply, wrongly, a political commentary on the United States. Even so, *The Phantom of Liberty* was chosen to close the 1974 New York Film Festival as a tribute to Buñuel and what he again insisted was his last film.

Luis was present in Avery Fisher Hall for the screening on 13 October, but the audience was surprised by his failure to acknowledge their applause, or even stand or smile. Nor did he show up for the press conference after the preview. He had other, more pressing concerns – his health. He had already been diagnosed as diabetic, and ordered to cut down on drinking and smoking. In *Phantom*, a doctor is shown using every euphemism in the dictionary to avoid telling a patient that he has cancer of the liver. The incident came from life. During the writing of the screenplay, Buñuel had difficulty digesting, especially after he had been drinking. His doctor and old friend, José-Luis Barros diagnosed a cyst, but Luis had been sufficiently scared to give up alcohol for the first time since the age of eighteen.

When he started to drink again, his head for liquor had gone. Concorde had begun flying the Mexico City–Paris route, and he and Carrière tried out its luxury service, more than lavish enough to keep Luis anaesthetized during the hated air journey. When they arrived at Roissy, however, Carrière had to help him off the plane. 'I'm so ashamed,' Silberman murmured in embarrassment as they half-carried him, rowdy and singing, to the car. On the same New York visit, Buñuel paid an unannounced sentimental visit to MoMA. Librarian Charles Silver was astonished to see the familiar figure browsing about. Knowing the library had a copy of *L'Age d'Or* but no rights to show it, he hurriedly improvised a contract for Buñuel to sign.

Silberman was again pressing for a new film so Buñuel and Carrière went to Madrid in February 1975 to think about it. Under the new liberal regime, Luis was more than welcome in Spain, and he took advantage of the changed political climate. Most of the old Order of Toledo was gone, but he recalled some of its former glory by hiring a castle just outside Madrid and holding a party for those friends who still remained, including Bergamin, Rey and Barros. The entertainment was provided by a troupe of drummers from Calanda, whose music reduced the group to tears.

Moving into their Guadarrama hotel, Buñuel and Carrière began work on the most promising project, Huysmans's *Là-Bas*. Gérard Départieu had agreed to star in the double role of Gilles de Rais, the lieutenant of Joan of Arc who became a torturer and murderer as Marshal of France but redeemed himself before death, and Huysmans's autobiographical hero Durtal, a modern writer led into Devil worship by his mistress.

It was a project Buñuel had nursed for decades and he was eager now to make the film, but before they were halfway through the first draft, Carrière knew he would never shoot it. As his official reason for stopping, Buñuel claimed he no longer felt able, at his age, to handle the intricacies of a medieval setting. Carrière has since admitted, however, that as they began writing the scenes of de Rais at a black mass, Luis felt ill. *The Monk* had scenes of Devil worship and it had never been made. Perhaps this film would not be finished either. In Madrid, Barros reassured him that his liver trouble was not life-threatening, but Luis was unconvinced. Abandoning the project, he flew back to Mexico and the calm of Cerrada de Felix Cuevas.

In the explosive development of Mexico City, however, what had once been a sleepy area on the edge of the town was now crowded with new and ugly apartment blocks. Breeze-block walls and a line of eucalypts to some extent protected his privacy, but the small garden with its outdoor barbecue increasingly became an island of calm in a busy suburb.

With nothing to occupy him, Buñuel fidgeted. He started make-work projects, paging through old photo albums and arranging his accumulations of snapshots, often annotating them as he did so. He indexed his library, painstakingly recording titles, even publishers and dates, in a notebook. Though he always professed to scorn critical assessments, he had copies of almost every book on his work and every major magazine survey. He also listed the honours won by his films, and typed out the list, pecking two-fingered on the old typewriter in his study.

After a few months, Silberman, divining that Buñuel was vegetating, followed him there, bringing Carrière with him. Buñuel, though delighted to see them, complained to an old friend, George L. George, 'Friends keep coming to see me with new projects, new ideas, new offers. I finally give in – just for friendship's sake.' Accusations of exploitation surfaced again, but, in fairness to Silberman, the producer had no particular need to make a Buñuel film at that time in order to generate cash, since his production of René Clément's thriller *Rider on the Rain* with Charles Bronson was a major commercial hit. Working with Buñuel, on the other hand, was a matter of honour and friendship. If he did not make films with him, someone less scrupulous would. Or, worse, Buñuel would not make films at all. As Luis told a journalist during the promotion of *Discreet Charm* in New York, 'Serge is not just a producer, he is my friend. He is making my life shorter. He is keeping me young.'

If Luis didn't want to make *Là-Bas*, wheedled Silberman, why not choose another subject, something less dark, less sinister? The three of them went to San José Purua to think about it. There they encountered yet another bad omen. In the hotel's remodelling, his favourite bar overlooking the tree-filled canyon had disappeared.

Grudgingly, Buñuel sorted through his memory and came up with another project abandoned years before. Pierre Louÿs's erotic novel *La Femme et le Pantin* had been filmed a number of times. Josef von Sternberg used Marlene Dietrich as the trashy *poule-de-luxe* Conchita, turning her into a lambent and elusive image of sexuality. Playing the same role for Duvivier, Bardot had embodied her pouting and nude, but as the same dazzling object of desire. Perhaps it was time for a new look at the sexual object, a peep at the shadowy side; a film, in fact, about a dark lady, ambivalent and contradictory: an *obscure* object of desire.

When Buñuel and Carrière started work on the script, neither of them anticipated the twist that was to make it one of Bunuel's most unorthodox films. Buñuel's determination to create a Conchita who combined overt sexuality with a hidden melancholy complicated the writing. 'One day,' said Carrière, 'it was raining, and you know how it is; nothing goes right and you get bored and discouraged and you want to give everything up, and to throw the script through the window. Luis said, and it was one idea out of a thousand: "Why don't we give the role to two different actors?" We spent two or three hours dividing the script into two parts, one scene for one woman and one for the other. One would be vulgar, attractive, fat, of lower-class origin, and the other much more distinguished, aristocratic. There would have been two different *characters*, you understand. And at the end of it Luis dismissed the idea as "the whim of a rainy day". We forgot about it and wrote the script for one actress.

'When the script was over, he started looking in Paris for an actress, and the first one to come to the mind of the producers was Isabelle Adjani.' The most promising young actress of her generation, Adjani had startled the theatrical establishment by being invited to join France's prestigious but ultra-conservative national theatre, the Comédie Française, at eighteen, then scandalized it by resigning at twenty to make *The Story of Adèle H* with Truffaut.

'So she was contacted,' continued Carrière, 'and someone said that Buñuel would like very much to see her. And she answered: "If he wants to see me, let him see one of my movies." This was reported to Buñuel, who found the answer absolutely logical, and he went to see her in *The Story of Adèle H*. We saw the film together, and he liked her. Back at the office he told them he'd seen the film and wanted very much to meet her. From that day on, there was no answer.'

Since Adjani apparently was not interested, Buñuel started looking at tests. 'He saw tests of Angela Molina, Maria Schneider, Carole Bouquet and many others – about eight or nine,' says Carrière. 'All the dark brunette French and Spanish actresses from that period. He chose Maria Schneider, who was good in the test.'

The daughter of actor Daniel Gelin, Maria Schneider had created a sensation in Bernardo Bertolucci's *Last Tango in Paris* as the promiscuous girl who has a no-holds-barred affair with bereaved stranger Marlon Brando. The suggestion to cast her as Conchita came originally from Juan Luis, who had thought of her for one of his own films. He went to Barcelona, where she was shooting Antonioni's *The Passenger* with Jack Nicholson, and talked to her, but was not impressed. She seemed to him a re-actor rather than an actor, and inappropriate to a role that would require her to behave like a fiery Spanish girl and even dance flamenco. Her well-publicized drug history had also damaged her health. She was pale and sweating, and her teeth had begun to deteriorate. Luis, however, was more than happy with the tests, and decided to go ahead with her as Conchita.

'They started to shoot in Madrid,' said Carrière, 'and after three days he couldn't get anything out of her. She had been on drugs; everyone knows that – it's no secret. I liked her very much. She was a brilliant young actress. But she was lacklustre, dull.

'Silberman went to see the rushes, and he and Luis agreed that night in the bar that he could not continue. And, to Buñuel's mind, came back this memory of the rainy afternoon in San José Purua. He said to Silberman: "Serge, do you know a woman who could be all the women in the world?" Silberman looked puzzled. Luis went on: "This woman is difficult to cast because one day she's like this, the next like that." And Serge understood. He said: "You want to do it with two different actresses?".'*

They chose olive-skinned Angela Molina, who had made a couple of minor Spanish films, and Carole Bouquet, a frosty ingénue of nineteen who had done only one small TV role. At Epinay they rebuilt all the sets, Silberman taking the opportunity to make them much larger than those in Madrid. Bouquet says she played the entire role in a state of terror, convinced that she would be fired, as Schneider had been, but Buñuel was content. A role played by two utterly different actresses at the same time offered a confirmed Surrealist all the oddity he could desire. It also illustrated what Octavio Paz had said in his essay 'Buñuel's Philosophical Cinema', about 'the duality that governs his entire work. On one hand, ferocity and lyricism, a world of dreams and blood . . . On the other hand, a bare, spare style that is not at all Baroque and results in a sort of exaggerated sobriety. The straight line, not the Surrealist arabesque.'

As he began shooting *That Obscure Object of Desire*, Luis had been chilled by a premonition that he would never finish the film. He refused to work unless Juan Luis and Pierry Lary were on the set. They came in each morning and sat reading the paper over coffee for an hour, then slipped away. 'He didn't need us,' said Juan Luis. 'He was fine.'

---

* Silberman's account differs in only one detail. He says Luis asked him: 'Have you ever read *Doctor Jekyll and Mister Hyde*?'

In fact, Luis was in worse health than he realized. His diabetes increasingly affected his eyes, making reading difficult, and also sapped his strength. After shooting finished he returned to Mexico City where increasingly he spent his time at home, fretting over his declining powers. The medical dictionary on his shelf became well-thumbed as he checked the progress of his various ailments, and plotted the inevitable end.

Carrière tried to involve him in a new script. A phrase of Paz, that all a chained man had to do to make himself free was close his eyes, suggested the theme of *The Sumptuous Ceremony*. A young, attractive terrorist is sentenced to a long term of imprisonment, but the moment she is locked in her cell, her erotic dreams and nightmare imaginings invade it. It was soon obvious to Carrière, however, that Buñuel's health was too frail, and they stopped working by mutual consent.

Buñuel could almost certainly have found money to finance the film in Mexico, since its movie industry was flourishing with the forced draught of heavy government subsidy. Churubusco had been nationalized in 1960. In 1970 Luis Echeverria Alvarez became president and promptly appointed his brother Rodolfo, an ex-movie actor and Jorge Negrete's successor as head of the movie union ANDA, to run the Banco Cinematografico.

By the early 1970s Mexico was turning out more than seventy features a year. Arturo Ripstein, Luis Alcoriza and Alberto Isaac were all working consistently. Foreign directors found it an increasingly attractive location. Joseph Losey was still trying to float a version of Lowry's *Under the Volcano*, though Buñuel, when Losey had discussed the project with him in Paris in January 1974, had told him discouragingly that he'd already read eight screenplays from the novel, and none worked. (John Huston finally made an unsatisfactory version in 1984.)

In June 1975 Echeverria convened a conference on the political problems of cinema. Buñuel, along with John Huston, Losey, Roman Polanski, Sergio Leone, Costa-Gavras and Frank Capra, was guest at a brunch where the President attacked 'the manipulation of cinema by international political tendencies, aiming to use it as an instrument to dominate developing nations'. To Buñuel, these pious concepts sorted ill with Echeverria's history, since it had been he who made the decision in 1968 to fire on protesting students in the Plaza of Three Cultures when they seemed to threaten the forthcoming Olympic Games. Three hundred died.

Luis had no energy left for indignation. He was succumbing to what Juan Luis called *la bola des años*: the weight of the years. His persistent diabetes was diagnosed as an inoperable cancer of the bile duct which had spread to his liver. By his birthday in February 1983 it was evident he might not see another. He needed nursing care and constant medication. Aware that a national hero was failing, the Mexican Republic made a graceful, if belated gesture of recognition. President Miguel de la Madrid visited Buñuel at home to congratulate him.

Sickness drew Luis and Jeanne into an intimacy they had never shared before. He became totally dependent on her, to the extent that he could not bear for her to leave the house. When she tried to go out on one occasion, for medicines, he wept – only the second time she had seen him in tears. The first had been the death of their dog Tristana. 'I didn't weep for the death of my brother,' Luis mused, 'yet I did for this little dog. But then she did live with us for eight years.'

As he became weaker, Luis asked for one of his pistols to be placed in the bedside table. Jeanne feared he intended to commit suicide. After his death, she found a sealed envelope with the gun. It said simply, 'Nobody is guilty of my death. I alone am responsible.'

It was a typically rational gesture by Buñuel to prepare a suicide note in advance, just in case. As he'd shown at Breton's burial, he had no time for the polite conventions of death. When Michel Piccoli had asked him to go on French radio to talk about their mutual friend André de Richaux, whose *Les Reliques* he'd once wanted to film, Buñuel refused with a quip. 'No. I never speak about dead friends. I just give stars as you would a restaurant. Sadoul, 5. De Richaux, 4.'

A few days later, Luis called for his doctors to visit him, and told them collectively he had decided not to accept any further treatment. They protested that much could still be done, but Luis was tired. Old friends were invited to call for a last visit. In June, European papers even carried a report that Buñuel was finally ready to be reconciled with Dali, and had invited him to Mexico. But Gala had died on 10 June 1982 and Dali had slipped into a senile decline. He wasn't going anywhere, least of all Mexico.

After Dali's death, a bizarre memento of their feud was found in his house. As he grew older, Dali had become obsessed with fakes, and had commissioned a collection of copies of famous old master paintings. In the autumn of 1969 he had gone one further and shot a fake Buñuel film. called *La Brouette de la Chair (The Wheelbarrow of Flesh)*, it was intended for release after Buñuel's death. When the expected acclaim was at its height, Dali would step in and reveal his authorship. Few people, however, are likely to have been fooled by Dali's clumsy pastiche, especially since it began with a few frames of his dream sequence from *Spellbound*. Only an apparent landscape of leaning trees which resolves itself into the eyebrows and lips of a reclining girl shows any of Buñuel's (or Dali's) flair.

For those who did call on him in his last days, Luis had a courteous farewell. 'He gave each of us something that had accompanied him for years,' says José de la Colina, 'and he said goodbye with a very precise request that we no longer come to call.' Serge Silberman was among those summoned. Luis still drank a couple of glasses of wine each day, but for Silberman he prepared the ritual midday martini of his great days. Since he could not drink it, however, he asked his old friend to dip his finger in the cocktail, and touch it to his lips.

He made no will, though he always joked about the reading of this fictional document. The family would be gathered but the lawyer would refuse to start 'until Mr Rockefeller arrived'. When Nelson Rockefeller swept up in his limousine, it would be revealed that Luis had left all his worldly goods to him.

Ironically, Luis's last months were made more agreeable by his friendship with a Catholic priest. Luis had met Father Julian Pablo at Alatriste's home, and the thin, balding, faintly effeminate priest became a regular visitor at the Buñuel house, though always, in deference to Luis's convictions, in civilian clothes. A familiar face around the movie business, he had ambitions to become a film-maker, and did go on to produce and direct a few films.

Many regarded Pablo as a somewhat sinister force in Luis's life but, as his health worsened, Buñuel came to depend on these visits. If Pablo had not arrived by 5 p.m., he began to fret. Often they simply sat in silence, but if they did wrangle it was mostly over points of Catholic dogma. Agnostic friends worried that the priest might be persuading Luis to make his peace with the Church, but both men denied it. 'He knows more about the Church and its doctrines than I do,' Pablo admitted.

Juan Luis was shooting a film in Paris, but in July Rafael cabled to say he was coming home.

'He's coming to see me die,' Luis said.

Jeanne laughed this off, but the night of Rafael's arrival, Luis fell into a diabetic coma. He was rushed to hospital, where the staff managed to revive him.

As he woke, Luis sleepily demanded a cigar from his bedside table. Jeanne explained that he was in hospital.

'What hospital?'

'The English Hospital.'

'That's going to be expensive,' he said, provident to the end. When his physician came in, he demanded a cigar. 'Why not?' the doctor said, giving him one of his own. It could hardly do any harm now.

On 29 July 1983, in the morning, the nurse turned Luis on to his side. Jeanne, who had been sitting up with him, took his hands.

'How are you, Luis?' she asked.

'I'm dying,' he said. She felt his pulse slowing, and though she called the doctors, it was too late.

'There's a place near where we live in Mexico,' Juan Luis Buñuel said, 'the Gayosso, where all bodies have to be taken. It's the law. The body lay there in a casket. Then my brother took it and had him cremated.' No formal funeral took place, only a simple ceremony at which President de la Madrid delivered the eulogy. As Luis wished, there was no memorial, headstone or tomb, and Jeanne has never revealed what was done with the ashes. They were probably, as Luis asked, simply scattered. 'When I'm dead I hope they burn everything I ever made,' he said. 'I share the feelings of the Marquis de Sade. I want them to burn me and throw me to the four winds. I want to disappear completely, without trace.' 'He was a true atheist,' says Juan Luis.

'He knew human behaviour, human feelings,' Stephane Audran said of Buñuel. 'He was more than a film-maker. He was an artist, a poet. He had a vision. A poet to me is someone who is closer to reality than anybody else. He saw reality like children. He wasn't *attached* to anything. His vision of human beings was . . . amused. Like God, watching us doing crazy things, but with love. He was an example of a real man, a human being. He was very special. I never met anyone like him in my life.'

An actress, a member of a class he despised, having the last word on his life! How Luis Buñuel would have smiled.

Select Bibliography

In addition to the many published screenplays for Buñuel films, and *My Last Breath*, by Luis Buñuel and Jean-Claude Carrière (Cape, London, 1984), the following books were consulted and are, in some cases, quoted:

L'Age d'Or: Correspondence Luis Buñuel–Charles de Noailles. Lettres et Documents (1929–1976). Centre Georges Pompidou, 1994.

Au Coeur du Temps. Denise Tual. Carrere, Paris, 1987.

Bad Boy of Music. Georges Antheil. Hurst and Blackett, London, nd.

Buñuel en Mexico. Victor Fuentes. Instituto de Estudios Turolenses, Zaragoza, 1993.

Le Cinéma Mexicain. Cinemathèque Française. Centre Georges Pompidou, Paris, 1992.

Crevel. François Buot. Grasset, Paris, 1991.

Cocteau. Francis Steegmuller. Macmillan, London, 1970.

Déjà Jadis. Georges Ribemont-Dessaignes. Julliard, Paris, 1958.

Dialogues Egoistes. Michel Piccoli. Orban, Paris, 1976.

Diary of a Genius. Salvador Dali. Doubleday, NY, 1965.

Eli Lotar. Programme of exhibition at Centre Georges Pompidou. Edited by Annick Lionel-Marie, 1994.

Elsa Lanchester Herself. Elsa Lanchester. St Martins, NY, 1983.

Entretiens avec Max Aub. Belfond, Paris, 1991.

Federico Garcia Lorca. Ian Gibson. Faber, London, 1989.

Goya. Luis Buñuel. Screenplay, edited and annotated by Christian Garcia Buñuel. Instituto de Estudios Turolenses, Zaragoza, 1992.

Hollywood: Ville Mirage. Joseph Kessel. Gallimard, Paris, 1936.

Immortal Memories. Sergei Eisenstein. Translated by Herbert Marshall. Houghton Miffin, Boston, 1983.

Johnny Got His Gun. Dalton Trumbo and Luis Buñuel. Screenplay, edited and annotated by Christian Garcia Buñuel. Instituto de Estudios Turolenses, Zaragoza, 1993.

La Fabrica de Sueños: Estudios Churubasco 1945–1985. Imcine, Mexico City, 1985.

Letters to Gala. Paul Eluard. Translated by Jesse Browner. Paragon, NY, 1989.

The Lives of Elsa Triolet. Lachlan MacKinnon. Chatto & Windus, London, 1992.

Luis Buñuel. Raymond Durgnat. University of California Press, LA, 1990.

Memorias de una Mujer sin Piano. Jeanne Rucar de Buñuel and Marisol Martin del Campo. Alianza, Mexico City, 1990.

Mexican Cinema: Reflections of a Society 1896–1988. Carl J. Mora. University of California, LA, 1982.

Monsieur Vanel. Jacqueline Cartier. Laffont, Paris, 1989.

Nancy Cunard. Anne Chisholm. Sidgwick & Jackson, London, 1979.

Objects of Desire: Conversations with Luis Buñuel. José de la Colina and Tomas Perez Turrent. Edited and translated by Paul Lenti. Marsilio, NY, 1992.

Out of the Past: Spanish Cinema after Franco. John Hopewell. BFI, London, 1986.

The Politics of Surrealism. Helena Lewis. Paragon, NY, 1988.

Le Provocateur. Michel Piccoli. France-Empire, Paris. 1989.

Les Producteurs: Les Risques d'un Métier. Yonnick Flot. Hatier, Paris, 1986.

Rencontres I: Chroniques et Entretiens. Georges Sadoul. Denoël, Paris, 1984.

Self Portrait. Man Ray. Little, Brown, NY, 1963.

What is Cinema? vol. II. André Bazin. Translated by Hugh Gray. University of California, LA, 1971.

With Eisenstein in Hollywood. Ivor Montagu. International, NY, 1969.

The World of Luis Buñuel. Edited by Joan Mellen. OUP, NY, 1978.

Index